結界師

KEKKAISHI

12

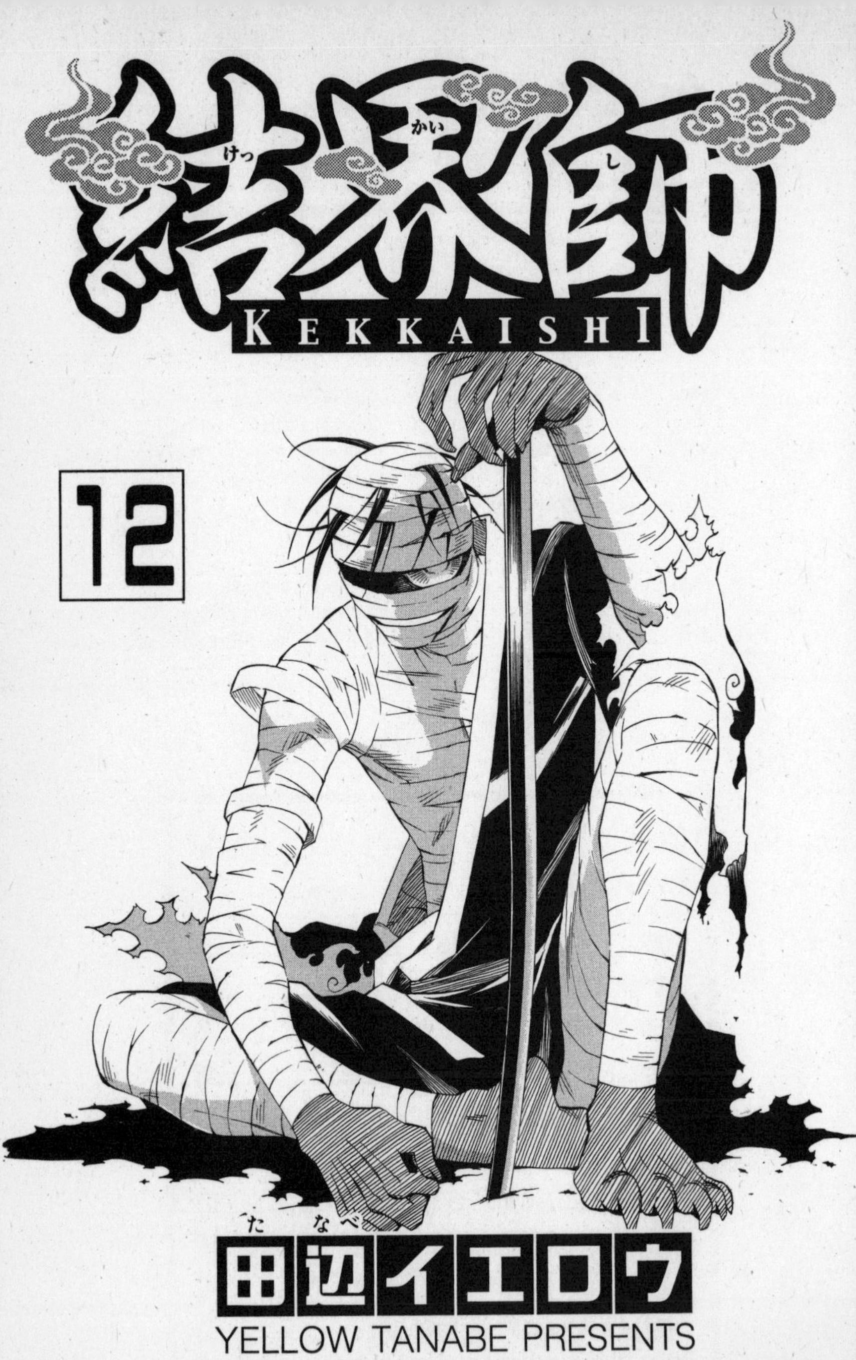

田辺イエロウ

YELLOW TANABE PRESENTS

THE STORY THUS FAR

Yoshimori Sumimura and Tokine Yukimura have an ancestral duty to protect the Karasumori Forest from supernatural beings called *ayakashi*. People with their gift for terminating ayakashi are called *kekkaishi*, or "barrier masters."

The Kokuboro, an organization of ayakashi, attack the Karasumori site. During a fierce battle, Yoshimori loses his dear friend and colleague, Gen Shishio.

Heartbroken over his friend's death, Yoshimori eventually channels his grief and rage into training to become an even greater kekkaishi. He vows to destroy Gen's killer, Kaguro, and in a ploy to gain entry into the Kokuboro castle, surrenders to his enemies. Sen Kagemiya, a member of the kekkaishi night troop, is captured as well.

Coincidentally, Yoshimori's grandfather's closest friend, Heisuke Matsudo—thought to be murdered by ayakashi—infiltrates the Kokuboro castle at the same time, with the intention of hunting down Byaku, a leader of the Kokuboro with whom Matsudo seems to have a longstanding feud.

Inside the Kokuboro castle, despite being at the mercy of his captors, Yoshimori confronts Kaguro while Matsudo prepares for his showdown with Byaku...

KEKKAISHI VOL. 12
TABLE OF CONTENTS

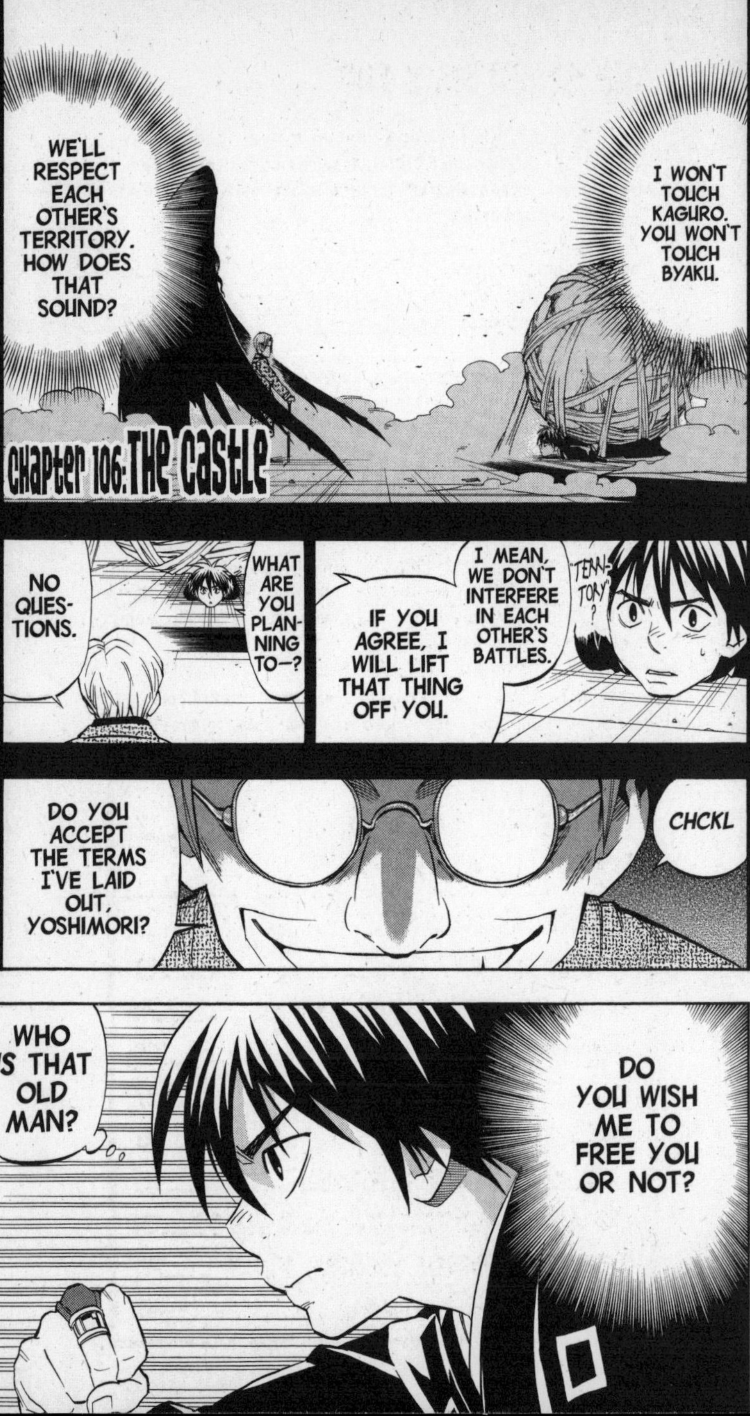
I WON'T TOUCH KAGURO. YOU WON'T TOUCH BYAKU.
WE'LL RESPECT EACH OTHER'S TERRITORY. HOW DOES THAT SOUND?
Chapter 106: The Castle
"TERRI-TORY"?
I MEAN, WE DON'T INTERFERE IN EACH OTHER'S BATTLES.
IF YOU AGREE, I WILL LIFT THAT THING OFF YOU.
WHAT ARE YOU PLAN-NING TO—?
NO QUES-TIONS.
CHCKL
DO YOU ACCEPT THE TERMS I'VE LAID OUT, YOSHIMORI?
DO YOU WISH ME TO FREE YOU OR NOT?
WHO *IS* THAT OLD MAN?

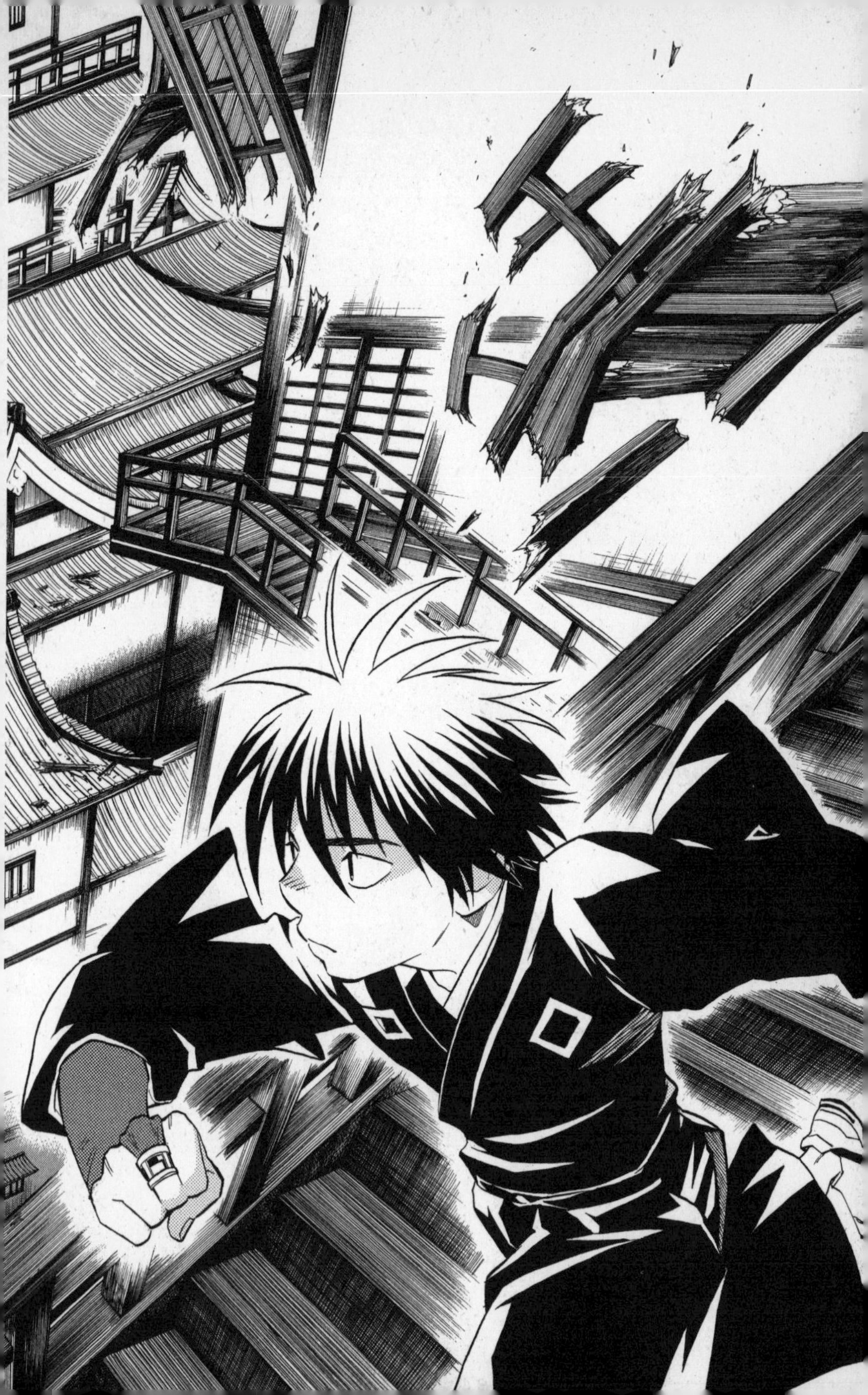

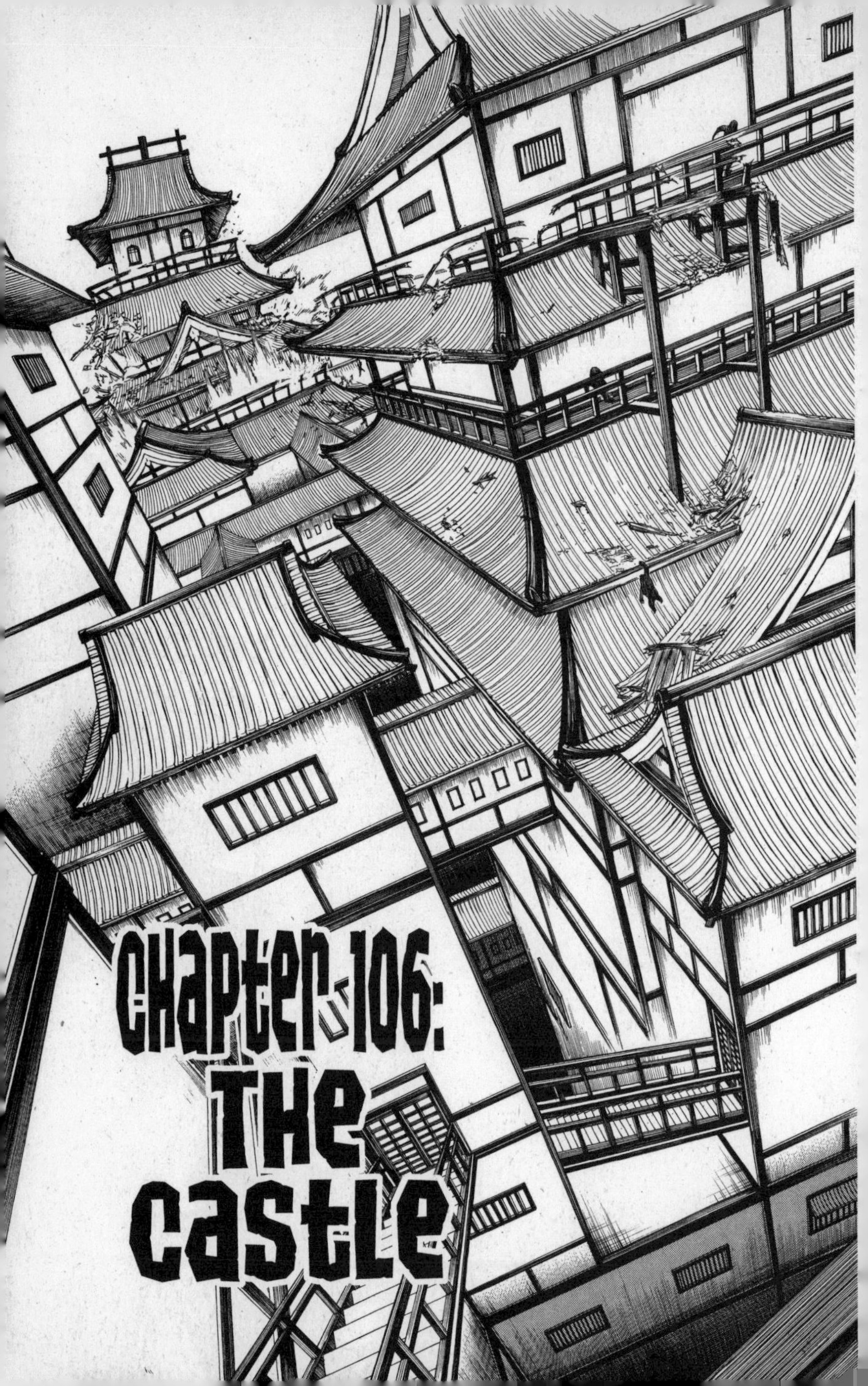
CHAPTER 106:
THE castle

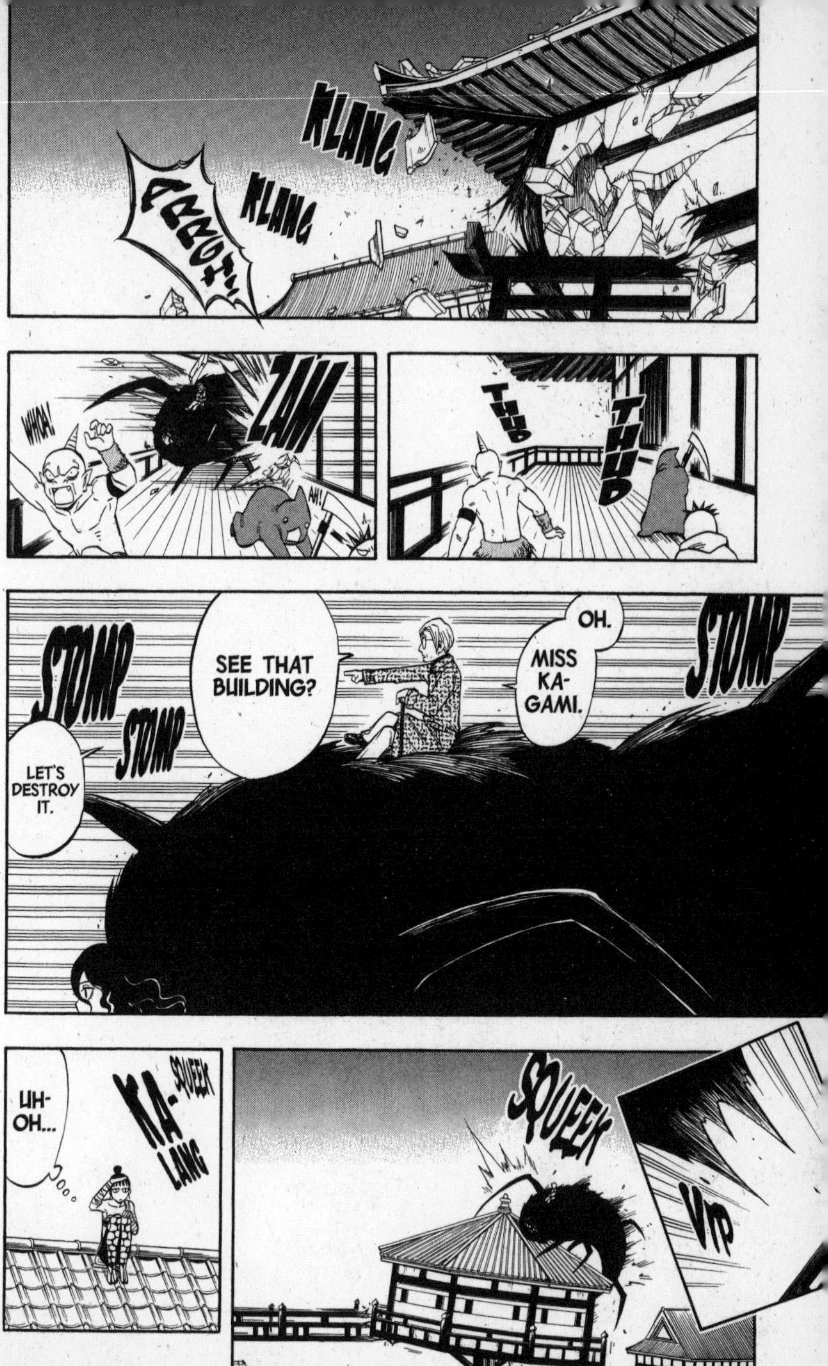
KLANG
KLANG
ARRGH!!
THUD
THUD
ZAM
WHOA!
AH!
OH.
MISS KA-GAMI.
STOMP
SEE THAT BUILDING?
STOMP
STOMP
LET'S DESTROY IT.
SQUEEK
VIP
SQUEEK
KA-LANG
UH-OH...

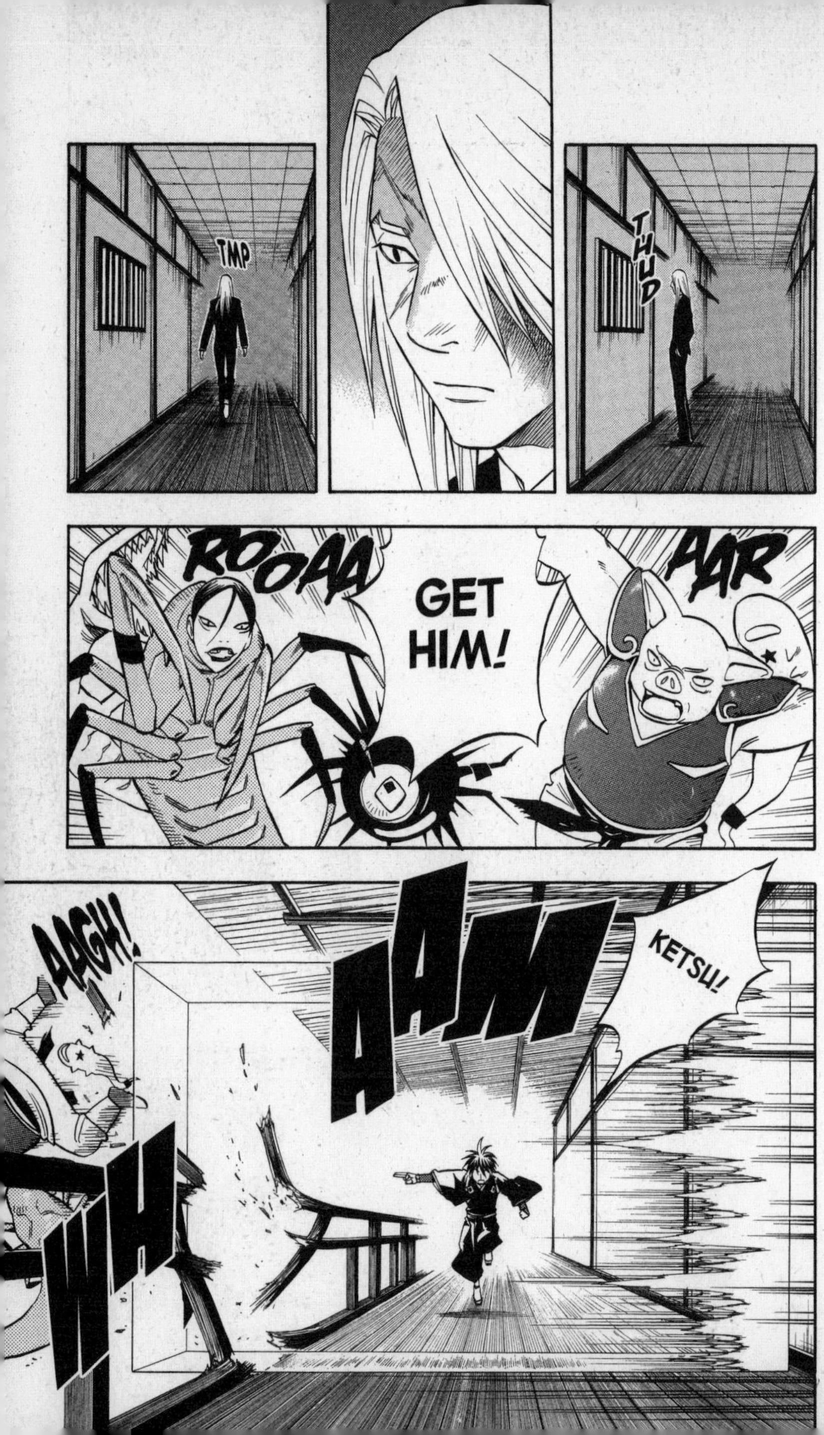
THUD
TMP
AAR
GET HIM!
ROOAA
KETSU!
AAM
AAGH!
WH

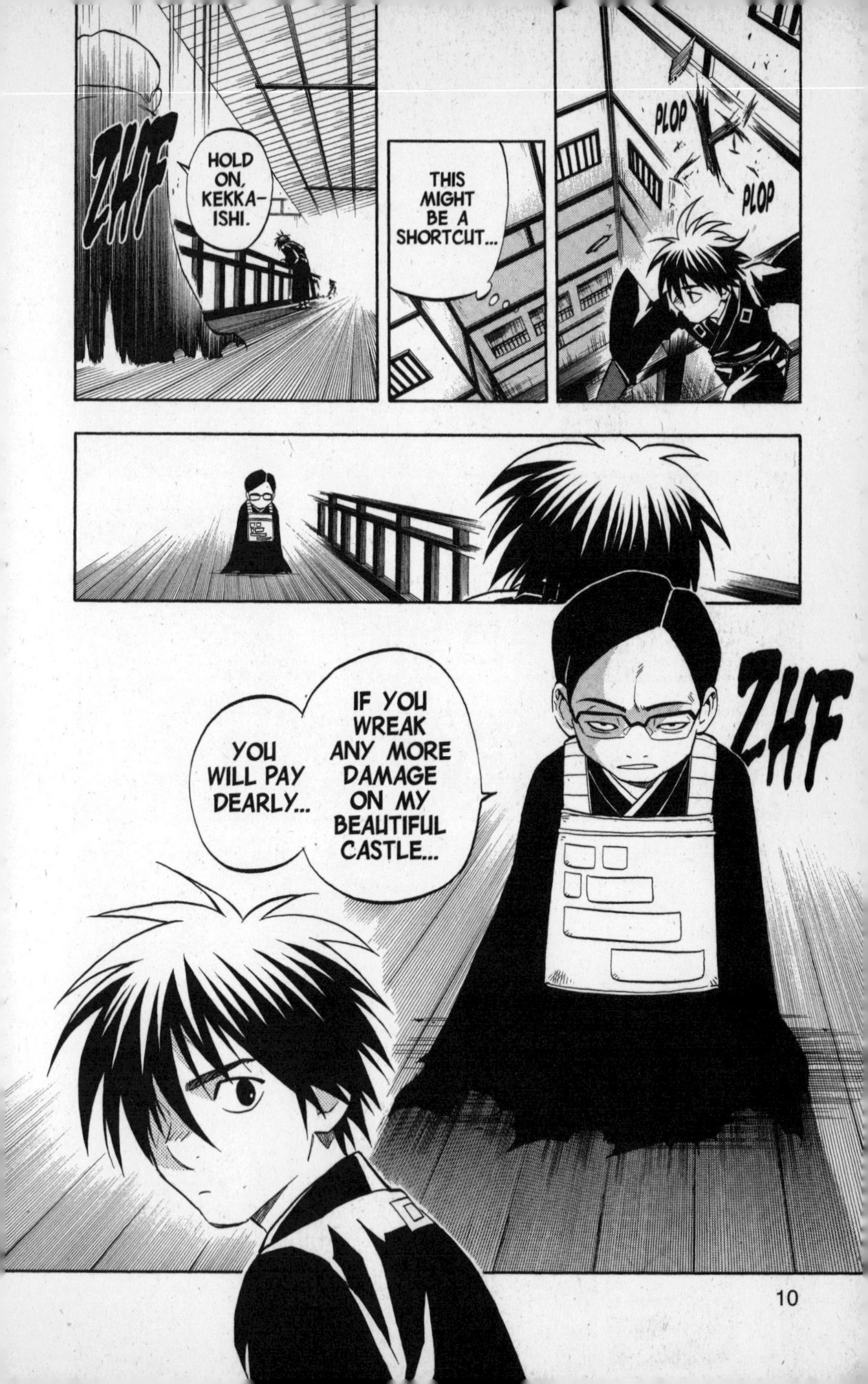
PLOP
PLOP
THIS MIGHT BE A SHORTCUT...
ZHF
HOLD ON, KEKKA-ISHI.
ZHF
IF YOU WREAK ANY MORE DAMAGE ON MY BEAUTIFUL CASTLE...
YOU WILL PAY DEARLY...

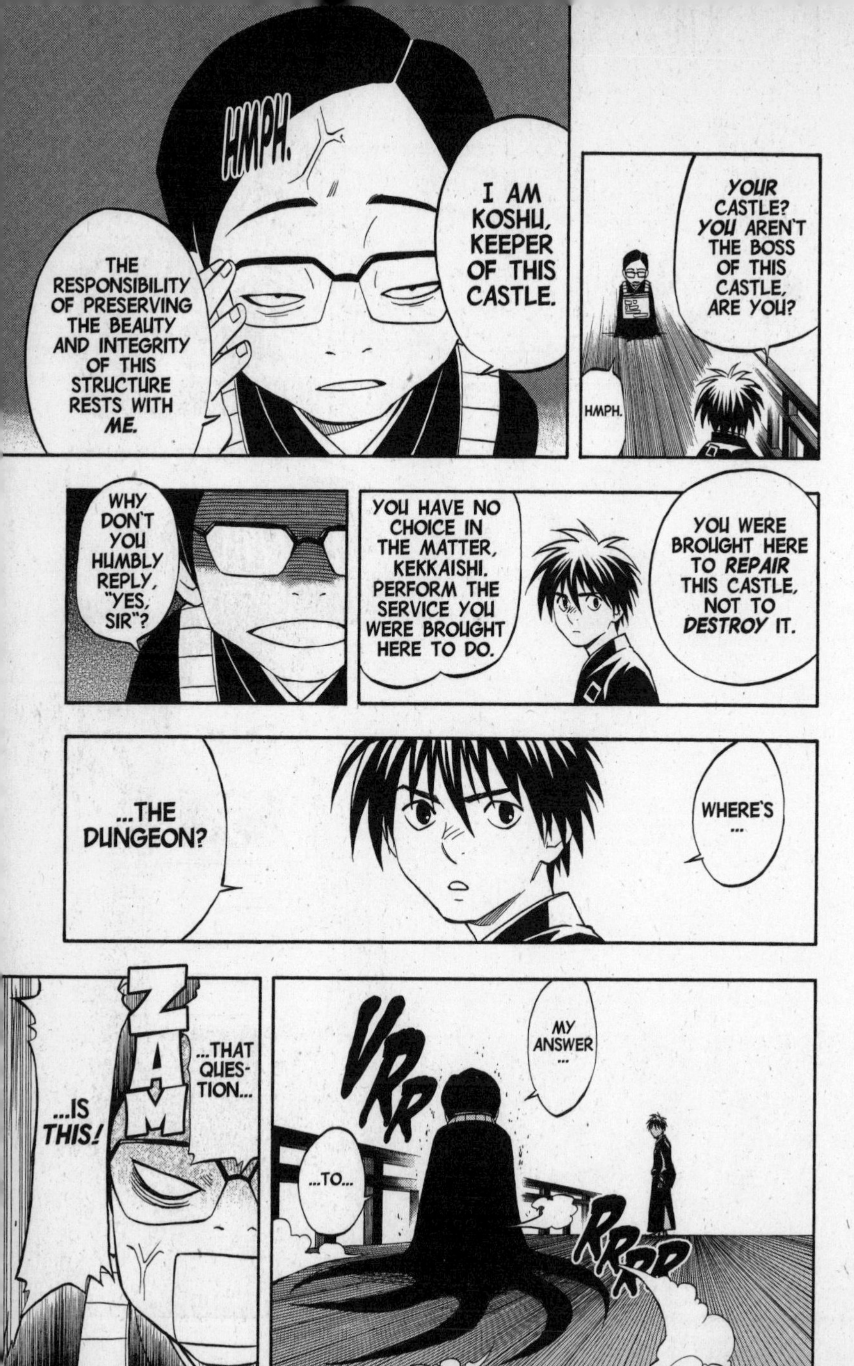
YOUR CASTLE? YOU AREN'T THE BOSS OF THIS CASTLE, ARE YOU?
HMPH.
HMPH.
I AM KOSHU, KEEPER OF THIS CASTLE.
THE RESPONSIBILITY OF PRESERVING THE BEAUTY AND INTEGRITY OF THIS STRUCTURE RESTS WITH ME.
YOU WERE BROUGHT HERE TO REPAIR THIS CASTLE, NOT TO DESTROY IT.
YOU HAVE NO CHOICE IN THE MATTER, KEKKAISHI. PERFORM THE SERVICE YOU WERE BROUGHT HERE TO DO.
WHY DON'T YOU HUMBLY REPLY, "YES, SIR"?
WHERE'S ...
...THE DUNGEON?
MY ANSWER ...
VRR
...TO...
RRRP
...THAT QUES-TION...
ZAM
...IS THIS!

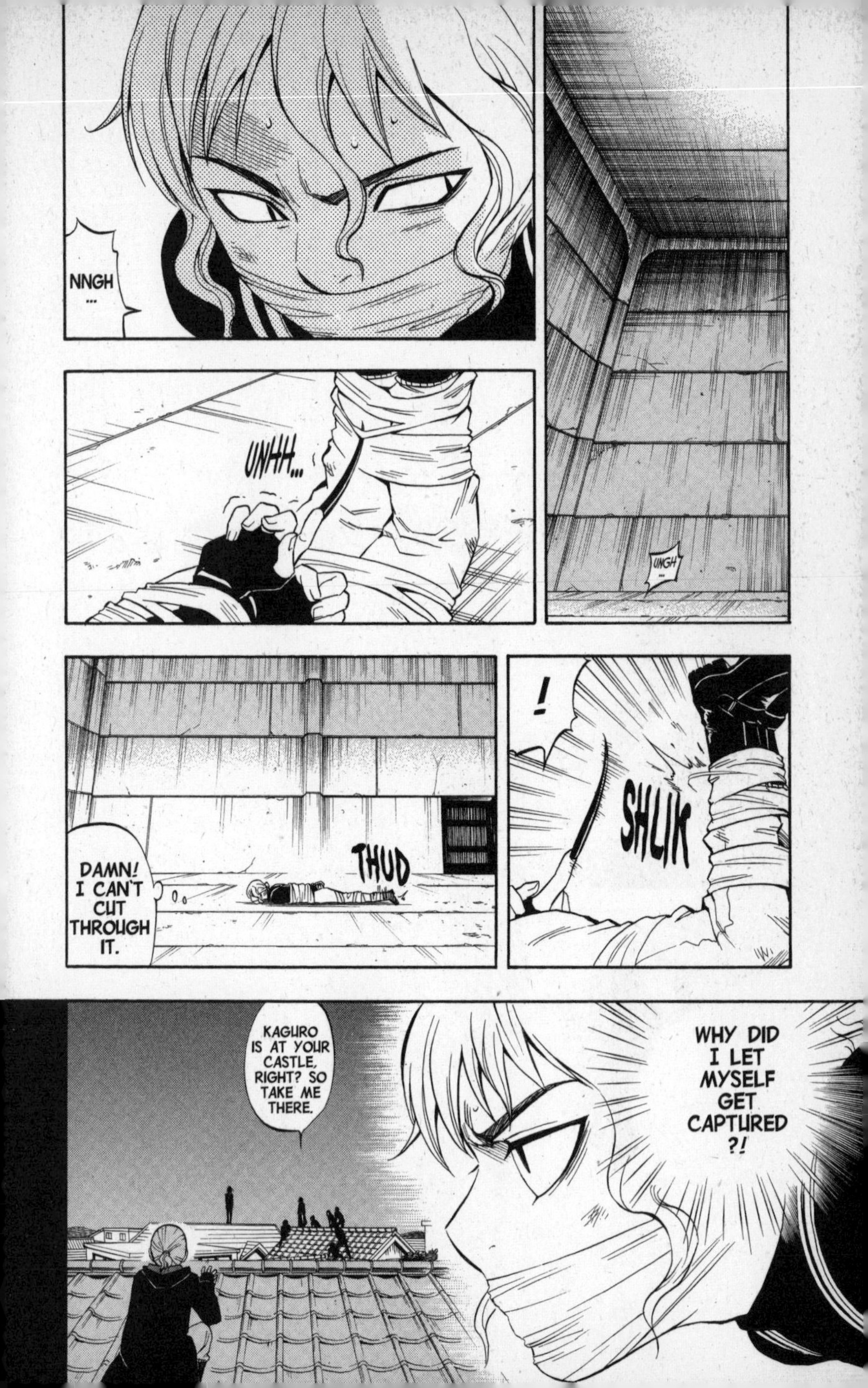
UNGH ...
NNGH ...
UNHH...
!
SHLIK
THUD
DAMN! I CAN'T CUT THROUGH IT.
WHY DID I LET MYSELF GET CAPTURED ?!
KAGURO IS AT YOUR CASTLE, RIGHT? SO TAKE ME THERE.

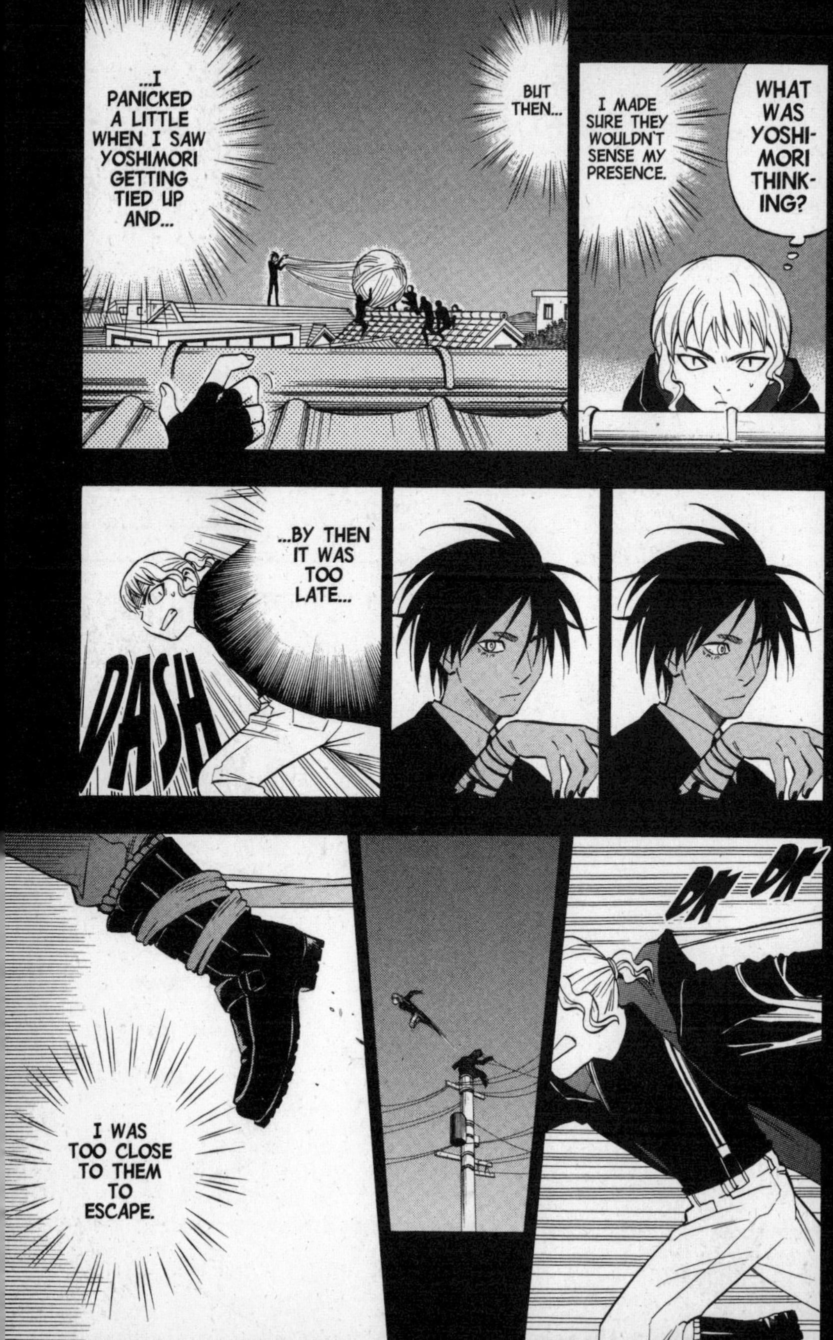
WHAT WAS YOSHIMORI THINKING?
I MADE SURE THEY WOULDN'T SENSE MY PRESENCE.
BUT THEN...
...I PANICKED A LITTLE WHEN I SAW YOSHIMORI GETTING TIED UP AND...
...BY THEN IT WAS TOO LATE...
DASH
DK DK
I WAS TOO CLOSE TO THEM TO ESCAPE.

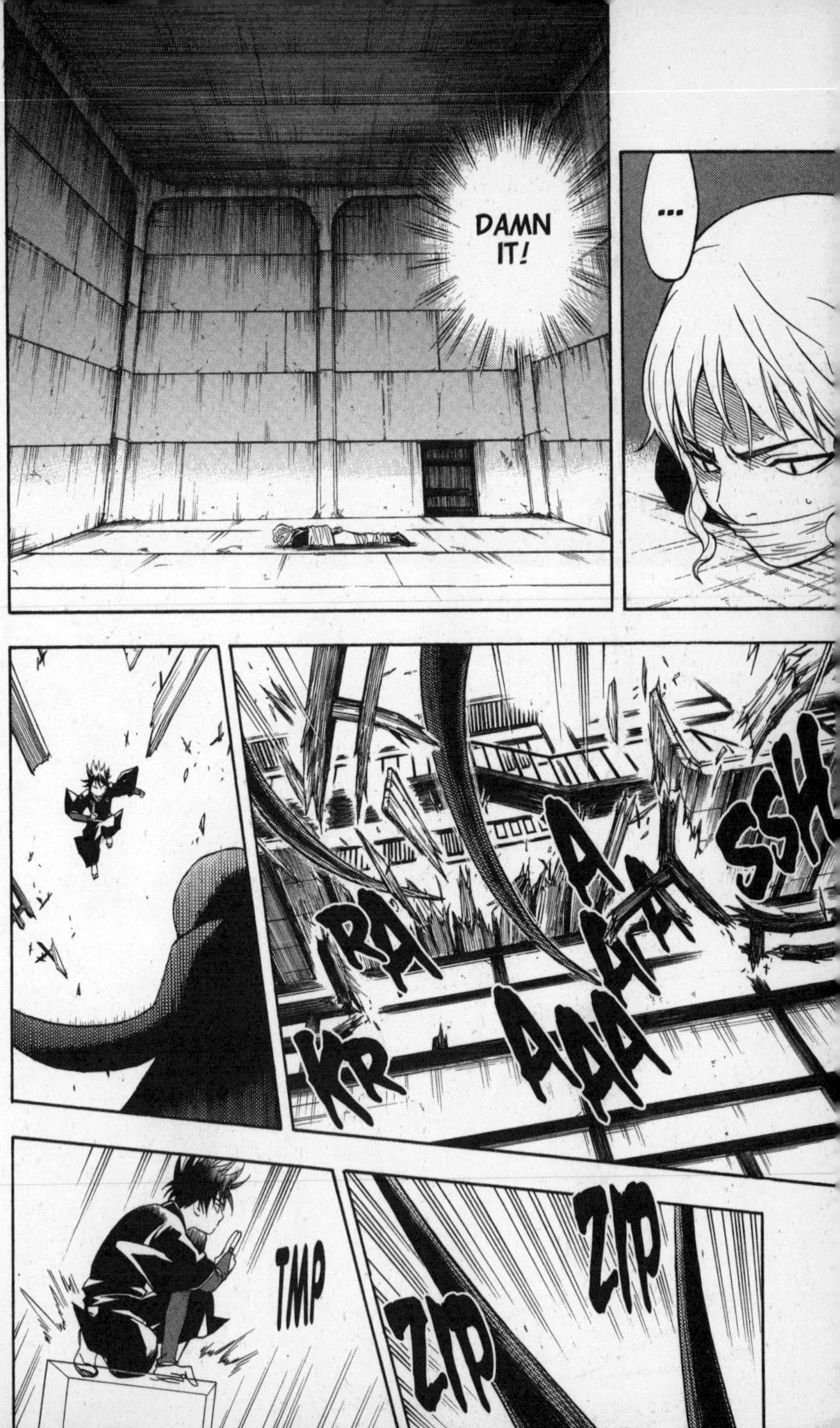
...
DAMN IT!
SSH
KR RA A AAA
ZIP
ZIP
TMP

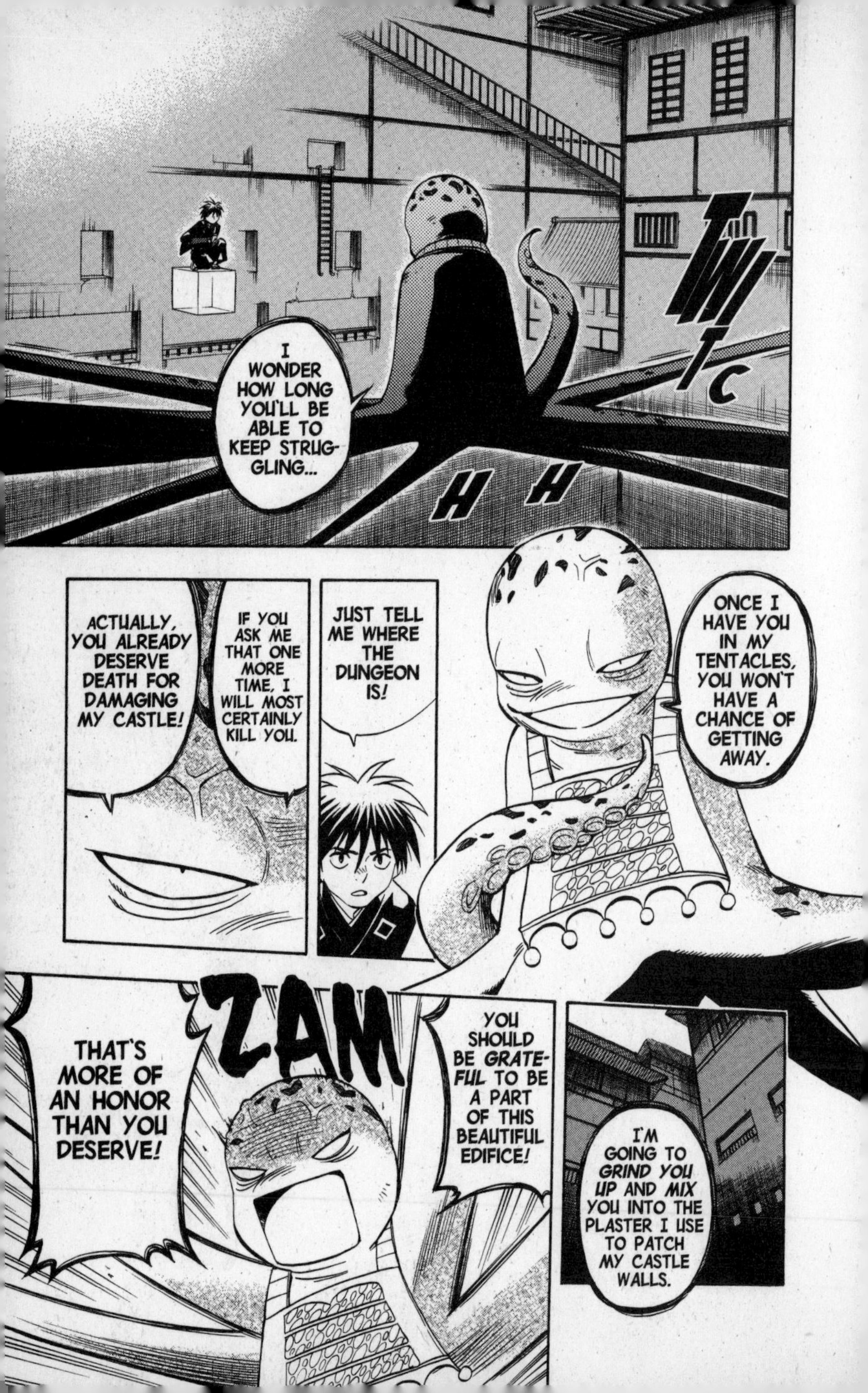
I WONDER HOW LONG YOU'LL BE ABLE TO KEEP STRUG-GLING...
ONCE I HAVE YOU IN MY TENTACLES, YOU WON'T HAVE A CHANCE OF GETTING AWAY.
JUST TELL ME WHERE THE DUNGEON IS!
IF YOU ASK ME THAT ONE MORE TIME, I WILL MOST CERTAINLY KILL YOU.
ACTUALLY, YOU ALREADY DESERVE DEATH FOR DAMAGING MY CASTLE!
I'M GOING TO *GRIND YOU UP* AND *MIX* YOU INTO THE PLASTER I USE TO PATCH MY CASTLE WALLS.
ZAM
YOU SHOULD BE *GRATE-FUL* TO BE A PART OF THIS BEAUTIFUL EDIFICE!
THAT'S MORE OF AN HONOR THAN YOU DESERVE!

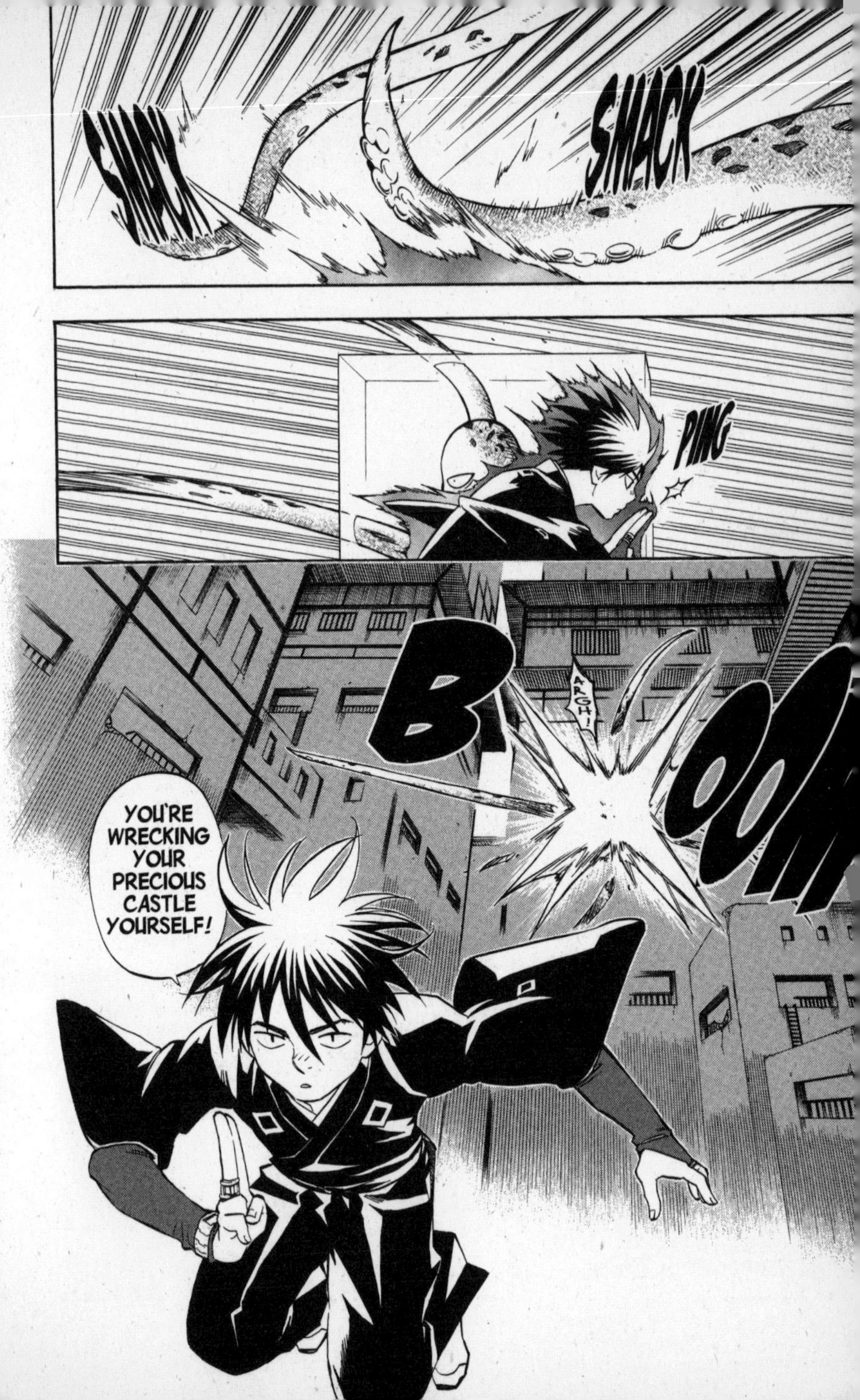
SMACK
SMACK
PING
B
ARGH!
OOOM
YOU'RE WRECKING YOUR PRECIOUS CASTLE YOURSELF!

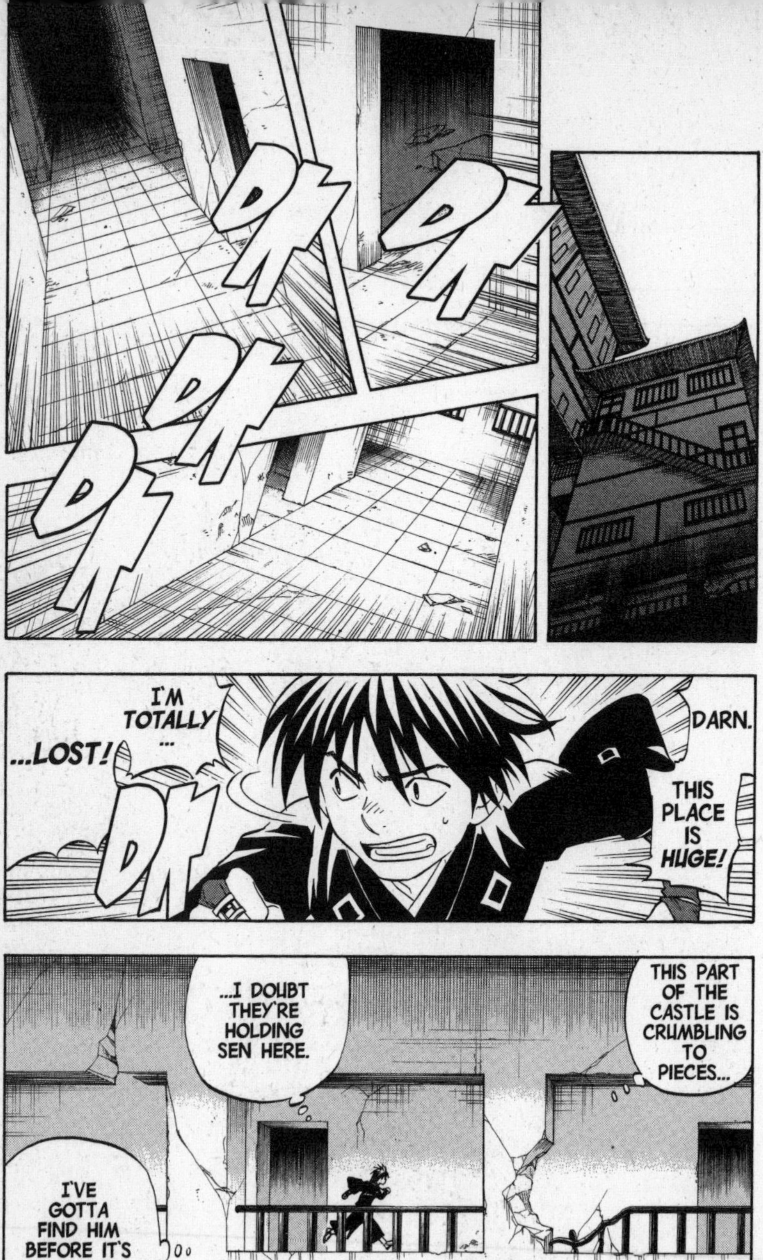
DK
DK
DK
DK
DARN.
THIS PLACE IS HUGE!
I'M TOTALLY ...
...LOST!
DK
THIS PART OF THE CASTLE IS CRUMBLING TO PIECES...
...I DOUBT THEY'RE HOLDING SEN HERE.
I'VE GOTTA FIND HIM BEFORE IT'S TOO LATE!

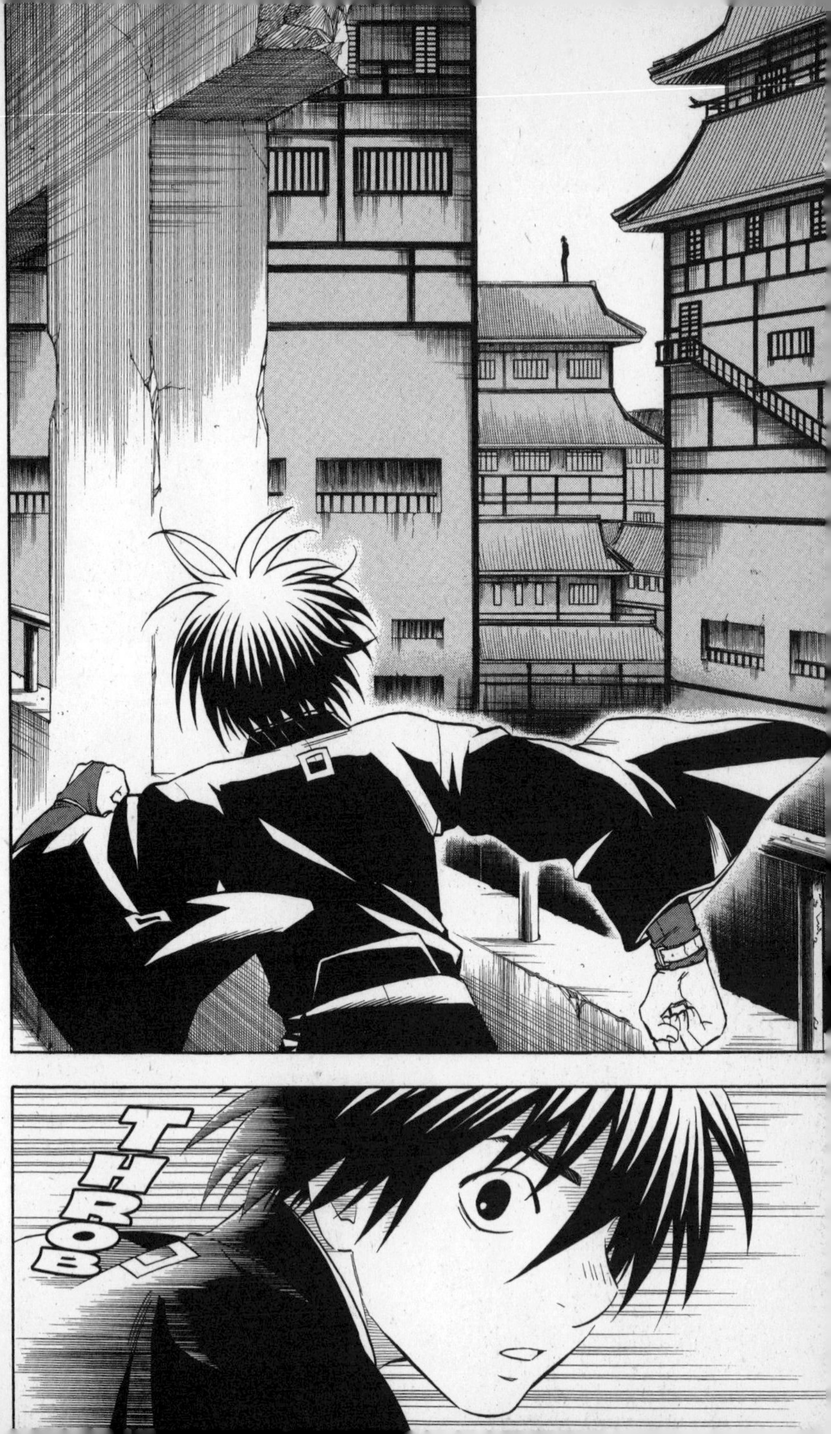
THROB

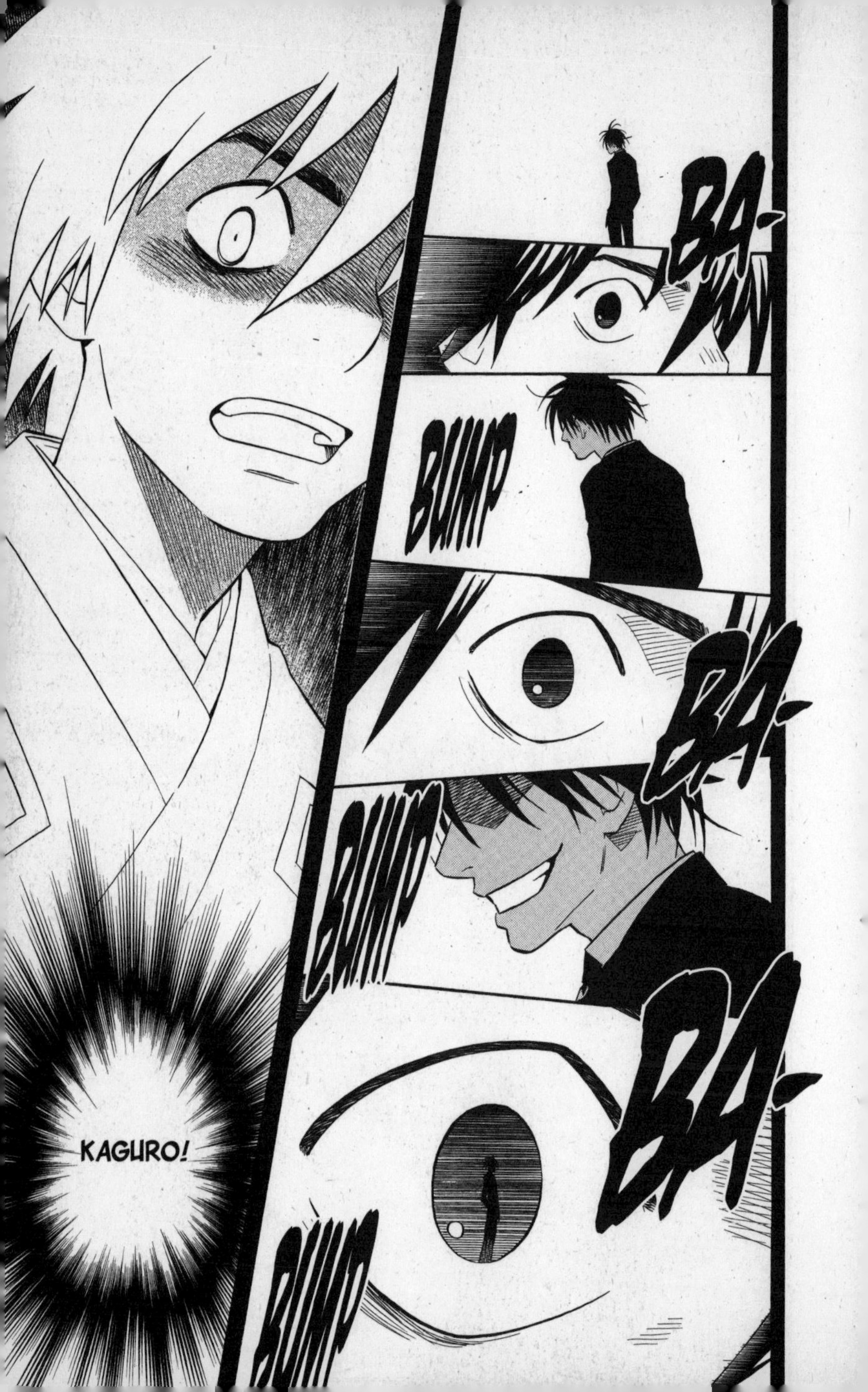
BA-
BUMP
BA-
BUMP
BA-
BUMP
KAGURO!

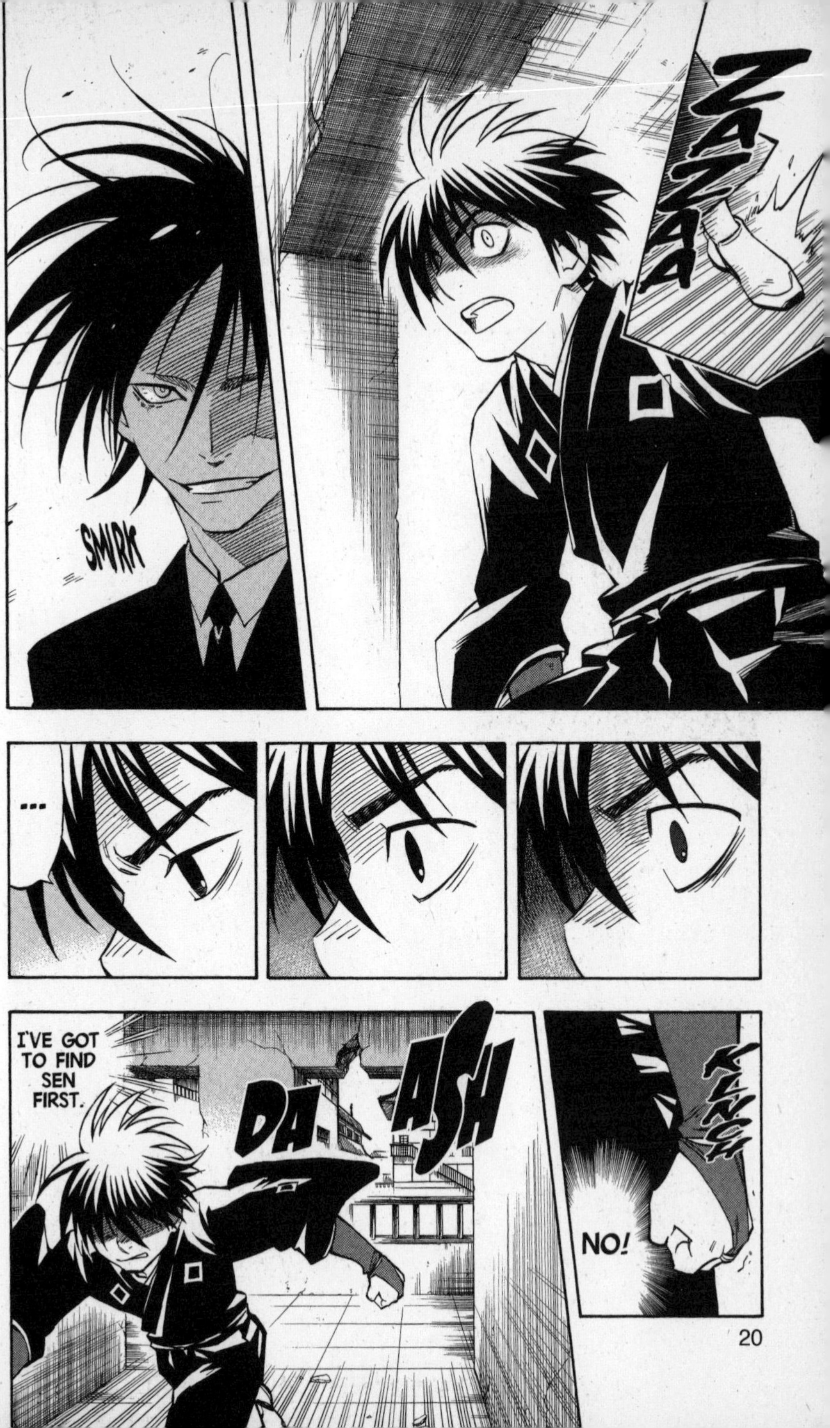
ZAZAA
SMIRK
...
NO!
KLINCH
I'VE GOT TO FIND SEN FIRST.
DA-ASH

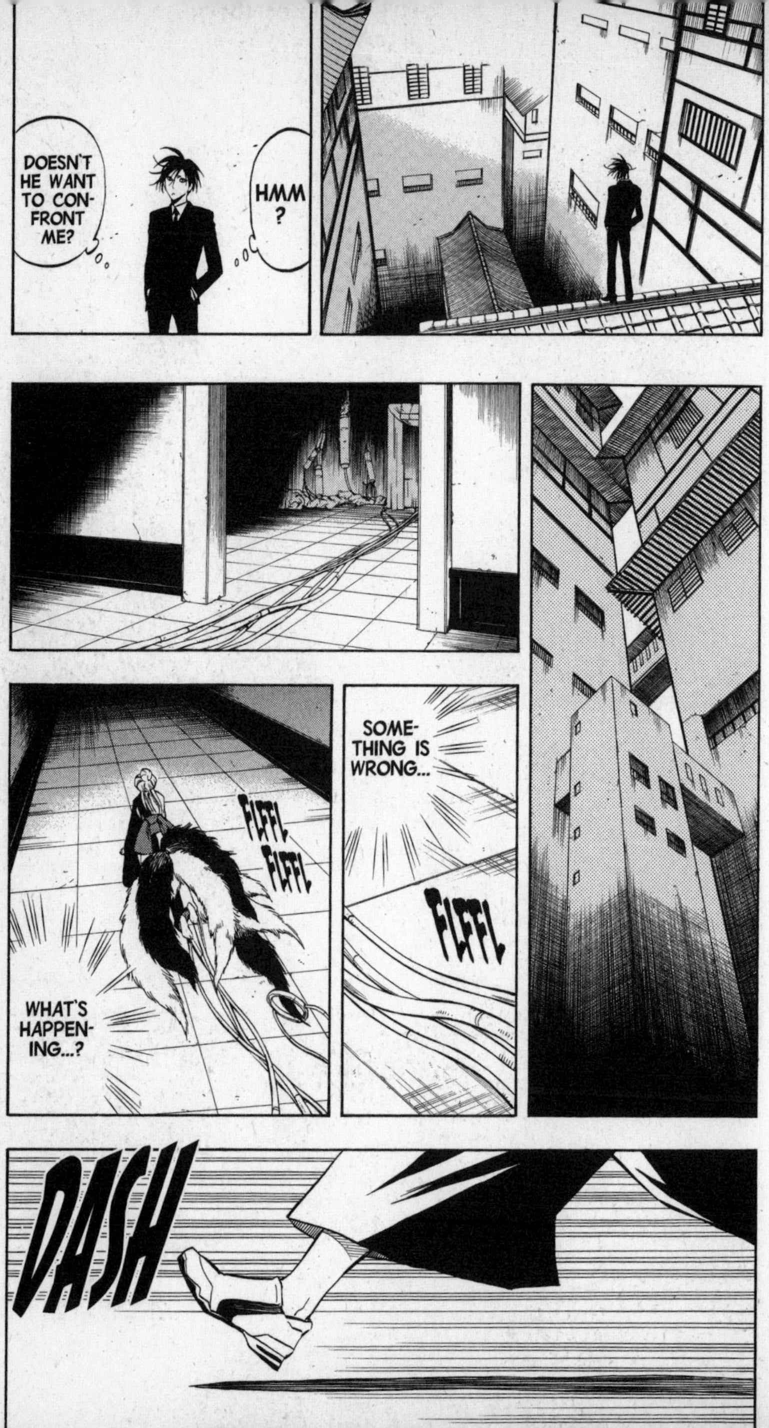
HMM ?
DOESN'T HE WANT TO CON-FRONT ME?
SOME-THING IS WRONG...
FLFFL
FLFFL FLFFL
WHAT'S HAPPEN-ING...?
DASH

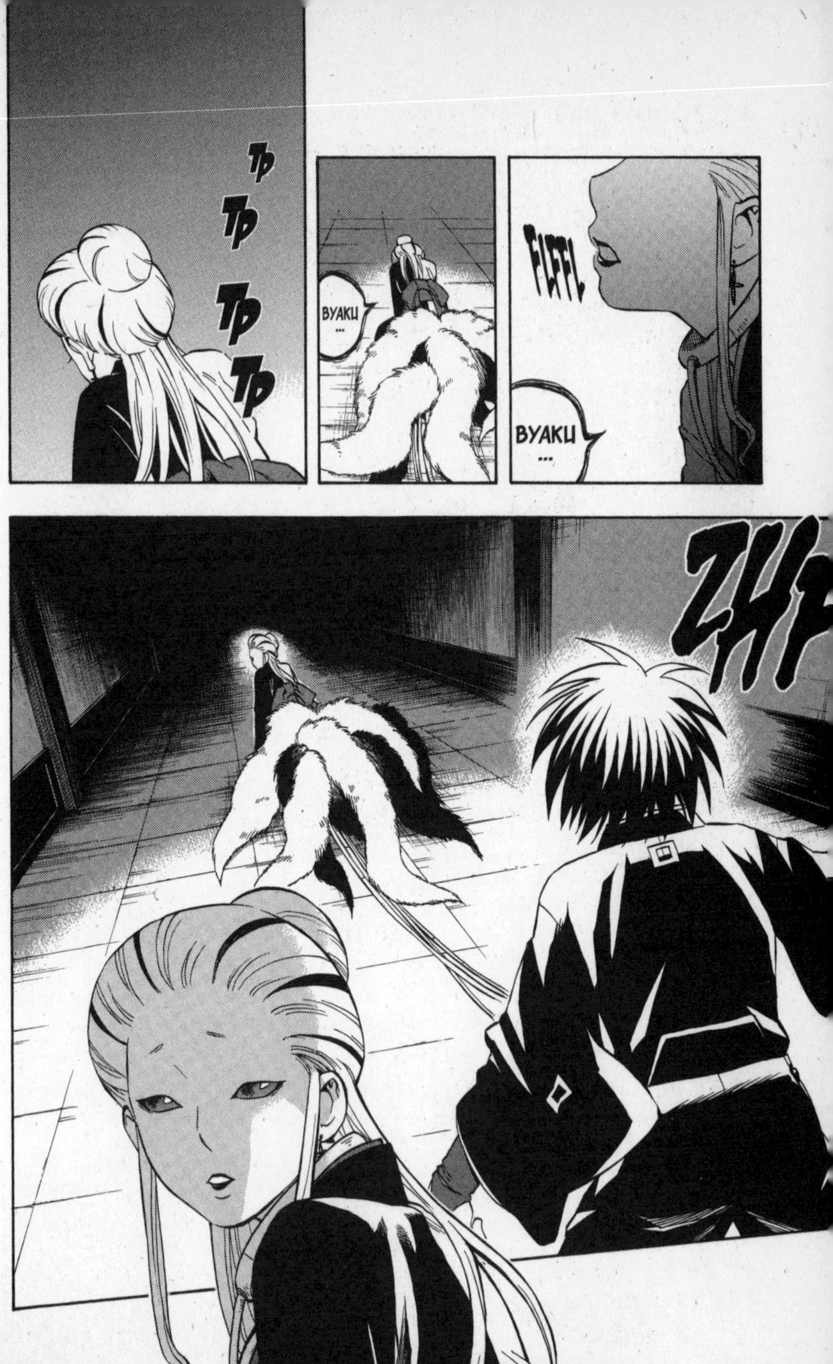
FLFFL
BYAKU ...
BYAKU ...
TP
TP
TP
TP
ZH

Chapter 107: Rescue

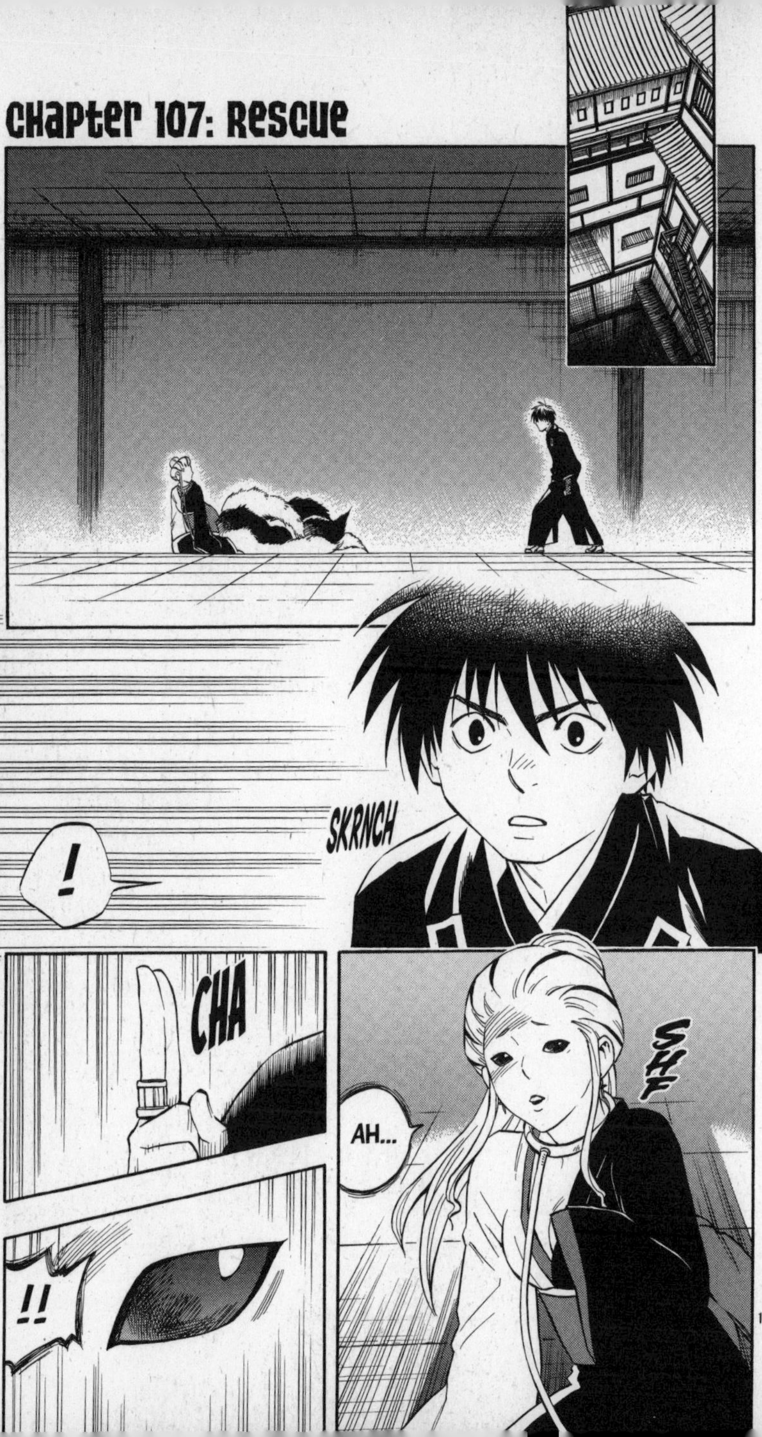
SKRNCH
!
SHF
AH...
CHA
!!

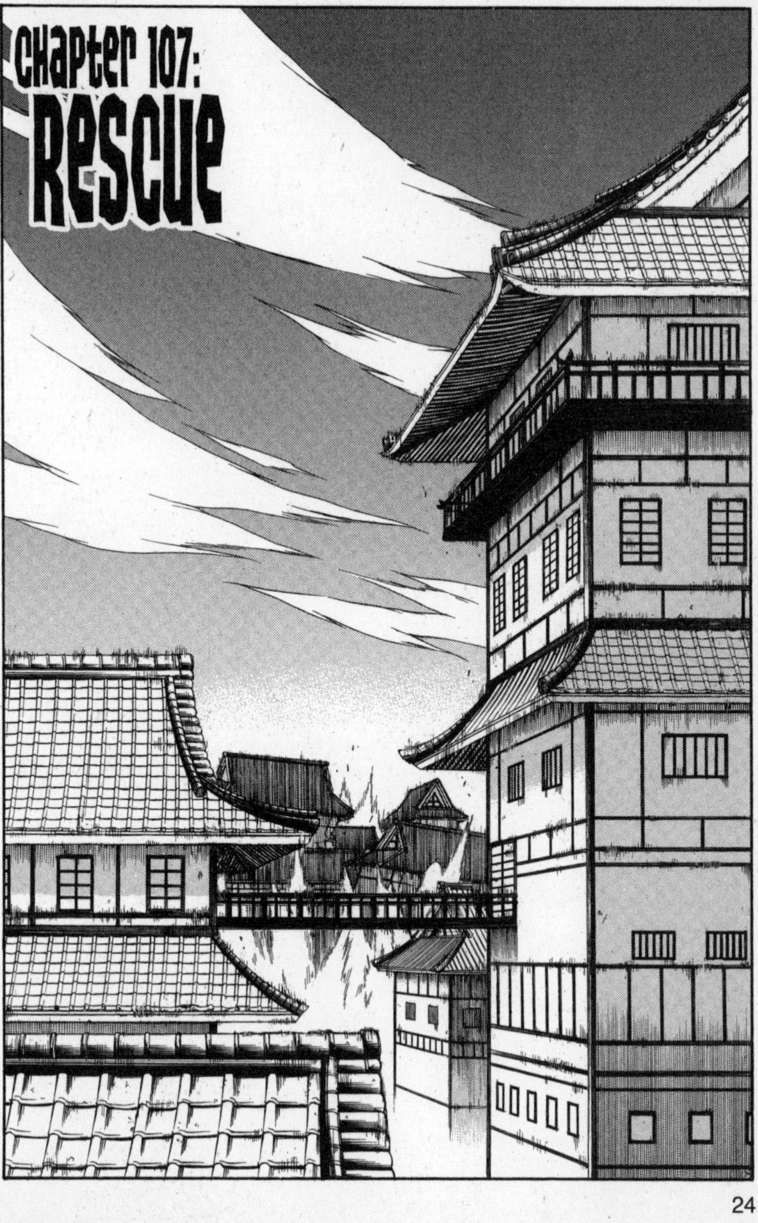
Chapter 107:
Rescue
2

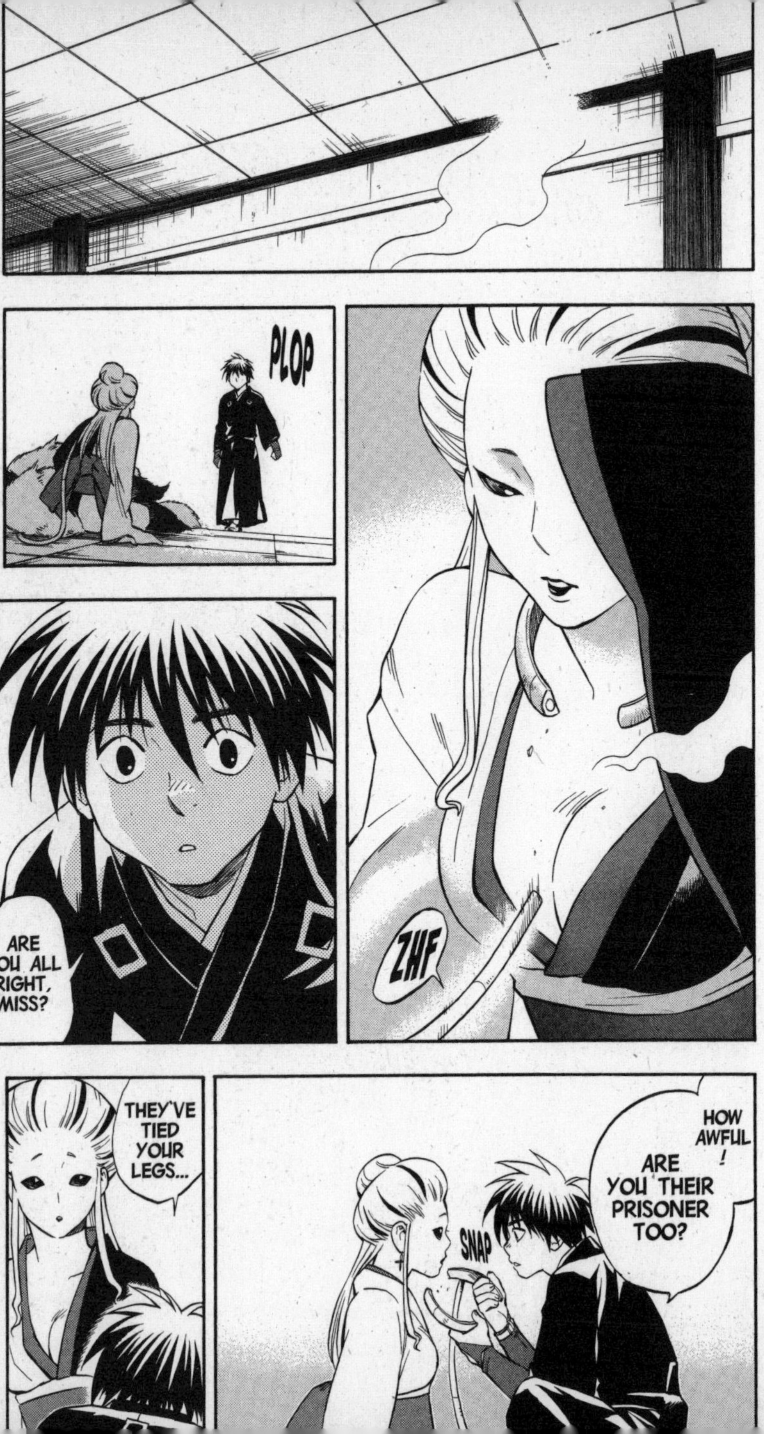
ZHF
PLOP
ARE YOU ALL RIGHT, MISS?
HOW AWFUL!
ARE YOU THEIR PRISONER TOO?
SNAP
THEY'VE TIED YOUR LEGS...

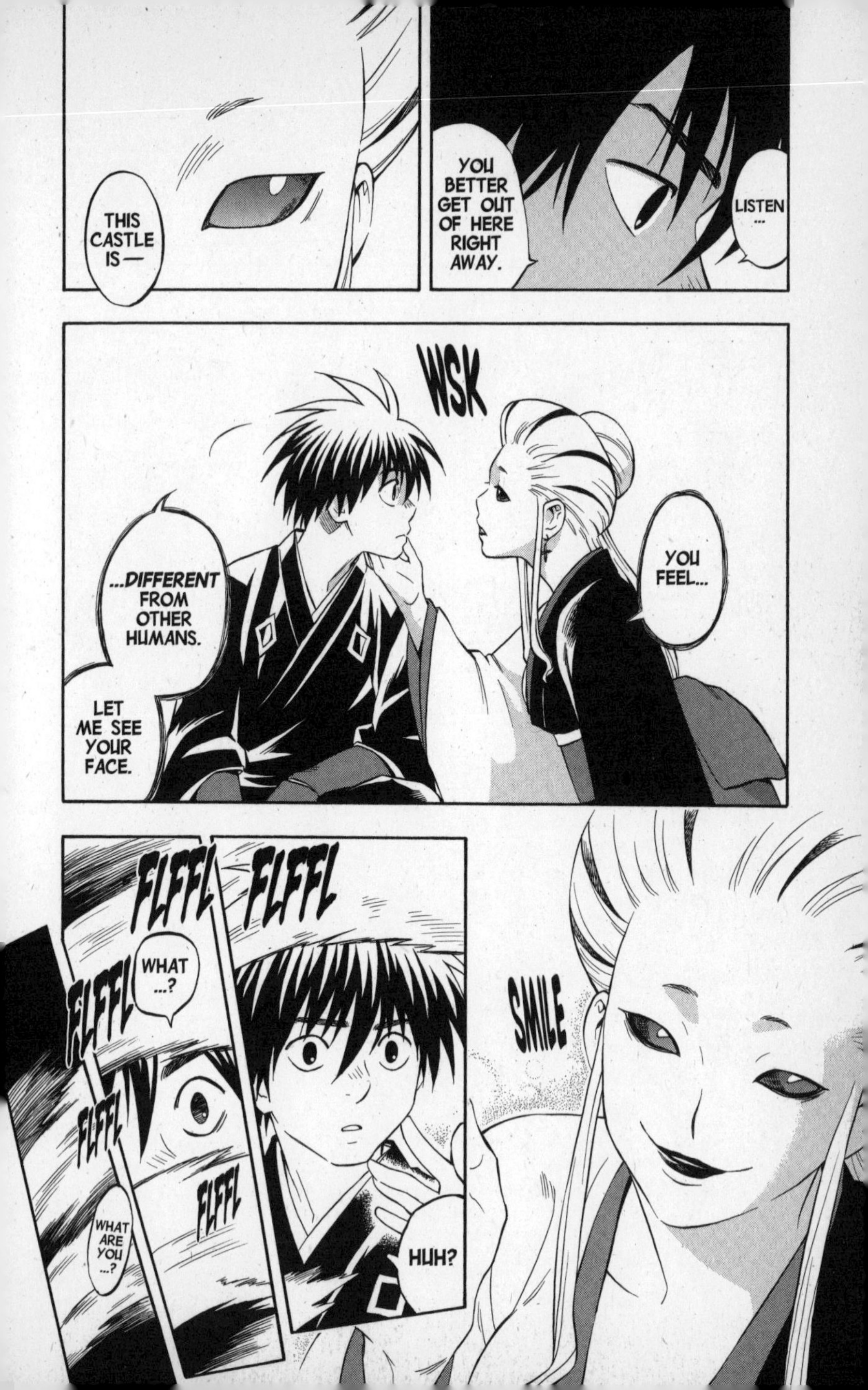
LISTEN ...
YOU BETTER GET OUT OF HERE RIGHT AWAY.
THIS CASTLE IS—
WSK
YOU FEEL...
...DIFFERENT FROM OTHER HUMANS.
LET ME SEE YOUR FACE.
SMILE
FLFFL
FLFFL
WHAT ...?
HUH?
FLFFL
FLFFL
FLFFL
WHAT ARE YOU ...?

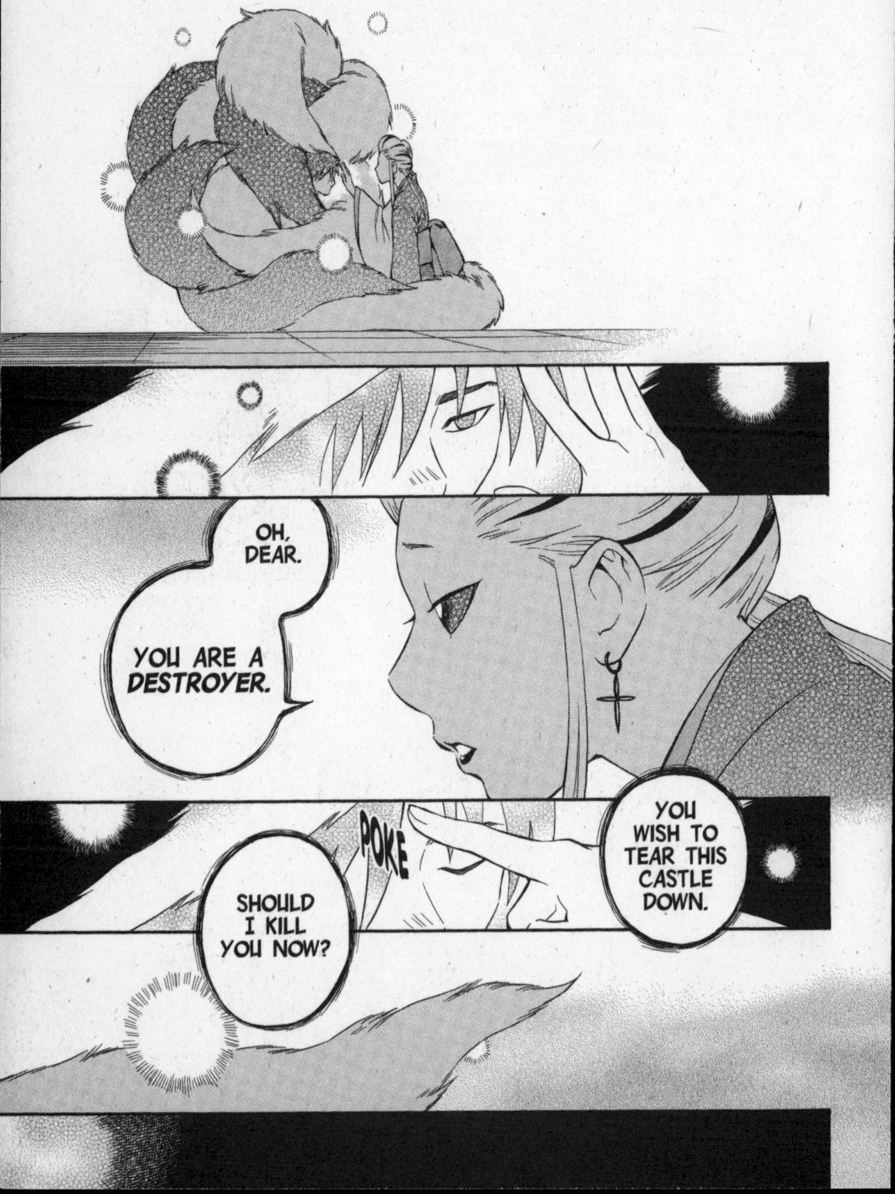
OH, DEAR.
YOU ARE A **DESTROYER.**
YOU WISH TO TEAR THIS CASTLE DOWN.
POKE
SHOULD I KILL YOU NOW?

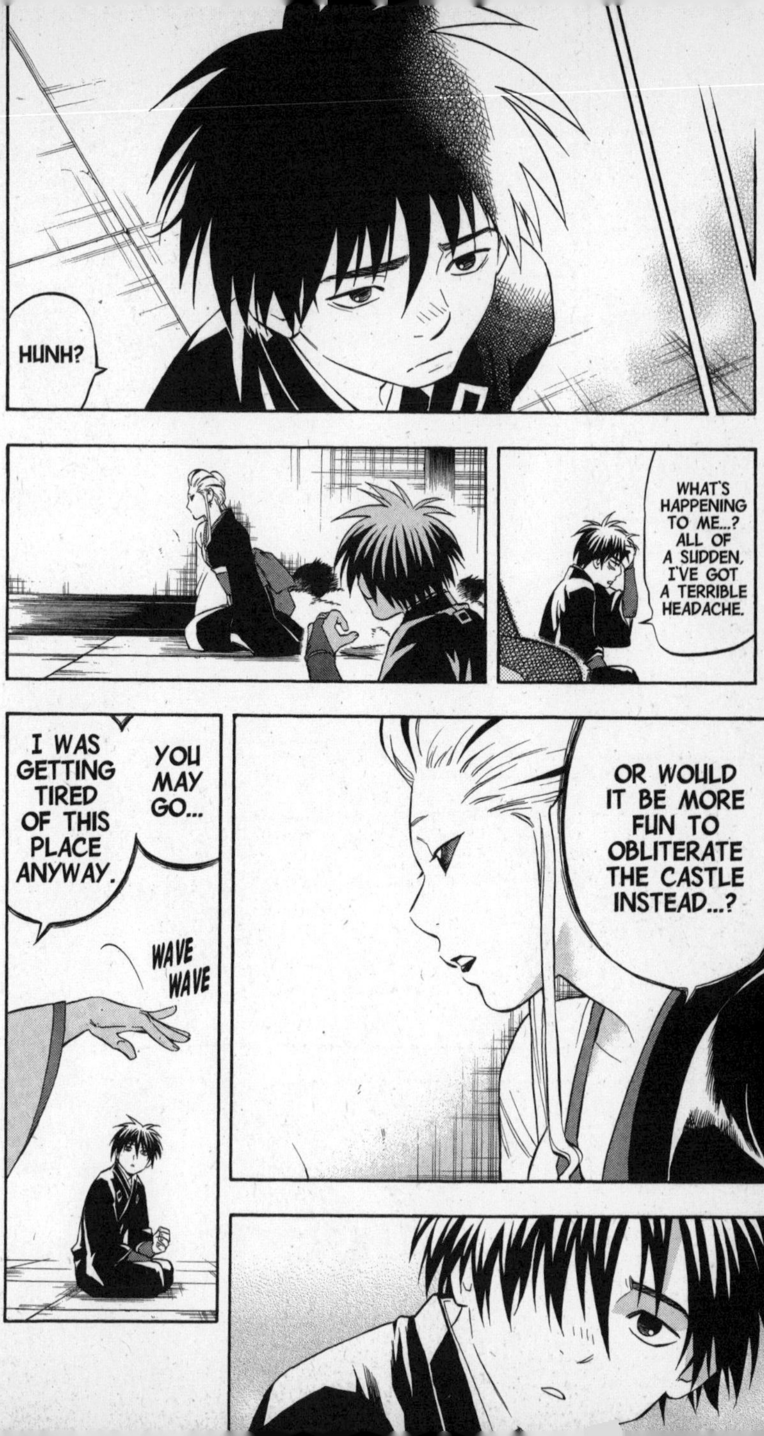
HUNH?
WHAT'S HAPPENING TO ME...? ALL OF A SUDDEN, I'VE GOT A TERRIBLE HEADACHE.
OR WOULD IT BE MORE FUN TO OBLITERATE THE CASTLE INSTEAD...?
YOU MAY GO...
I WAS GETTING TIRED OF THIS PLACE ANYWAY.
WAVE WAVE

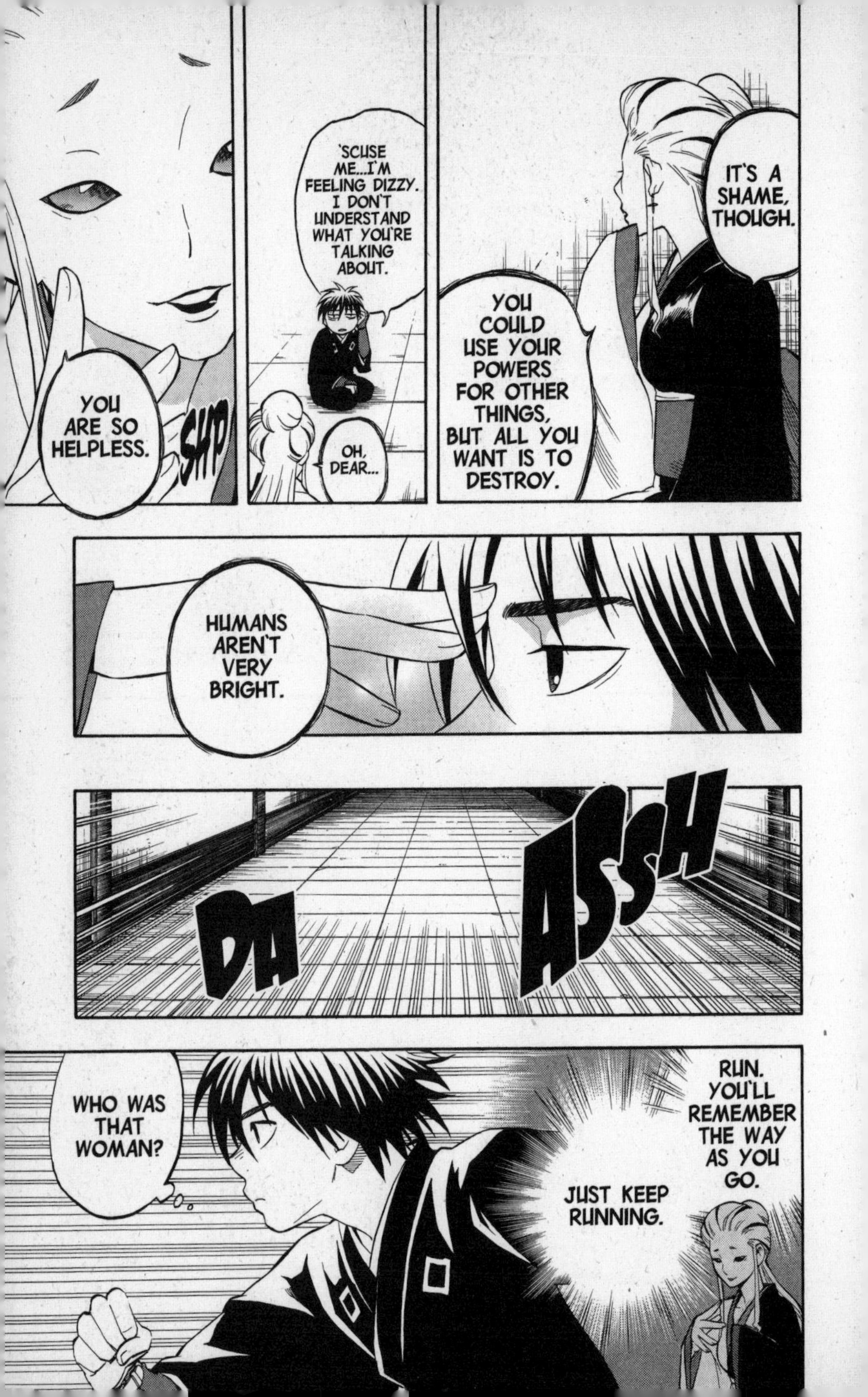
IT'S A SHAME, THOUGH.
YOU COULD USE YOUR POWERS FOR OTHER THINGS, BUT ALL YOU WANT IS TO DESTROY.
'SCUSE ME...I'M FEELING DIZZY. I DON'T UNDERSTAND WHAT YOU'RE TALKING ABOUT.
OH, DEAR...
SHP
YOU ARE SO HELPLESS.
HUMANS AREN'T VERY BRIGHT.
DA
ASSH
RUN. YOU'LL REMEMBER THE WAY AS YOU GO.
JUST KEEP RUNNING.
WHO WAS THAT WOMAN?

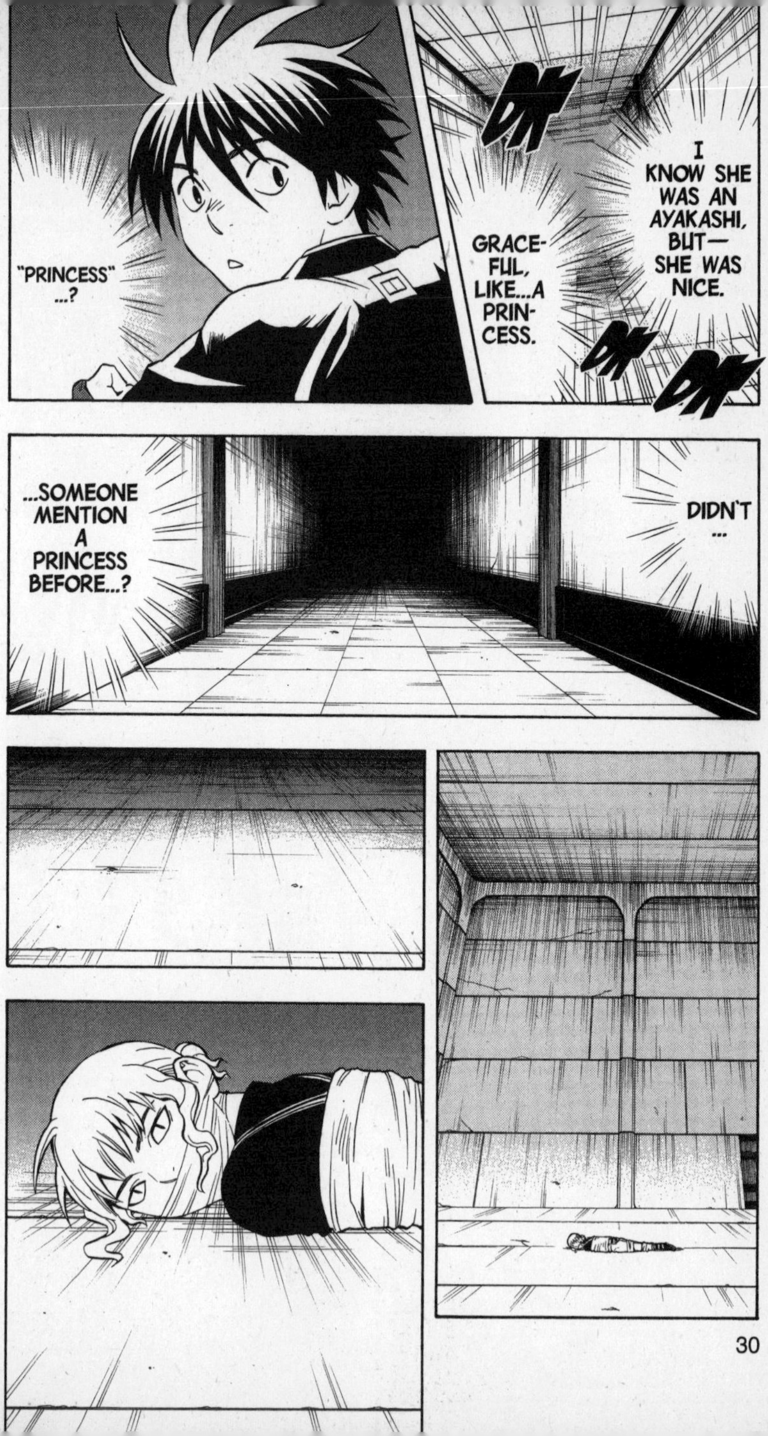
DK
I KNOW SHE WAS AN AYAKASHI, BUT— SHE WAS NICE.
GRACE-FUL, LIKE...A PRIN-CESS.
DK
DK
"PRINCESS" ...?
DIDN'T ...
...SOMEONE MENTION A PRINCESS BEFORE...?

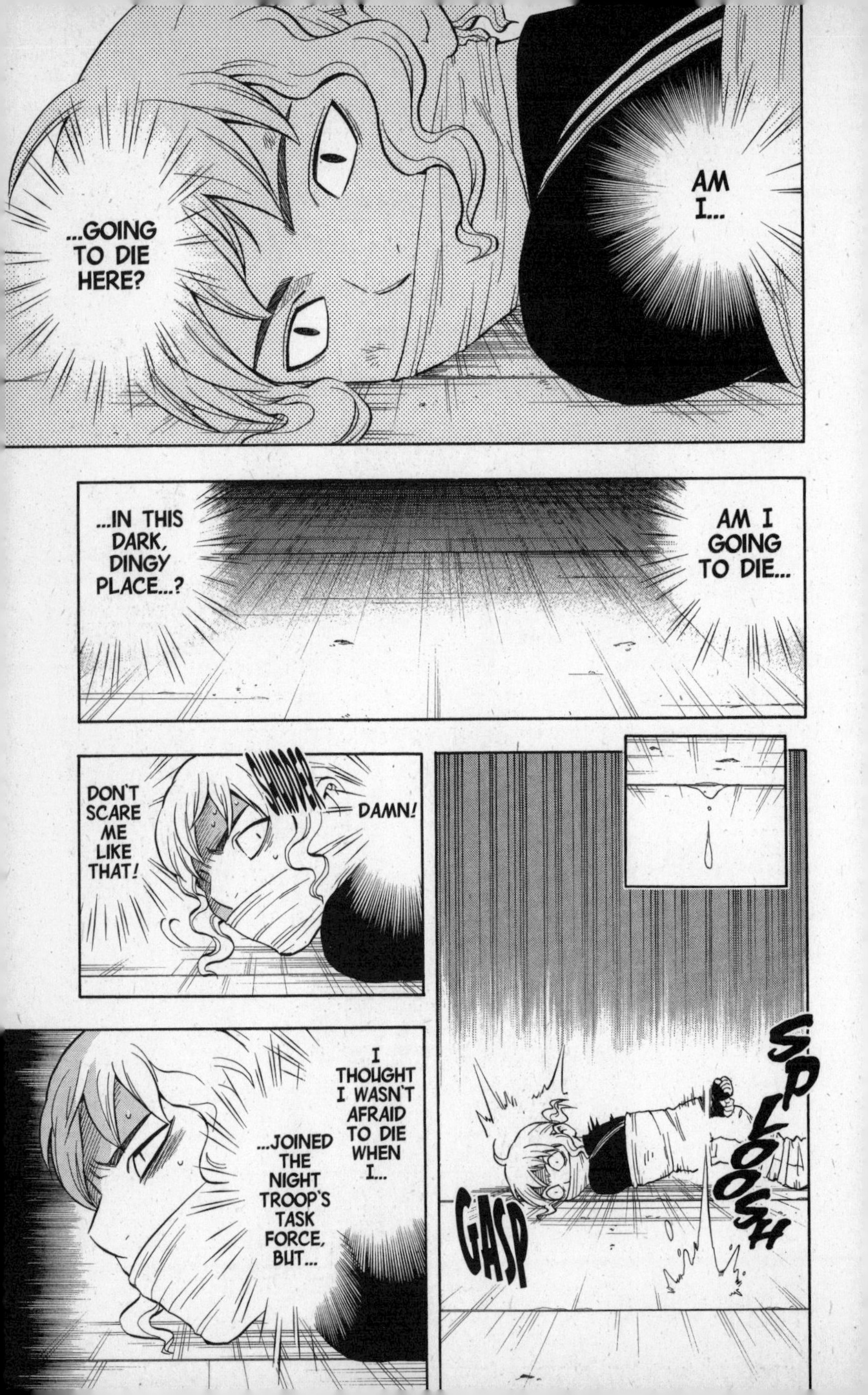
AM I...
...GOING TO DIE HERE?
AM I GOING TO DIE...
...IN THIS DARK, DINGY PLACE...?
SPLOOSH
GASP
SHUDDER
DAMN!
DON'T SCARE ME LIKE THAT!
I THOUGHT I WASN'T AFRAID TO DIE WHEN I...
...JOINED THE NIGHT TROOP'S TASK FORCE, BUT...

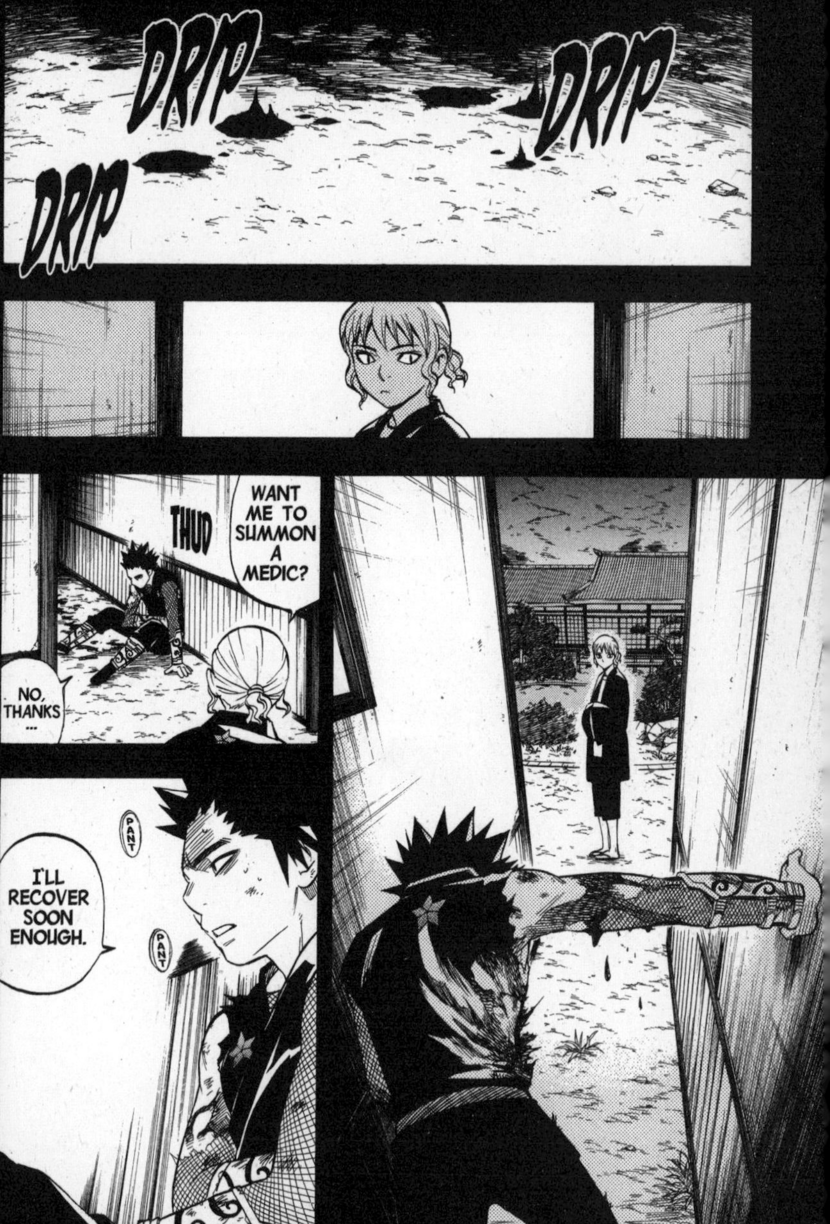
DRIP
DRIP
DRIP
WANT ME TO SUMMON A MEDIC?
THUD
NO, THANKS...
PANT
I'LL RECOVER SOON ENOUGH.
PANT

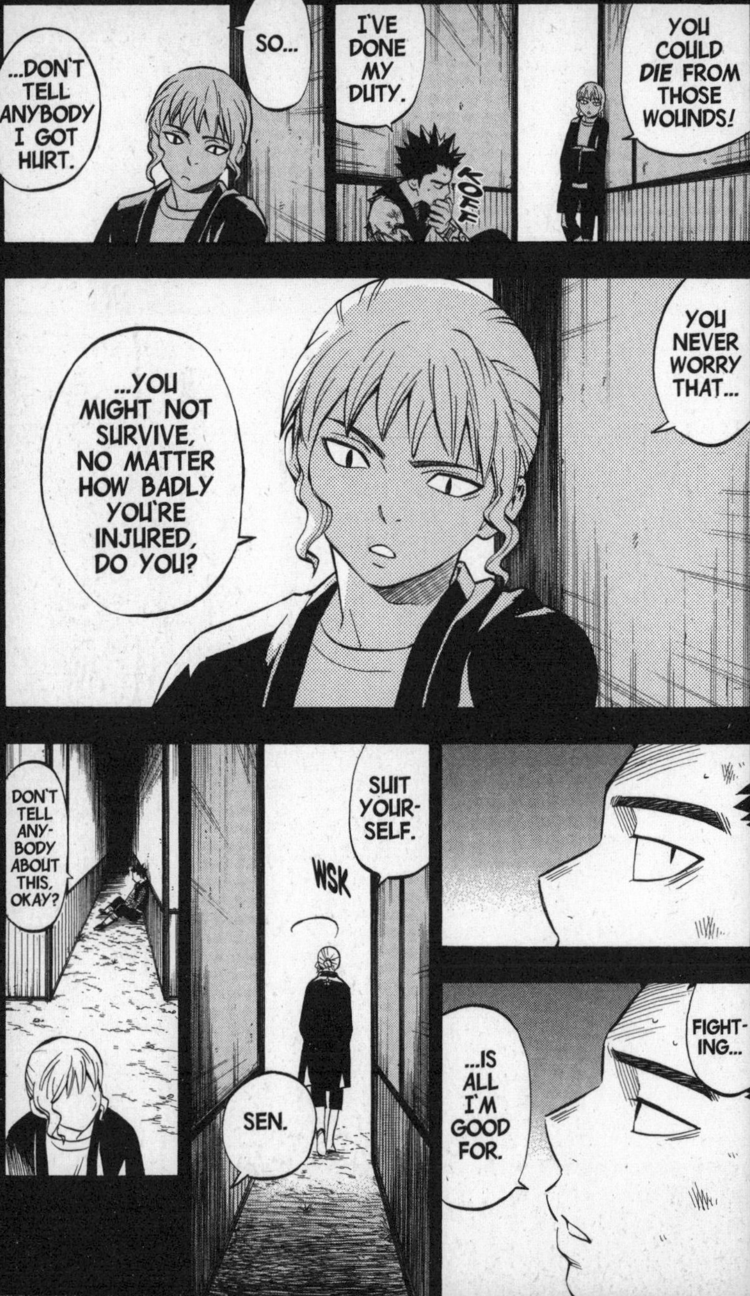
YOU COULD DIE FROM THOSE WOUNDS!
I'VE DONE MY DUTY.
KOFF
SO...
...DON'T TELL ANYBODY I GOT HURT.
YOU NEVER WORRY THAT...
...YOU MIGHT NOT SURVIVE, NO MATTER HOW BADLY YOU'RE INJURED, DO YOU?
FIGHT-ING...
...IS ALL I'M GOOD FOR.
SUIT YOUR-SELF.
WSK
SEN.
DON'T TELL ANY-BODY ABOUT THIS, OKAY?

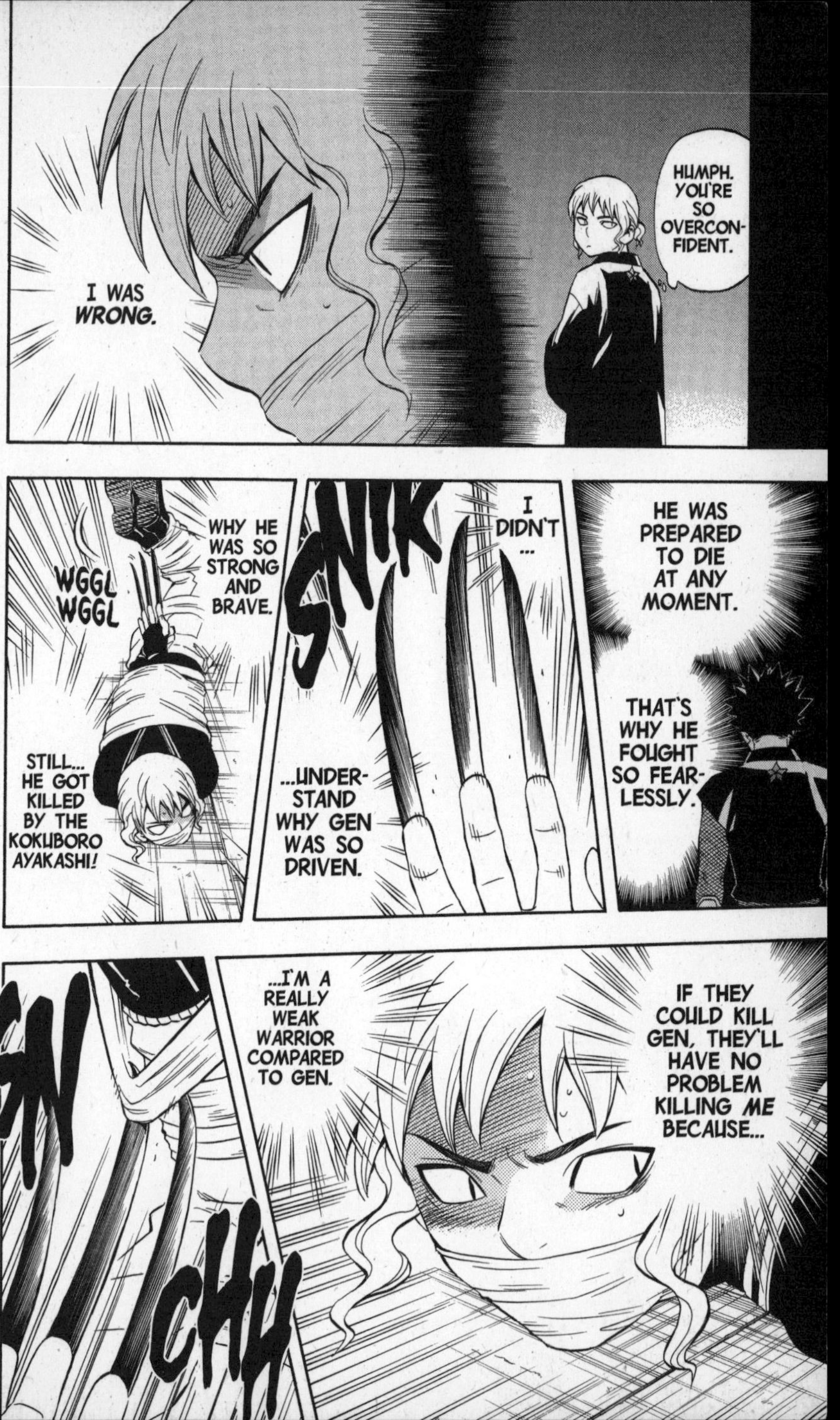
HUMPH. YOU'RE SO OVERCON-FIDENT.
I WAS *WRONG.*
HE WAS PREPARED TO DIE AT ANY MOMENT.
THAT'S WHY HE FOUGHT SO FEAR-LESSLY.
I DIDN'T ...
SNIK
...UNDER-STAND WHY GEN WAS SO DRIVEN.
WHY HE WAS SO STRONG AND BRAVE.
WGGL WGGL
STILL... HE GOT KILLED BY THE KOKUBORO AYAKASHI!
IF THEY COULD KILL GEN, THEY'LL HAVE NO PROBLEM KILLING *ME* BECAUSE...
...I'M A REALLY WEAK WARRIOR COMPARED TO GEN.
SN CHH

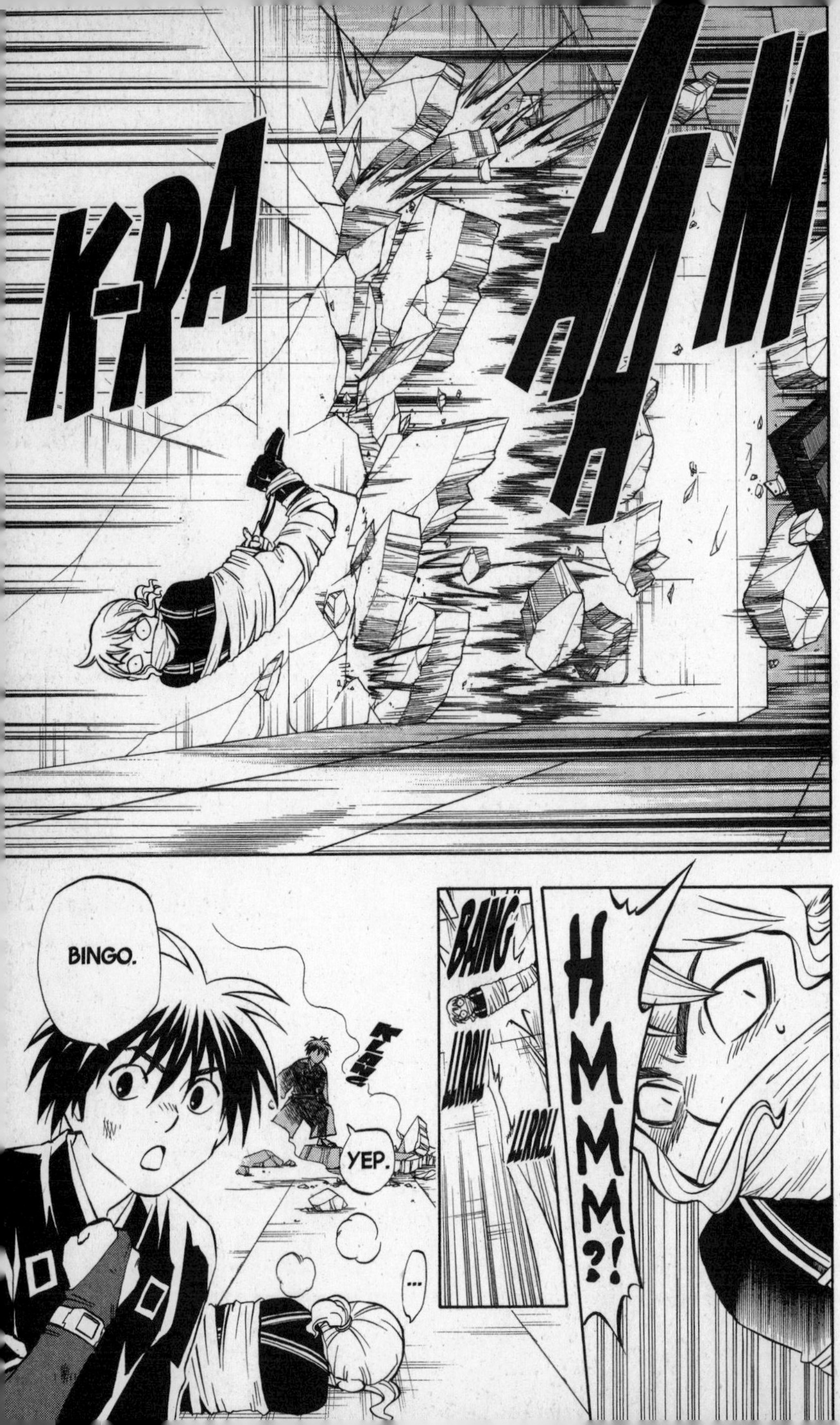
K-RA
HMMMM?!
BANG
LLRRLL
LLRRLL
BINGO.
KLANG
YEP.
...

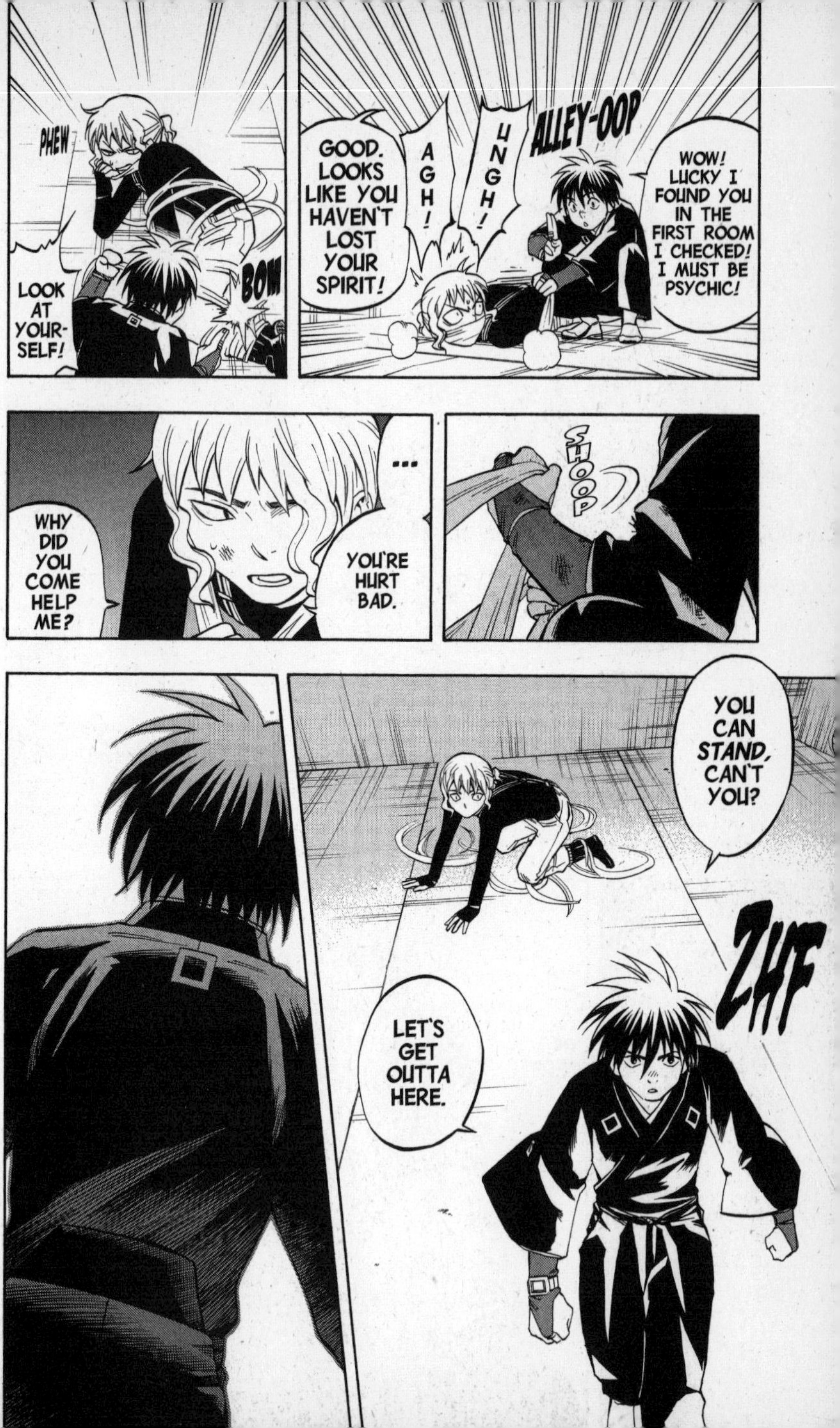
WOW! LUCKY I FOUND YOU IN THE FIRST ROOM I CHECKED! I MUST BE PSYCHIC!
ALLEY-OOP
UNGH!
AGH!
GOOD. LOOKS LIKE YOU HAVEN'T LOST YOUR SPIRIT!
BOM
LOOK AT YOURSELF!
PHEW
SHOOP
...
YOU'RE HURT BAD.
WHY DID YOU COME HELP ME?
YOU CAN STAND, CAN'T YOU?
ZHF
LET'S GET OUTTA HERE.

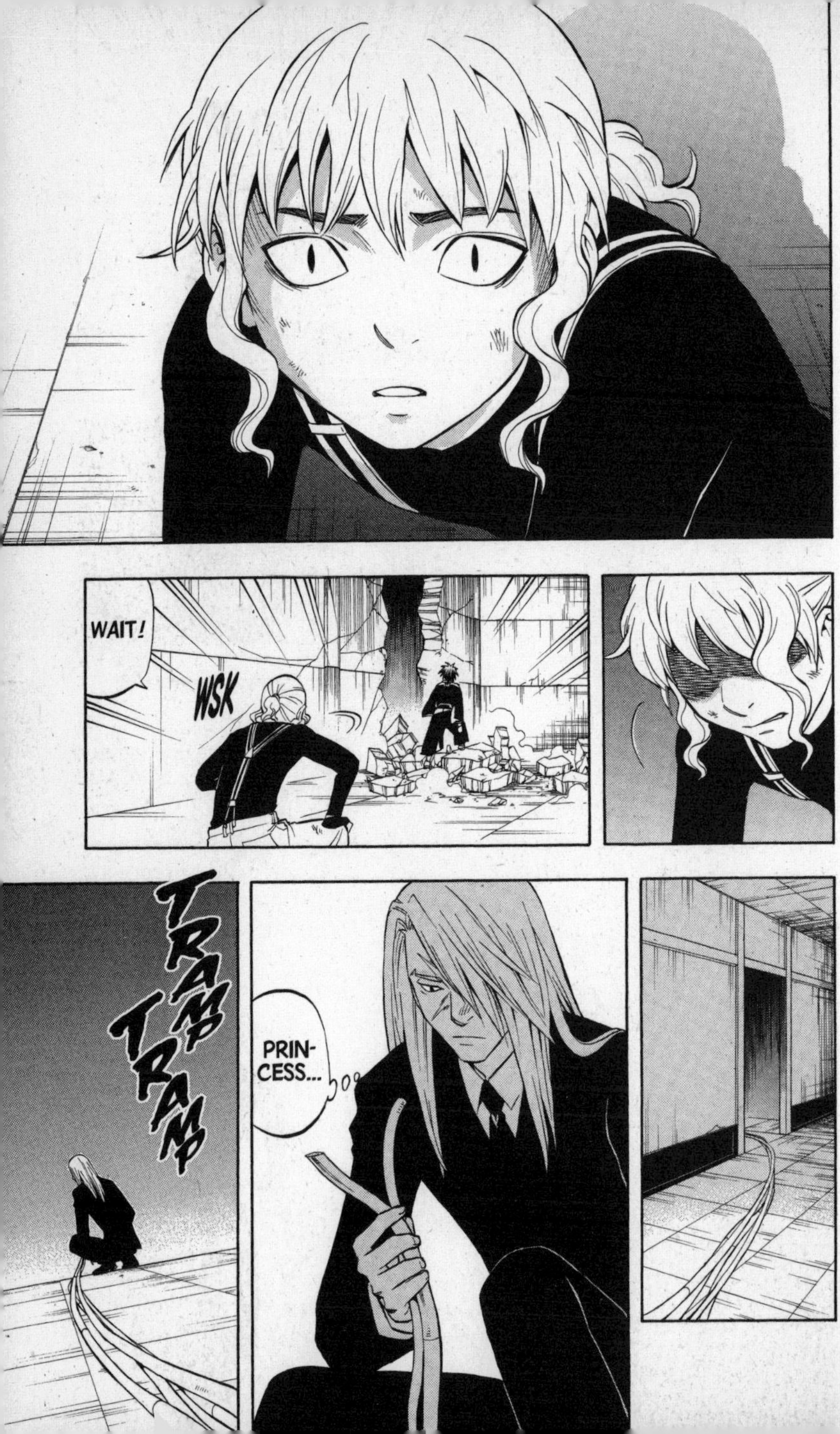
WAIT!
WSK
PRIN-CESS...
TRAMP TRAMP

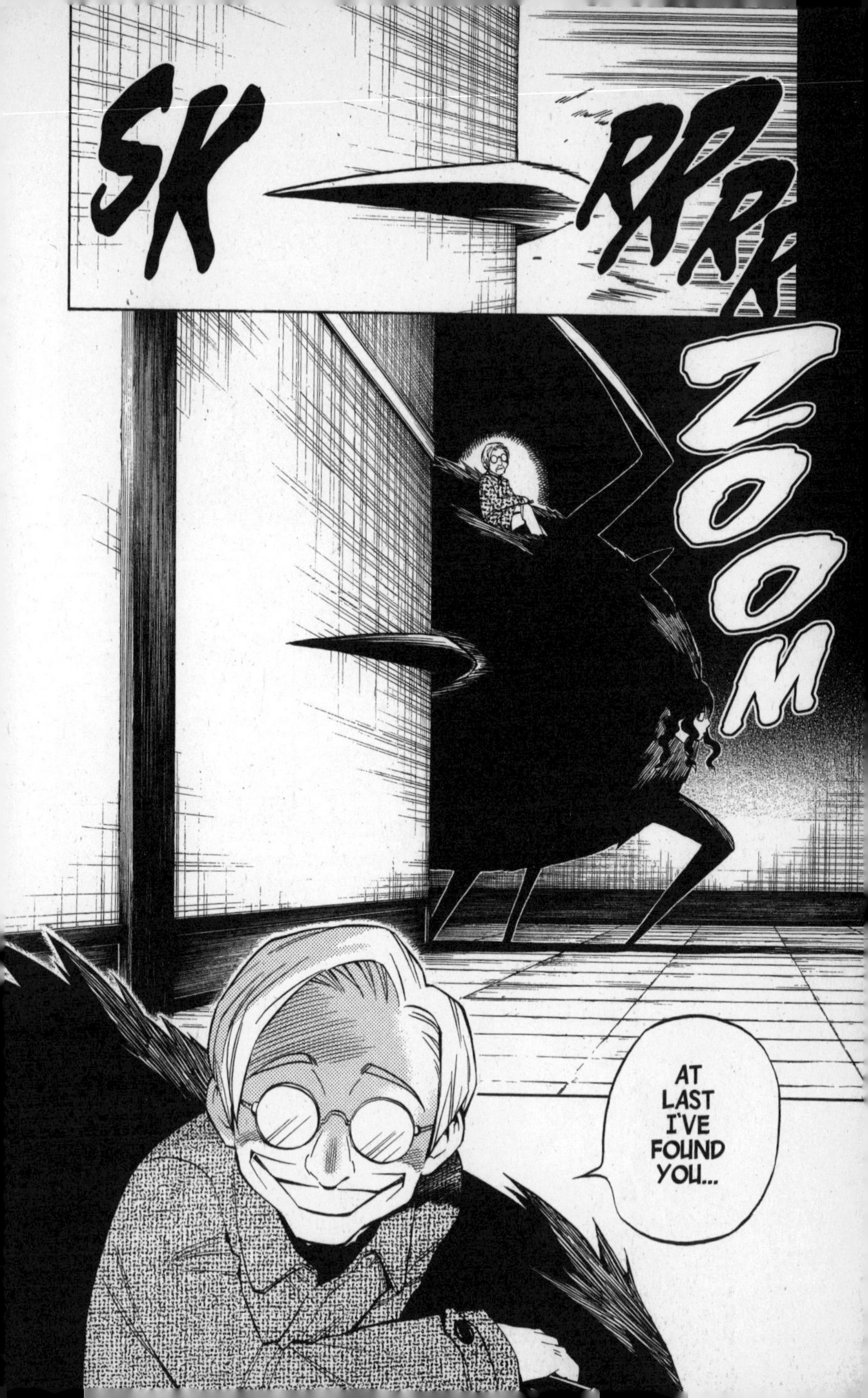
SK
RRRR
ZOOOM
AT LAST I'VE FOUND YOU...

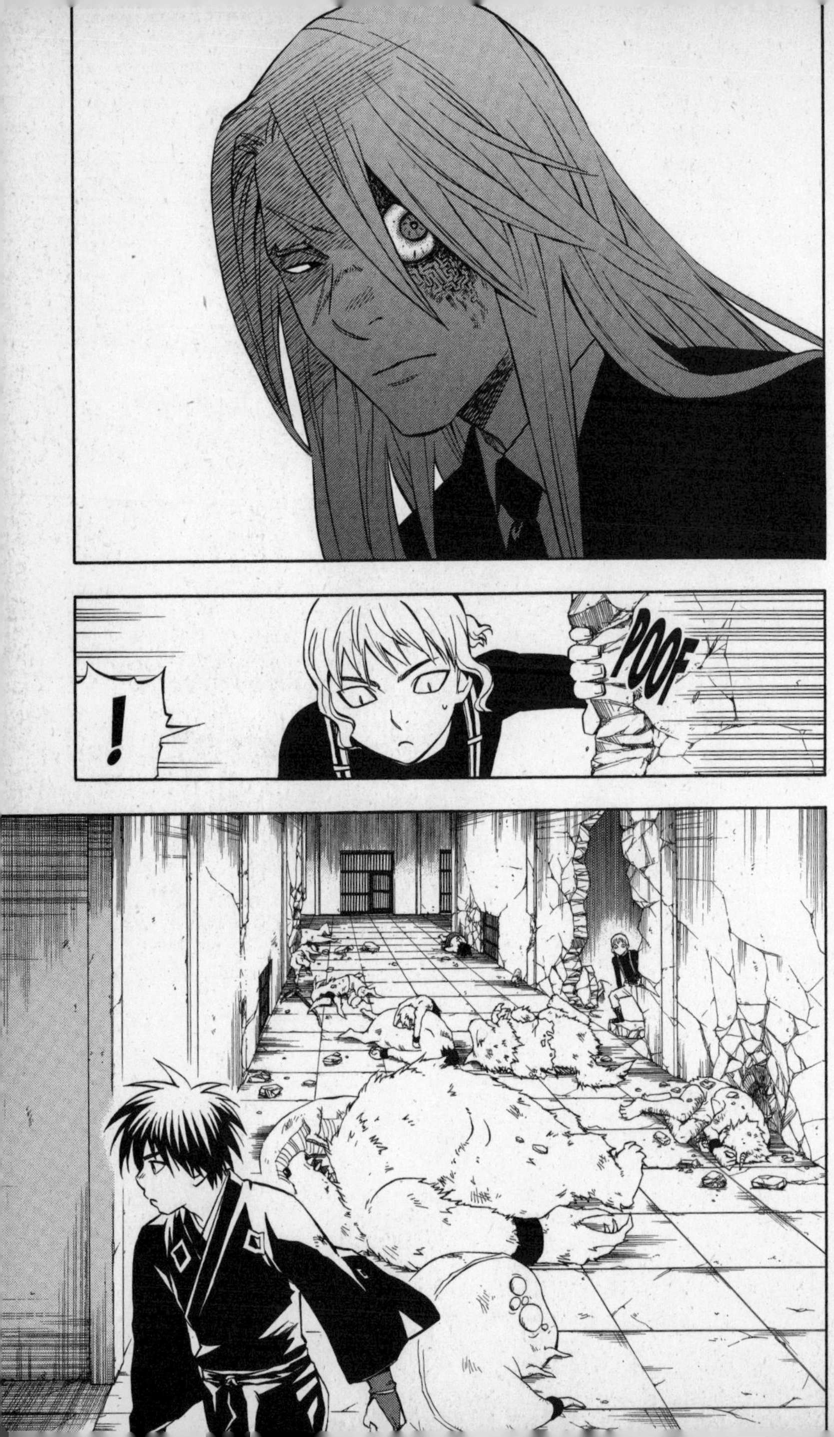
POOF
!

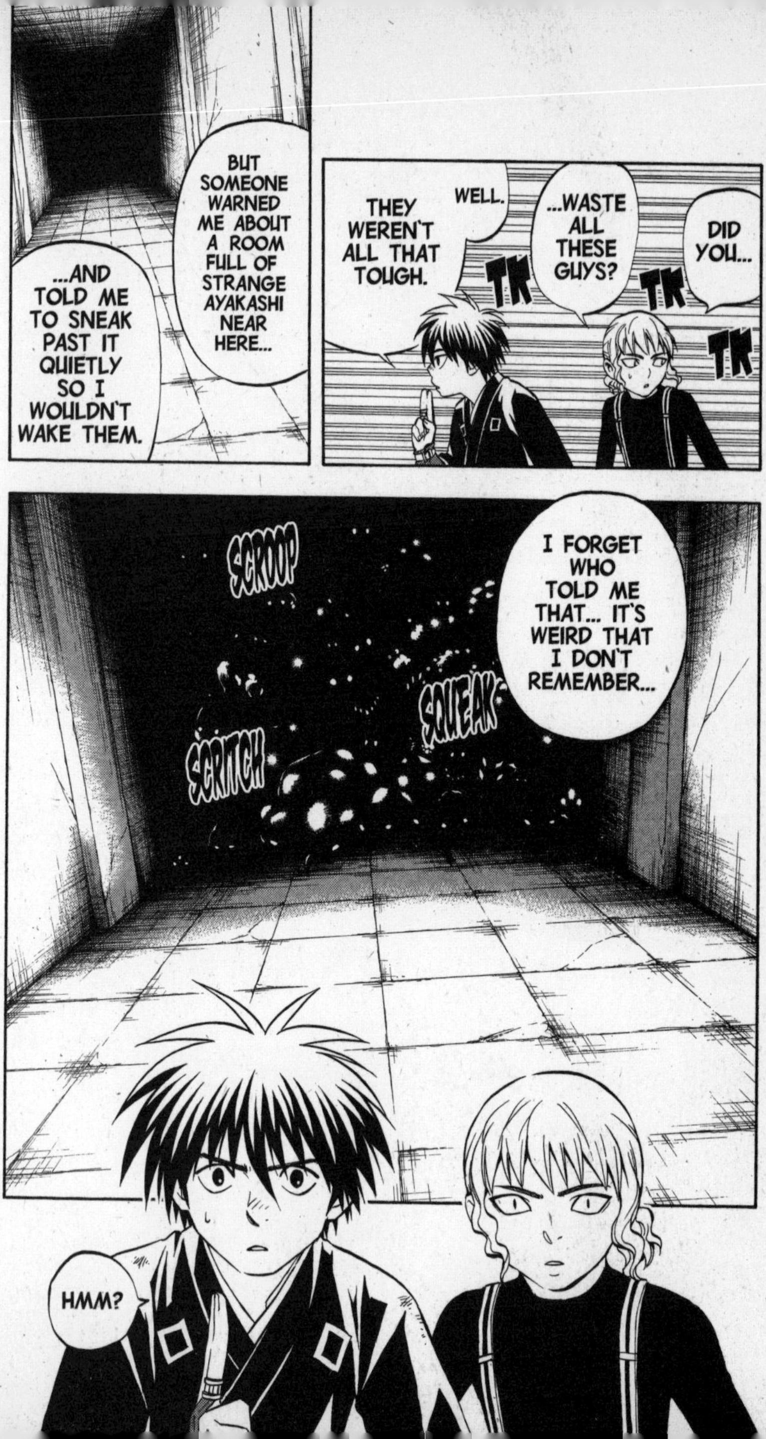
DID YOU...
TK
...WASTE ALL THESE GUYS?
TK
TK
WELL.
THEY WEREN'T ALL THAT TOUGH.
BUT SOMEONE WARNED ME ABOUT A ROOM FULL OF STRANGE AYAKASHI NEAR HERE...
...AND TOLD ME TO SNEAK PAST IT QUIETLY SO I WOULDN'T WAKE THEM.
I FORGET WHO TOLD ME THAT... IT'S WEIRD THAT I DON'T REMEMBER...
SQUEAK
SCROOP
SCRITCH
HMM?

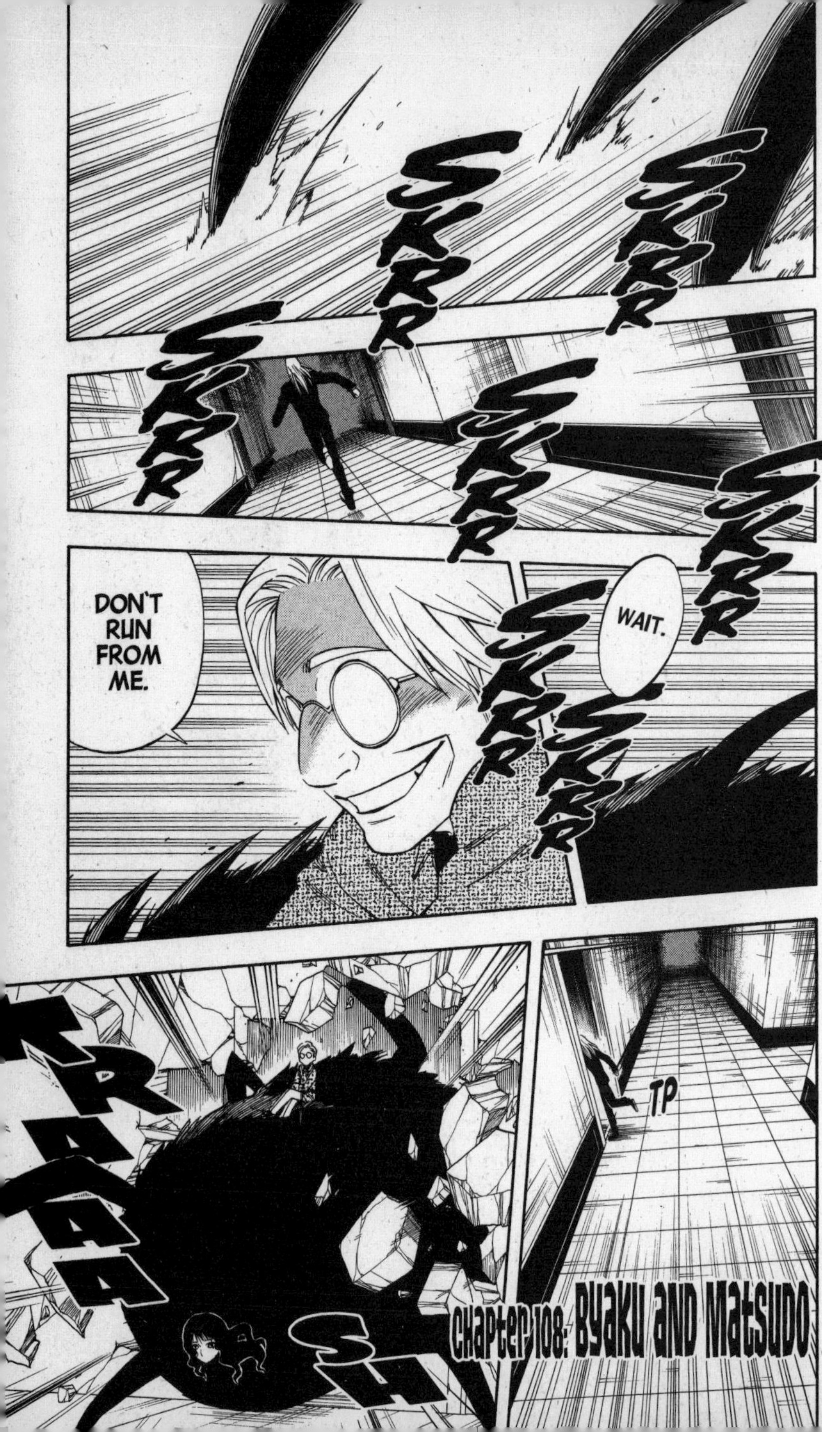

SKRR
SKRR
SKRR
SKRR
SKRR
WAIT.
SKRR
SKRR
DON'T RUN FROM ME.
TP
KRAAASH
Chapter 108: Byaku and Matsudo

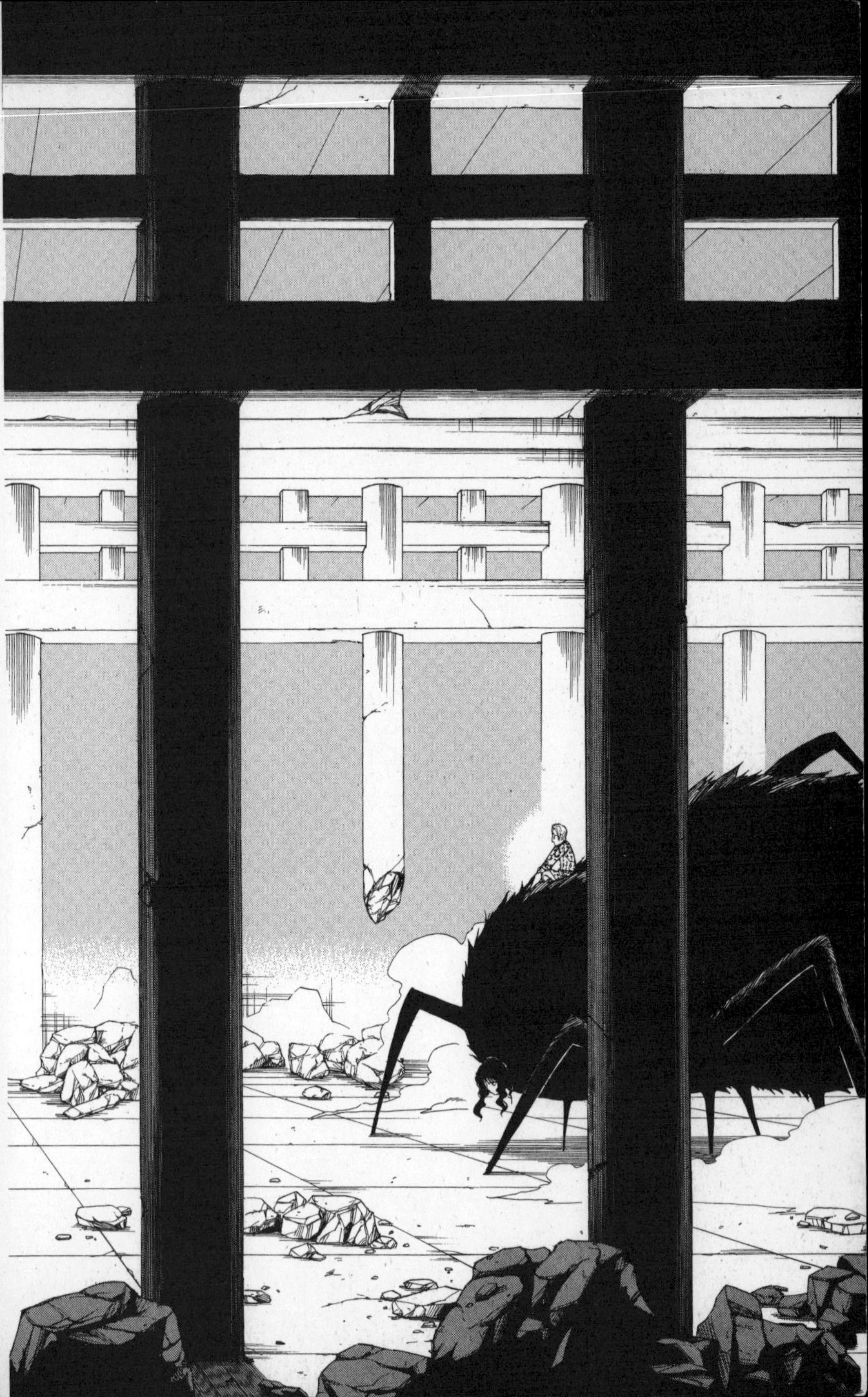

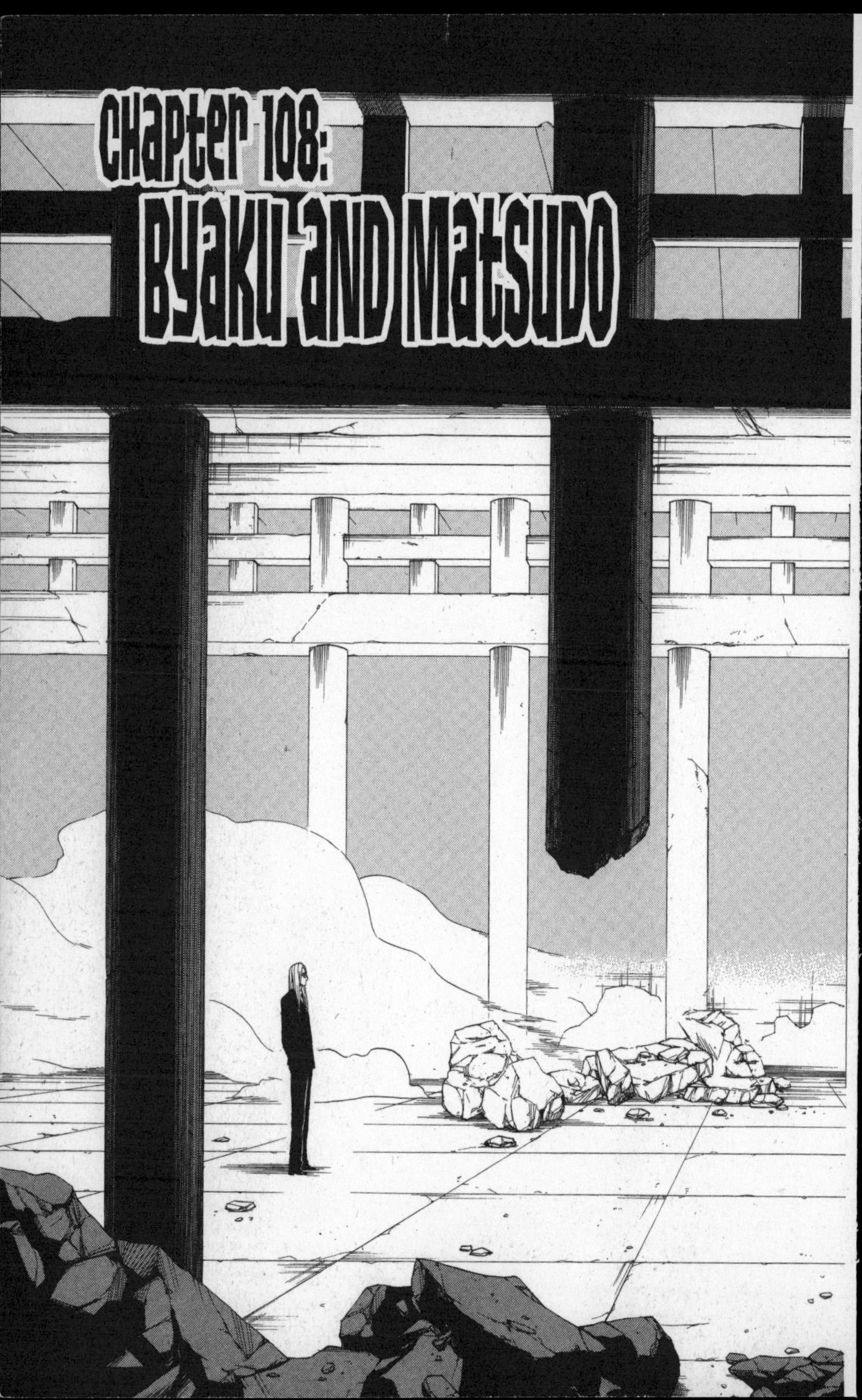
CHAPTER 108:
BYAKU AND MATSUDO

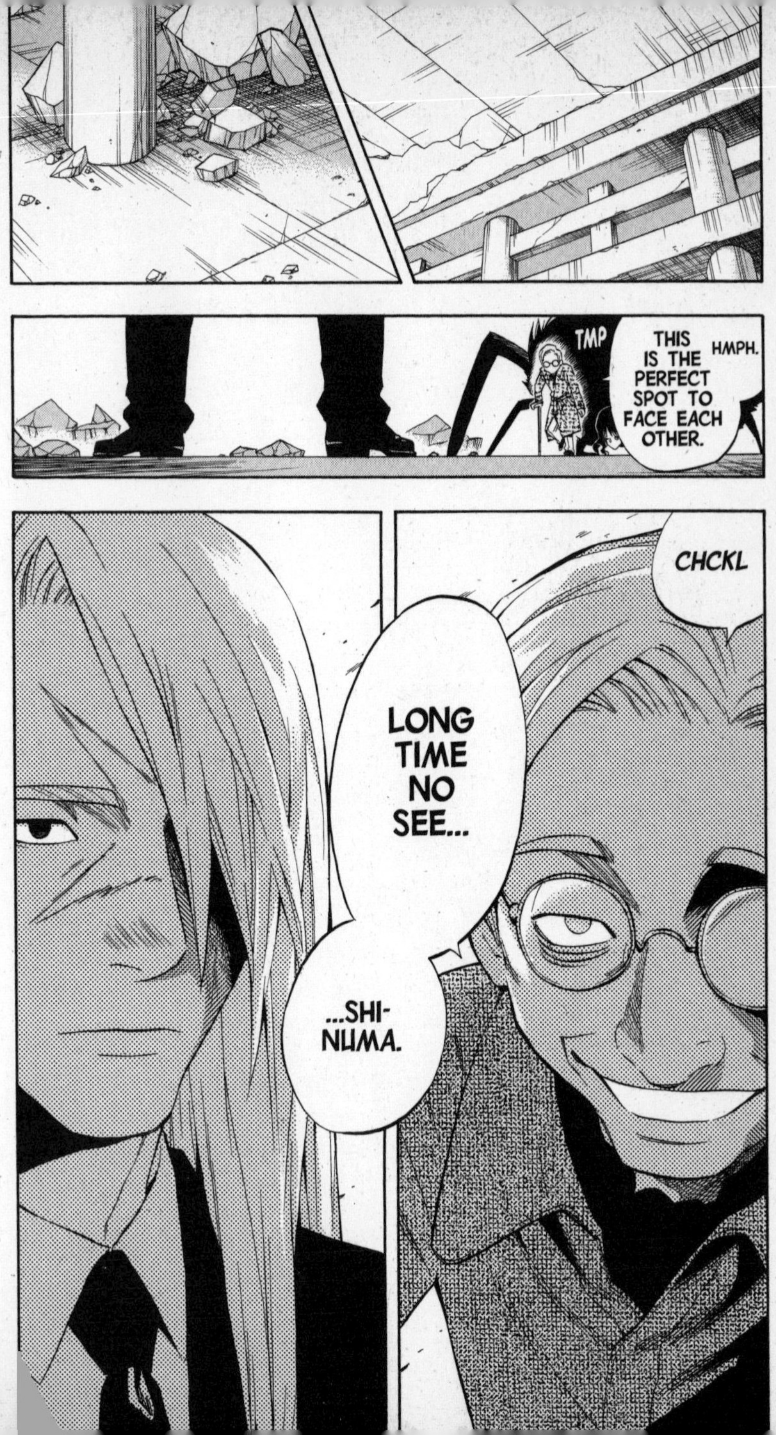
HMPH.
THIS IS THE PERFECT SPOT TO FACE EACH OTHER.
TMP
CHCKL
LONG TIME NO SEE...
...SHI-NUMA.

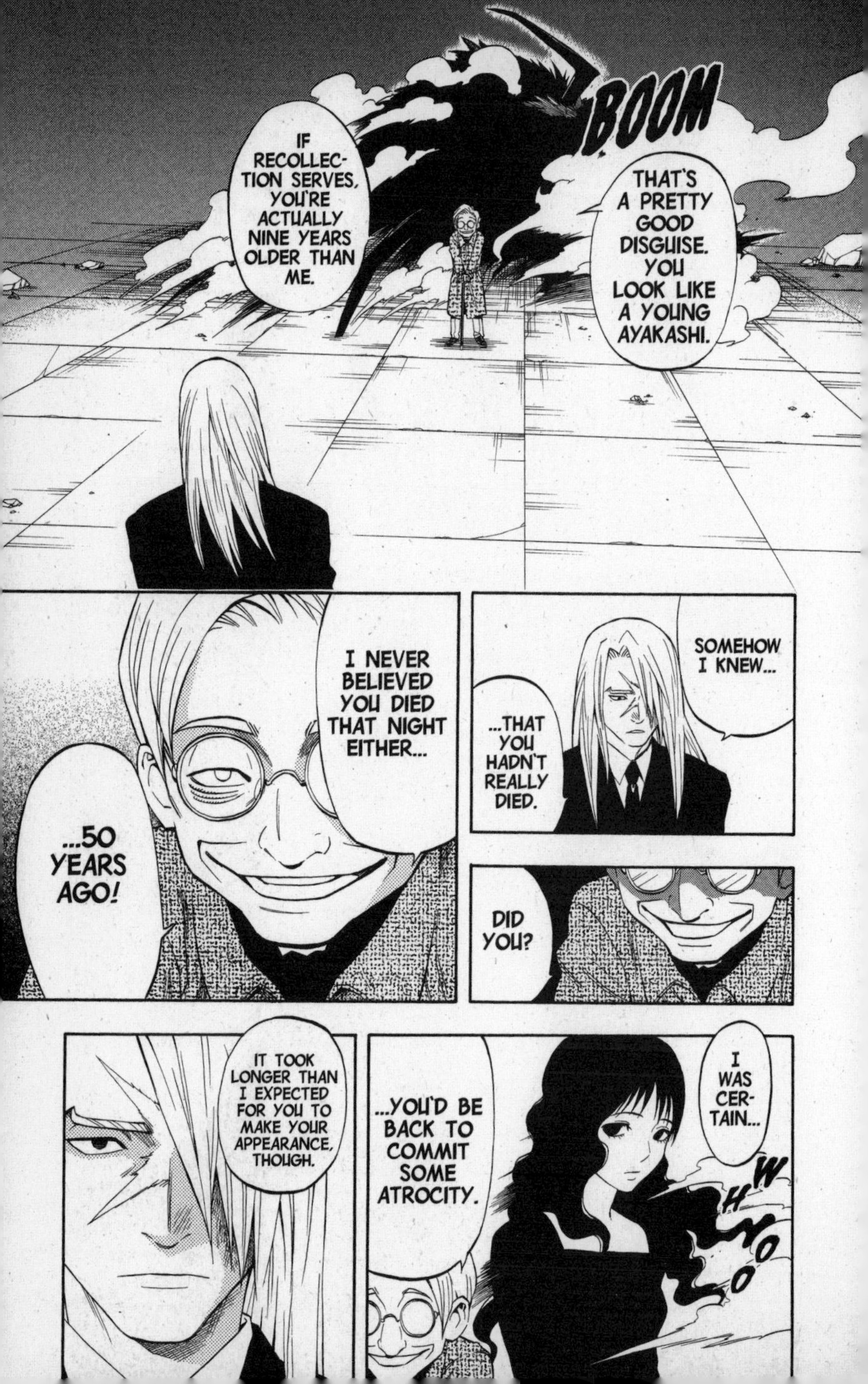
BOOM
THAT'S A PRETTY GOOD DISGUISE. YOU LOOK LIKE A YOUNG AYAKASHI.
IF RECOLLECTION SERVES, YOU'RE ACTUALLY NINE YEARS OLDER THAN ME.
SOMEHOW I KNEW...
...THAT YOU HADN'T REALLY DIED.
DID YOU?
I NEVER BELIEVED YOU DIED THAT NIGHT EITHER...
...50 YEARS AGO!
I WAS CERTAIN...
...YOU'D BE BACK TO COMMIT SOME ATROCITY.
WHOOO
IT TOOK LONGER THAN I EXPECTED FOR YOU TO MAKE YOUR APPEARANCE, THOUGH.

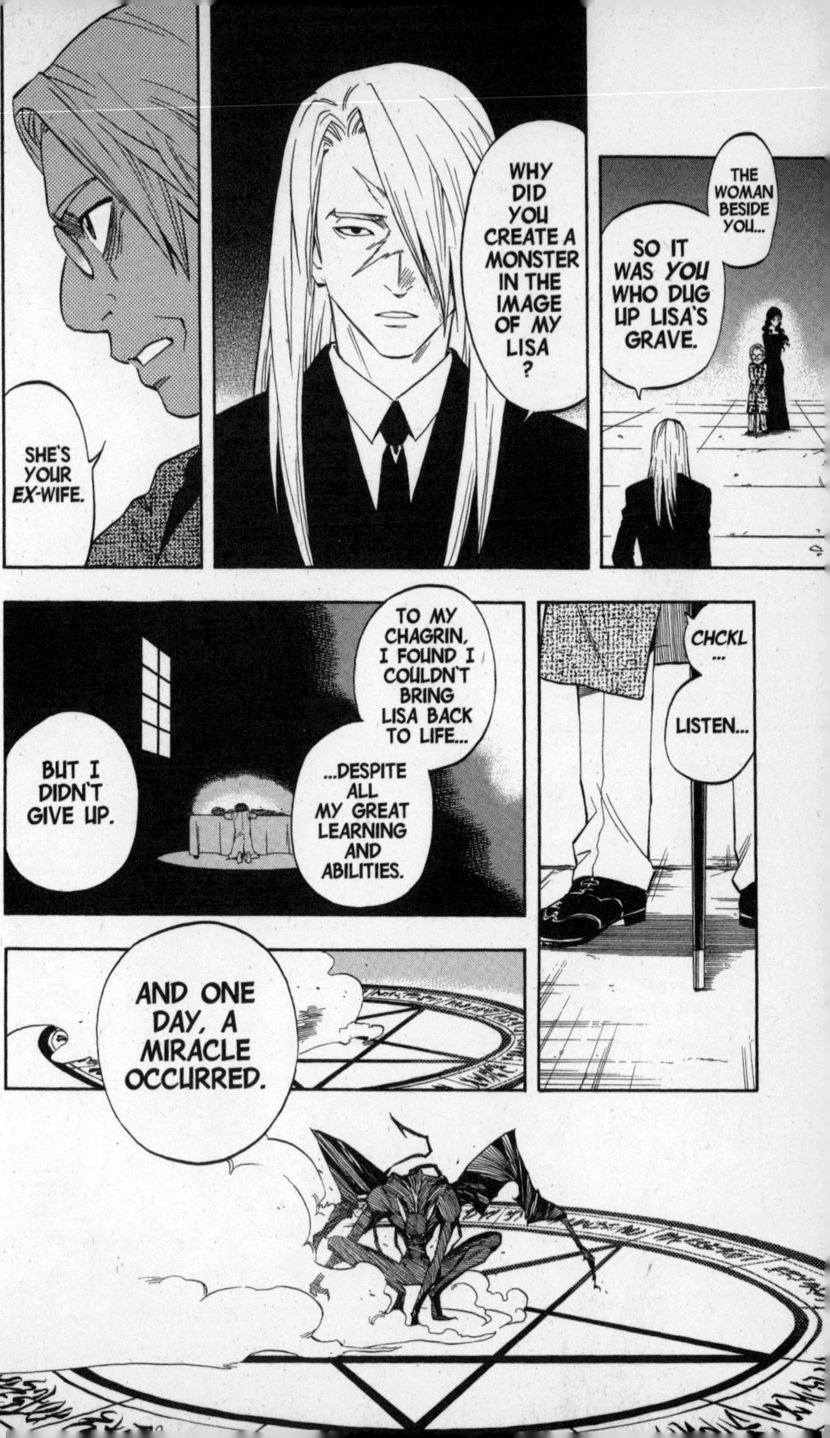
THE WOMAN BESIDE YOU...
SO IT WAS *YOU* WHO DUG UP LISA'S GRAVE.
WHY DID YOU CREATE A MONSTER IN THE IMAGE OF MY LISA?
SHE'S YOUR *EX*-WIFE.
CHCKL...
LISTEN...
TO MY CHAGRIN, I FOUND I COULDN'T BRING LISA BACK TO LIFE...
...DESPITE ALL MY GREAT LEARNING AND ABILITIES.
BUT I DIDN'T GIVE UP.
AND ONE DAY, A MIRACLE OCCURRED.

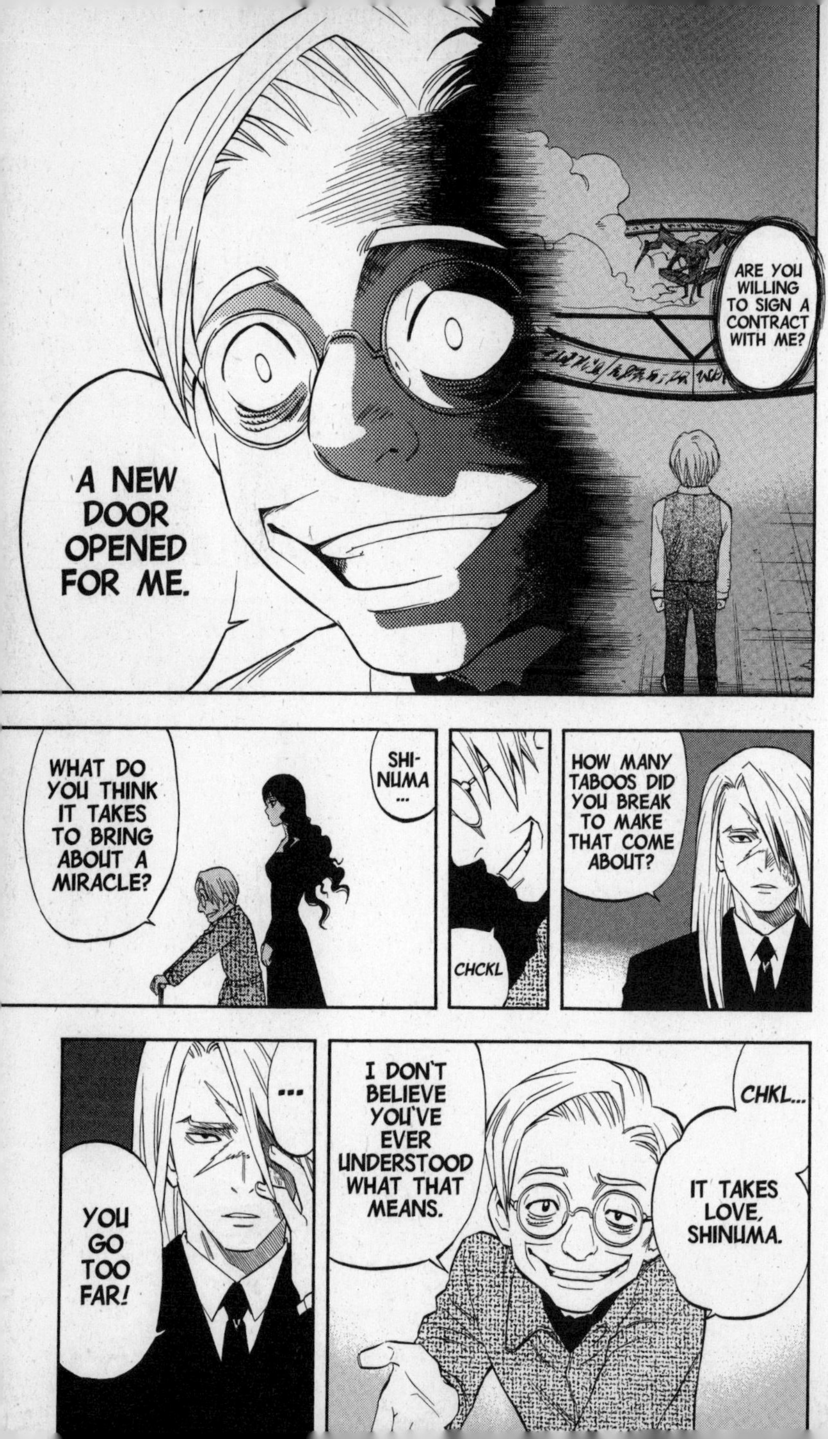
ARE YOU WILLING TO SIGN A CONTRACT WITH ME?
A NEW DOOR OPENED FOR ME.
HOW MANY TABOOS DID YOU BREAK TO MAKE THAT COME ABOUT?
CHCKL
SHI-NUMA...
WHAT DO YOU THINK IT TAKES TO BRING ABOUT A MIRACLE?
CHKL...
IT TAKES LOVE, SHINUMA.
I DON'T BELIEVE YOU'VE EVER UNDERSTOOD WHAT THAT MEANS.
...
YOU GO TOO FAR!

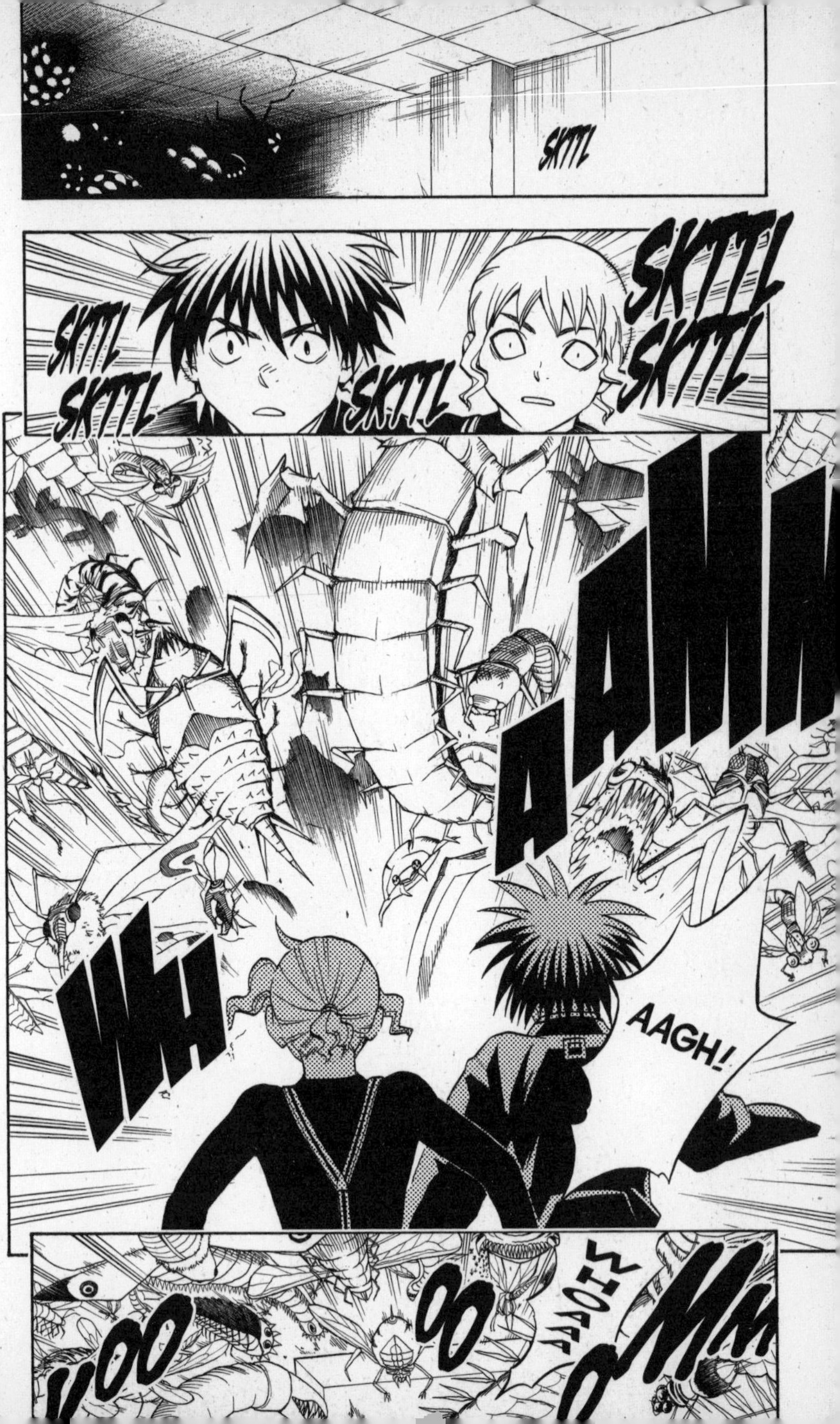
SKTTL
SKTTL SKTTL
SKTTL
SKTTL SKTTL
AAMM
AAGH!
WH
WHOAAA

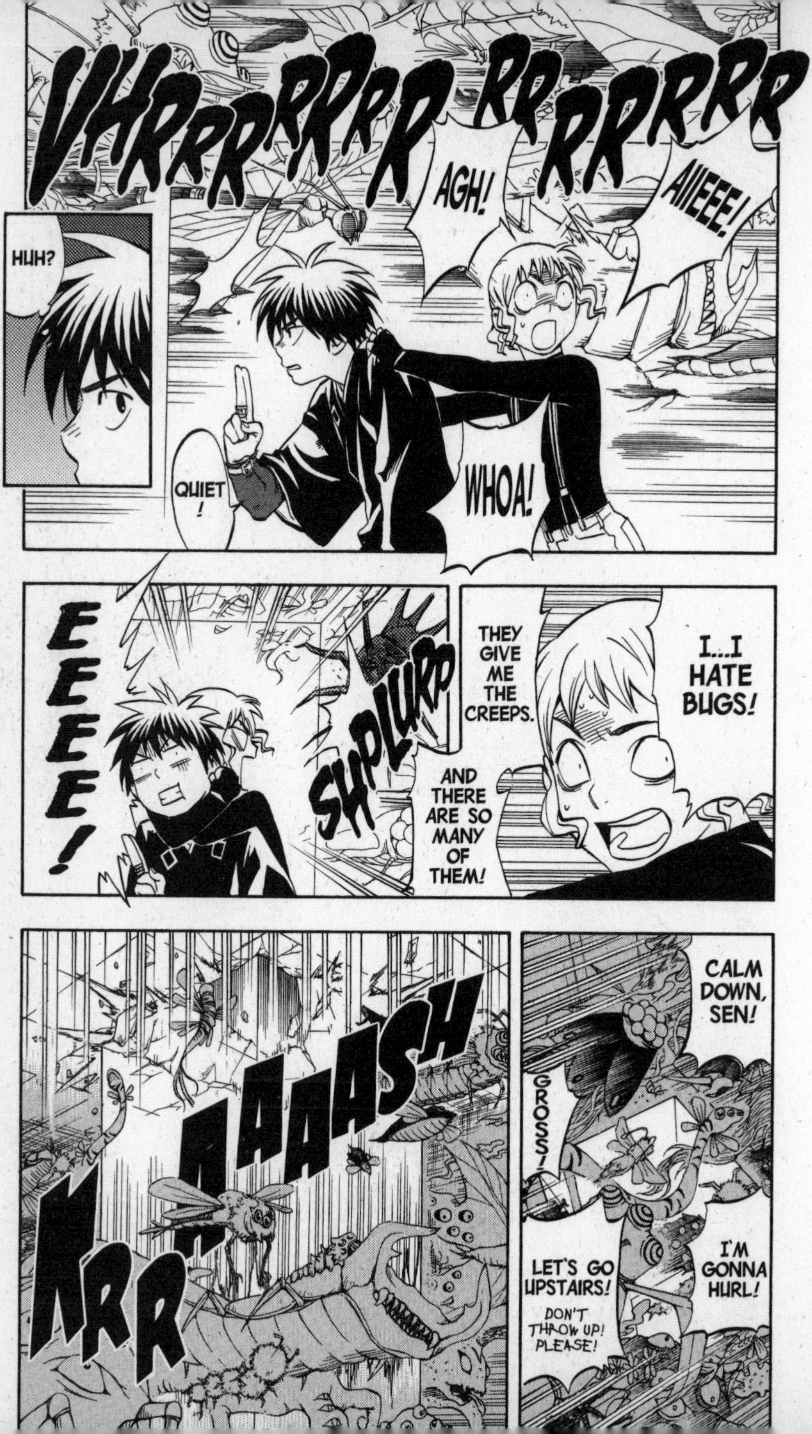
VHRRRRRRRR RRRRRRRR
AIEEE!
AGH!
WHOA!
QUIET!
HUH?
I...I HATE BUGS!
THEY GIVE ME THE CREEPS.
AND THERE ARE SO MANY OF THEM!
SHPLURP
EEEEE!
CALM DOWN, SEN!
GROSS!
I'M GONNA HURL!
LET'S GO UPSTAIRS!
DON'T THROW UP! PLEASE!
KRRAAAASH

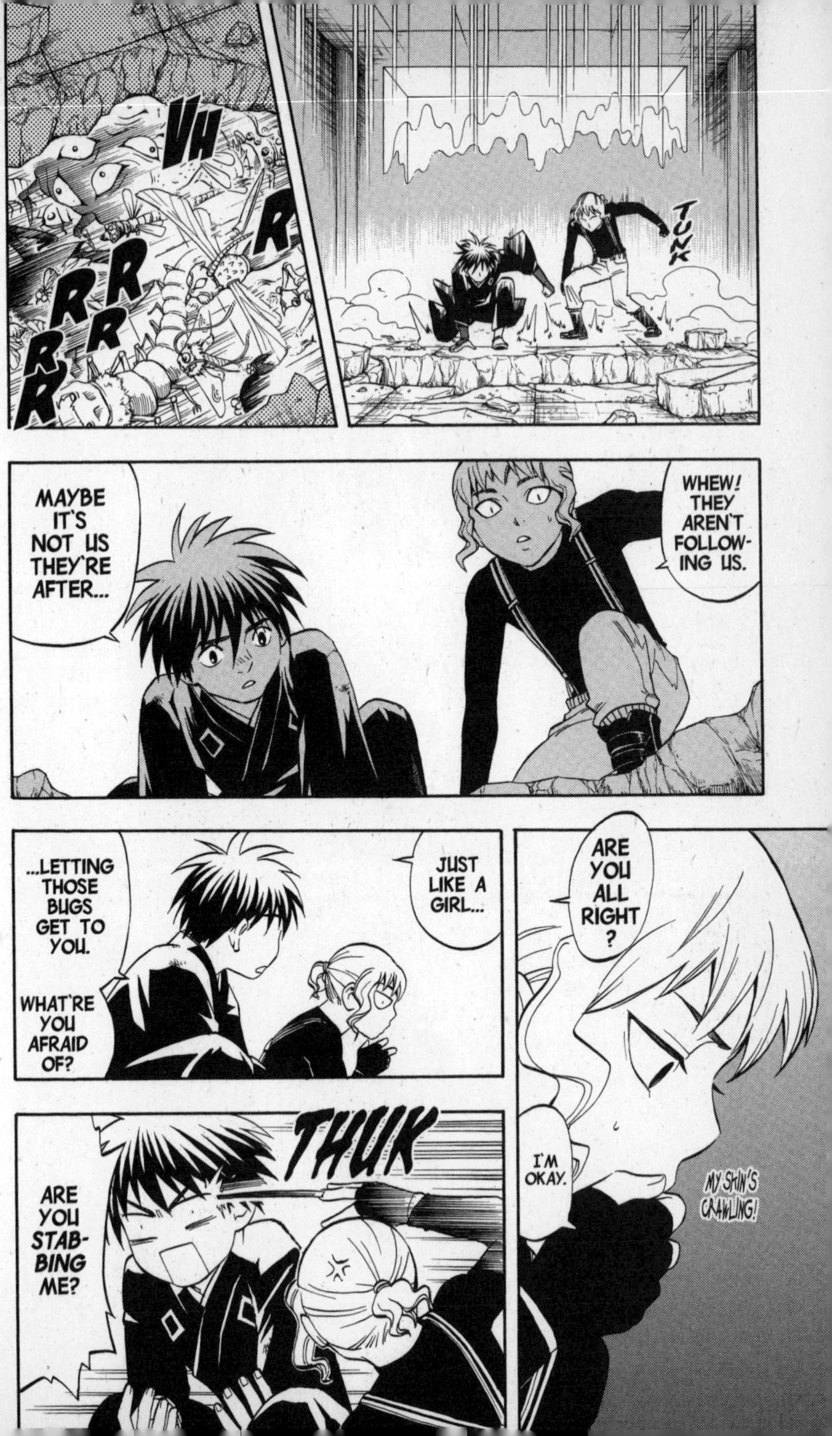
TUNK
VH
RRRRRRR
WHEW! THEY AREN'T FOLLOW-ING US.
MAYBE IT'S NOT US THEY'RE AFTER...
ARE YOU ALL RIGHT?
I'M OKAY.
MY SKIN'S CRAWLING!
JUST LIKE A GIRL...
...LETTING THOSE BUGS GET TO YOU.
WHAT'RE YOU AFRAID OF?
THUK
ARE YOU STAB-BING ME?

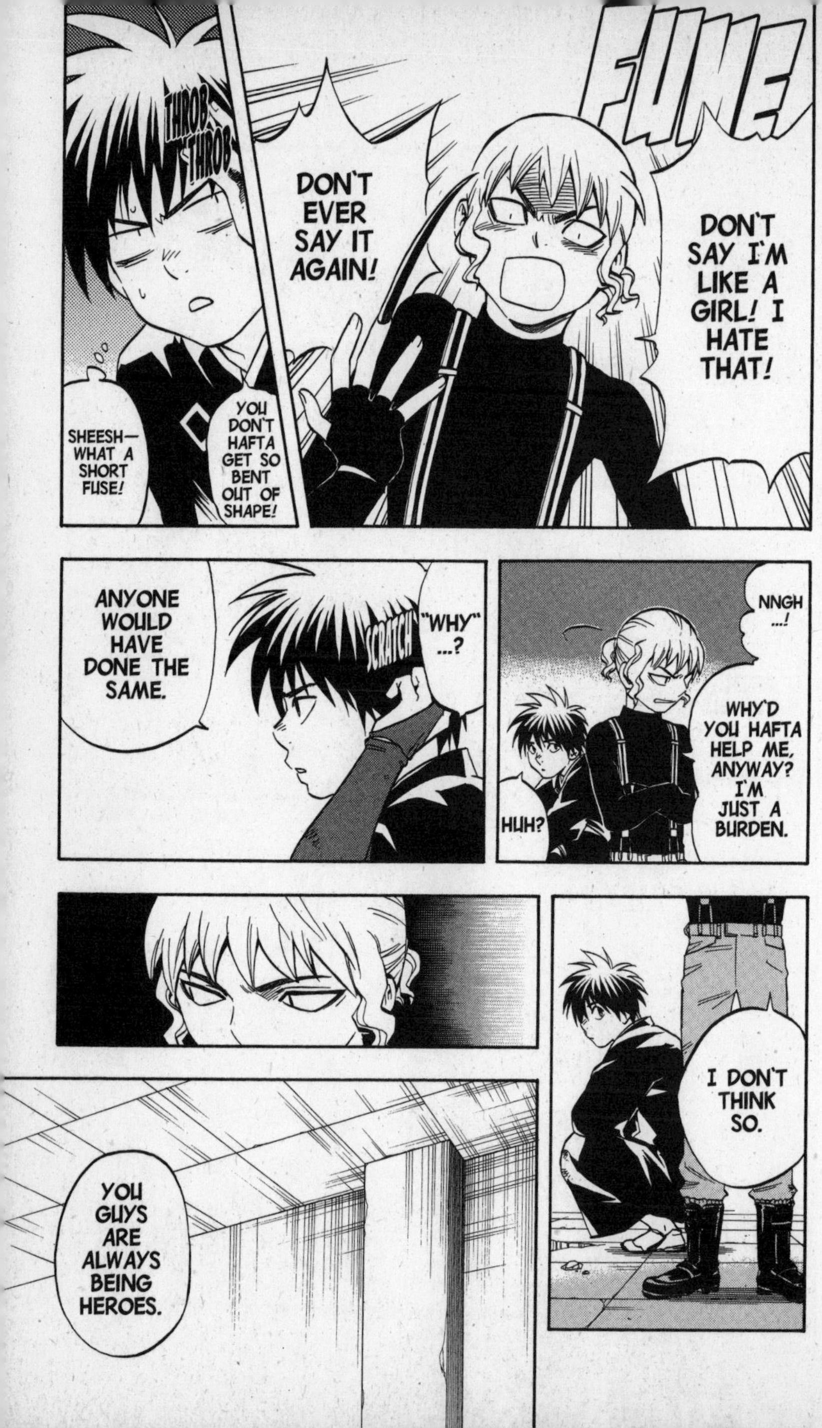
FUME!
DON'T SAY I'M LIKE A GIRL! I HATE THAT!
DON'T EVER SAY IT AGAIN!
THROB THROB
YOU DON'T HAFTA GET SO BENT OUT OF SHAPE!
SHEESH— WHAT A SHORT FUSE!
NNGH ...!
WHY'D YOU HAFTA HELP ME, ANYWAY? I'M JUST A BURDEN.
HUH?
"WHY" ...?
SCRATCH
ANYONE WOULD HAVE DONE THE SAME.
I DON'T THINK SO.
YOU GUYS ARE ALWAYS BEING HEROES.

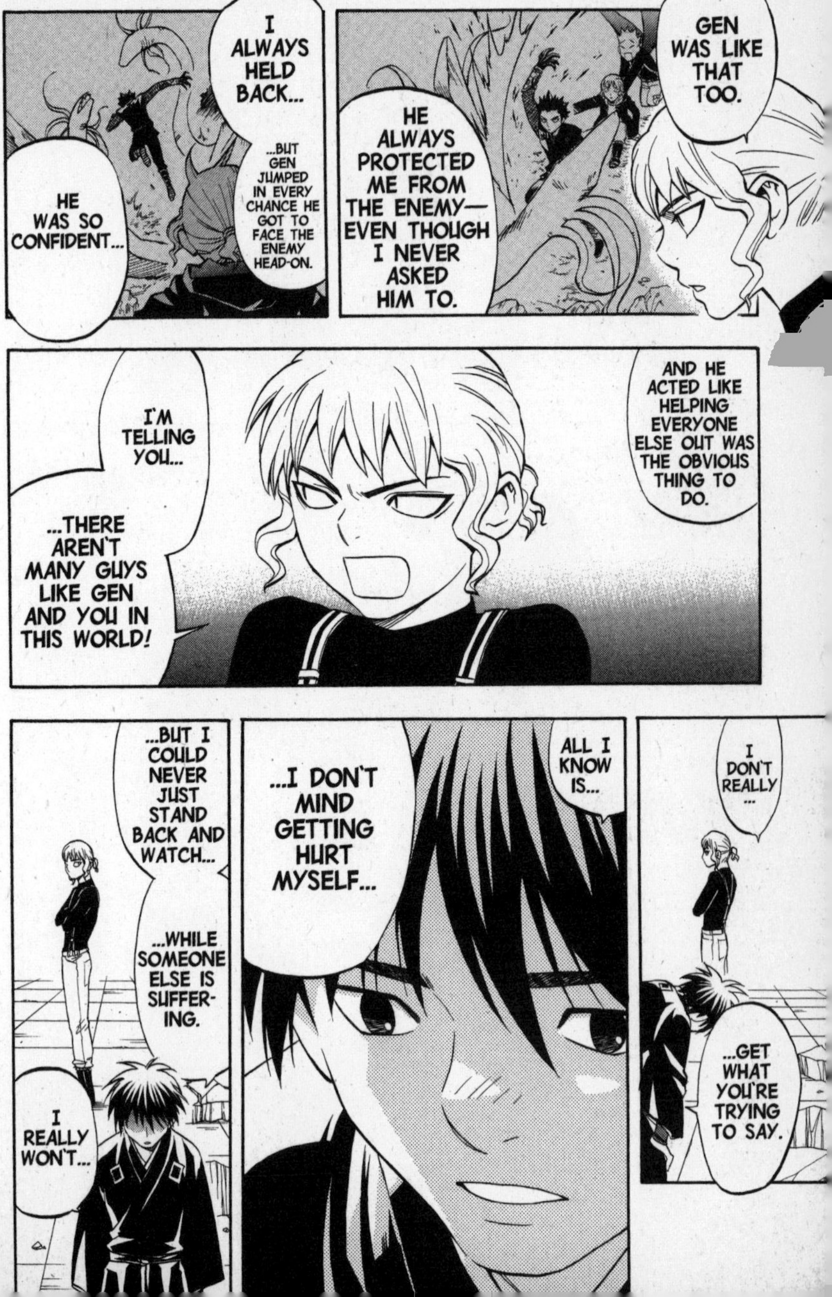
GEN WAS LIKE THAT TOO.
HE ALWAYS PROTECTED ME FROM THE ENEMY—EVEN THOUGH I NEVER ASKED HIM TO.
I ALWAYS HELD BACK...
...BUT GEN JUMPED IN EVERY CHANCE HE GOT TO FACE THE ENEMY HEAD-ON.
HE WAS SO CONFIDENT...
AND HE ACTED LIKE HELPING EVERYONE ELSE OUT WAS THE OBVIOUS THING TO DO.
I'M TELLING YOU...
...THERE AREN'T MANY GUYS LIKE GEN AND YOU IN THIS WORLD!
I DON'T REALLY...
...GET WHAT YOU'RE TRYING TO SAY.
ALL I KNOW IS...
...I DON'T MIND GETTING HURT MYSELF...
...BUT I COULD NEVER JUST STAND BACK AND WATCH...
...WHILE SOMEONE ELSE IS SUFFERING.
I REALLY WON'T...

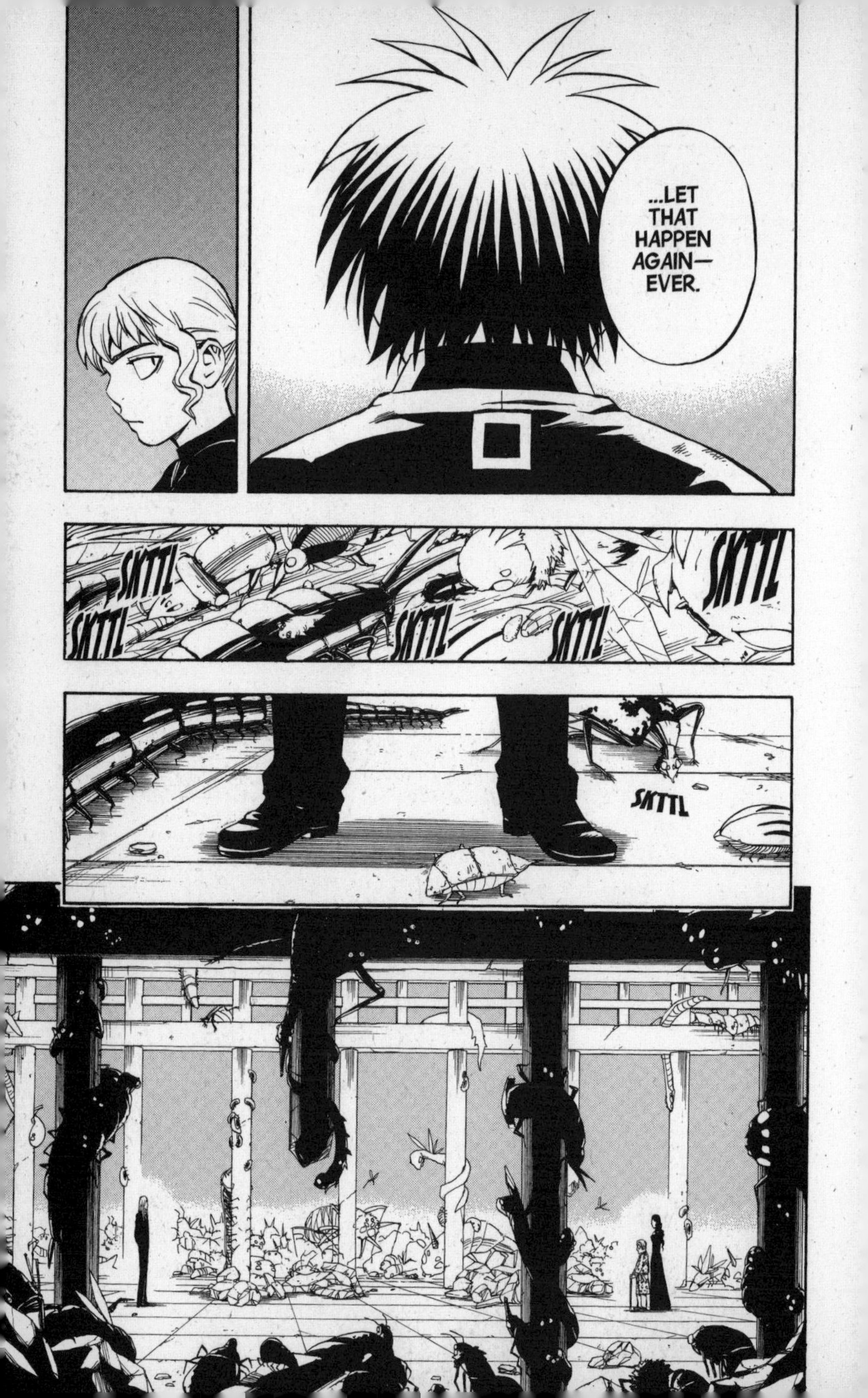
...LET THAT HAPPEN AGAIN—EVER.
SKTTL
SKTTL
SKTTL
SKTTL
SKTTL
SKTTL

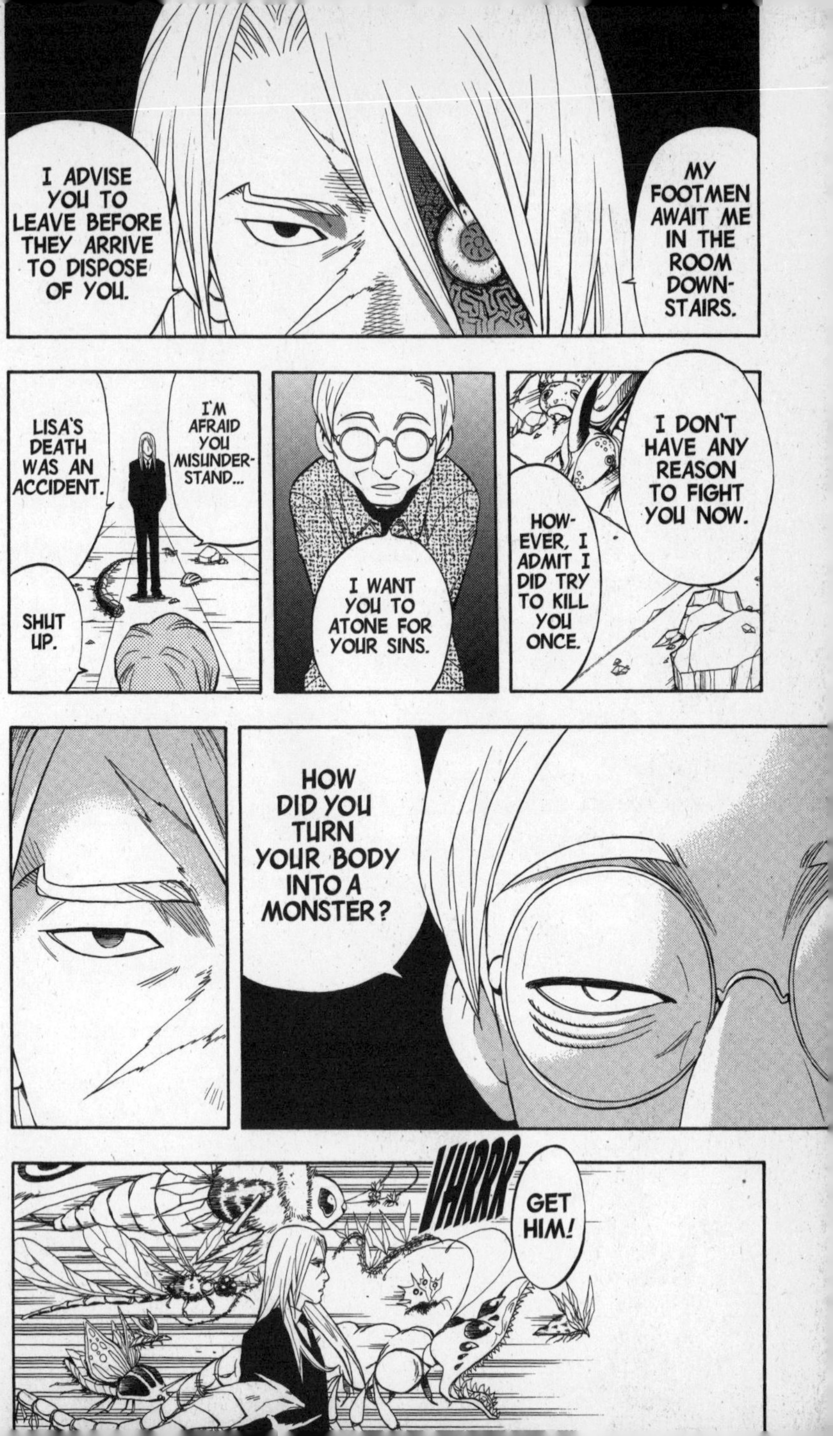
MY FOOTMEN AWAIT ME IN THE ROOM DOWN-STAIRS.
I ADVISE YOU TO LEAVE BEFORE THEY ARRIVE TO DISPOSE OF YOU.
I DON'T HAVE ANY REASON TO FIGHT YOU NOW.
HOW-EVER, I ADMIT I DID TRY TO KILL YOU ONCE.
I WANT YOU TO ATONE FOR YOUR SINS.
I'M AFRAID YOU MISUNDER-STAND...
LISA'S DEATH WAS AN ACCIDENT.
SHUT UP.
HOW DID YOU TURN YOUR BODY INTO A MONSTER?
VHRRR
GET HIM!

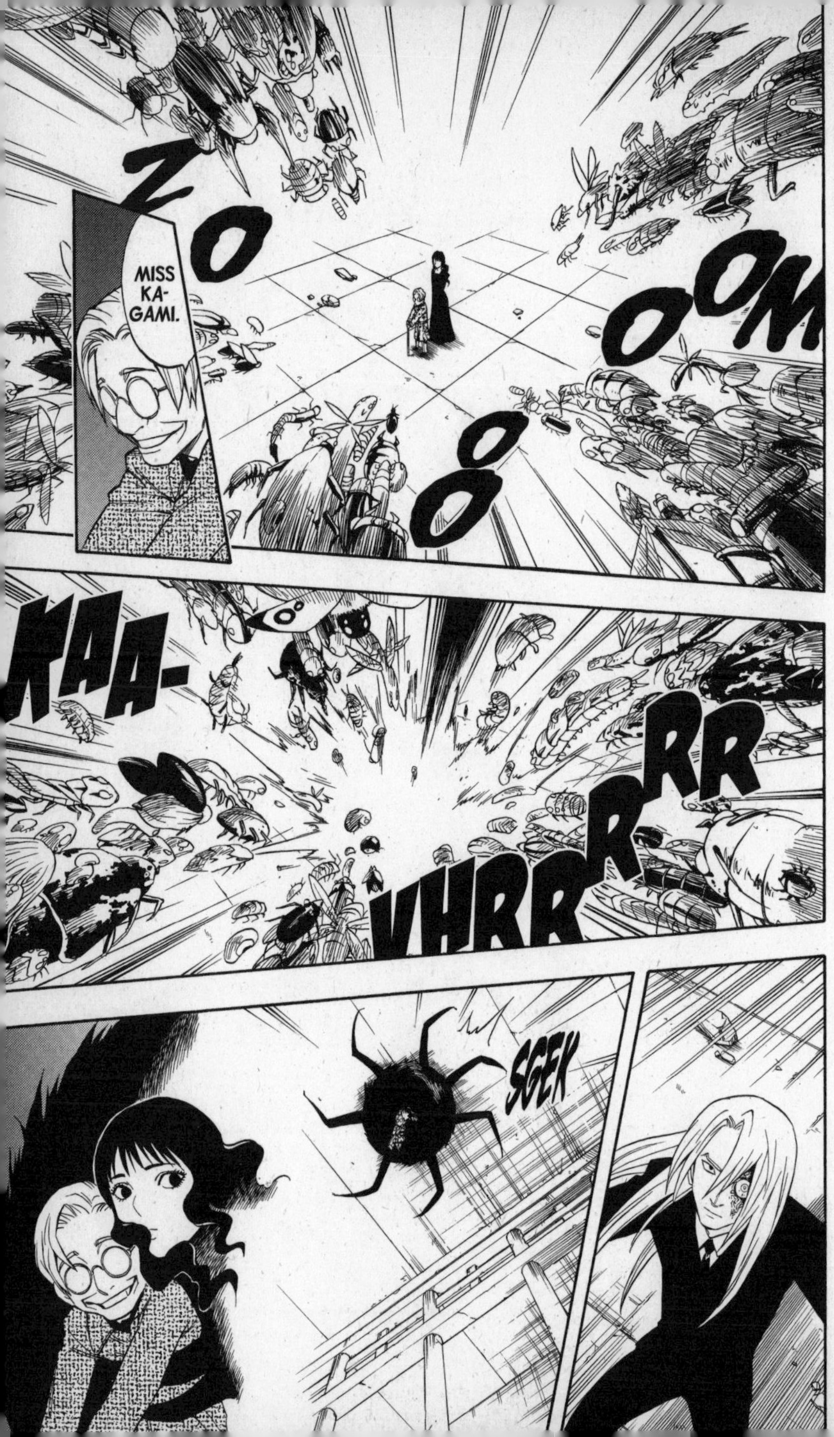
ZOOOOOOM
MISS KA-GAMI.
KAA-
VHRRRRRR
SGEK

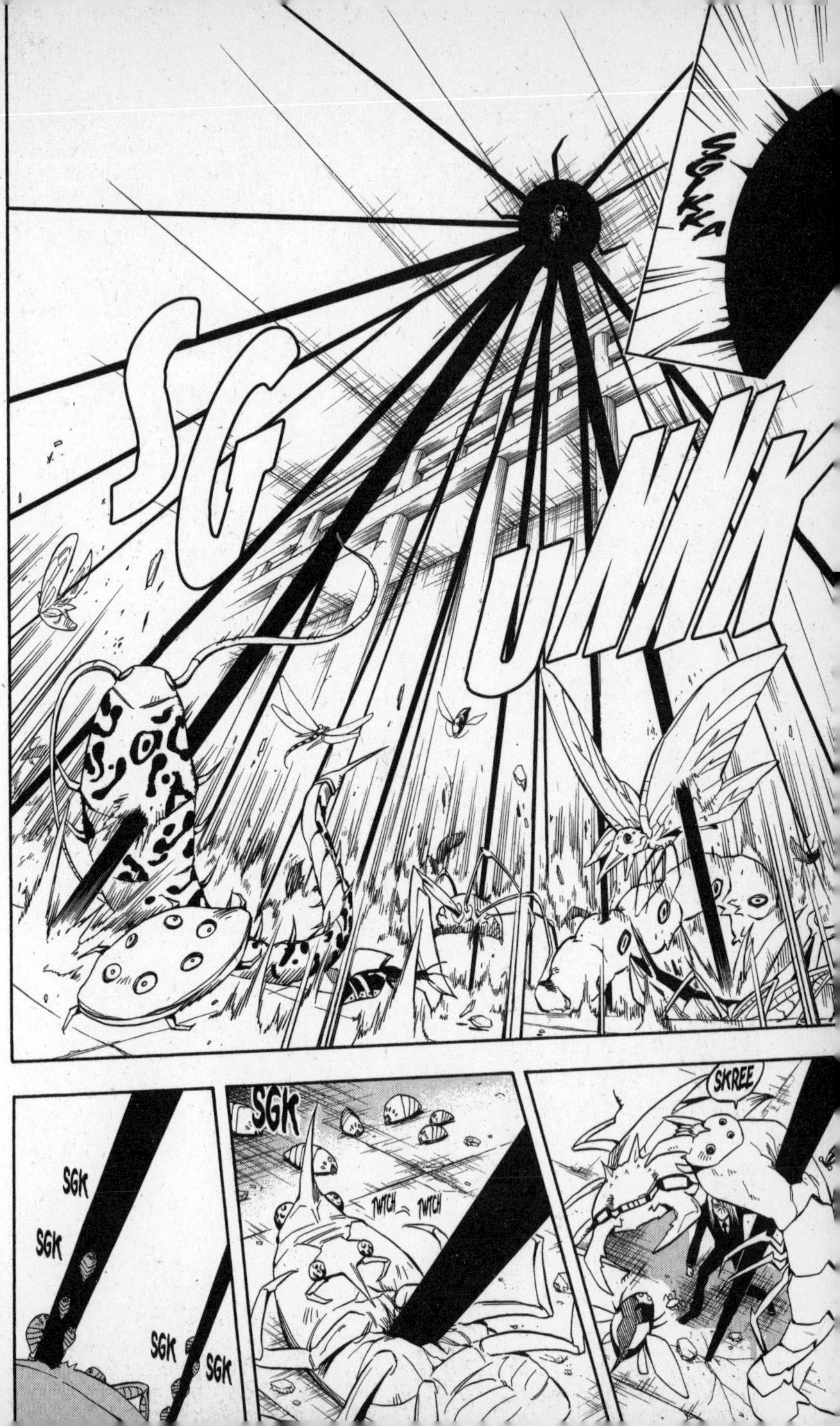
SGKKA
SGUNK
SKREE
SGK
TWITCH TWITCH
SGK
SGK
SGK
SGK

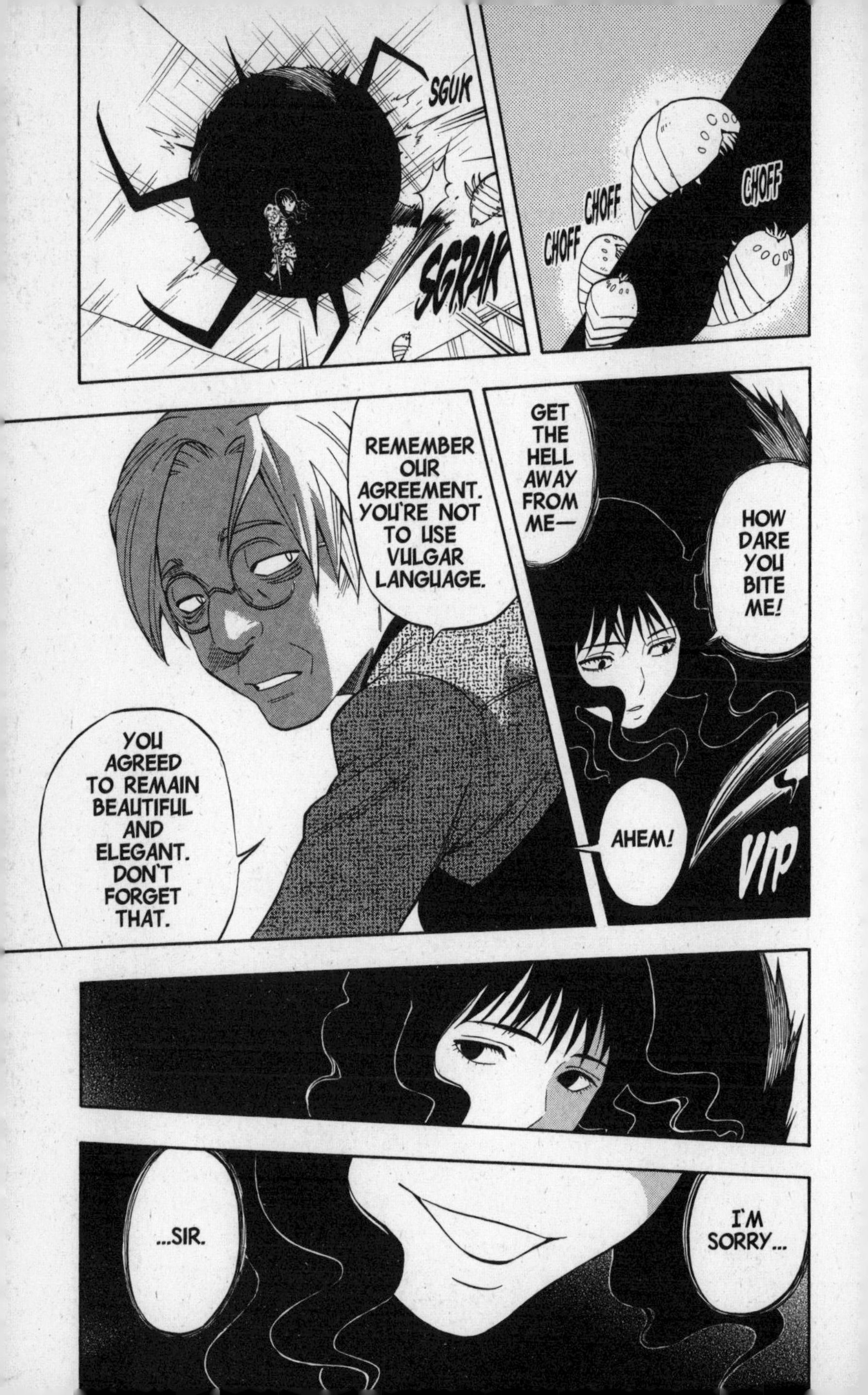
CHOFF
CHOFF
CHOFF
CHOFF
SGUK
SGRAK
GET THE HELL AWAY FROM ME—
HOW DARE YOU BITE ME!
AHEM!
VIP
REMEMBER OUR AGREEMENT. YOU'RE NOT TO USE VULGAR LANGUAGE.
YOU AGREED TO REMAIN BEAUTIFUL AND ELEGANT. DON'T FORGET THAT.
I'M SORRY...
...SIR.

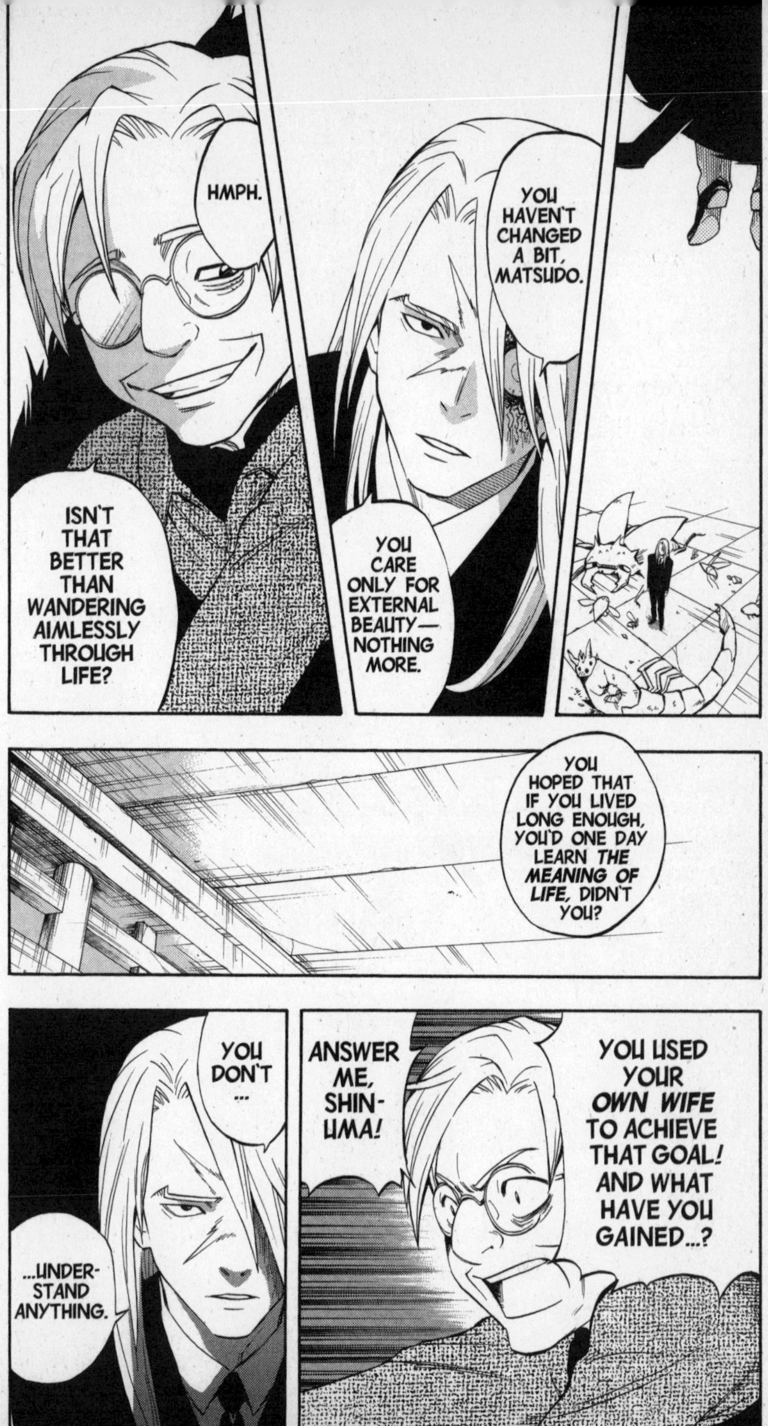
YOU HAVEN'T CHANGED A BIT, MATSUDO.
YOU CARE ONLY FOR EXTERNAL BEAUTY— NOTHING MORE.
HMPH.
ISN'T THAT BETTER THAN WANDERING AIMLESSLY THROUGH LIFE?
YOU HOPED THAT IF YOU LIVED LONG ENOUGH, YOU'D ONE DAY LEARN *THE MEANING OF LIFE,* DIDN'T YOU?
YOU USED YOUR *OWN WIFE* TO ACHIEVE THAT GOAL! AND WHAT HAVE YOU GAINED...?
ANSWER ME, SHIN-UMA!
YOU DON'T ...
...UNDER-STAND ANYTHING.

Chapter 109: Hollow Man

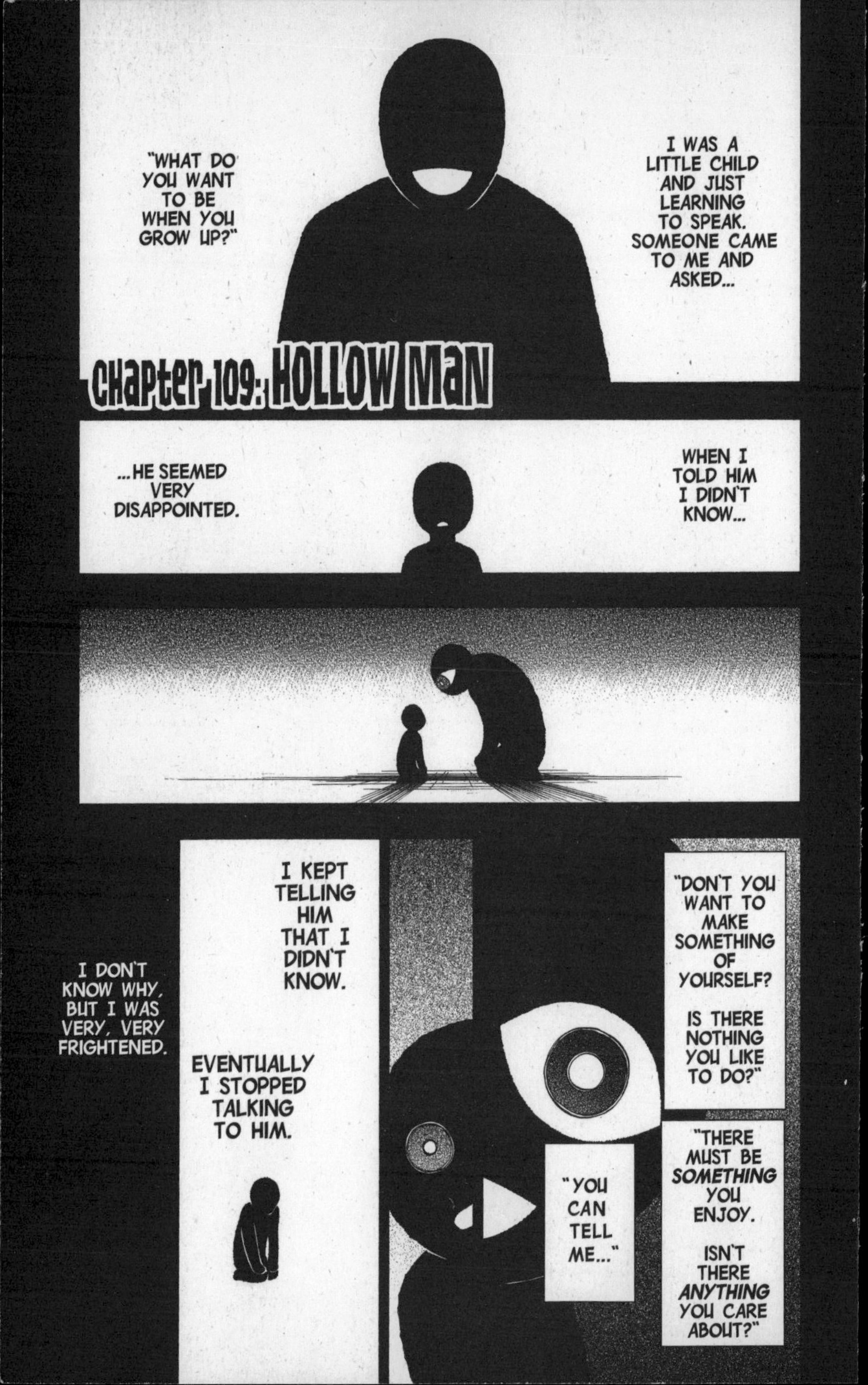

I WAS A LITTLE CHILD AND JUST LEARNING TO SPEAK. SOMEONE CAME TO ME AND ASKED...
"WHAT DO YOU WANT TO BE WHEN YOU GROW UP?"
WHEN I TOLD HIM I DIDN'T KNOW...
...HE SEEMED VERY DISAPPOINTED.
"DON'T YOU WANT TO MAKE SOMETHING OF YOURSELF? IS THERE NOTHING YOU LIKE TO DO?"
"THERE MUST BE *SOMETHING* YOU ENJOY. ISN'T THERE *ANYTHING* YOU CARE ABOUT?"
"YOU CAN TELL ME..."
I KEPT TELLING HIM THAT I DIDN'T KNOW.
EVENTUALLY I STOPPED TALKING TO HIM.
I DON'T KNOW WHY, BUT I WAS VERY, VERY FRIGHTENED.

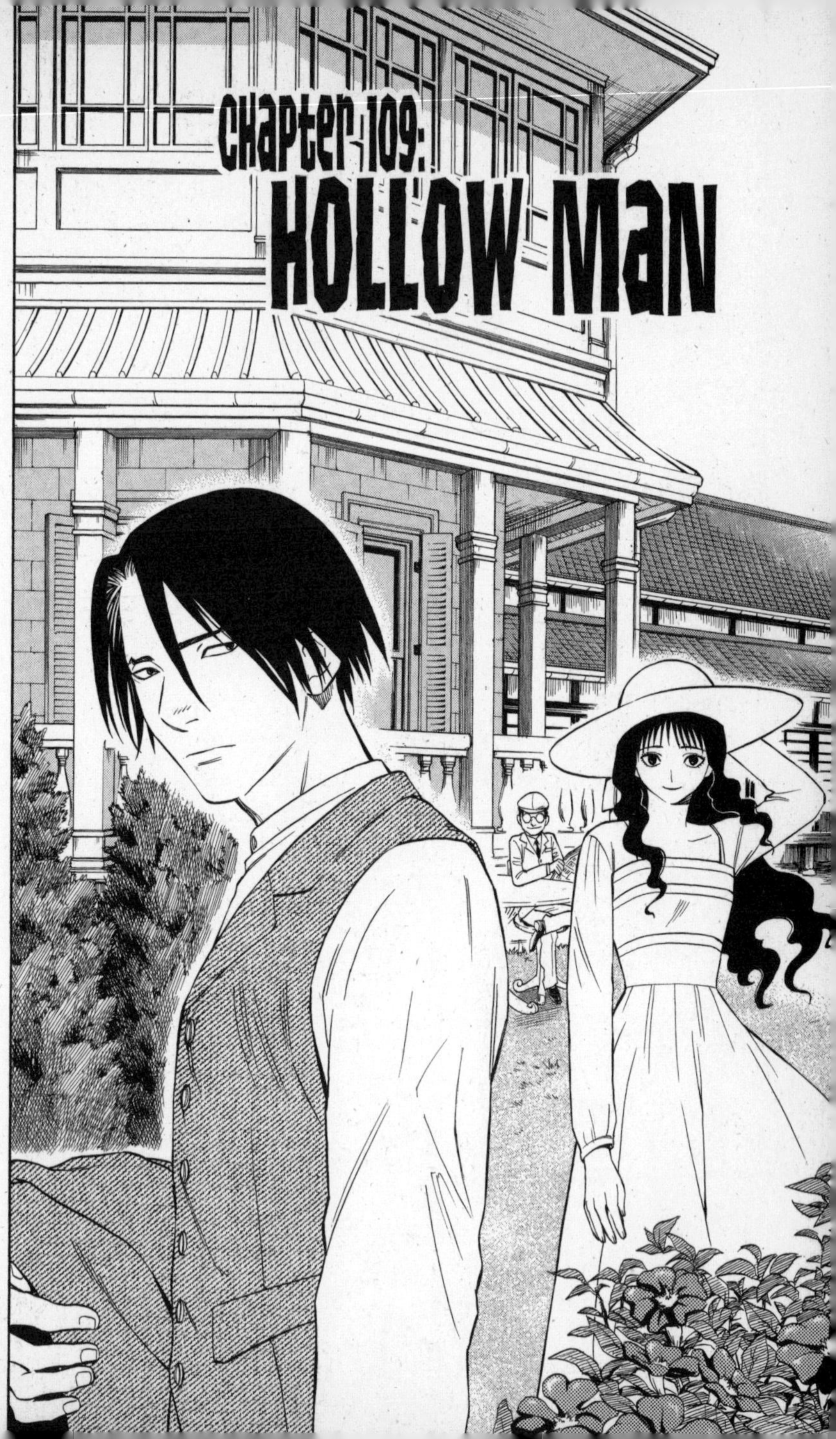
CHAPTER 109:
HOLLOW MAN

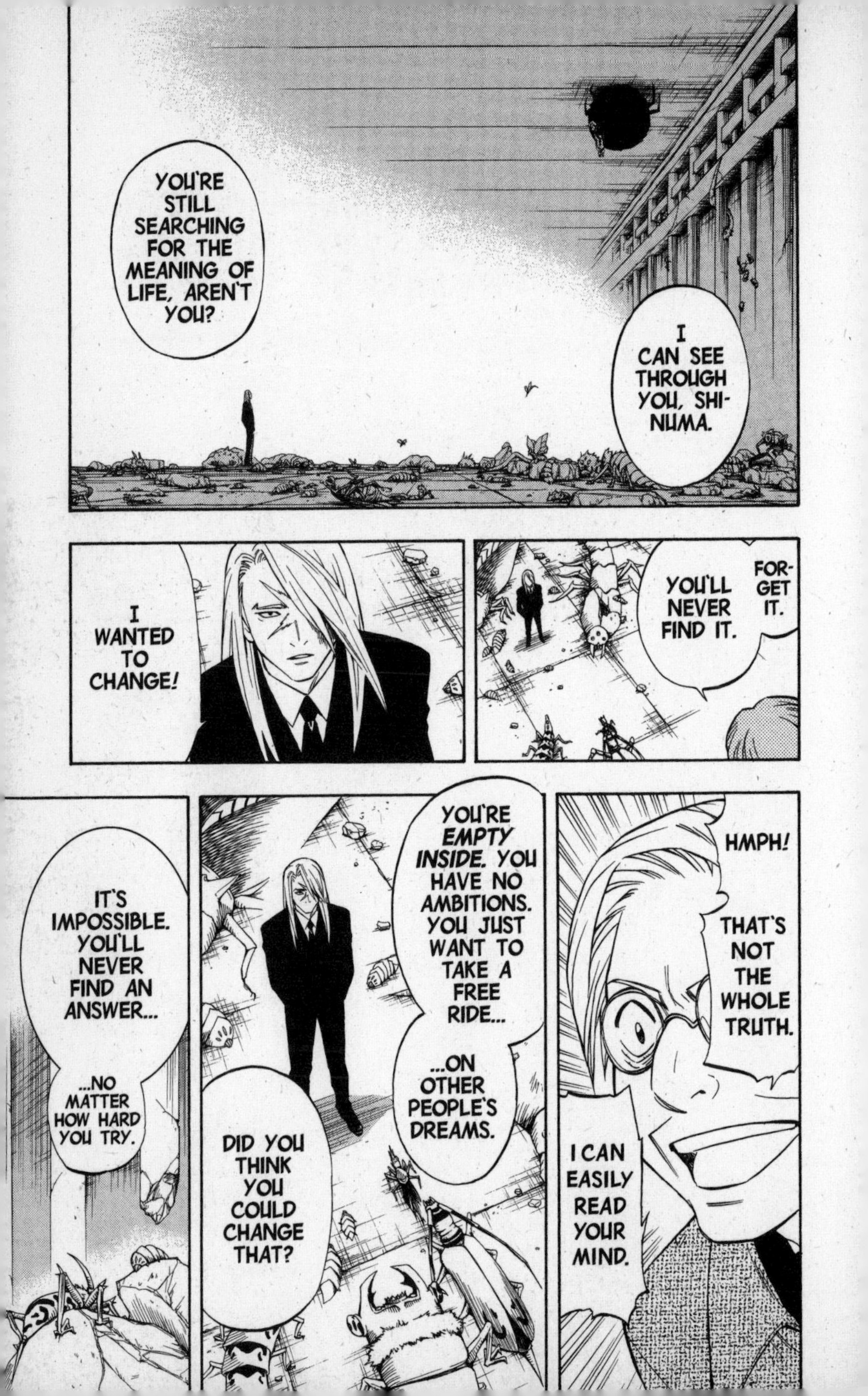
I CAN SEE THROUGH YOU, SHINUMA.
YOU'RE STILL SEARCHING FOR THE MEANING OF LIFE, AREN'T YOU?
FORGET IT.
YOU'LL NEVER FIND IT.
I WANTED TO CHANGE!
HMPH!
THAT'S NOT THE WHOLE TRUTH.
I CAN EASILY READ YOUR MIND.
YOU'RE *EMPTY INSIDE.* YOU HAVE NO AMBITIONS. YOU JUST WANT TO TAKE A FREE RIDE...
...ON OTHER PEOPLE'S DREAMS.
DID YOU THINK YOU COULD CHANGE THAT?
IT'S IMPOSSIBLE. YOU'LL NEVER FIND AN ANSWER...
...NO MATTER HOW HARD YOU TRY.

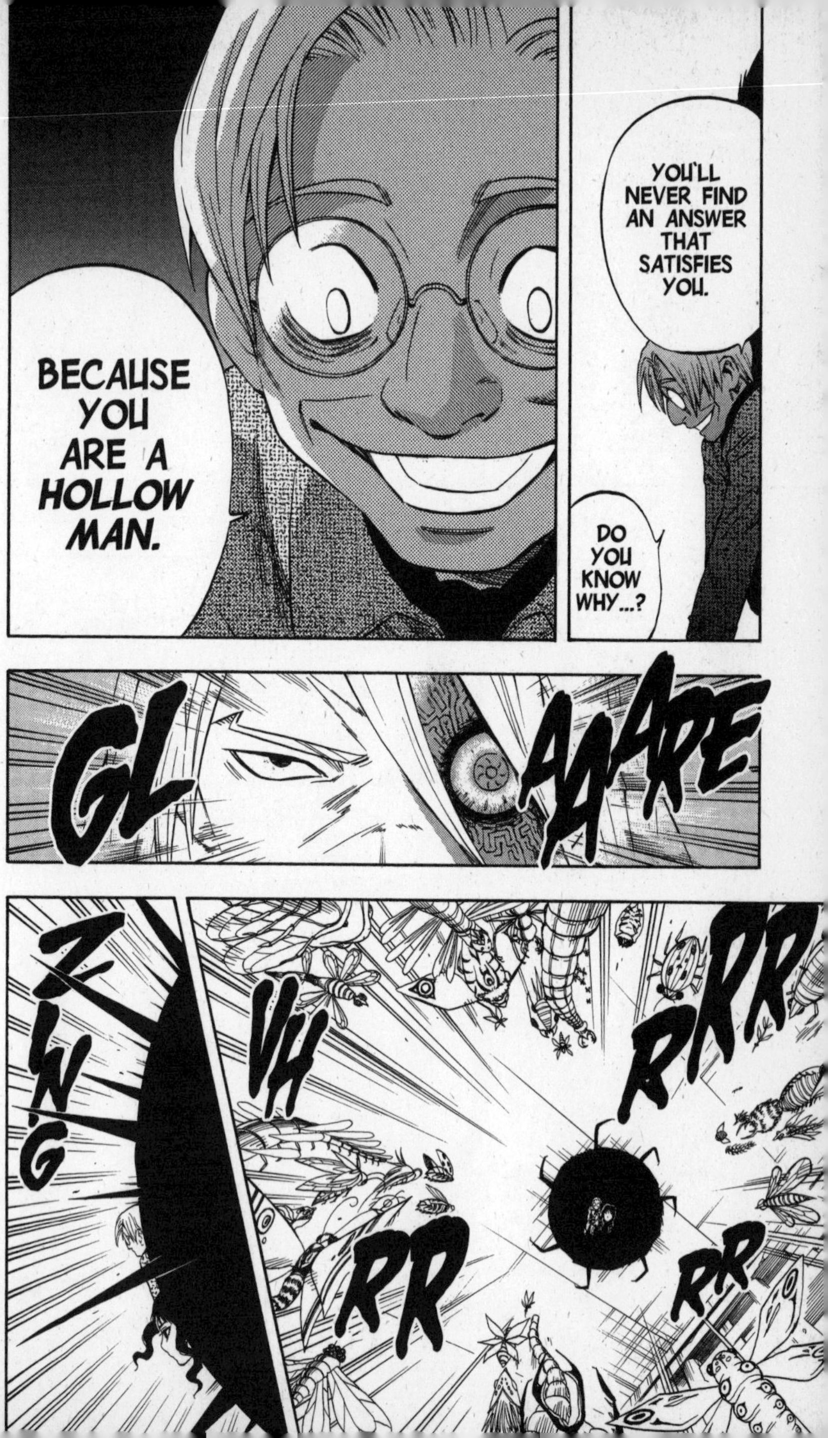
YOU'LL NEVER FIND AN ANSWER THAT SATISFIES YOU.
DO YOU KNOW WHY...?
BECAUSE YOU ARE A HOLLOW MAN.
GLAAARE
RRRR
RR
RR

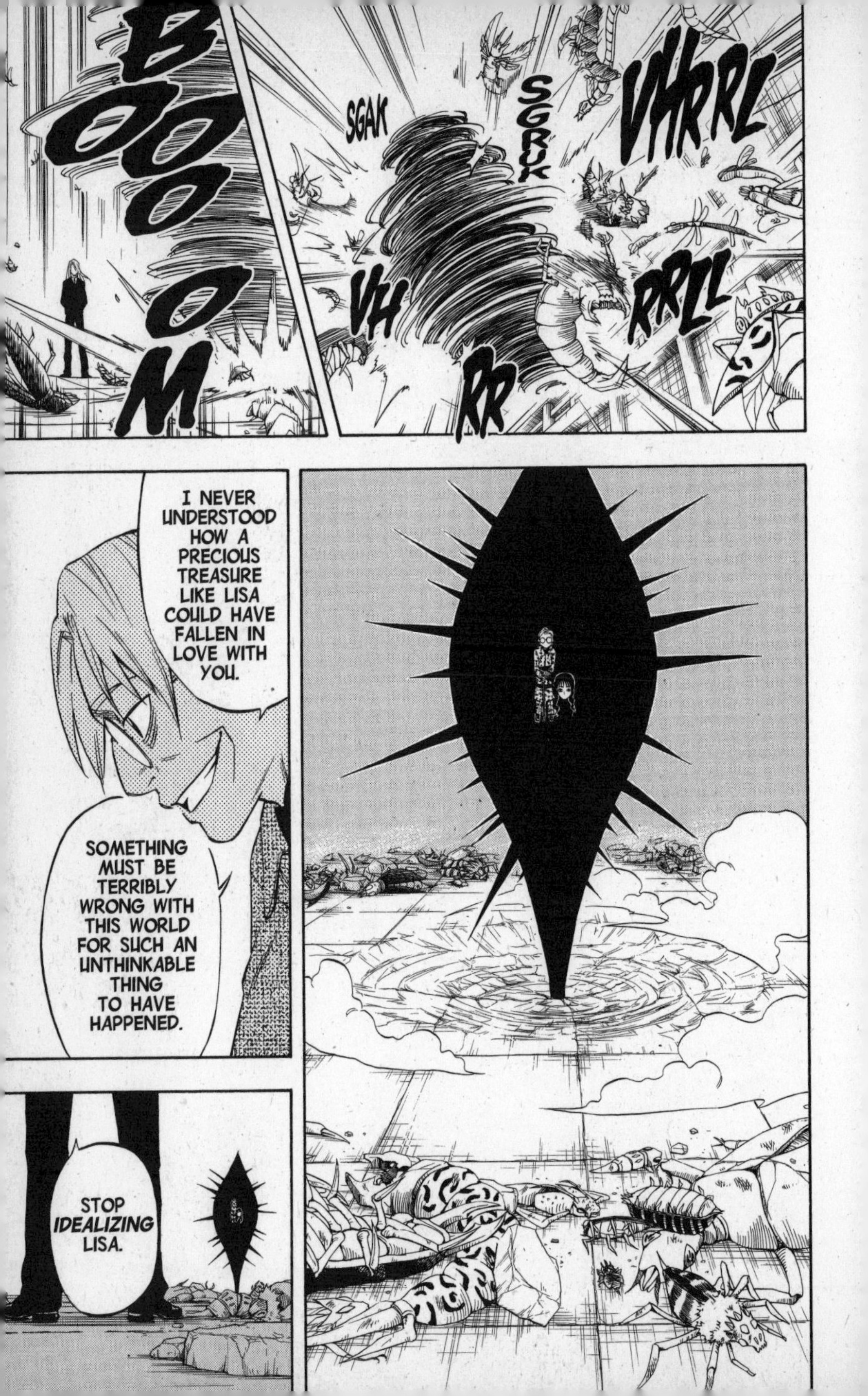
VHRRL
SGRUK
SGAK
RRLL
VH
RR
BOOOOOM
I NEVER UNDERSTOOD HOW A PRECIOUS TREASURE LIKE LISA COULD HAVE FALLEN IN LOVE WITH YOU.
SOMETHING MUST BE TERRIBLY WRONG WITH THIS WORLD FOR SUCH AN UNTHINKABLE THING TO HAVE HAPPENED.
STOP IDEALIZING LISA.

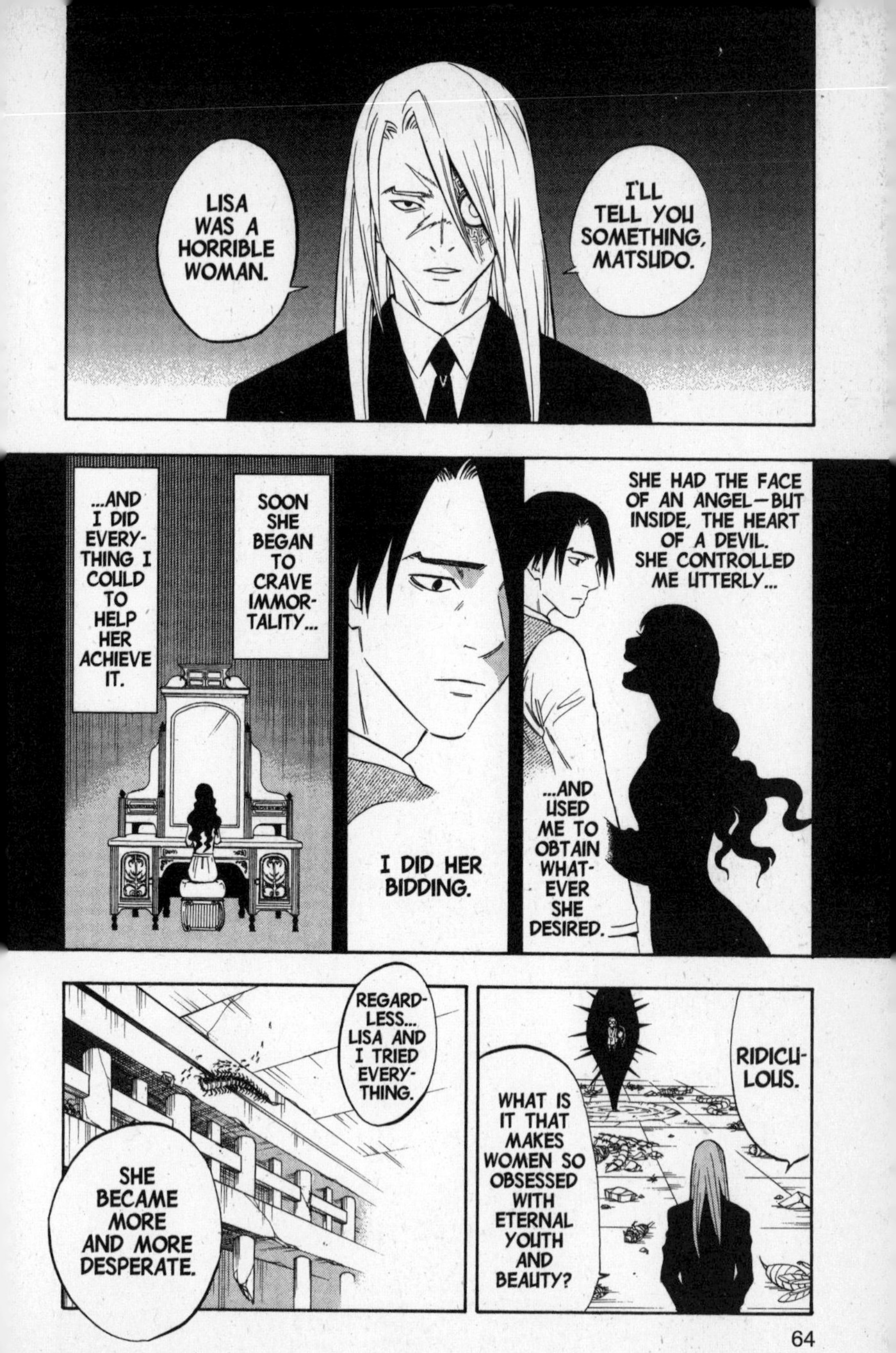
I'LL TELL YOU SOMETHING, MATSUDO.
LISA WAS A HORRIBLE WOMAN.
SHE HAD THE FACE OF AN ANGEL—BUT INSIDE, THE HEART OF A DEVIL. SHE CONTROLLED ME UTTERLY...
...AND USED ME TO OBTAIN WHAT-EVER SHE DESIRED.
I DID HER BIDDING.
SOON SHE BEGAN TO CRAVE IMMOR-TALITY...
...AND I DID EVERY-THING I COULD TO HELP HER ACHIEVE IT.
RIDICU-LOUS.
WHAT IS IT THAT MAKES WOMEN SO OBSESSED WITH ETERNAL YOUTH AND BEAUTY?
REGARD-LESS... LISA AND I TRIED EVERY-THING.
SHE BECAME MORE AND MORE DESPERATE.

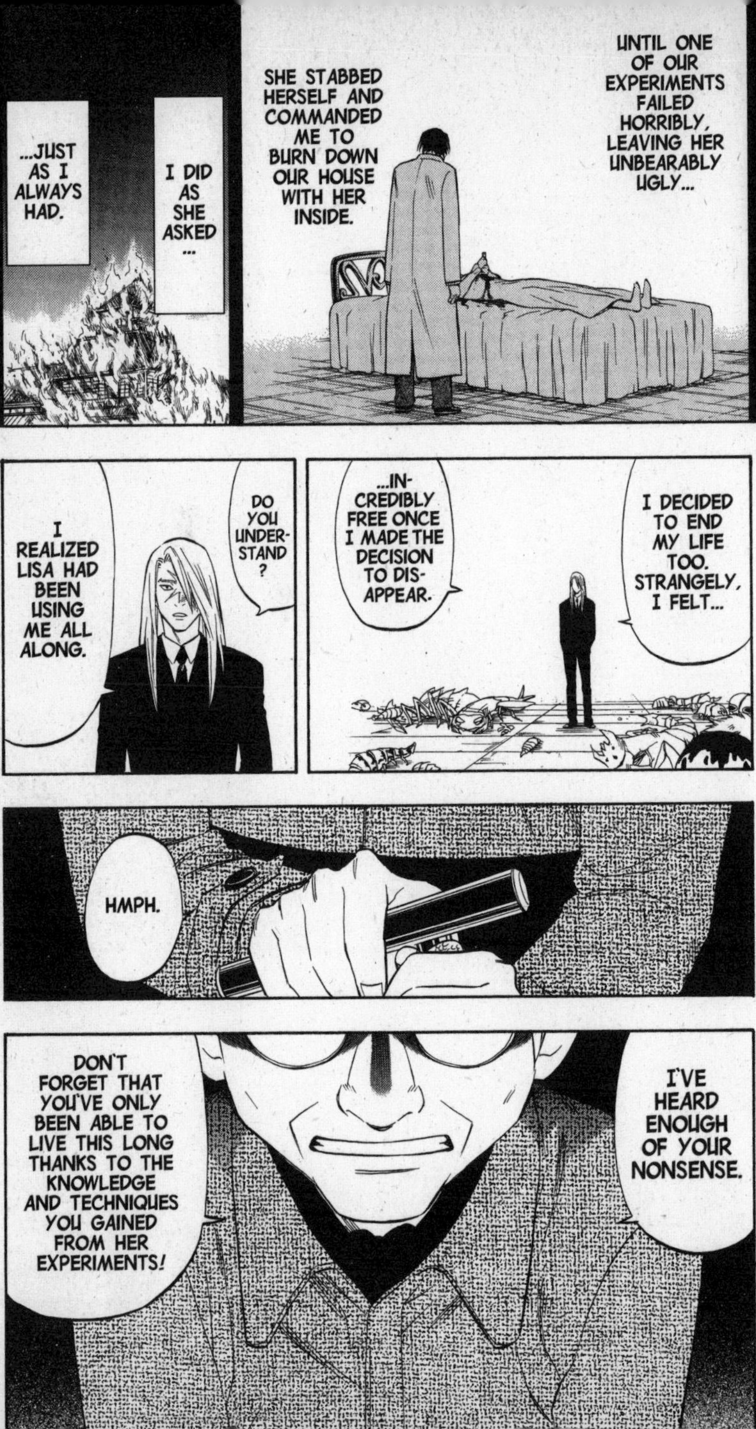
UNTIL ONE OF OUR EXPERIMENTS FAILED HORRIBLY, LEAVING HER UNBEARABLY UGLY...
SHE STABBED HERSELF AND COMMANDED ME TO BURN DOWN OUR HOUSE WITH HER INSIDE.
I DID AS SHE ASKED...
...JUST AS I ALWAYS HAD.
I DECIDED TO END MY LIFE TOO. STRANGELY, I FELT...
...IN-CREDIBLY FREE ONCE I MADE THE DECISION TO DIS-APPEAR.
DO YOU UNDER-STAND?
I REALIZED LISA HAD BEEN USING ME ALL ALONG.
HMPH.
I'VE HEARD ENOUGH OF YOUR NONSENSE.
DON'T FORGET THAT YOU'VE ONLY BEEN ABLE TO LIVE THIS LONG THANKS TO THE KNOWLEDGE AND TECHNIQUES YOU GAINED FROM HER EXPERIMENTS!

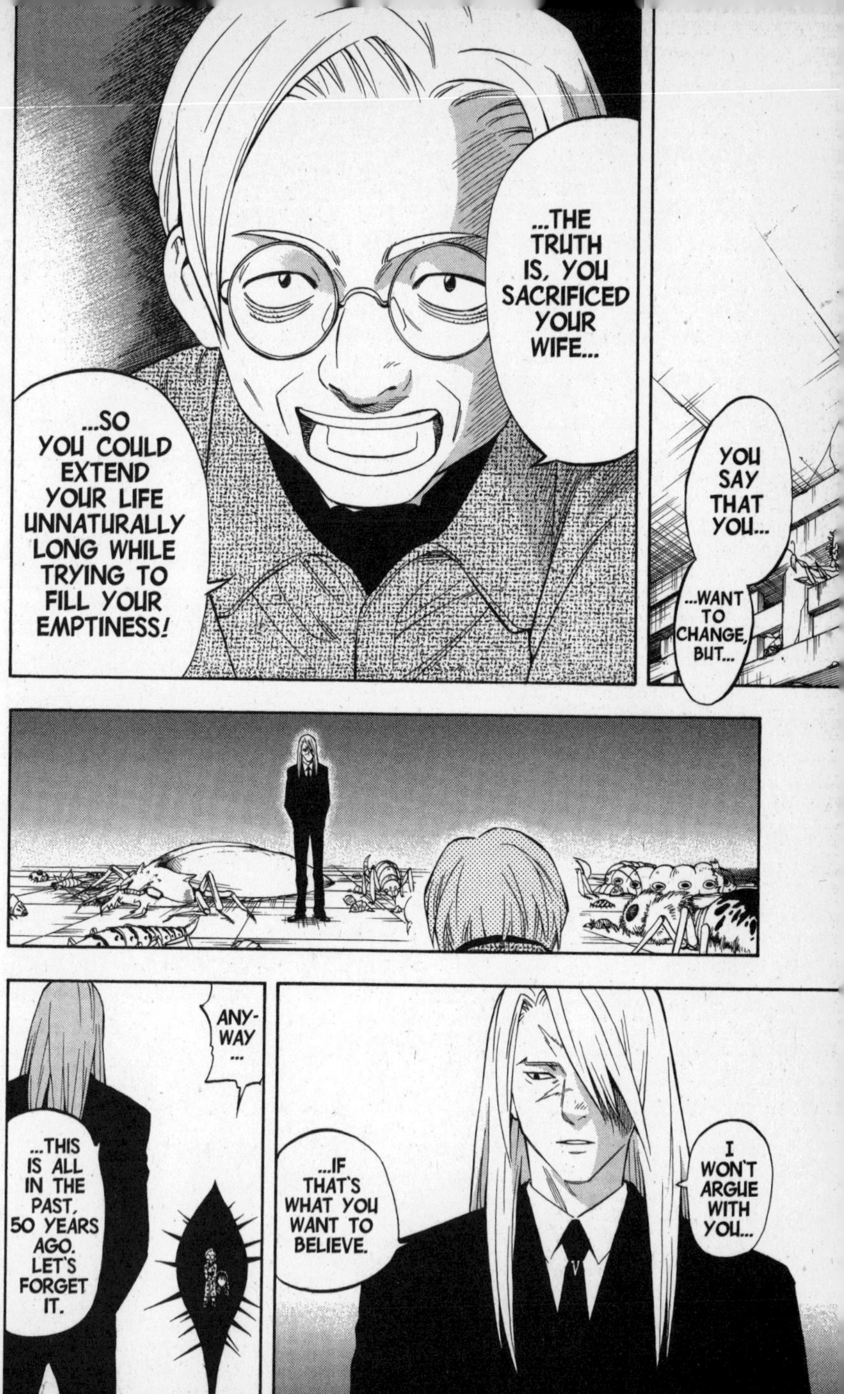
YOU SAY THAT YOU...
...WANT TO CHANGE, BUT...
...THE TRUTH IS, YOU SACRIFICED YOUR WIFE...
...SO YOU COULD EXTEND YOUR LIFE UNNATURALLY LONG WHILE TRYING TO FILL YOUR EMPTINESS!
I WON'T ARGUE WITH YOU...
...IF THAT'S WHAT YOU WANT TO BELIEVE.
ANY-WAY...
...THIS IS ALL IN THE PAST, 50 YEARS AGO. LET'S FORGET IT.

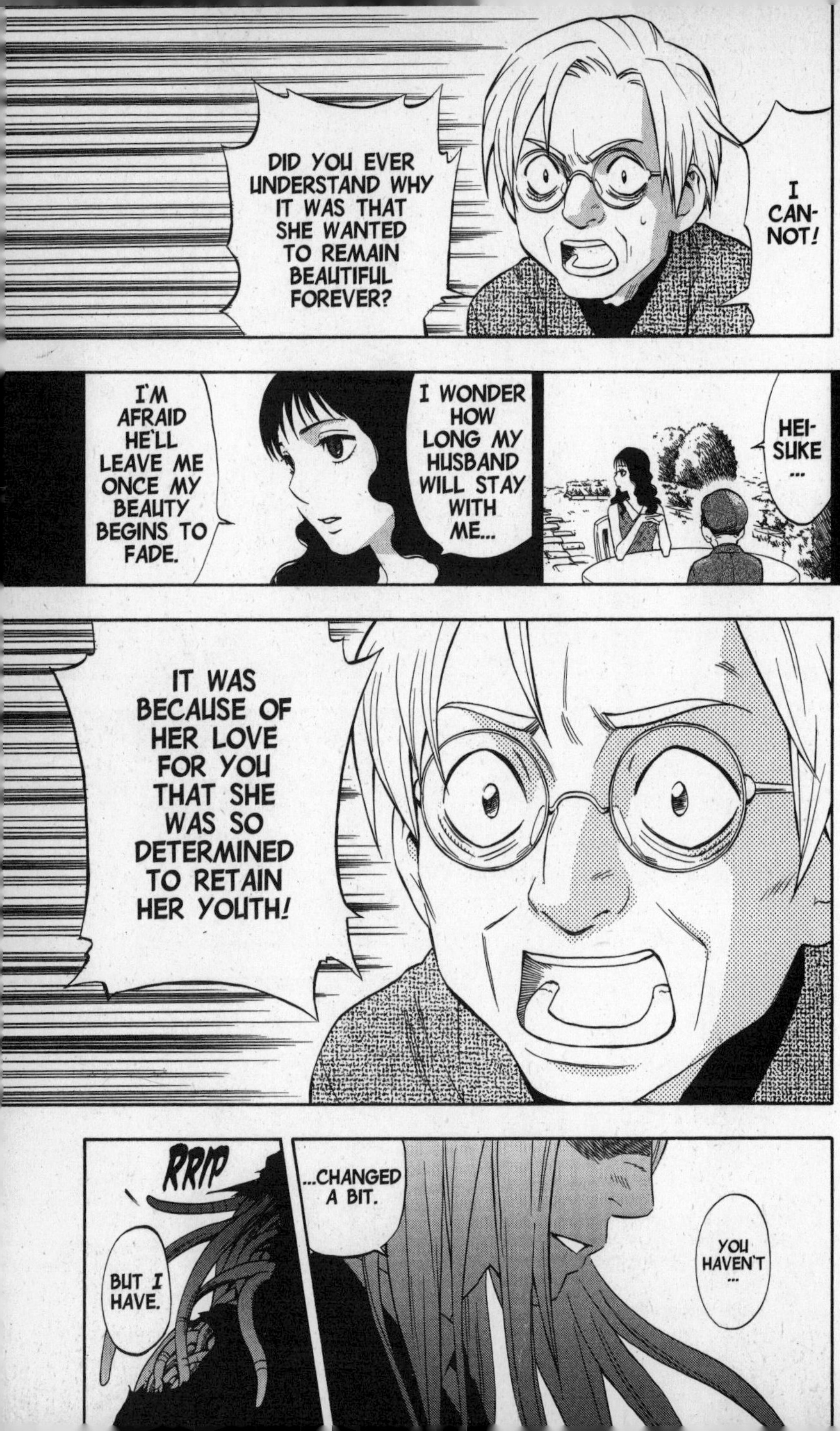
I CAN-NOT!
DID YOU EVER UNDERSTAND WHY IT WAS THAT SHE WANTED TO REMAIN BEAUTIFUL FOREVER?
HEI-SUKE ...
I WONDER HOW LONG MY HUSBAND WILL STAY WITH ME...
I'M AFRAID HE'LL LEAVE ME ONCE MY BEAUTY BEGINS TO FADE.
IT WAS BECAUSE OF HER LOVE FOR YOU THAT SHE WAS SO DETERMINED TO RETAIN HER YOUTH!
YOU HAVEN'T ...
...CHANGED A BIT.
RRIP
BUT I HAVE.

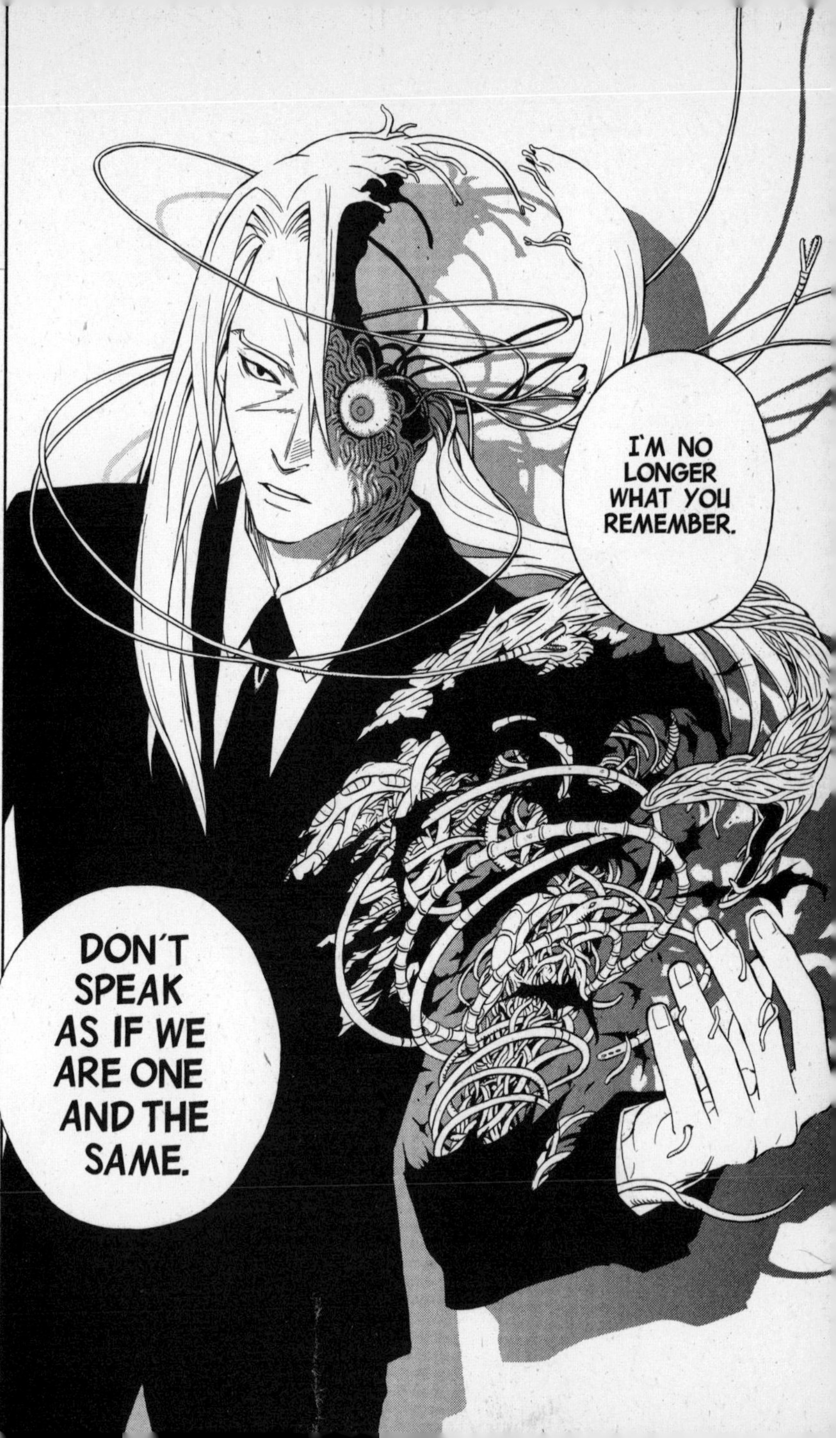
I'M NO LONGER WHAT YOU REMEMBER.
DON'T SPEAK AS IF WE ARE ONE AND THE SAME.

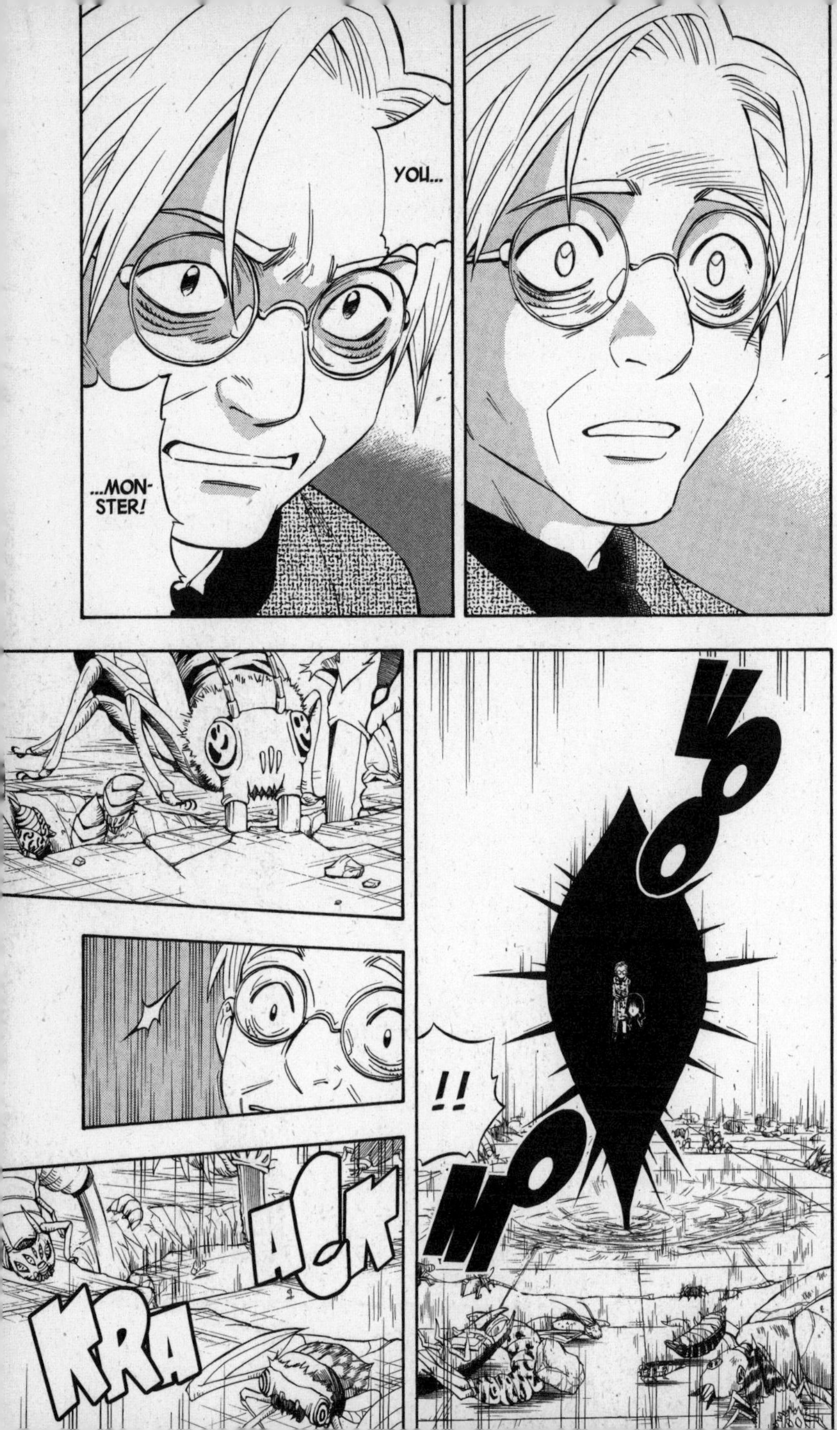
YOU...
...MON-
STER!
VOOOM
!!
KRAACK

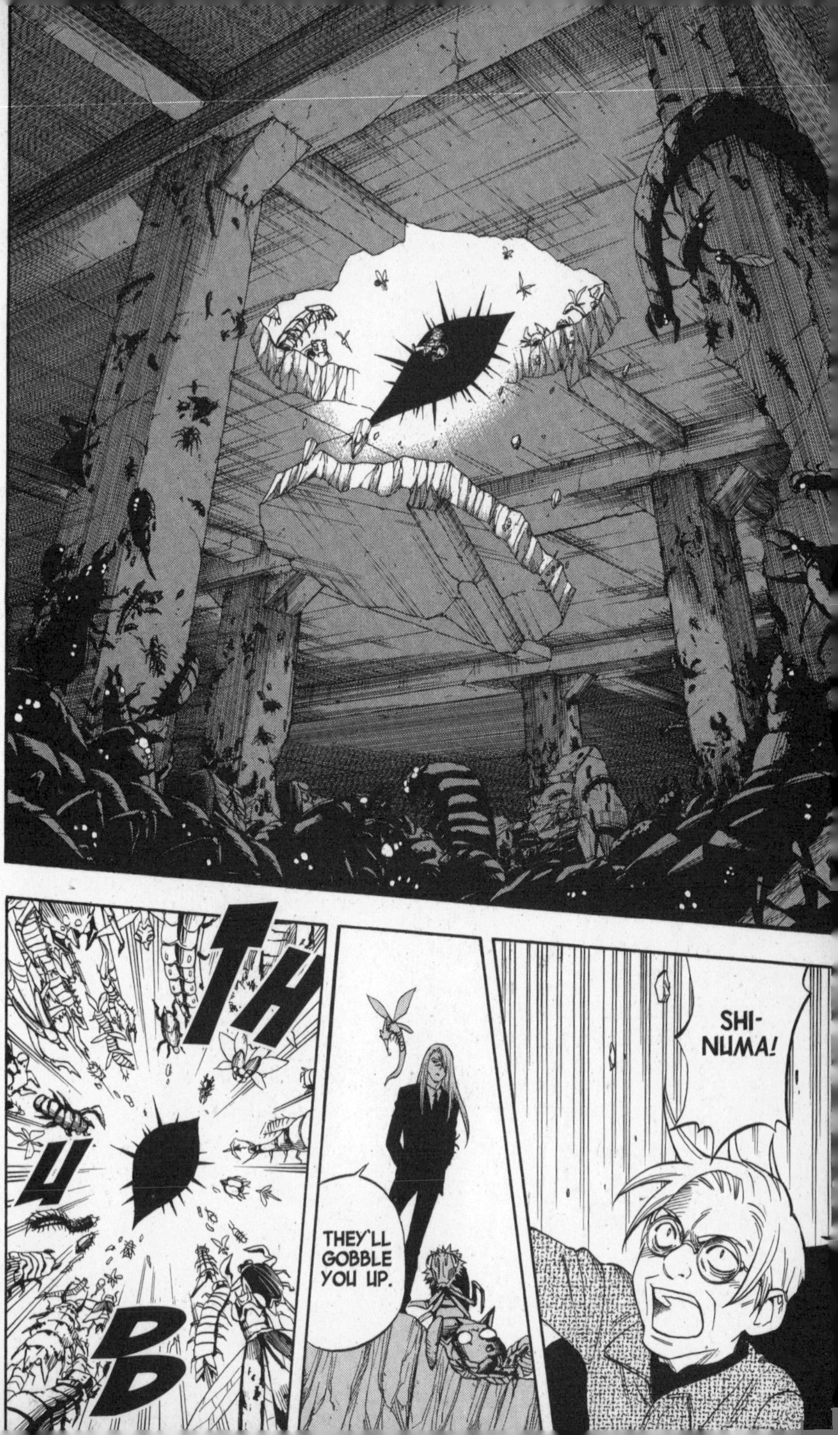
SHI-NUMA!
THEY'LL GOBBLE YOU UP.
THUD

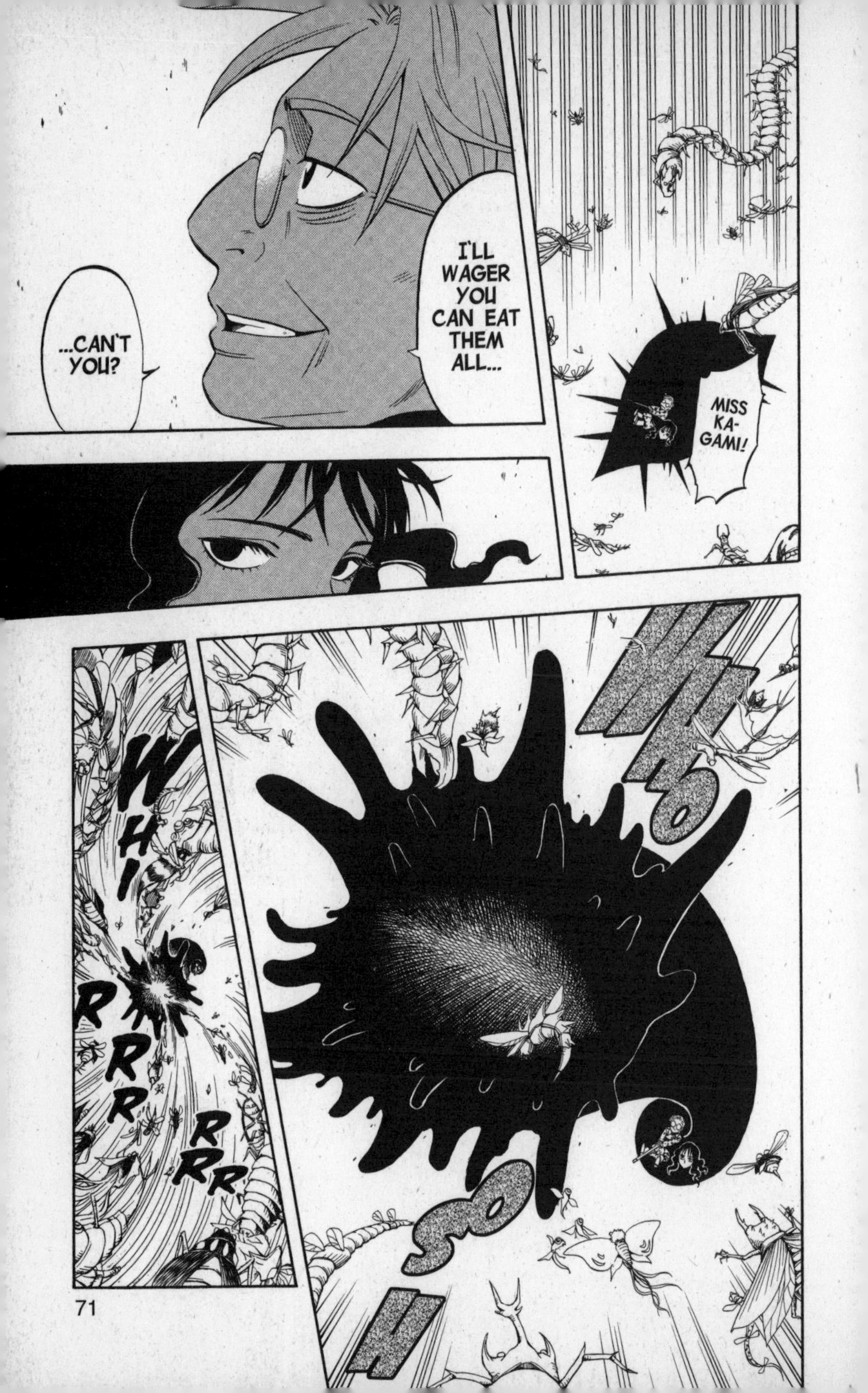
MISS KA-GAMI!
I'LL WAGER YOU CAN EAT THEM ALL...
...CAN'T YOU?
WHOOSH
WHIRRRRRRR

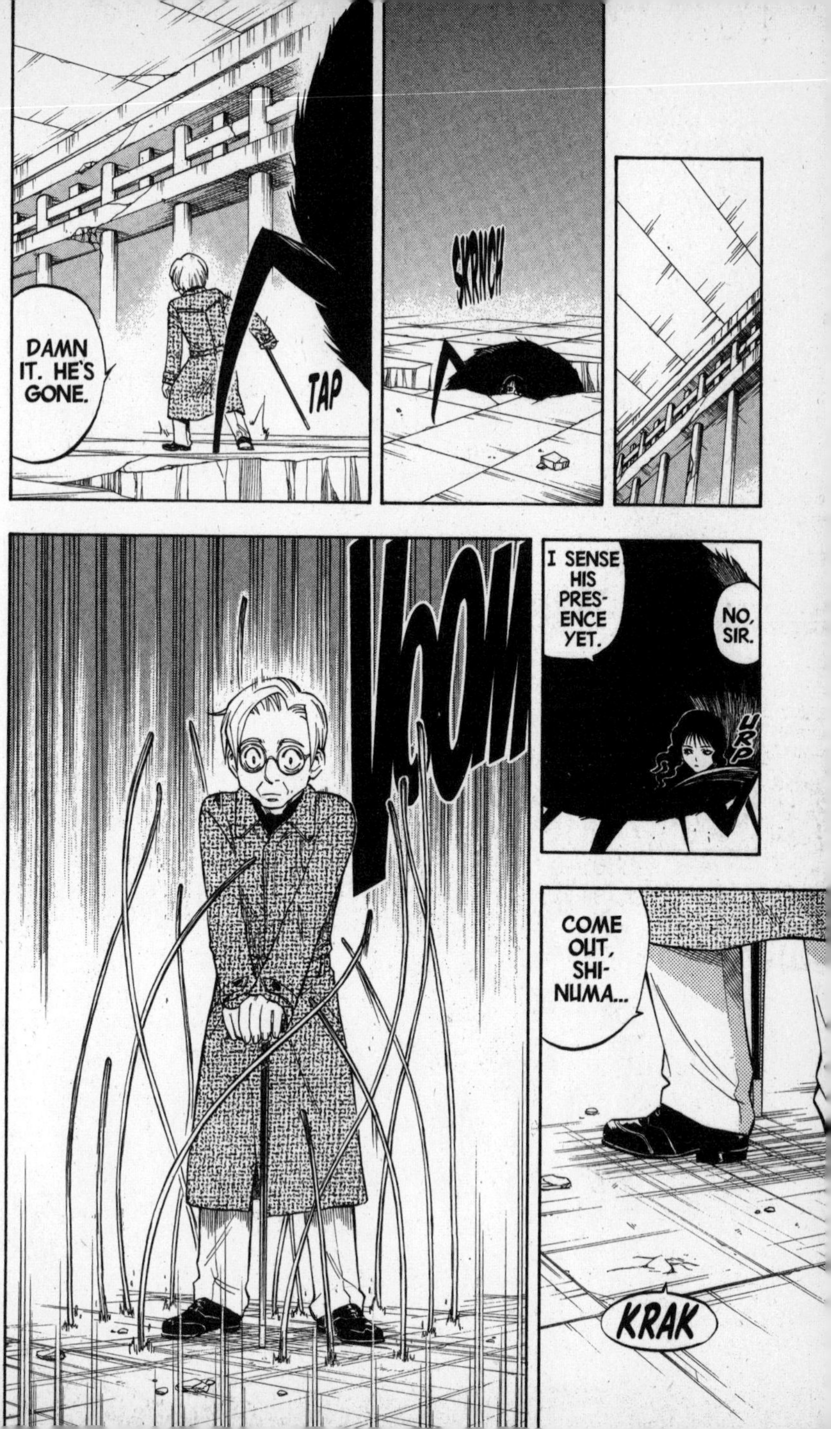
SKRNCH
DAMN IT. HE'S GONE.
TAP
I SENSE HIS PRES- ENCE YET.
NO, SIR.
URP
COME OUT, SHI- NUMA...
KRAK
VOOM

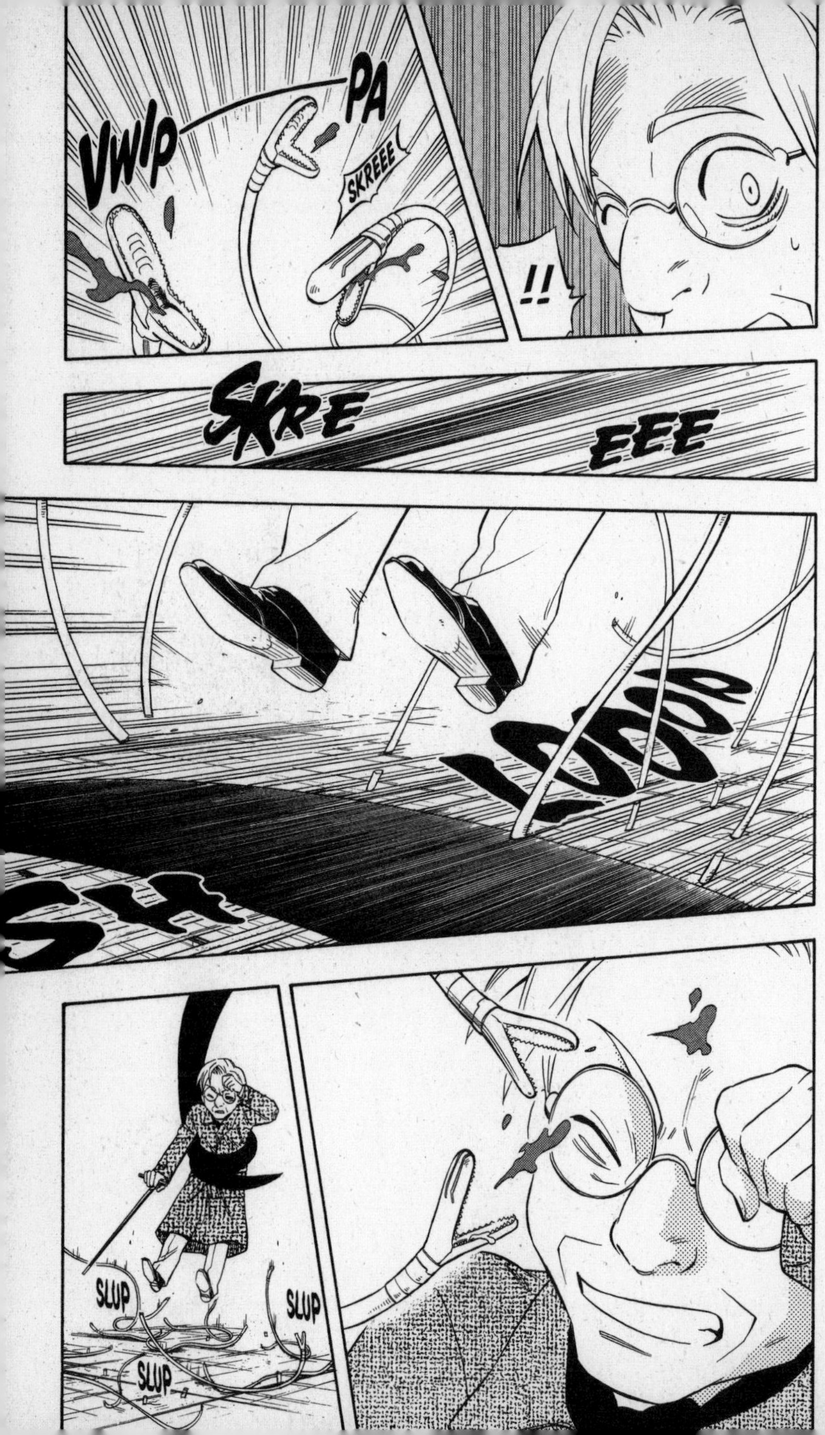
!!
VWIP
PA
SKREEE
SKRE
EEE
SLUP
SLUP
SLUP

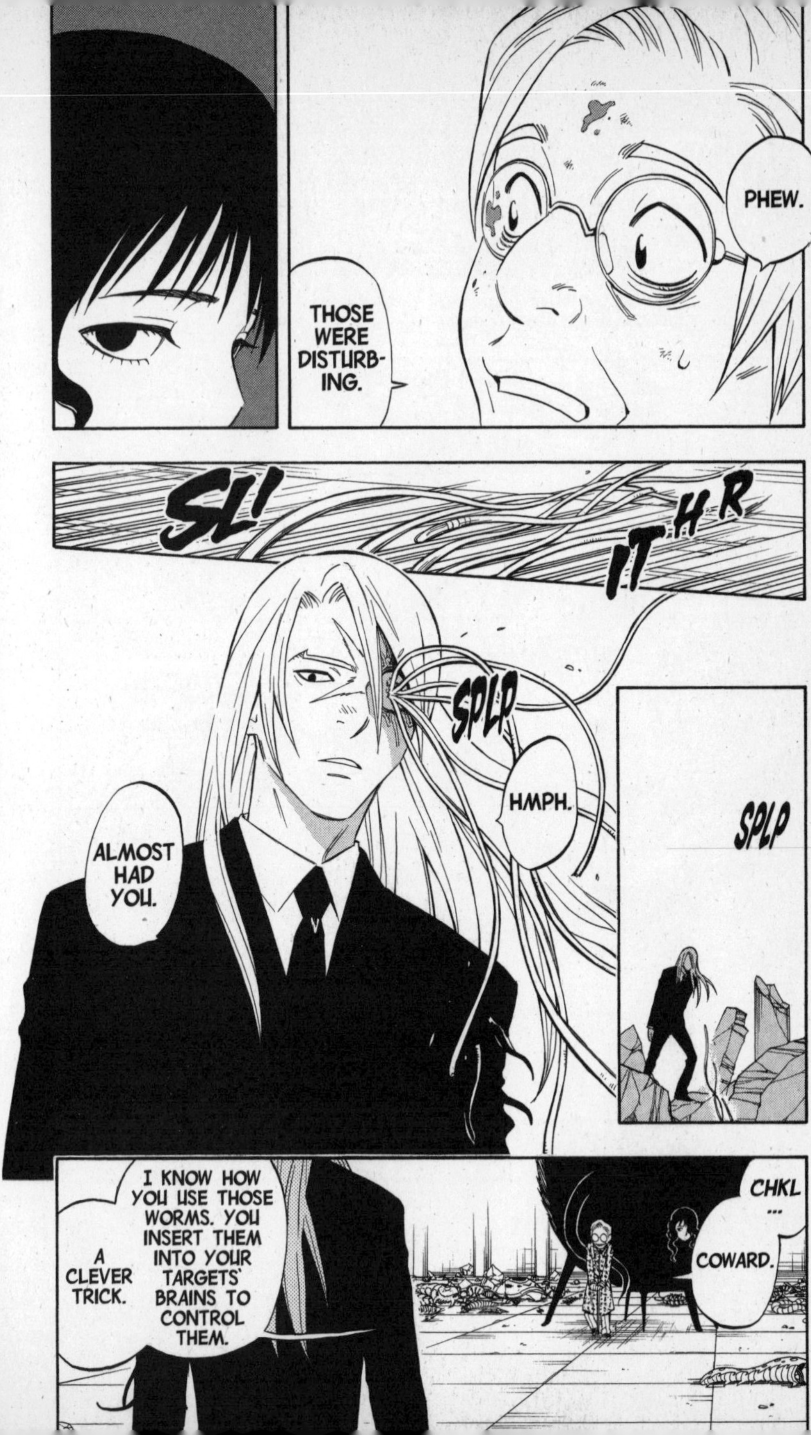
PHEW.
THOSE WERE DISTURB-ING.
SLITHR
SPLP
SPLP
HMPH.
ALMOST HAD YOU.
CHKL...
COWARD.
I KNOW HOW YOU USE THOSE WORMS. YOU INSERT THEM INTO YOUR TARGETS' BRAINS TO CONTROL THEM.
A CLEVER TRICK.

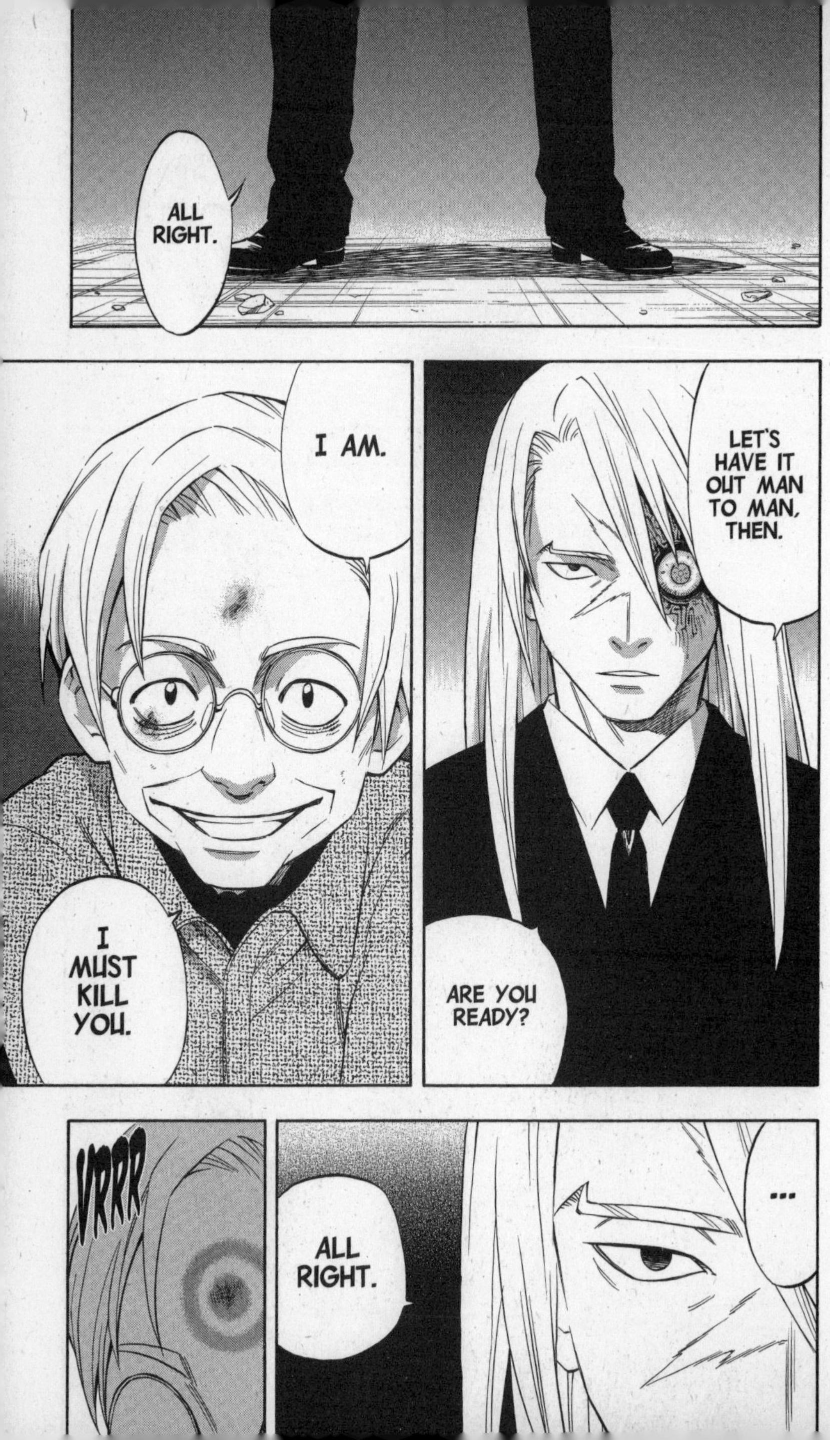
ALL RIGHT.
LET'S HAVE IT OUT MAN TO MAN, THEN.
ARE YOU READY?
I AM.
I MUST KILL YOU.
...
ALL RIGHT.
VRRR

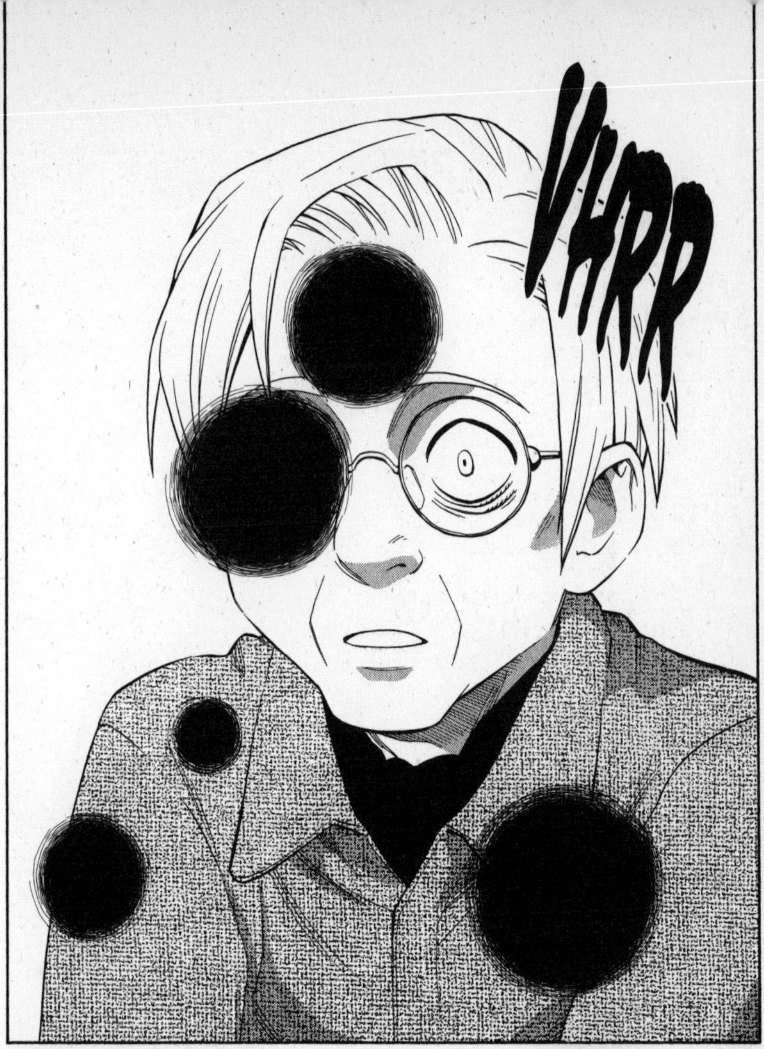
VHRR

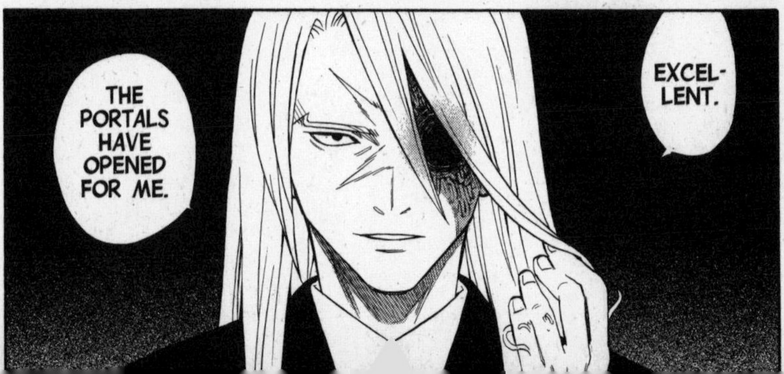
EXCEL-LENT.
THE PORTALS HAVE OPENED FOR ME.

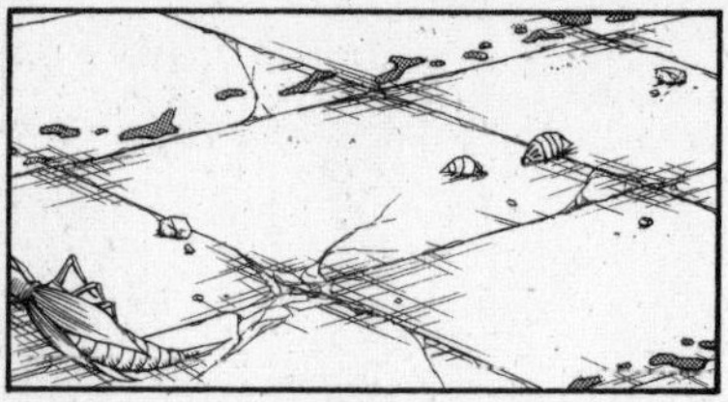
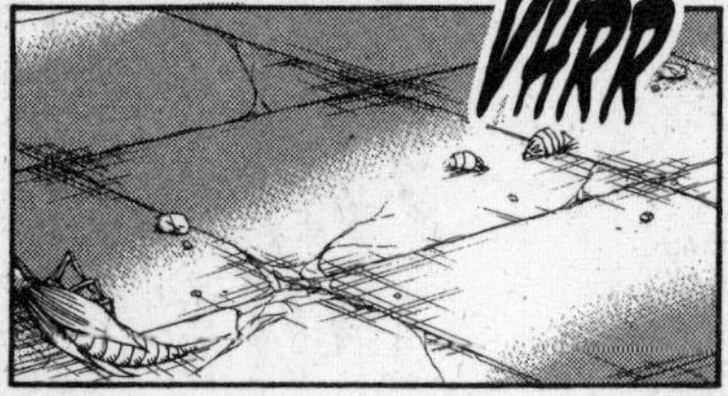
VHRR
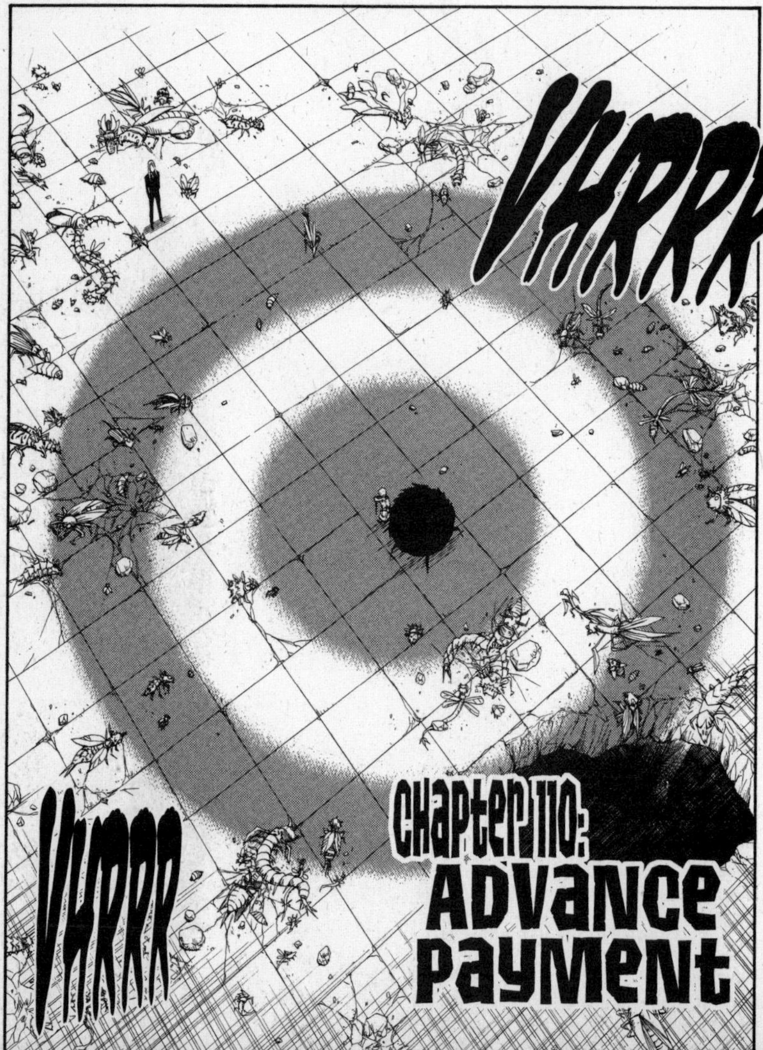
VHRRR
VHRRR
CHAPTER 110:
ADVANCE PAYMENT

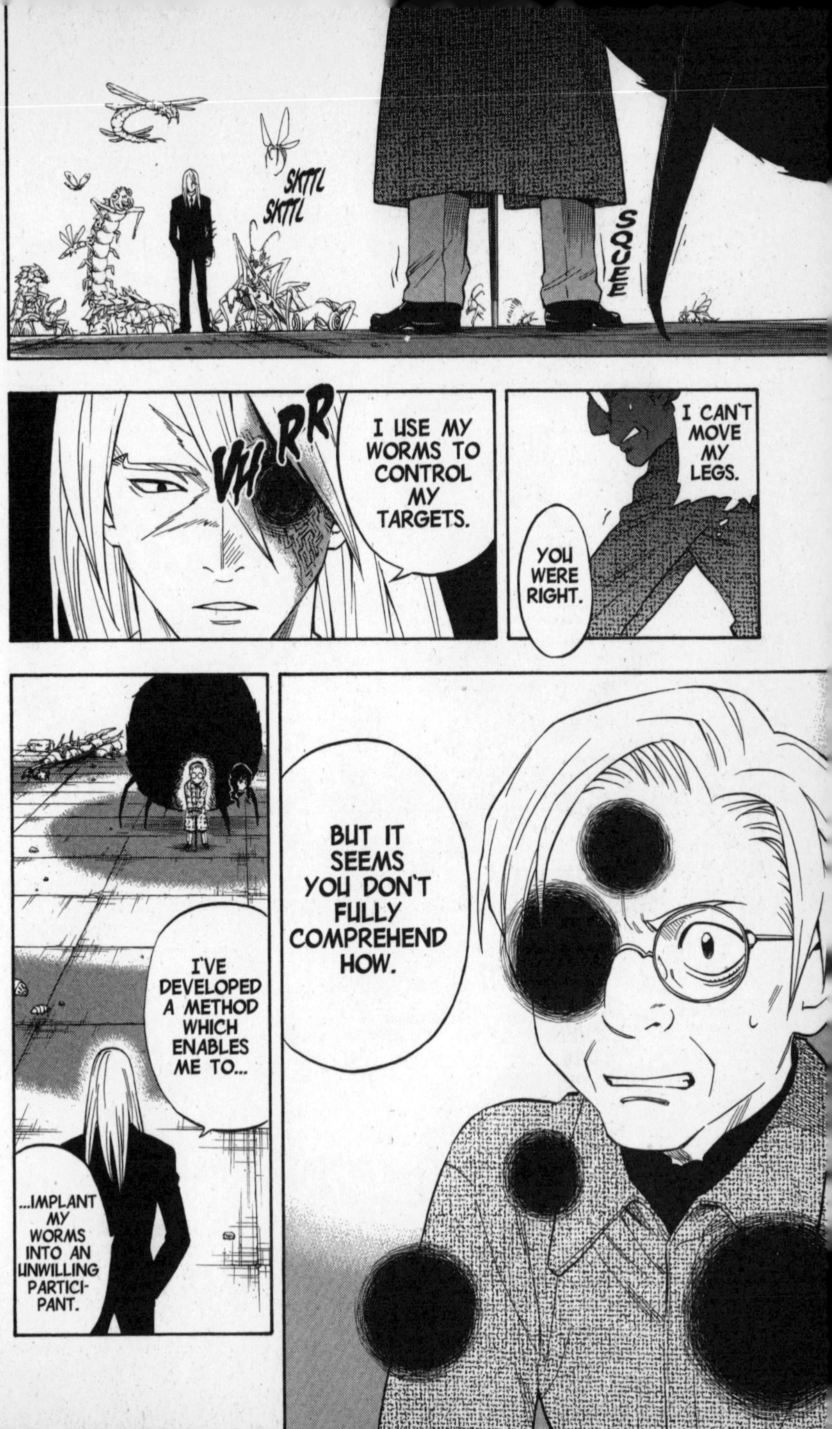
SQUEE
SKTTL SKTTL
I CAN'T MOVE MY LEGS.
YOU WERE RIGHT.
VHRR
I USE MY WORMS TO CONTROL MY TARGETS.
BUT IT SEEMS YOU DON'T FULLY COMPREHEND HOW.
I'VE DEVELOPED A METHOD WHICH ENABLES ME TO...
...IMPLANT MY WORMS INTO AN UNWILLING PARTICIPANT.

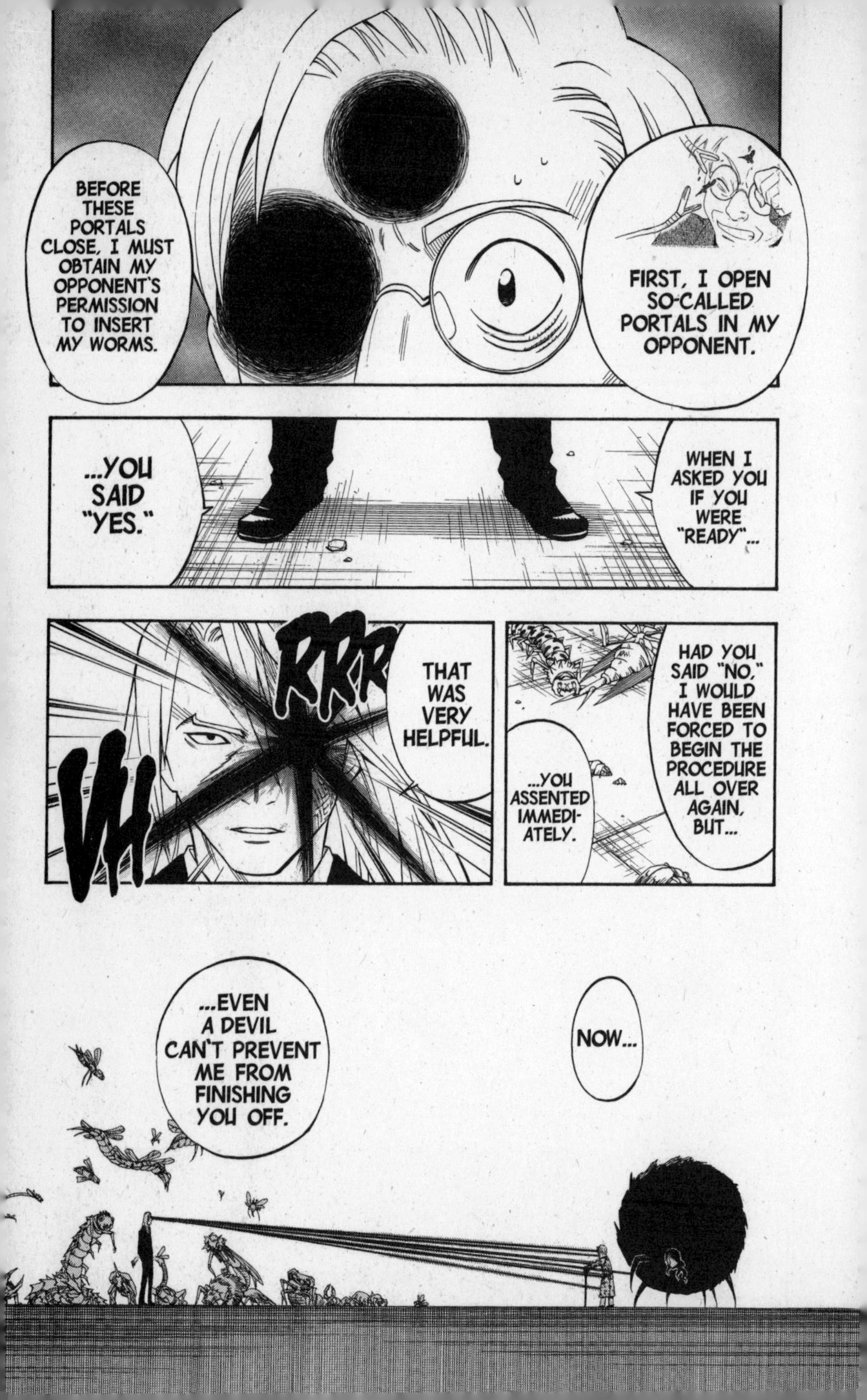
FIRST, I OPEN SO-CALLED PORTALS IN MY OPPONENT.
BEFORE THESE PORTALS CLOSE, I MUST OBTAIN MY OPPONENT'S PERMISSION TO INSERT MY WORMS.
WHEN I ASKED YOU IF YOU WERE "READY"...
...YOU SAID "YES."
HAD YOU SAID "NO," I WOULD HAVE BEEN FORCED TO BEGIN THE PROCEDURE ALL OVER AGAIN, BUT...
...YOU ASSENTED IMMEDIATELY.
THAT WAS VERY HELPFUL.
VHRRR
NOW...
...EVEN A DEVIL CAN'T PREVENT ME FROM FINISHING YOU OFF.

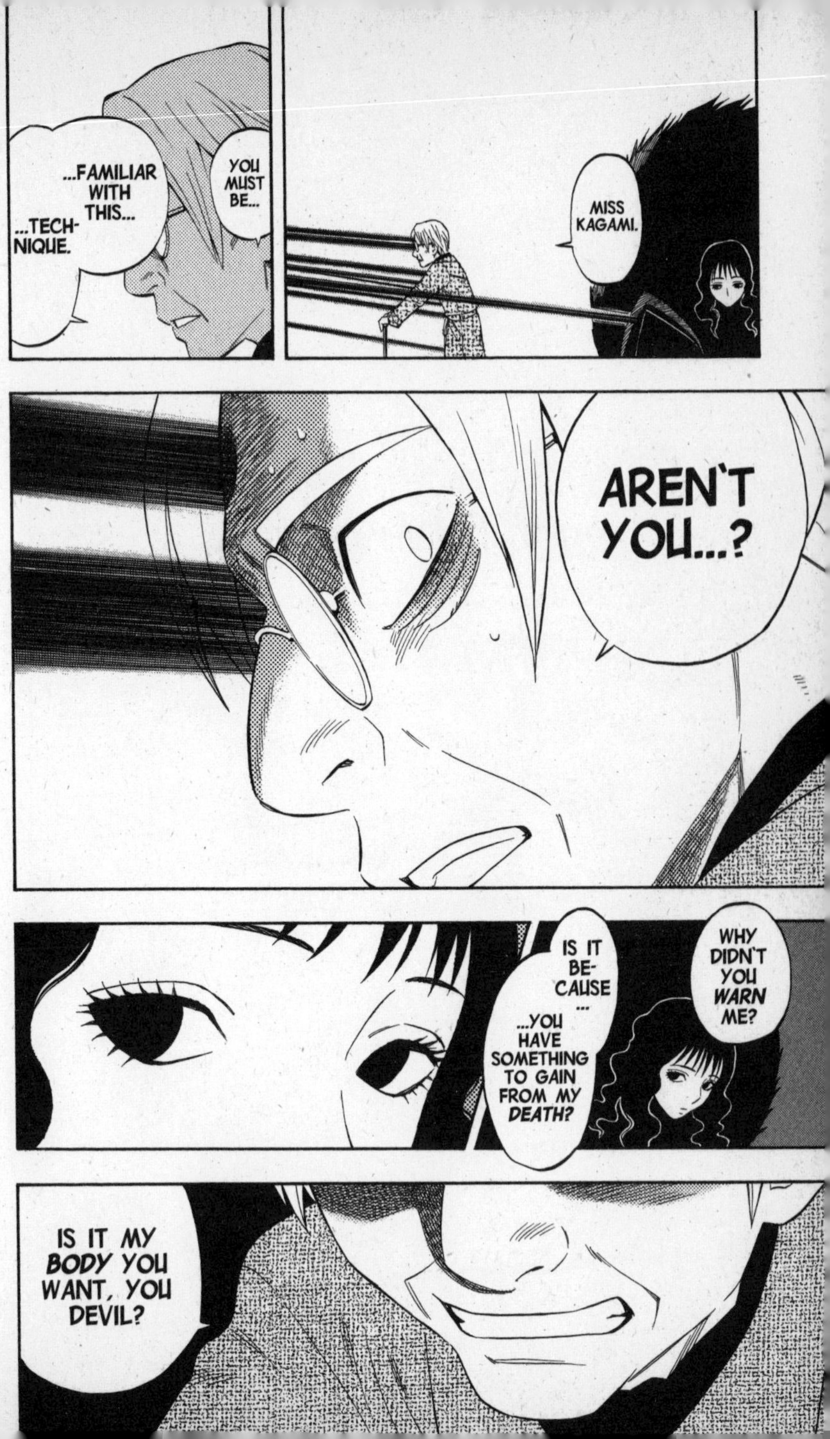
MISS KAGAMI.
YOU MUST BE...
...FAMILIAR WITH THIS...
...TECH-NIQUE.
AREN'T YOU...?
WHY DIDN'T YOU *WARN* ME?
IS IT BE-CAUSE ...
...YOU HAVE SOMETHING TO GAIN FROM MY *DEATH*?
IS IT MY *BODY* YOU WANT, YOU DEVIL?

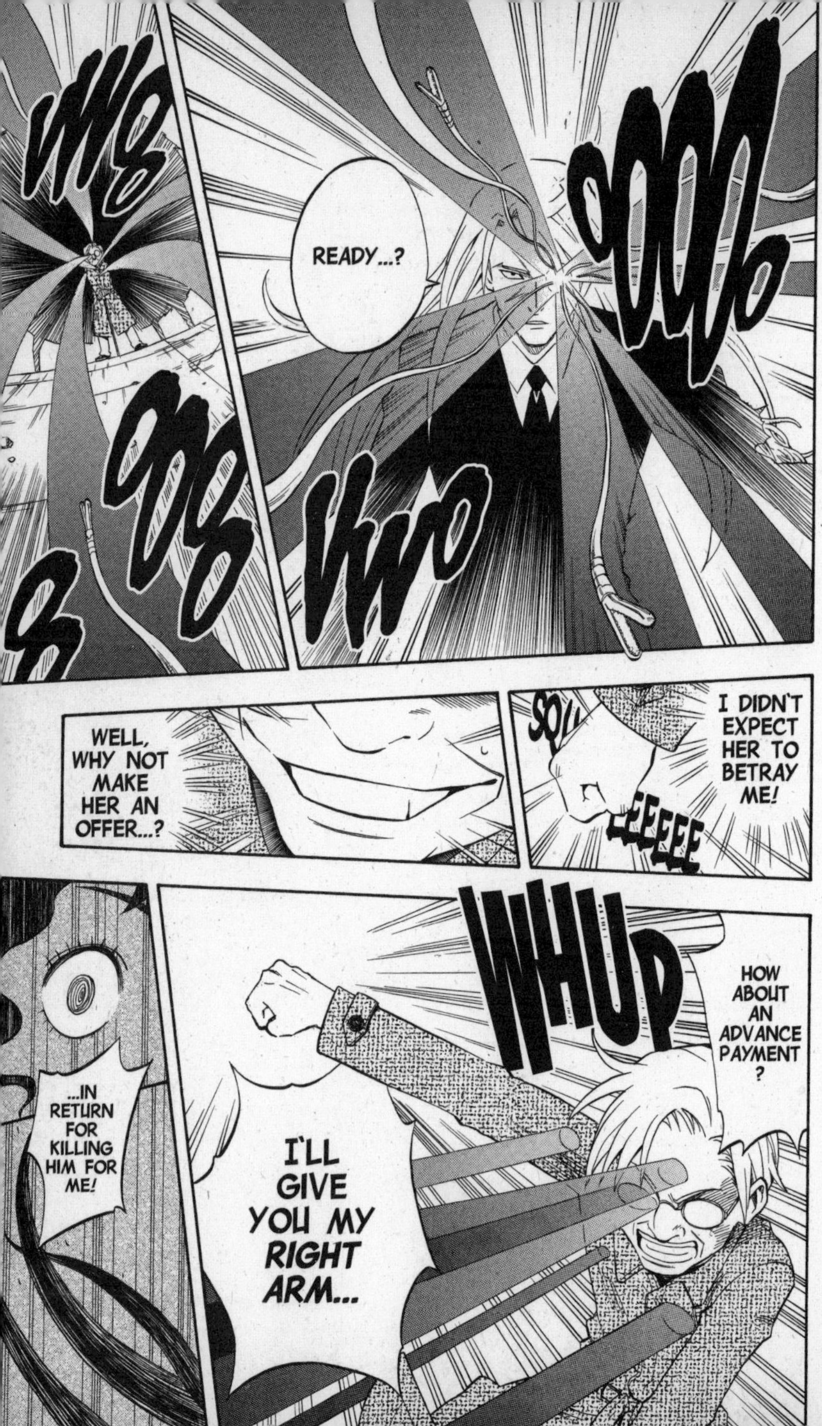
READY...?
I DIDN'T EXPECT HER TO BETRAY ME!
WELL, WHY NOT MAKE HER AN OFFER...?
HOW ABOUT AN ADVANCE PAYMENT?
WHUP
I'LL GIVE YOU MY RIGHT ARM...
...IN RETURN FOR KILLING HIM FOR ME!

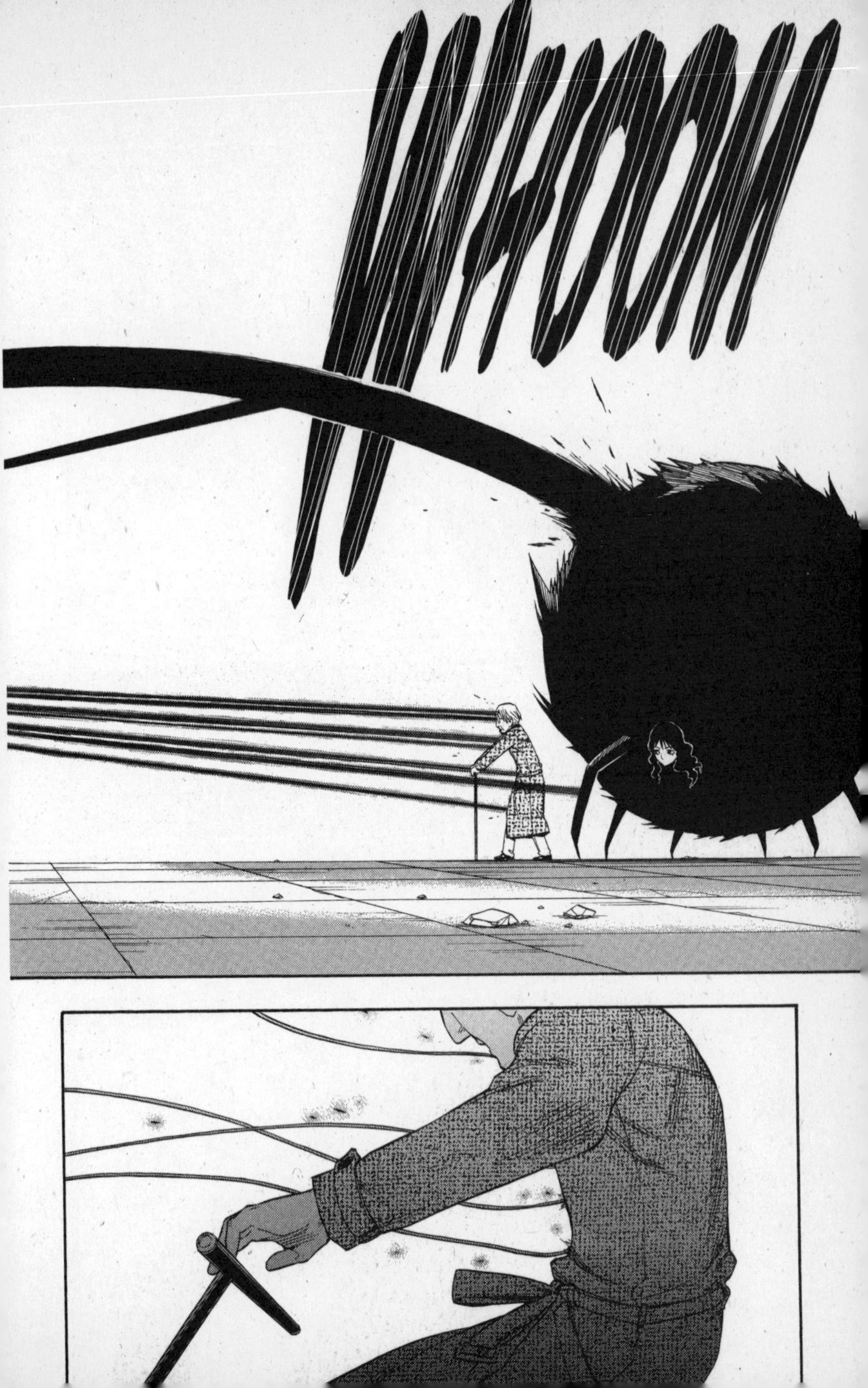
WHOOM

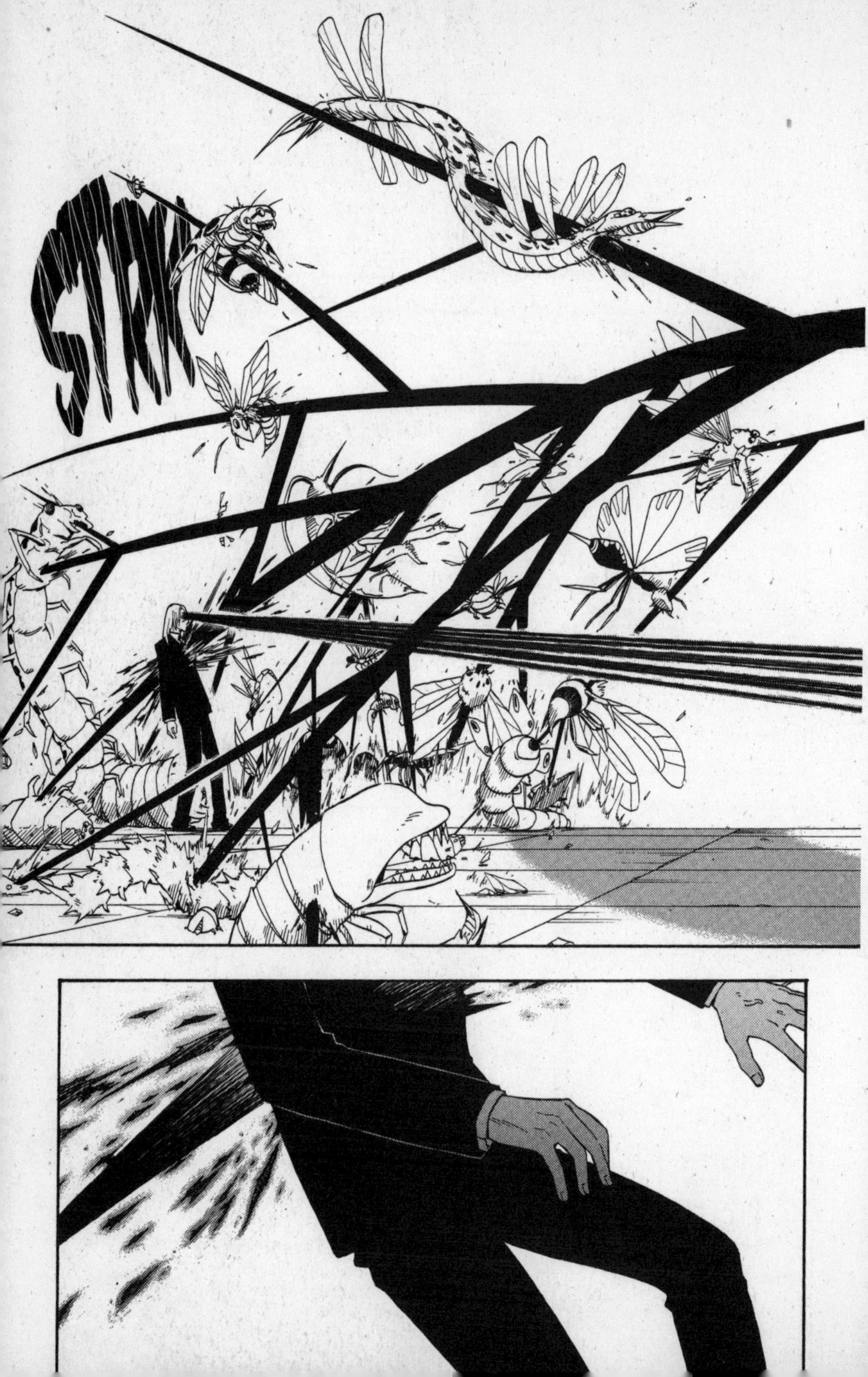
STRKK

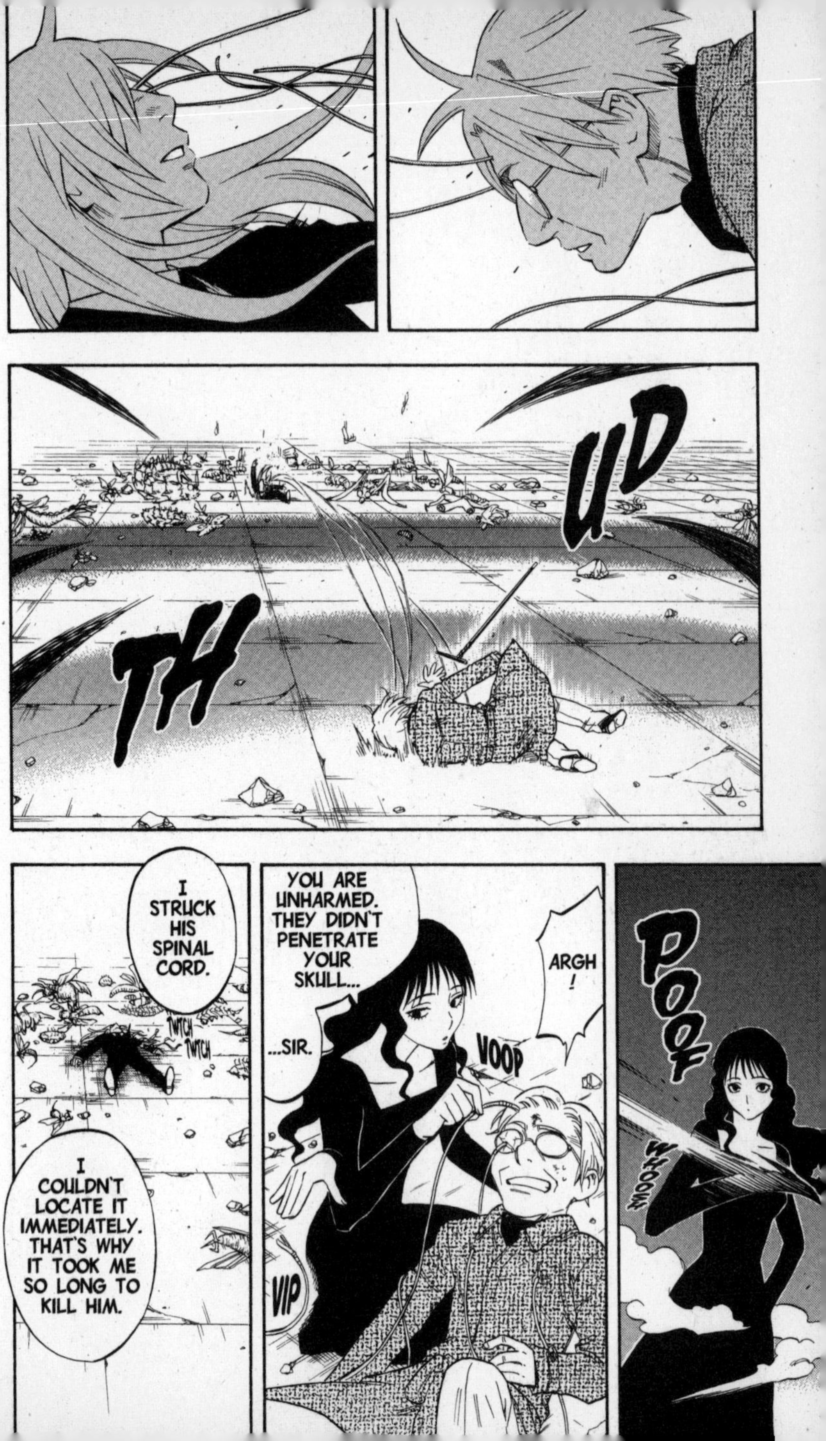
UD
TH
POOF
WHOOSH
ARGH!
YOU ARE UNHARMED. THEY DIDN'T PENETRATE YOUR SKULL...
...SIR.
VOOP
VIP
I STRUCK HIS SPINAL CORD.
TWITCH
TWITCH
I COULDN'T LOCATE IT IMMEDIATELY. THAT'S WHY IT TOOK ME SO LONG TO KILL HIM.

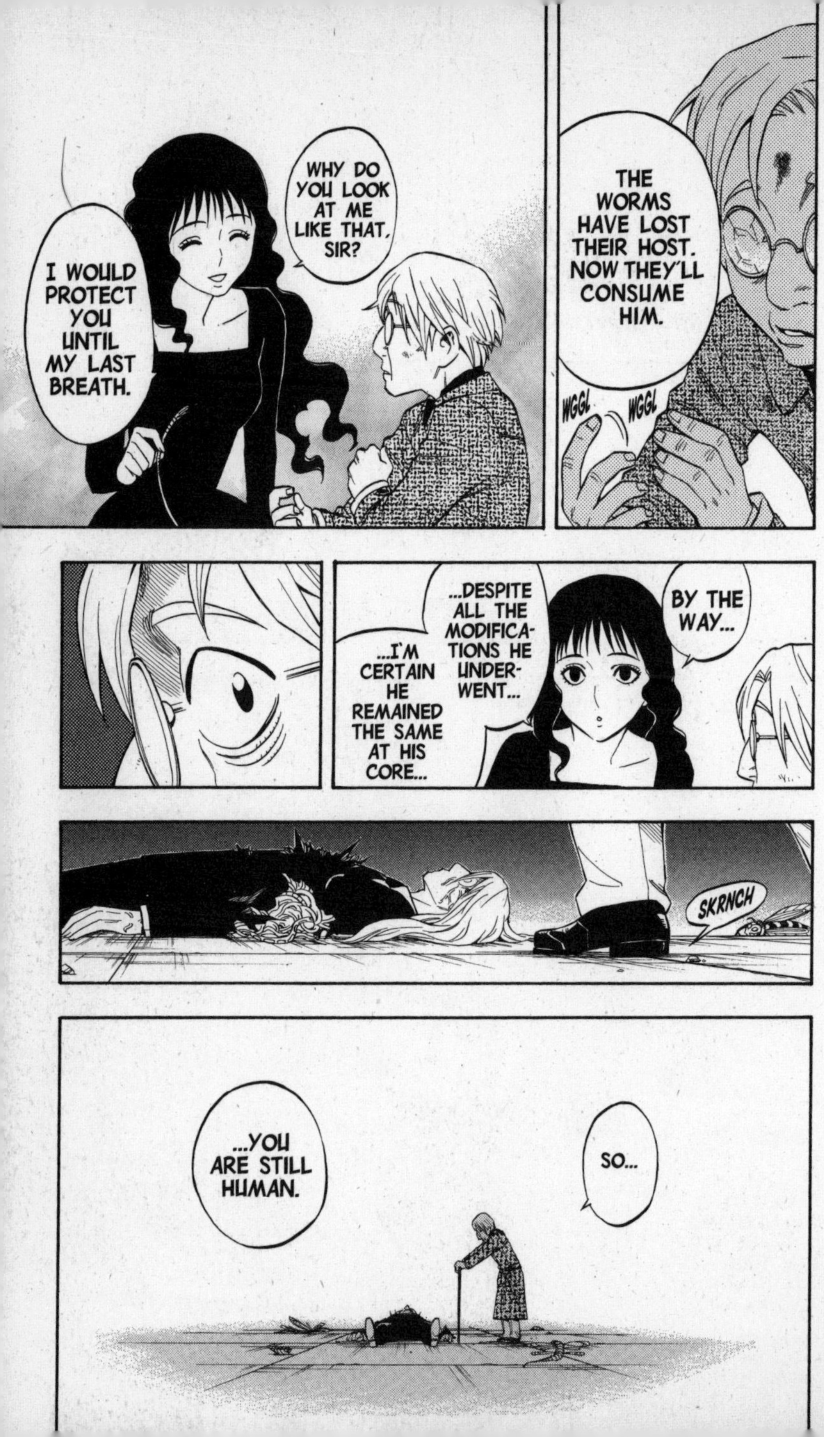
THE WORMS HAVE LOST THEIR HOST. NOW THEY'LL CONSUME HIM.
WGGL
WGGL
WHY DO YOU LOOK AT ME LIKE THAT, SIR?
I WOULD PROTECT YOU UNTIL MY LAST BREATH.
BY THE WAY...
...DESPITE ALL THE MODIFICATIONS HE UNDERWENT...
...I'M CERTAIN HE REMAINED THE SAME AT HIS CORE...
SKRNCH
SO...
...YOU ARE STILL HUMAN.

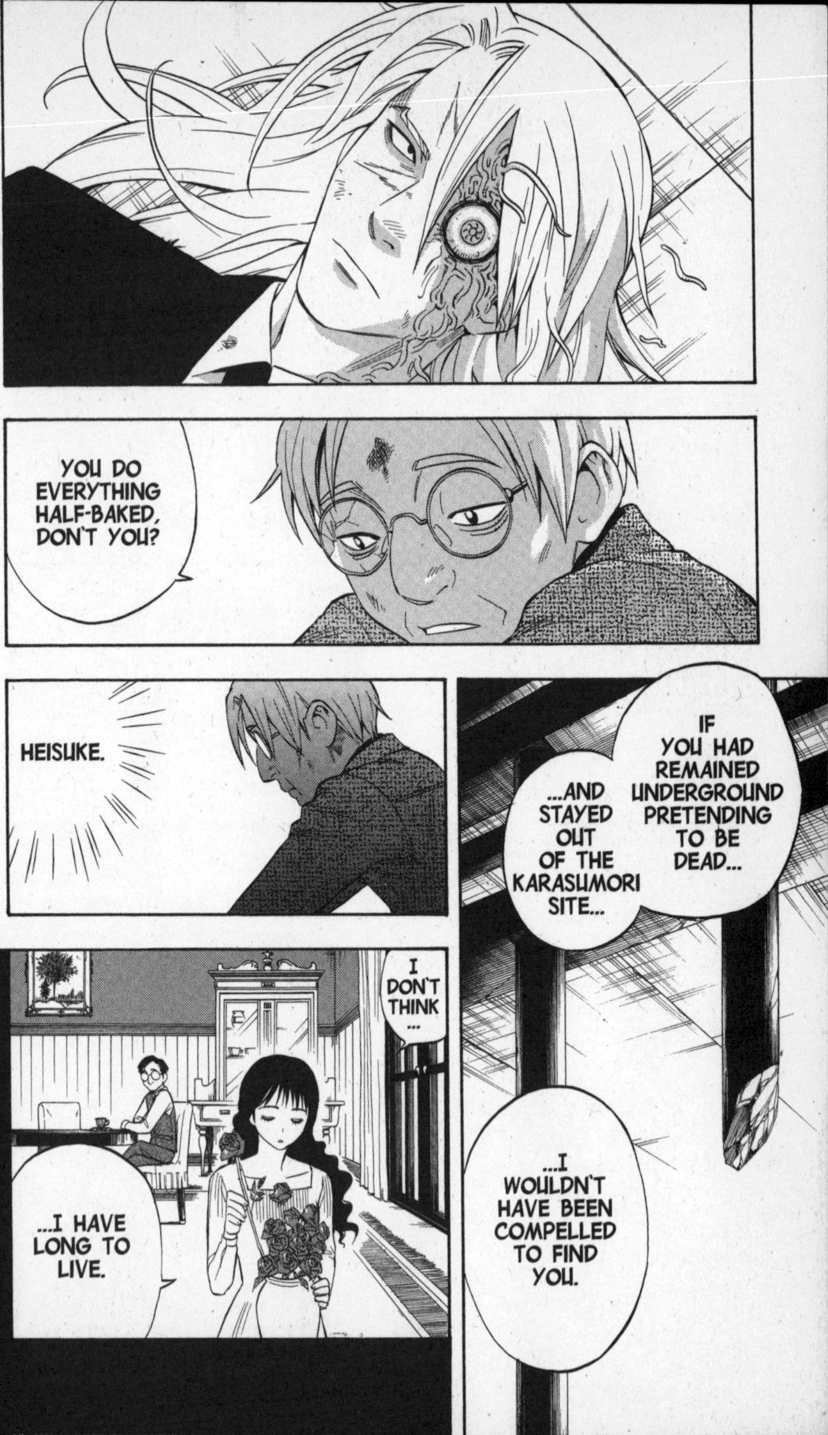
YOU DO EVERYTHING HALF-BAKED, DON'T YOU?
IF YOU HAD REMAINED UNDERGROUND PRETENDING TO BE DEAD...
...AND STAYED OUT OF THE KARASUMORI SITE...
...I WOULDN'T HAVE BEEN COMPELLED TO FIND YOU.
HEISUKE.
I DON'T THINK...
...I HAVE LONG TO LIVE.

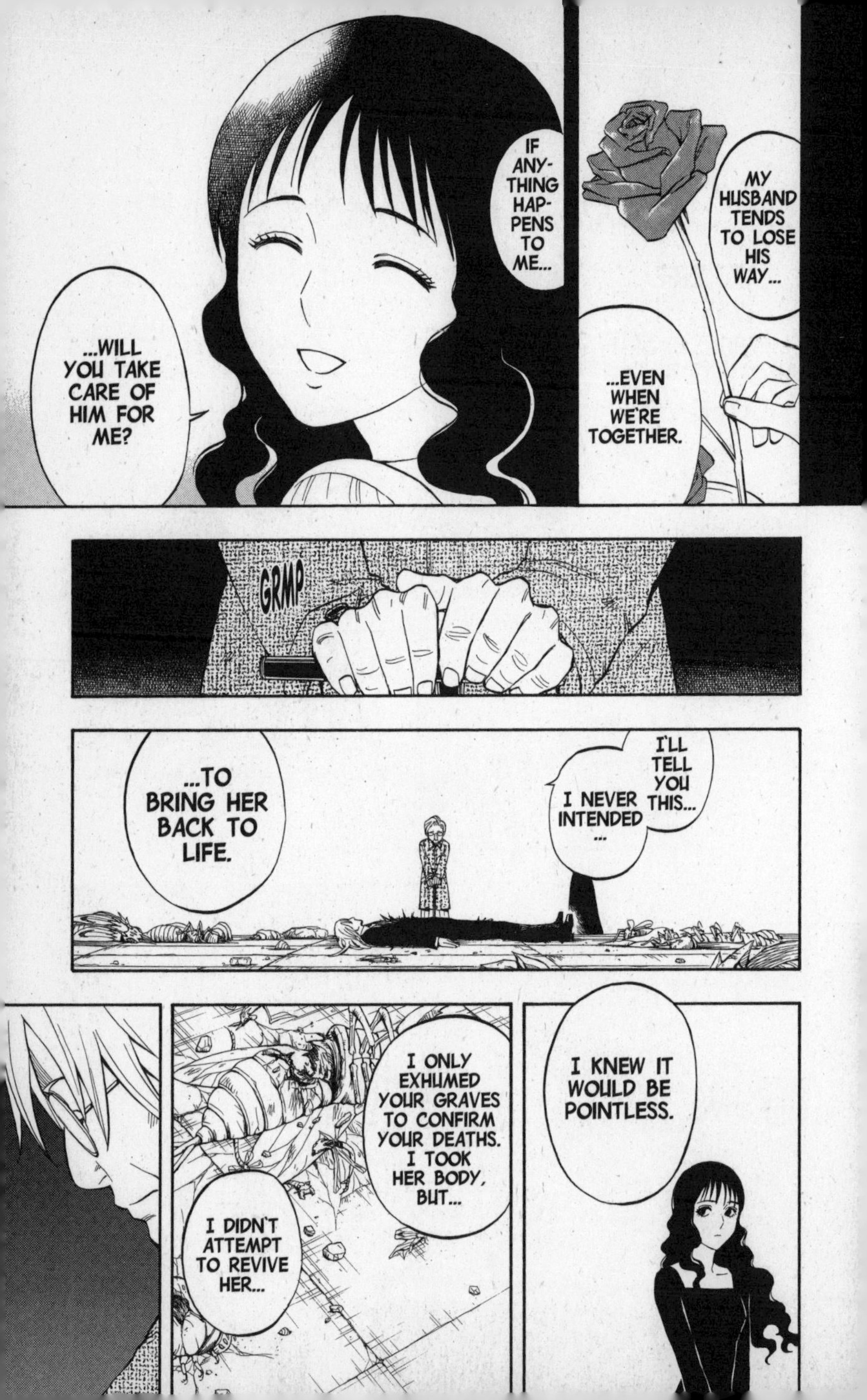
MY HUSBAND TENDS TO LOSE HIS WAY...
...EVEN WHEN WE'RE TOGETHER.
IF ANYTHING HAPPENS TO ME...
...WILL YOU TAKE CARE OF HIM FOR ME?
GRMP
I'LL TELL YOU THIS...
I NEVER INTENDED...
...TO BRING HER BACK TO LIFE.
I KNEW IT WOULD BE POINTLESS.
I ONLY EXHUMED YOUR GRAVES TO CONFIRM YOUR DEATHS. I TOOK HER BODY, BUT...
I DIDN'T ATTEMPT TO REVIVE HER...

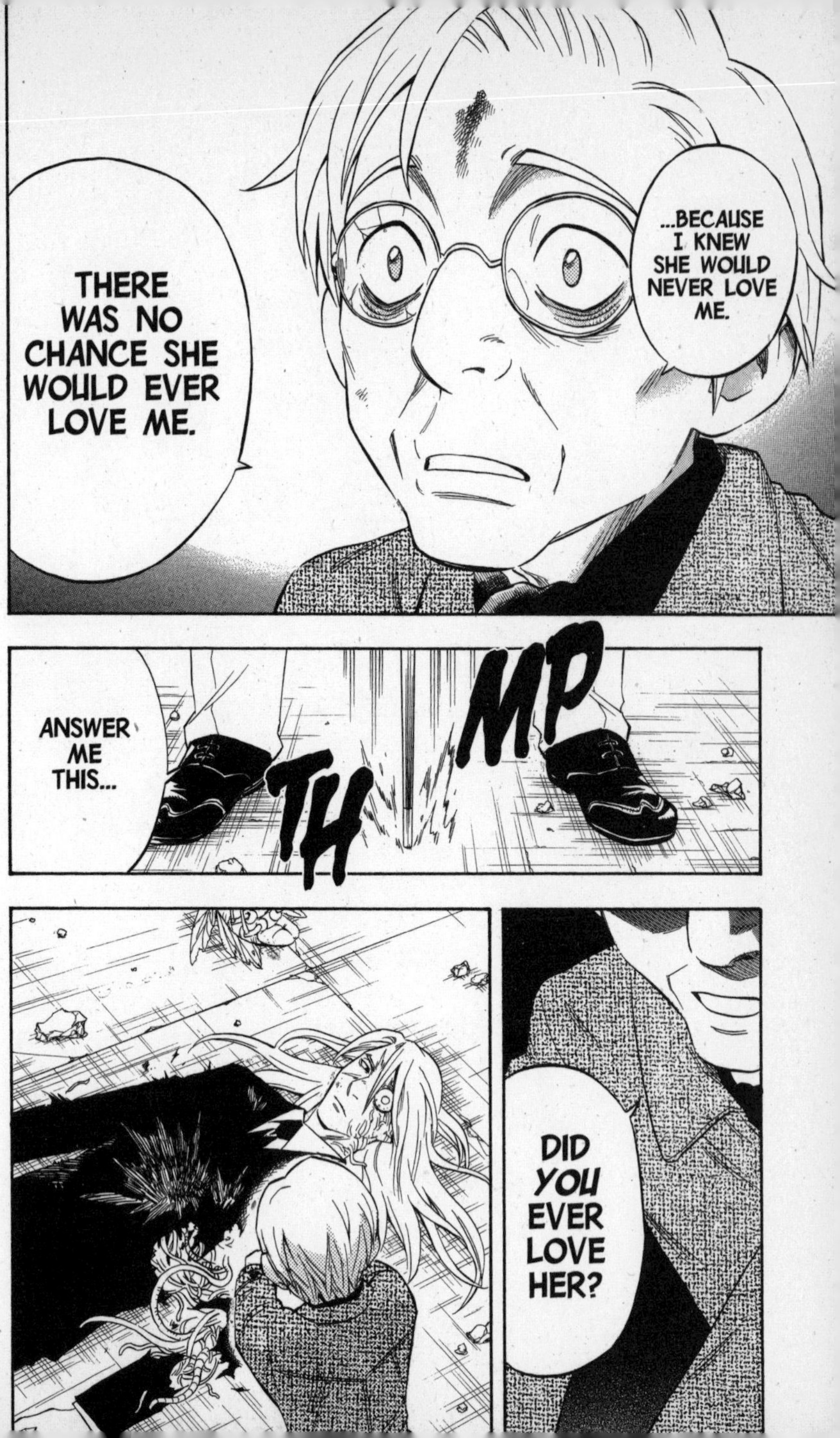
...BECAUSE I KNEW SHE WOULD NEVER LOVE ME.
THERE WAS NO CHANCE SHE WOULD EVER LOVE ME.
TH MP
ANSWER ME THIS...
DID *YOU* EVER LOVE HER?

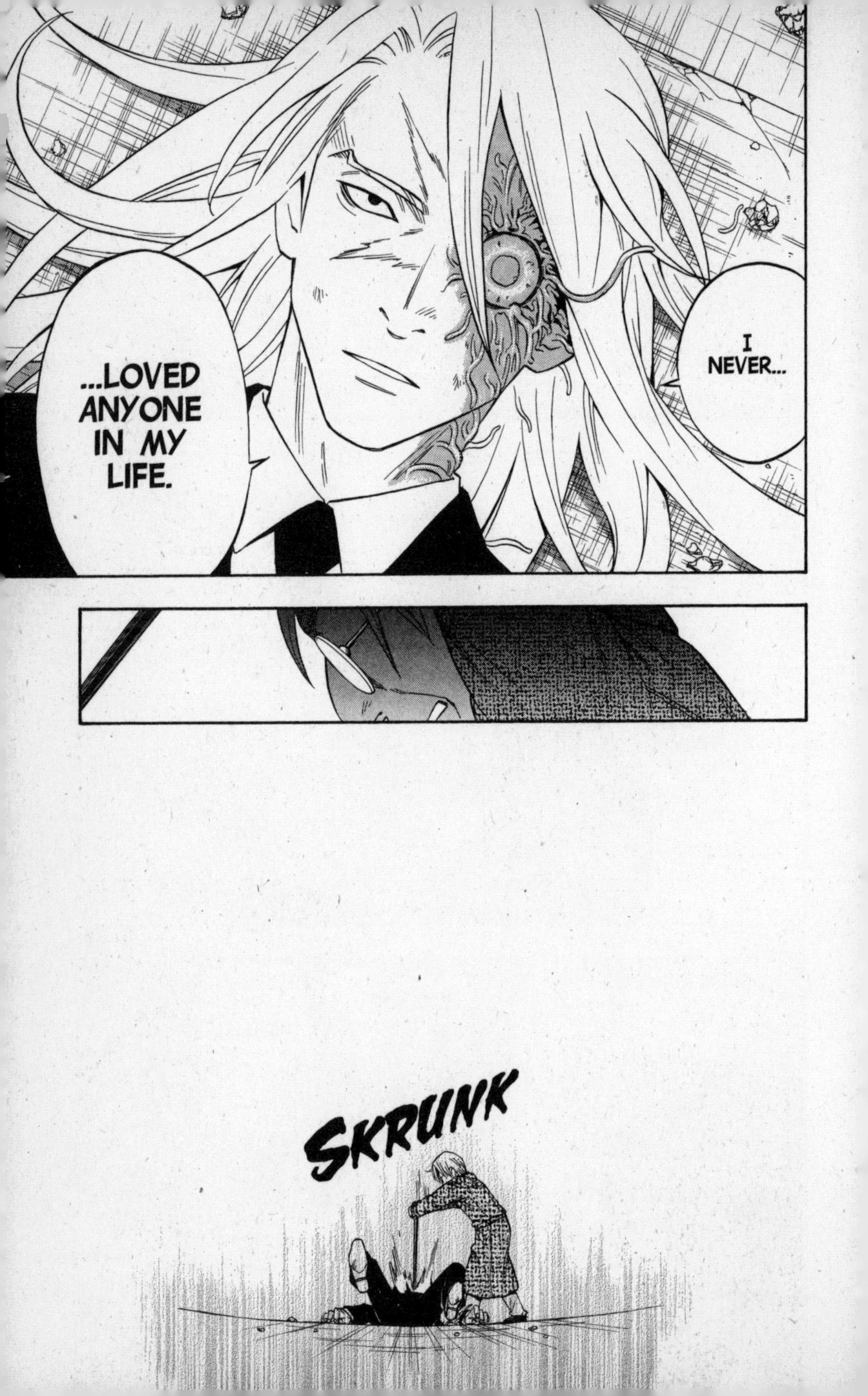
I NEVER...
...LOVED ANYONE IN MY LIFE.
SKRUNK

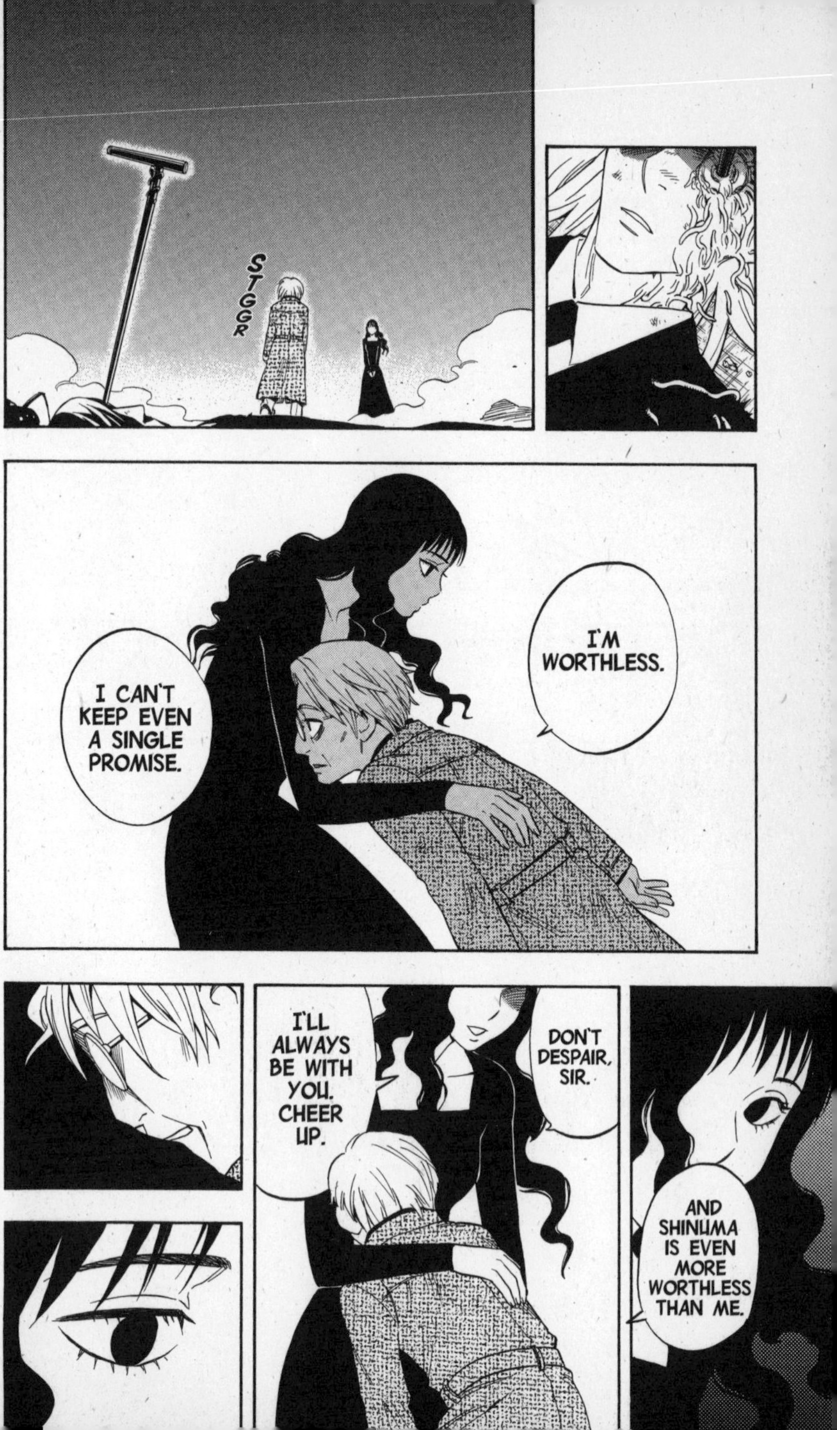
STGGR
I'M WORTHLESS.
I CAN'T KEEP EVEN A SINGLE PROMISE.
AND SHINUMA IS EVEN MORE WORTHLESS THAN ME.
DON'T DESPAIR, SIR.
I'LL ALWAYS BE WITH YOU. CHEER UP.

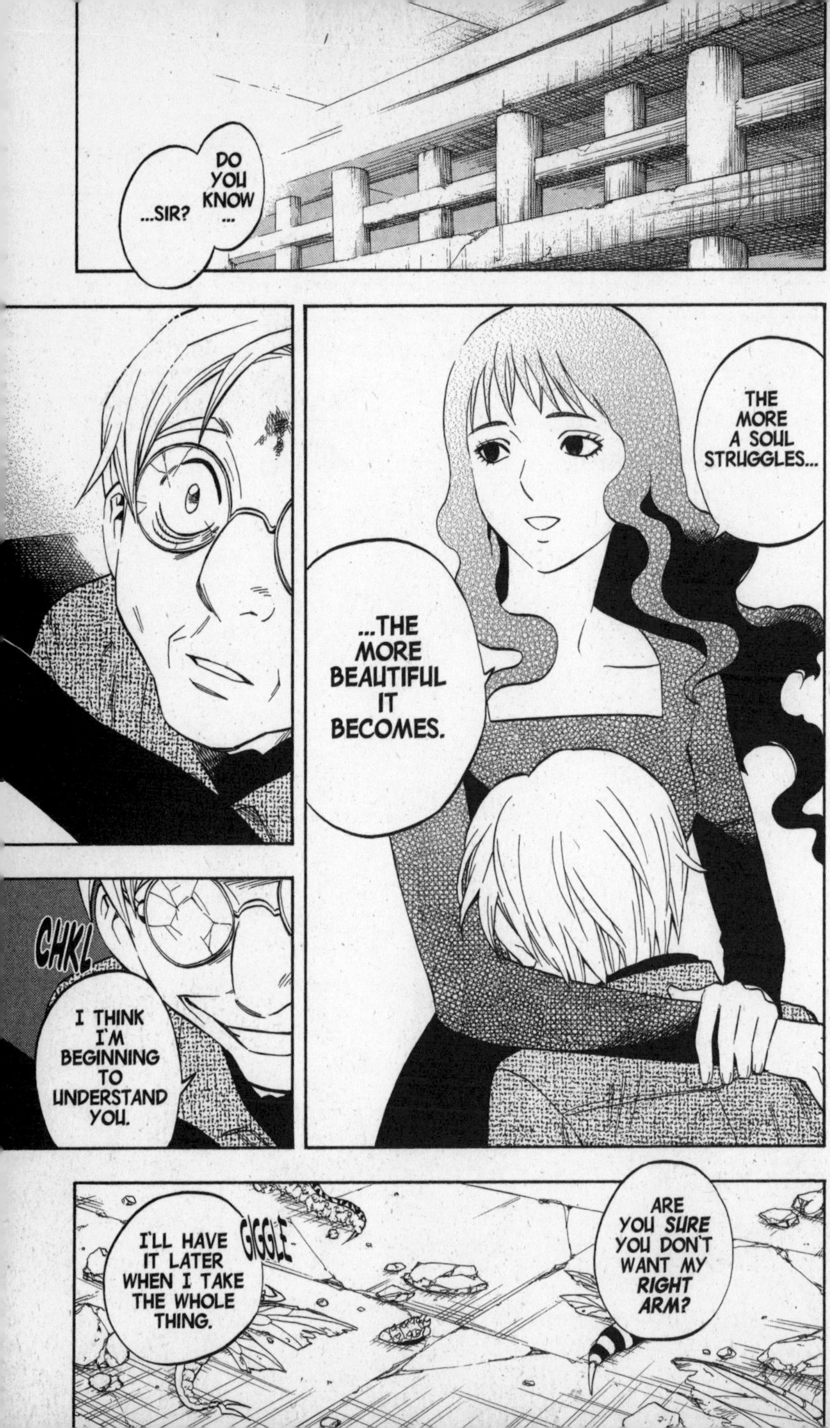
DO YOU KNOW ... ...SIR?
THE MORE A SOUL STRUGGLES...
...THE MORE BEAUTIFUL IT BECOMES.
CHKL
I THINK I'M BEGINNING TO UNDERSTAND YOU.
ARE YOU SURE YOU DON'T WANT MY RIGHT ARM?
GIGGLE
I'LL HAVE IT LATER WHEN I TAKE THE WHOLE THING.

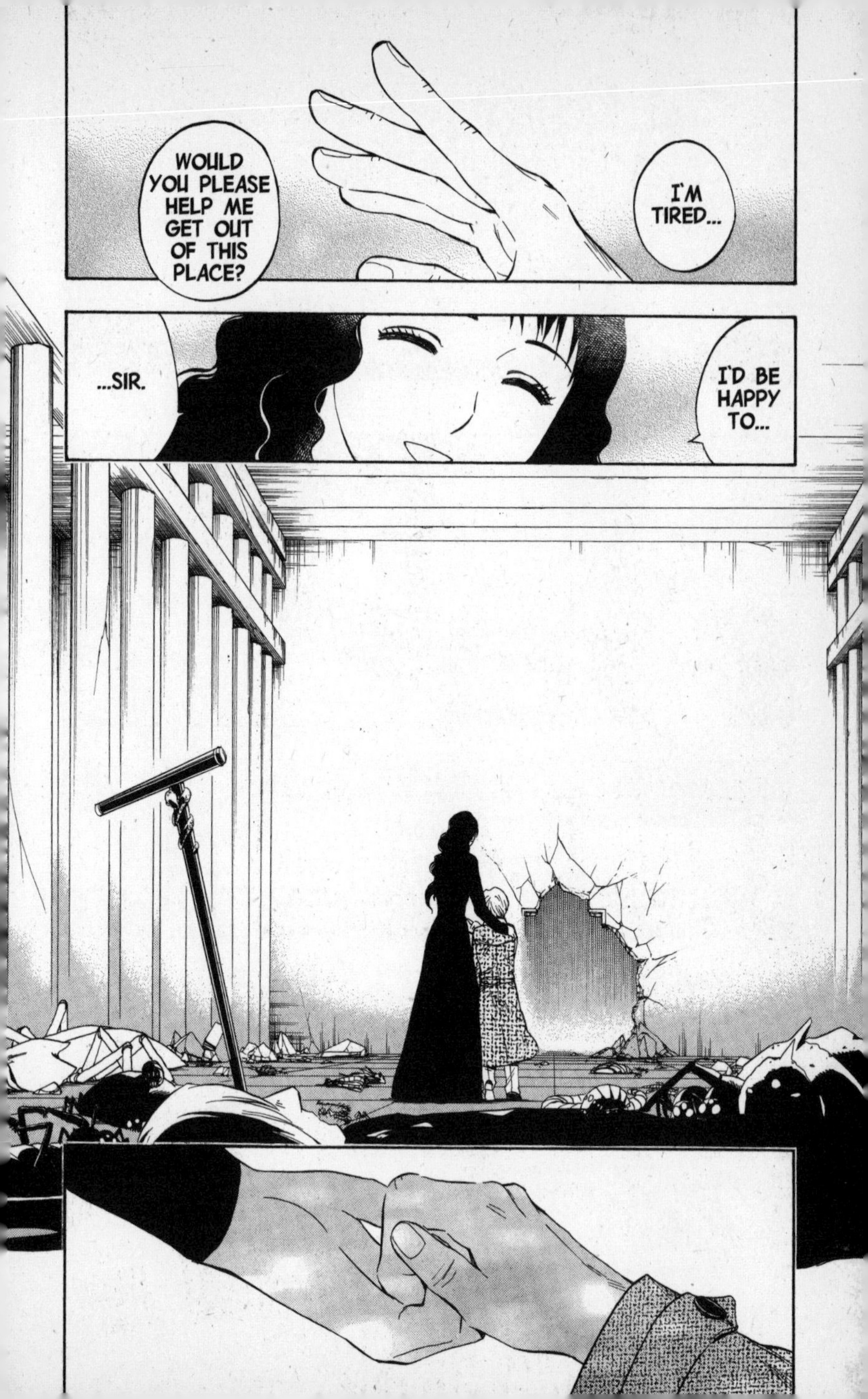
I'M TIRED...
WOULD YOU PLEASE HELP ME GET OUT OF THIS PLACE?
I'D BE HAPPY TO...
...SIR.

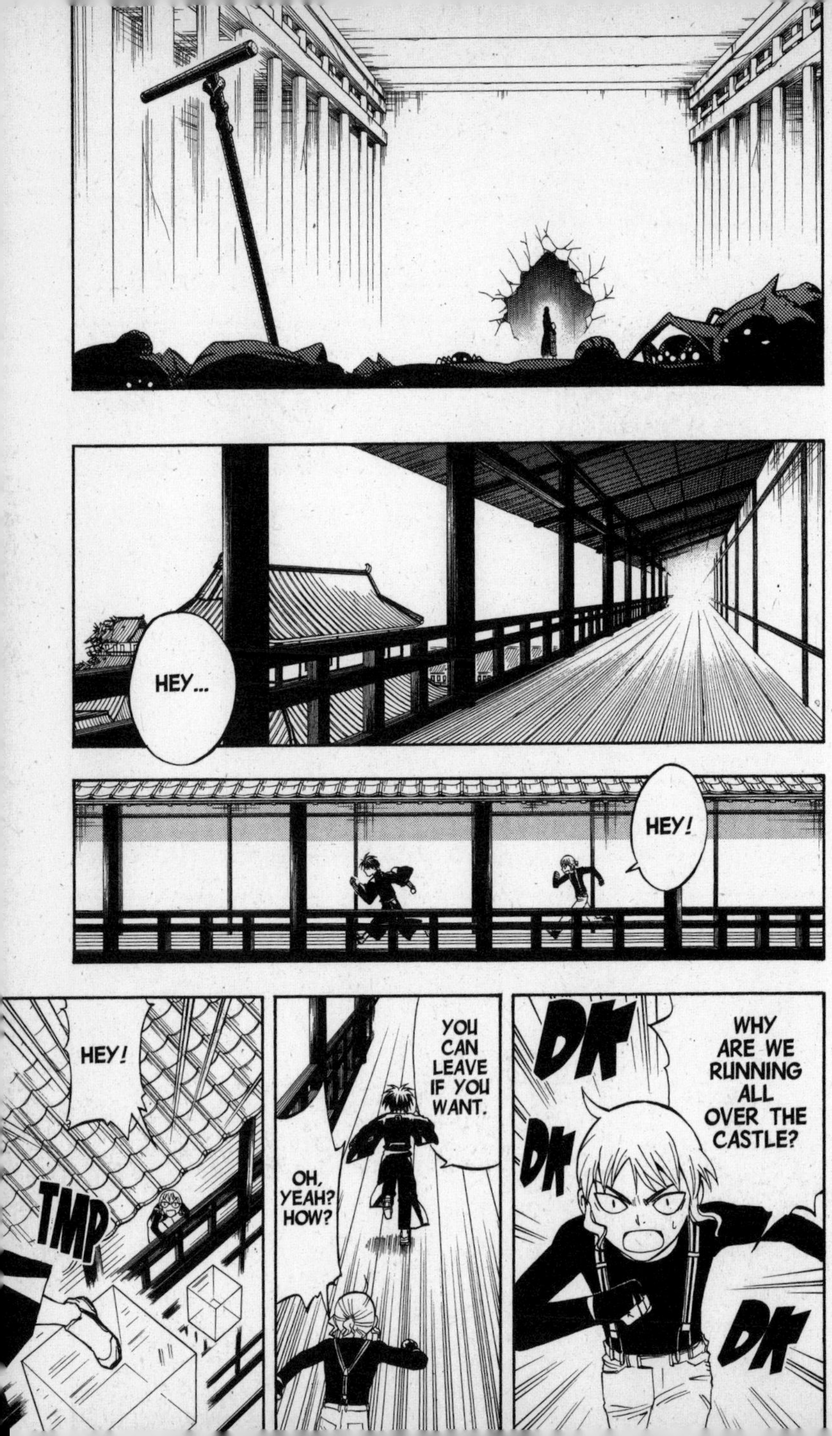
HEY...
HEY!
DK
DK
DK
WHY ARE WE RUNNING ALL OVER THE CASTLE?
YOU CAN LEAVE IF YOU WANT.
OH, YEAH? HOW?
HEY!
TMP

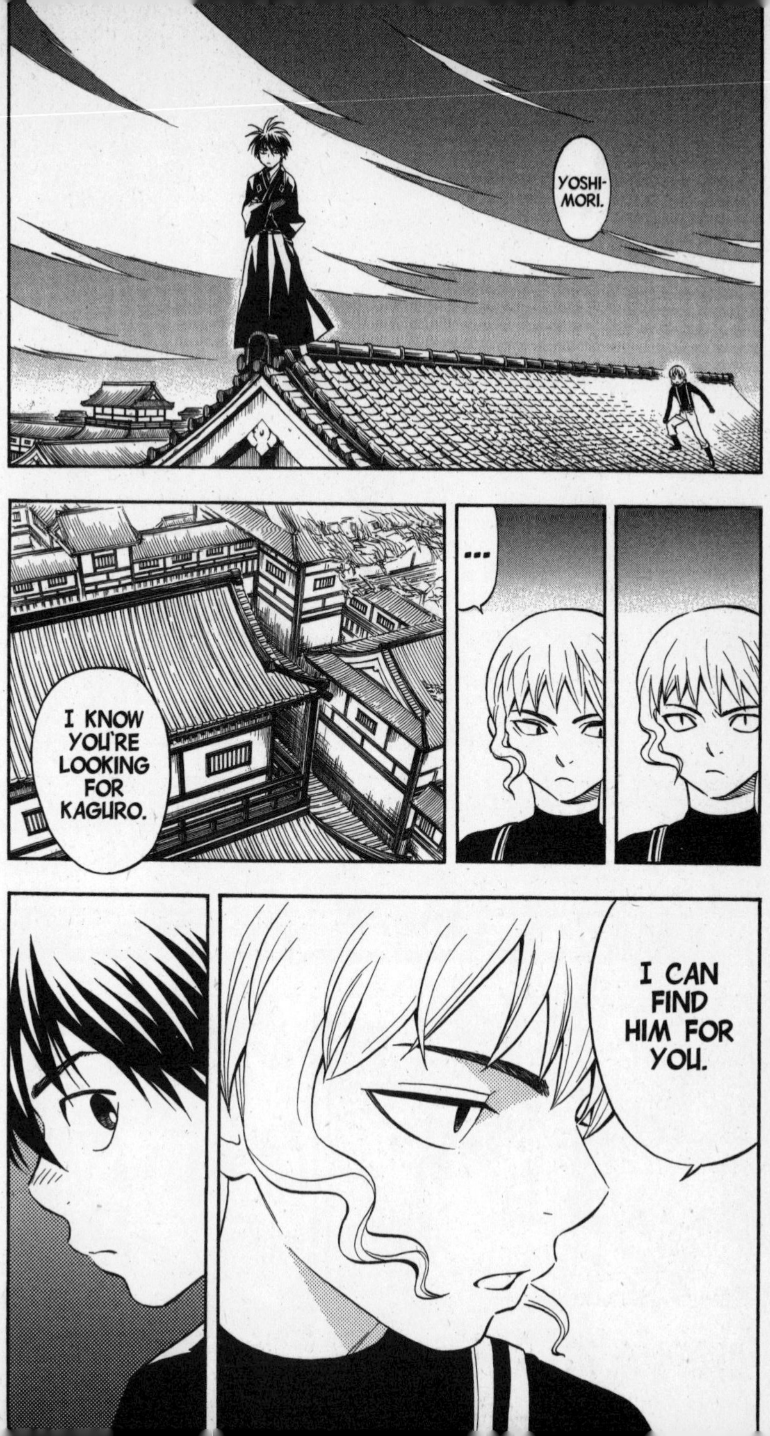
YOSHI-MORI.
...
I KNOW YOU'RE LOOKING FOR KAGURO.
I CAN FIND HIM FOR YOU.

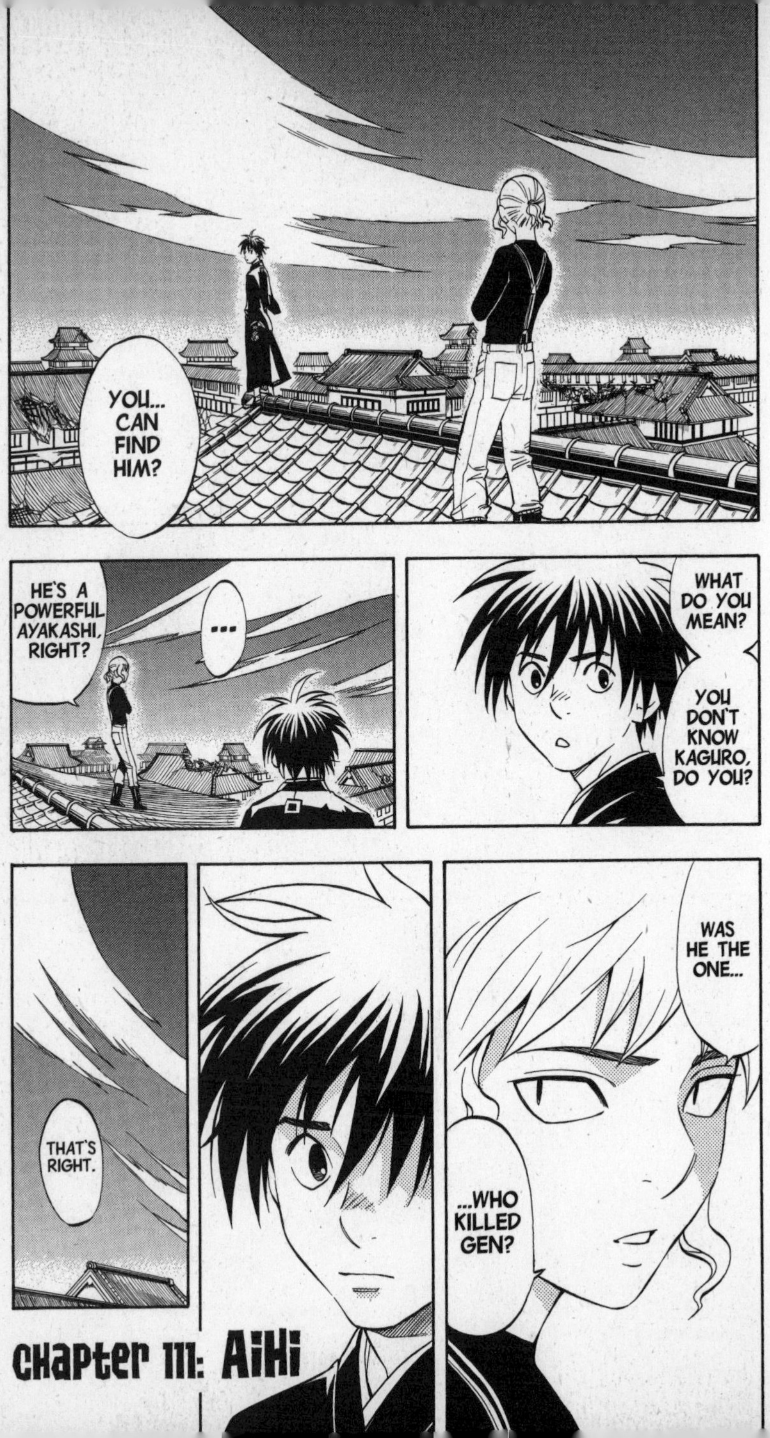
YOU... CAN FIND HIM?
WHAT DO YOU MEAN?
YOU DON'T KNOW KAGURO, DO YOU?
...
HE'S A POWERFUL AYAKASHI, RIGHT?
WAS HE THE ONE...
...WHO KILLED GEN?
THAT'S RIGHT.

Chapter 111: AiHi

CHAPTER 111:
AiHi

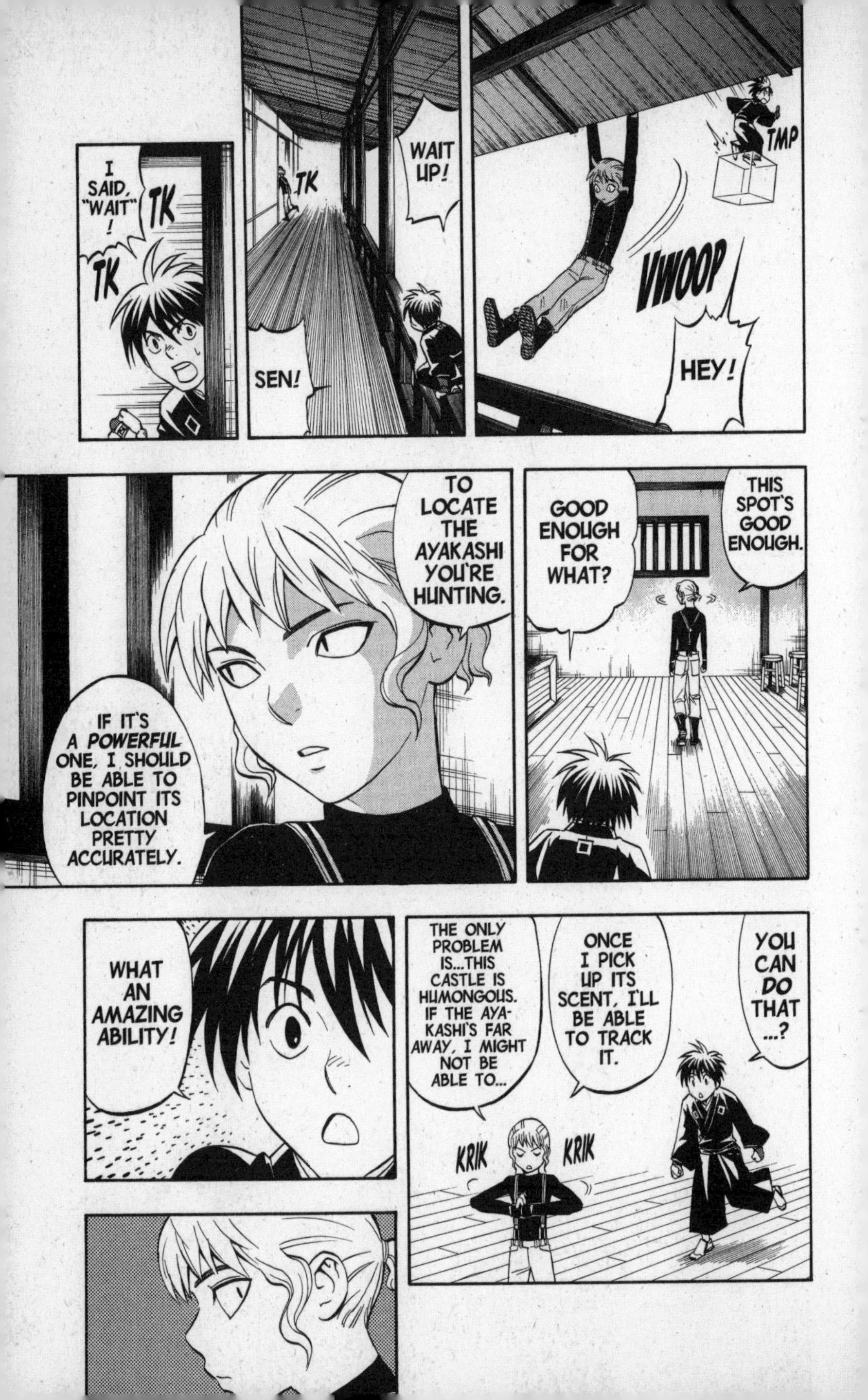
TMP
VWOOP
HEY!
WAIT UP!
TK
SEN!
I SAID, "WAIT"!
TK
TK
THIS SPOT'S GOOD ENOUGH.
GOOD ENOUGH FOR WHAT?
TO LOCATE THE AYAKASHI YOU'RE HUNTING.
IF IT'S A *POWERFUL* ONE, I SHOULD BE ABLE TO PINPOINT ITS LOCATION PRETTY ACCURATELY.
YOU CAN *DO* THAT...?
ONCE I PICK UP ITS SCENT, I'LL BE ABLE TO TRACK IT.
THE ONLY PROBLEM IS...THIS CASTLE IS HUMONGOUS. IF THE AYA-KASHI'S FAR AWAY, I MIGHT NOT BE ABLE TO...
KRIK
KRIK
WHAT AN AMAZING ABILITY!

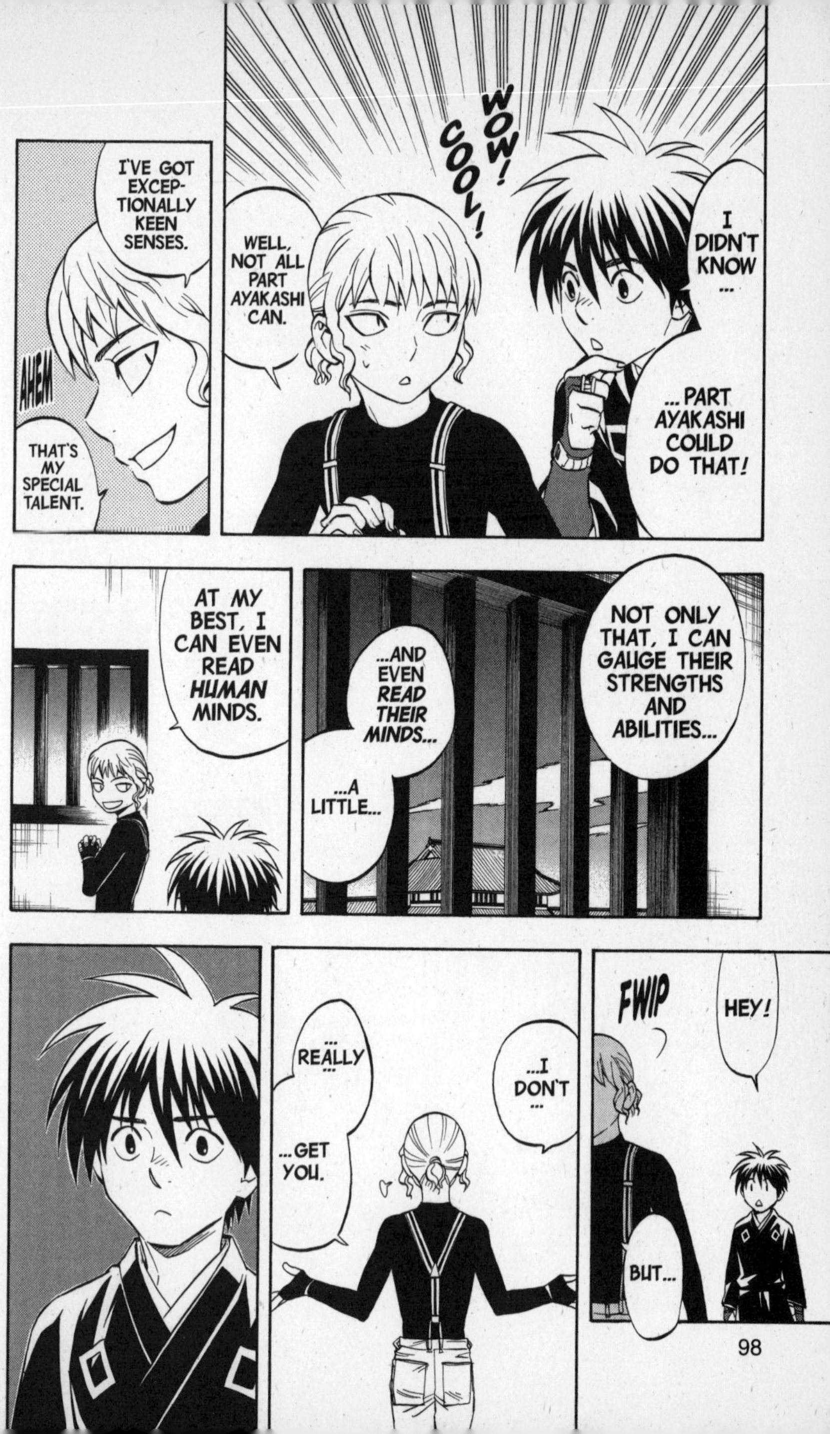
WOW! COOL!
I DIDN'T KNOW ...
... PART AYAKASHI COULD DO THAT!
WELL, NOT ALL PART AYAKASHI CAN.
I'VE GOT EXCEP-TIONALLY KEEN SENSES.
AHEM
THAT'S MY SPECIAL TALENT.
NOT ONLY THAT, I CAN GAUGE THEIR STRENGTHS AND ABILITIES...
...AND EVEN READ THEIR MINDS...
...A LITTLE...
AT MY BEST, I CAN EVEN READ HUMAN MINDS.
HEY!
FWIP
BUT...
...I DON'T ...
... REALLY ...
...GET YOU.

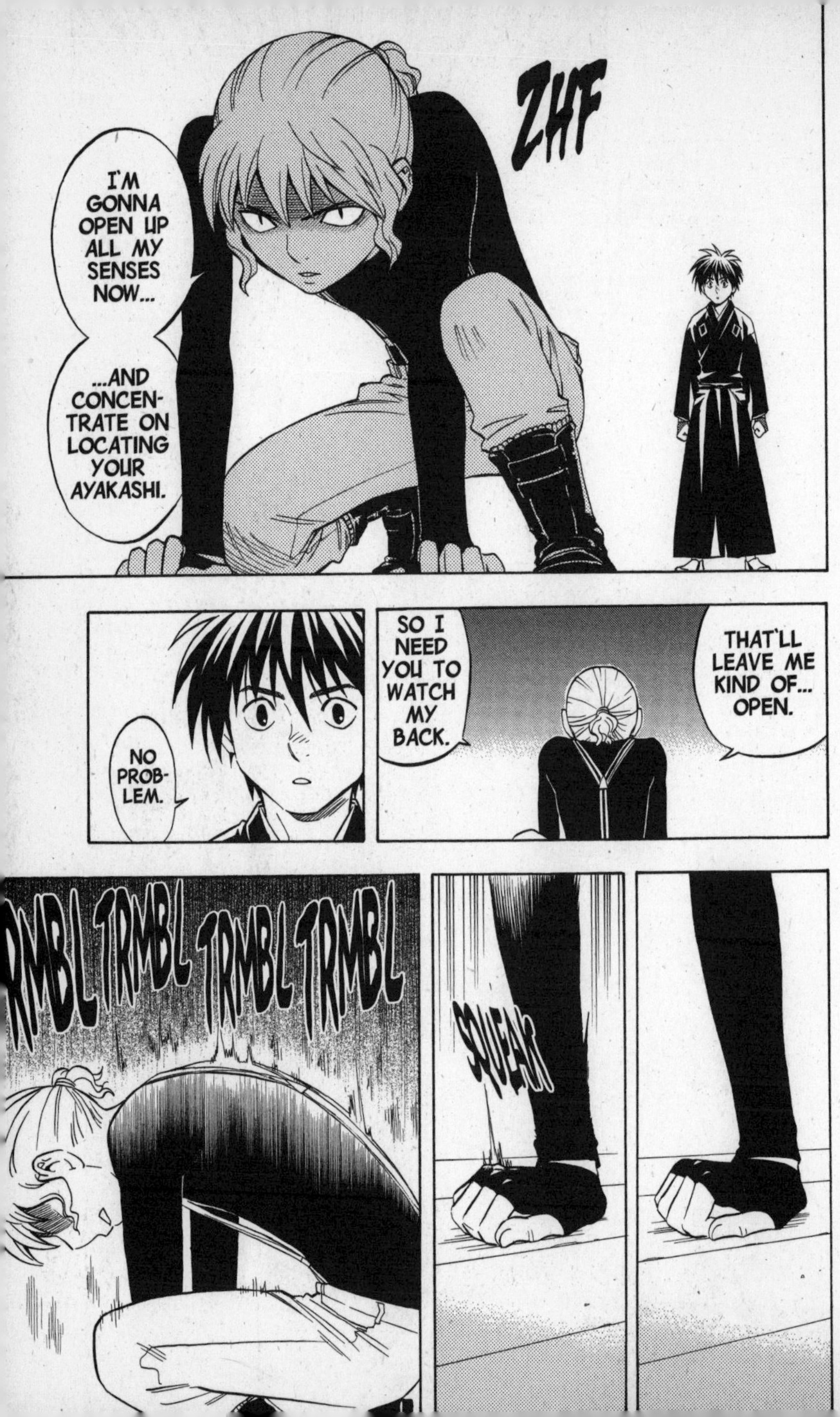
ZHF
I'M GONNA OPEN UP ALL MY SENSES NOW...
...AND CONCENTRATE ON LOCATING YOUR AYAKASHI.
THAT'LL LEAVE ME KIND OF... OPEN.
SO I NEED YOU TO WATCH MY BACK.
NO PROBLEM.
SQUEAK
RMBL TRMBL TRMBL TRMBL

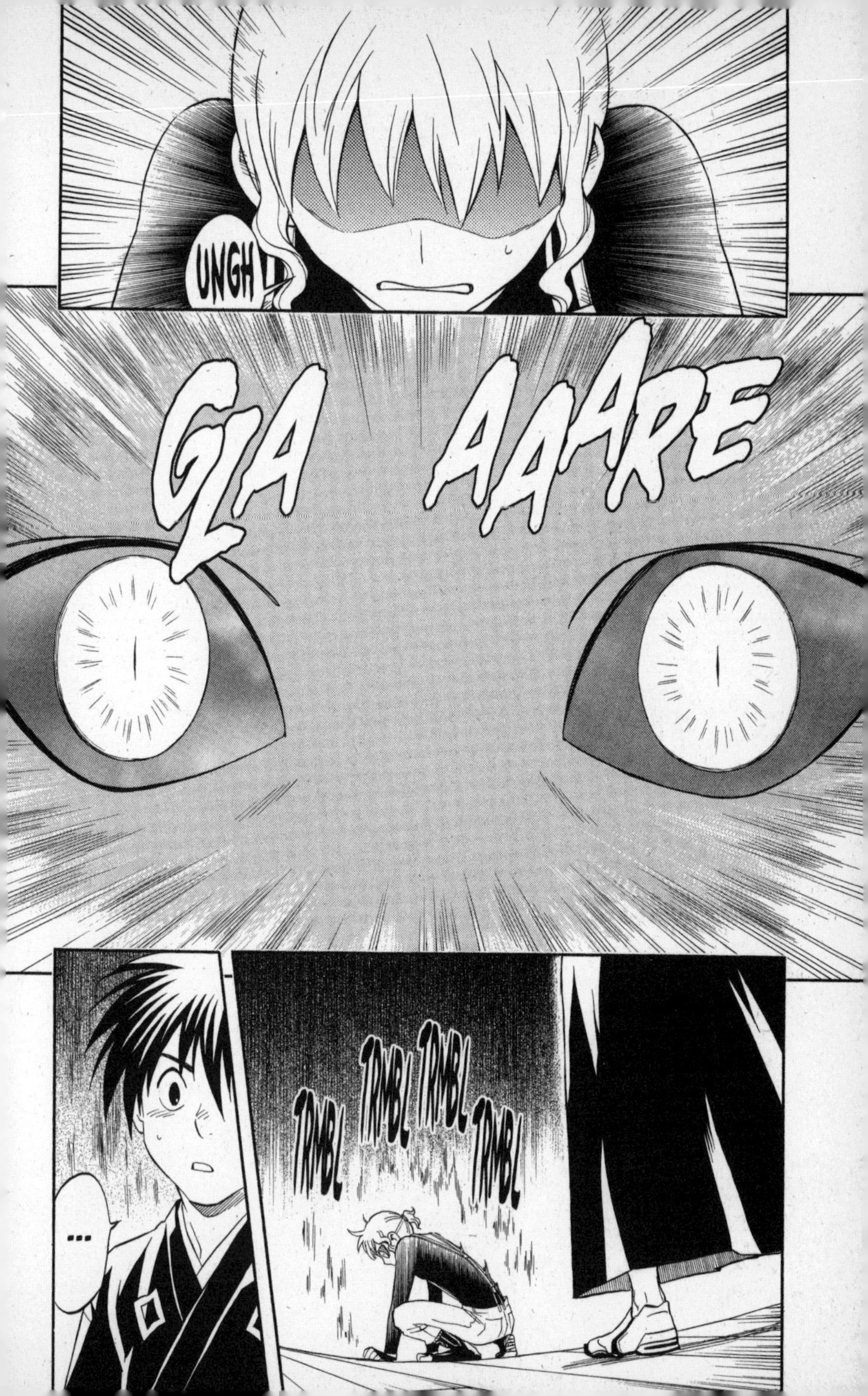
UNGH
GA AAARE
TRMBL TRMBL TRMBL TRMBL
...

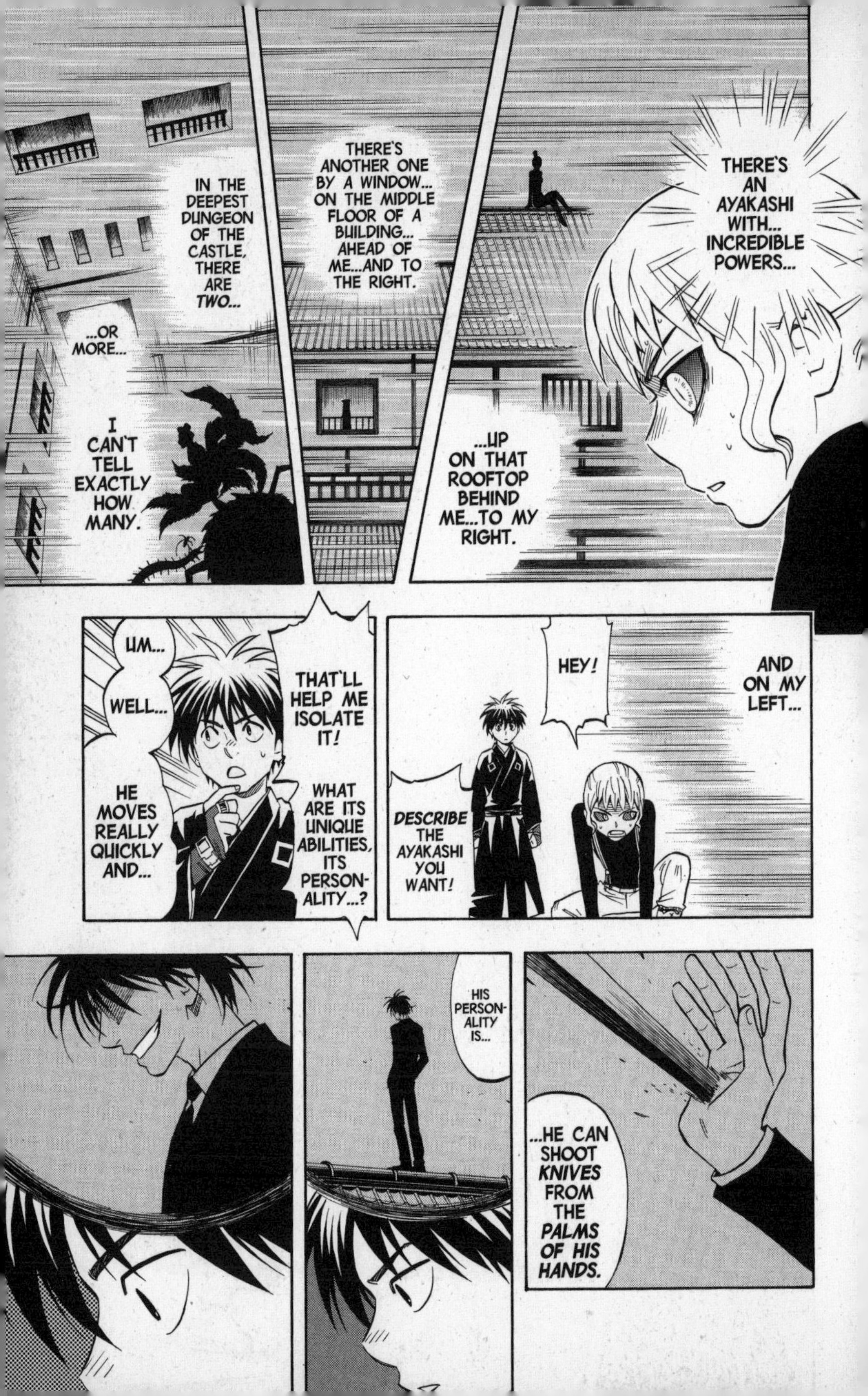
THERE'S AN AYAKASHI WITH... INCREDIBLE POWERS...
...UP ON THAT ROOFTOP BEHIND ME...TO MY RIGHT.
THERE'S ANOTHER ONE BY A WINDOW... ON THE MIDDLE FLOOR OF A BUILDING... AHEAD OF ME...AND TO THE RIGHT.
IN THE DEEPEST DUNGEON OF THE CASTLE, THERE ARE *TWO*...
...OR MORE...
I CAN'T TELL EXACTLY HOW MANY.
AND ON MY LEFT...
HEY!
DESCRIBE THE AYAKASHI YOU WANT!
THAT'LL HELP ME ISOLATE IT!
WHAT ARE ITS UNIQUE ABILITIES, ITS PERSON-ALITY...?
UM...
WELL...
HE MOVES REALLY QUICKLY AND...
...HE CAN SHOOT *KNIVES* FROM THE *PALMS* OF HIS HANDS.
HIS PERSON-ALITY IS...

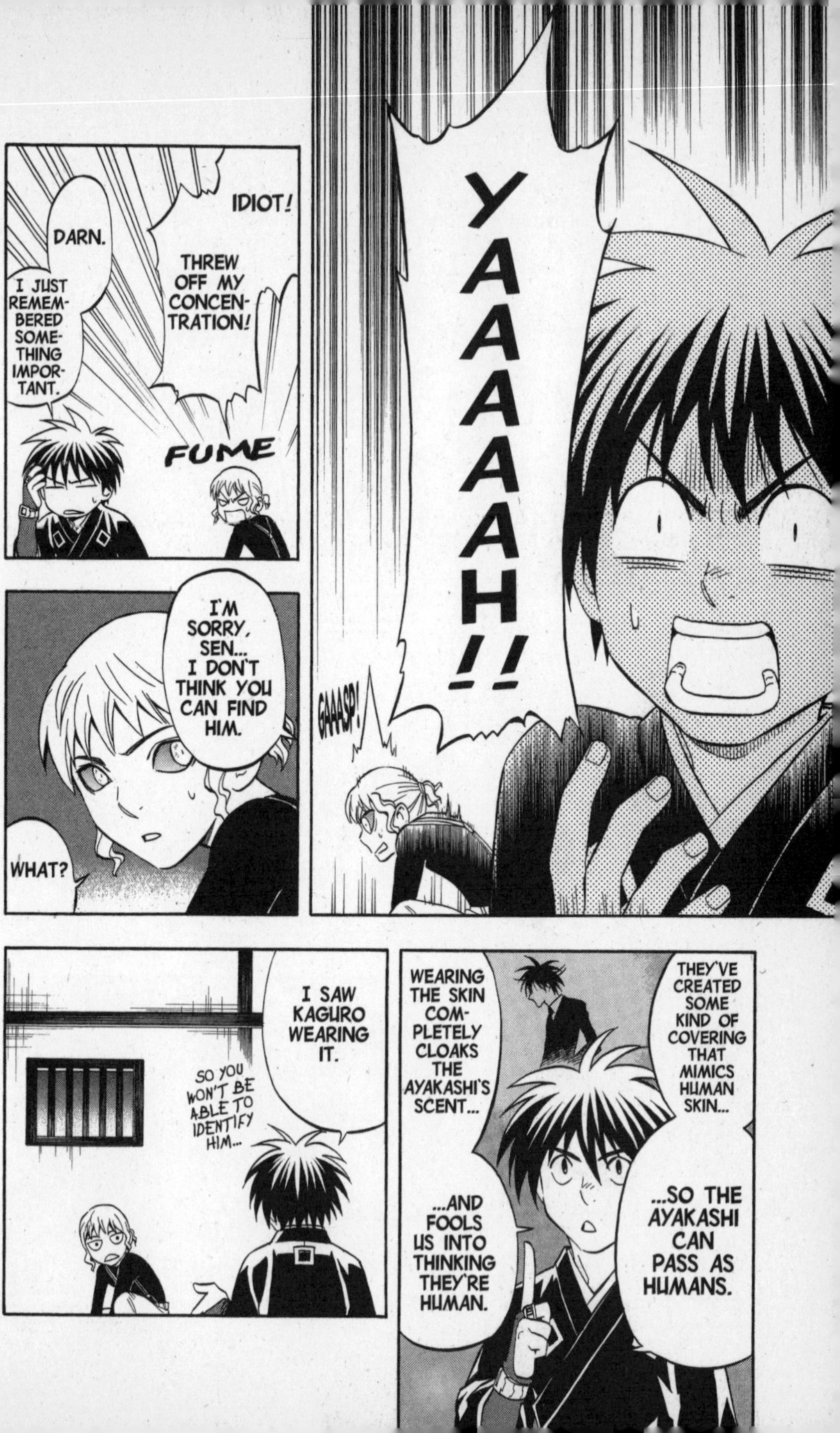
YAAAAAH!!
GAAASP!
IDIOT!
THREW OFF MY CONCENTRATION!
DARN.
I JUST REMEMBERED SOMETHING IMPORTANT.
FUME
I'M SORRY, SEN... I DON'T THINK YOU CAN FIND HIM.
WHAT?
THEY'VE CREATED SOME KIND OF COVERING THAT MIMICS HUMAN SKIN...
...SO THE AYAKASHI CAN PASS AS HUMANS.
WEARING THE SKIN COMPLETELY CLOAKS THE AYAKASHI'S SCENT...
...AND FOOLS US INTO THINKING THEY'RE HUMAN.
I SAW KAGURO WEARING IT.
SO YOU WON'T BE ABLE TO IDENTIFY HIM...

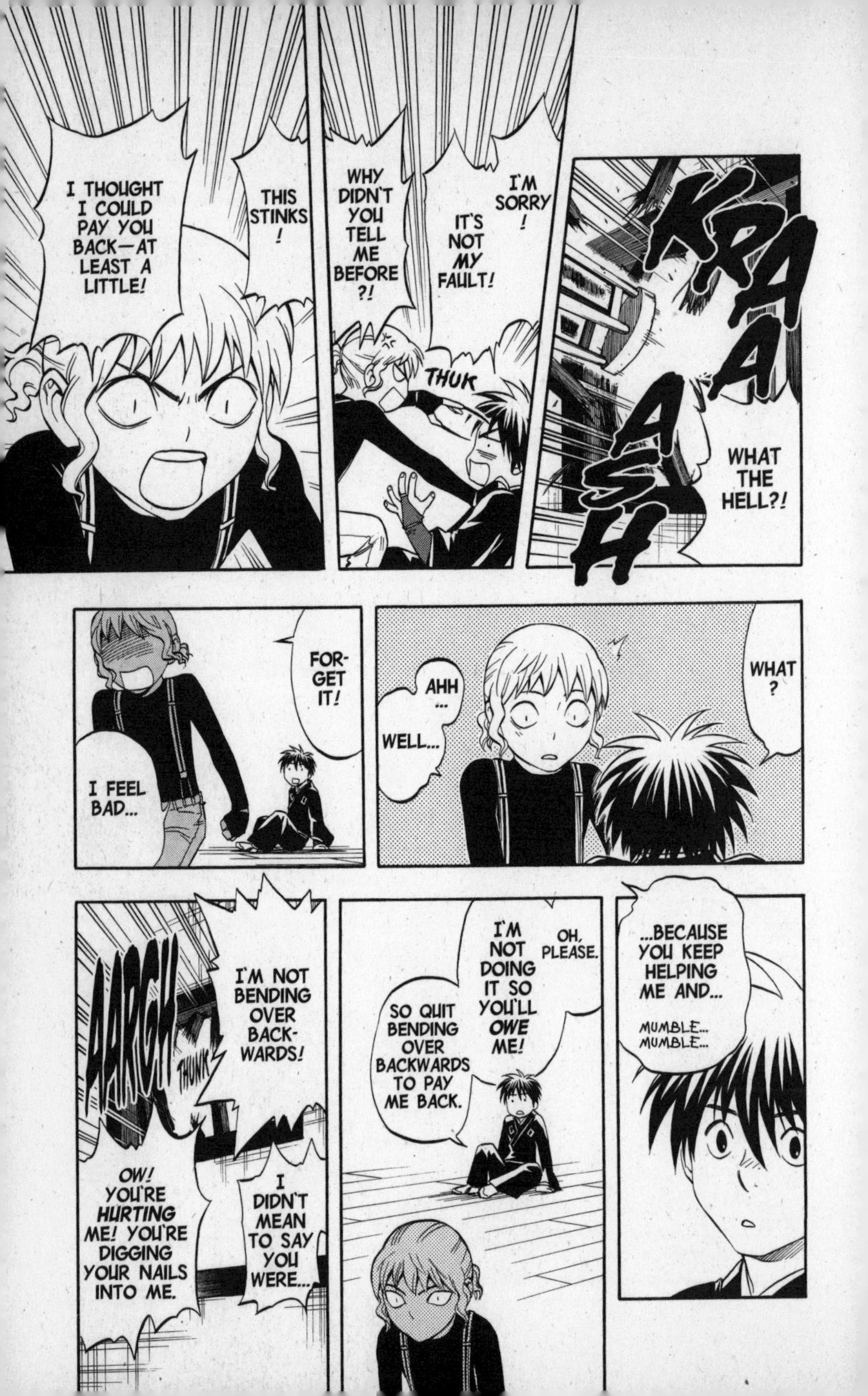
KRAAASH
WHAT THE HELL?!
I'M SORRY!
IT'S NOT MY FAULT!
WHY DIDN'T YOU TELL ME BEFORE?!
THUK
THIS STINKS!
I THOUGHT I COULD PAY YOU BACK—AT LEAST A LITTLE!
WHAT?
AHH... WELL...
FOR-GET IT!
I FEEL BAD...
...BECAUSE YOU KEEP HELPING ME AND...
MUMBLE... MUMBLE...
OH, PLEASE.
I'M NOT DOING IT SO YOU'LL OWE ME!
SO QUIT BENDING OVER BACKWARDS TO PAY ME BACK.
I'M NOT BENDING OVER BACK-WARDS!
AARGH
THUNK
I DIDN'T MEAN TO SAY YOU WERE...
OW! YOU'RE HURTING ME! YOU'RE DIGGING YOUR NAILS INTO ME.

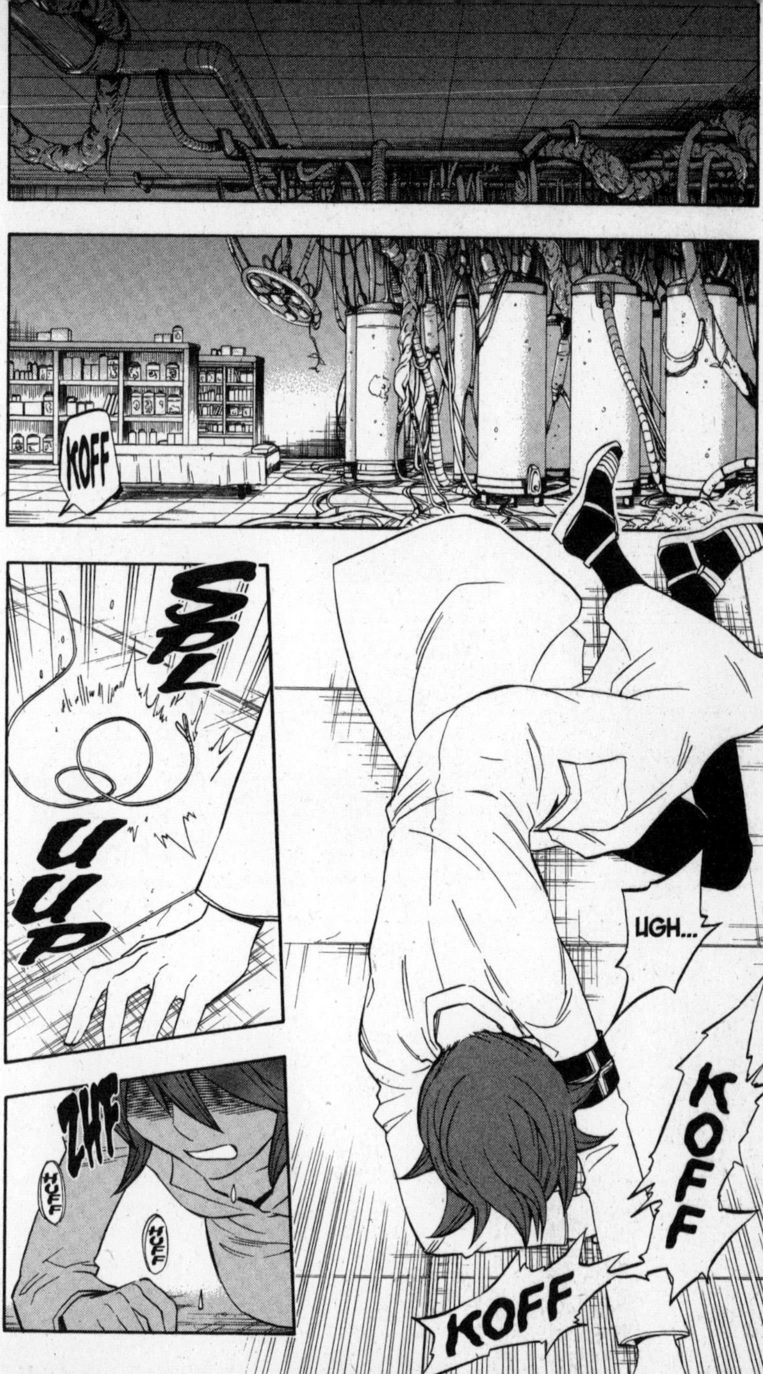
KOFF
UGH...
KOFF
KOFF
SPL
UUP
ZHF
HUFF
HUFF

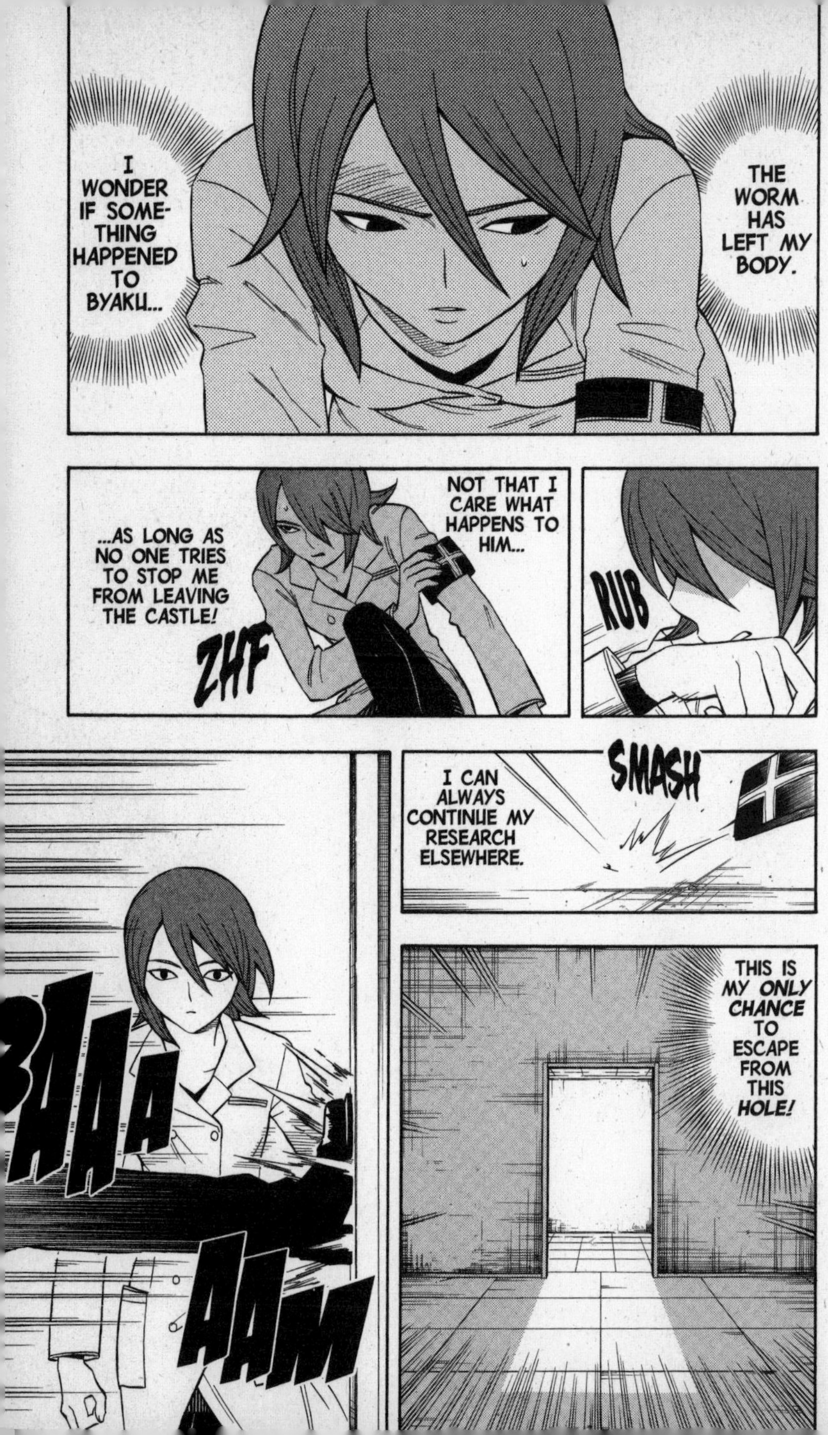
THE WORM HAS LEFT MY BODY.
I WONDER IF SOME-THING HAPPENED TO BYAKU...
RUB
NOT THAT I CARE WHAT HAPPENS TO HIM...
...AS LONG AS NO ONE TRIES TO STOP ME FROM LEAVING THE CASTLE!
ZHF
SMASH
I CAN ALWAYS CONTINUE MY RESEARCH ELSEWHERE.
THIS IS MY ONLY CHANCE TO ESCAPE FROM THIS HOLE!
BAAA
AAM

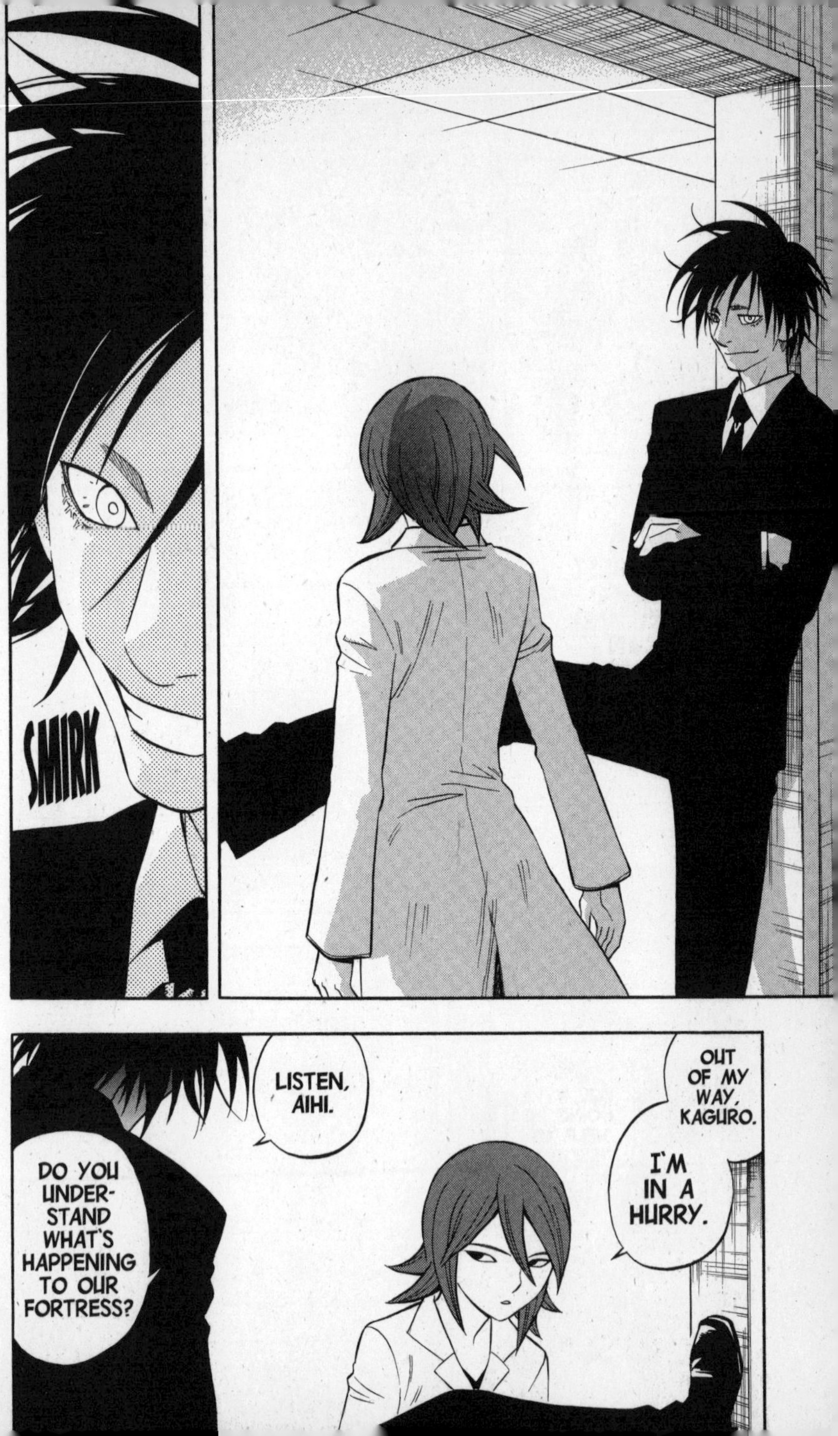
SMIRK
OUT OF MY WAY, KAGURO.
I'M IN A HURRY.
LISTEN, AIHI.
DO YOU UNDER-STAND WHAT'S HAPPENING TO OUR FORTRESS?

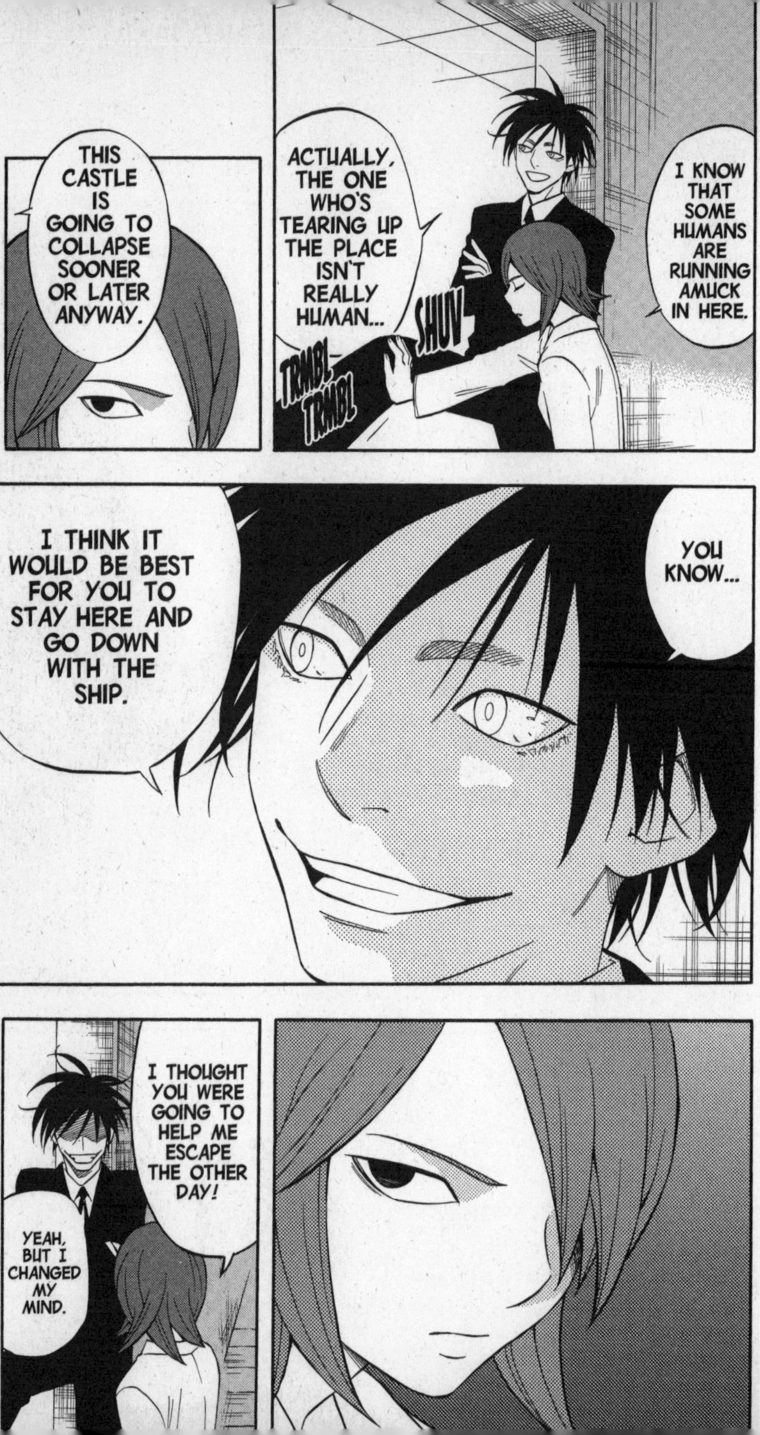
I KNOW THAT SOME HUMANS ARE RUNNING AMUCK IN HERE.
ACTUALLY, THE ONE WHO'S TEARING UP THE PLACE ISN'T REALLY HUMAN...
SHUV
TRMBL-TRMBL
THIS CASTLE IS GOING TO COLLAPSE SOONER OR LATER ANYWAY.
YOU KNOW...
I THINK IT WOULD BE BEST FOR YOU TO STAY HERE AND GO DOWN WITH THE SHIP.
I THOUGHT YOU WERE GOING TO HELP ME ESCAPE THE OTHER DAY!
YEAH, BUT I CHANGED MY MIND.

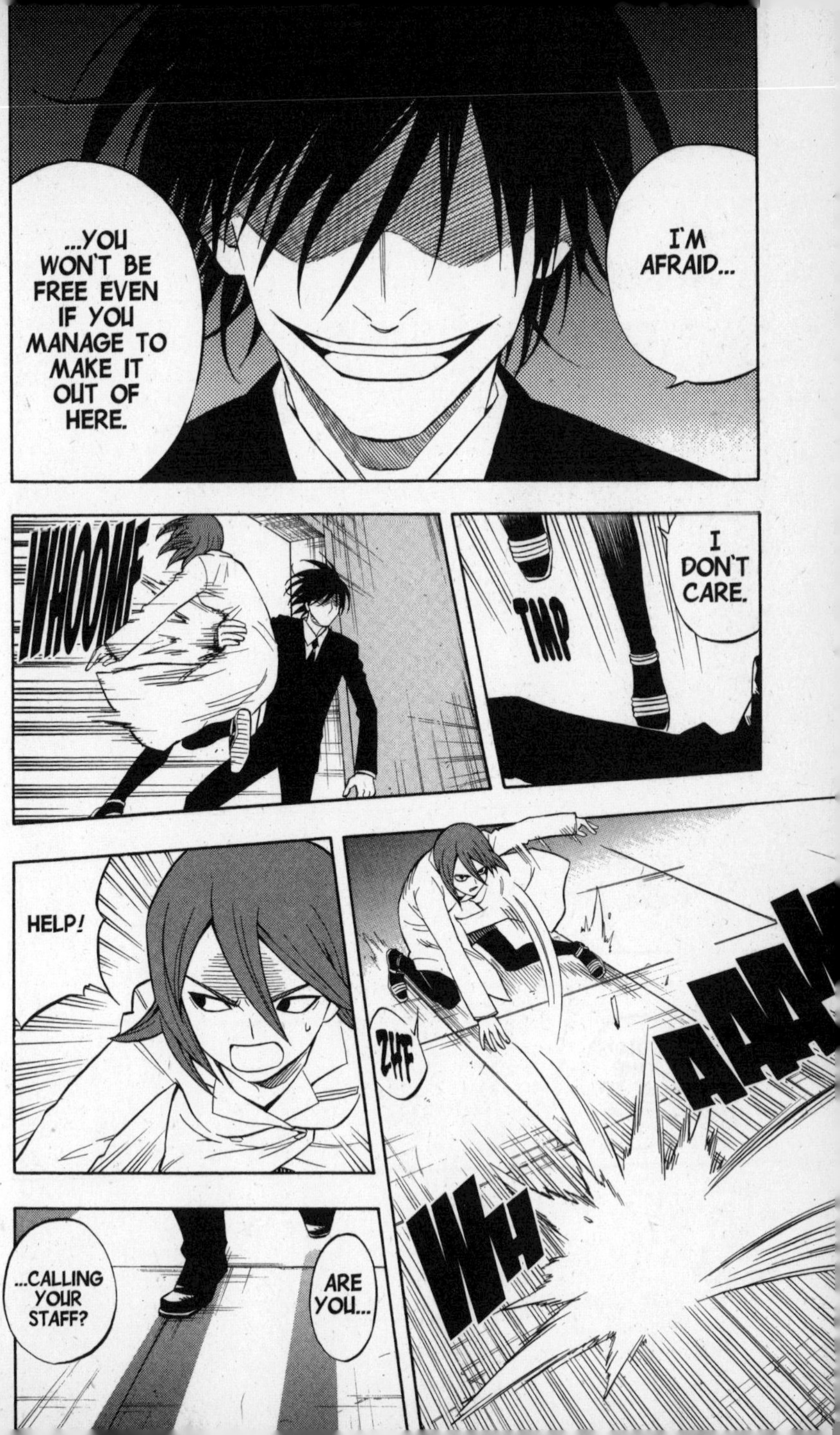
I'M AFRAID...
...YOU WON'T BE FREE EVEN IF YOU MANAGE TO MAKE IT OUT OF HERE.
I DON'T CARE.
TMP
WHOOMF
AAA
ZHF
WH
HELP!
ARE YOU...
...CALLING YOUR STAFF?

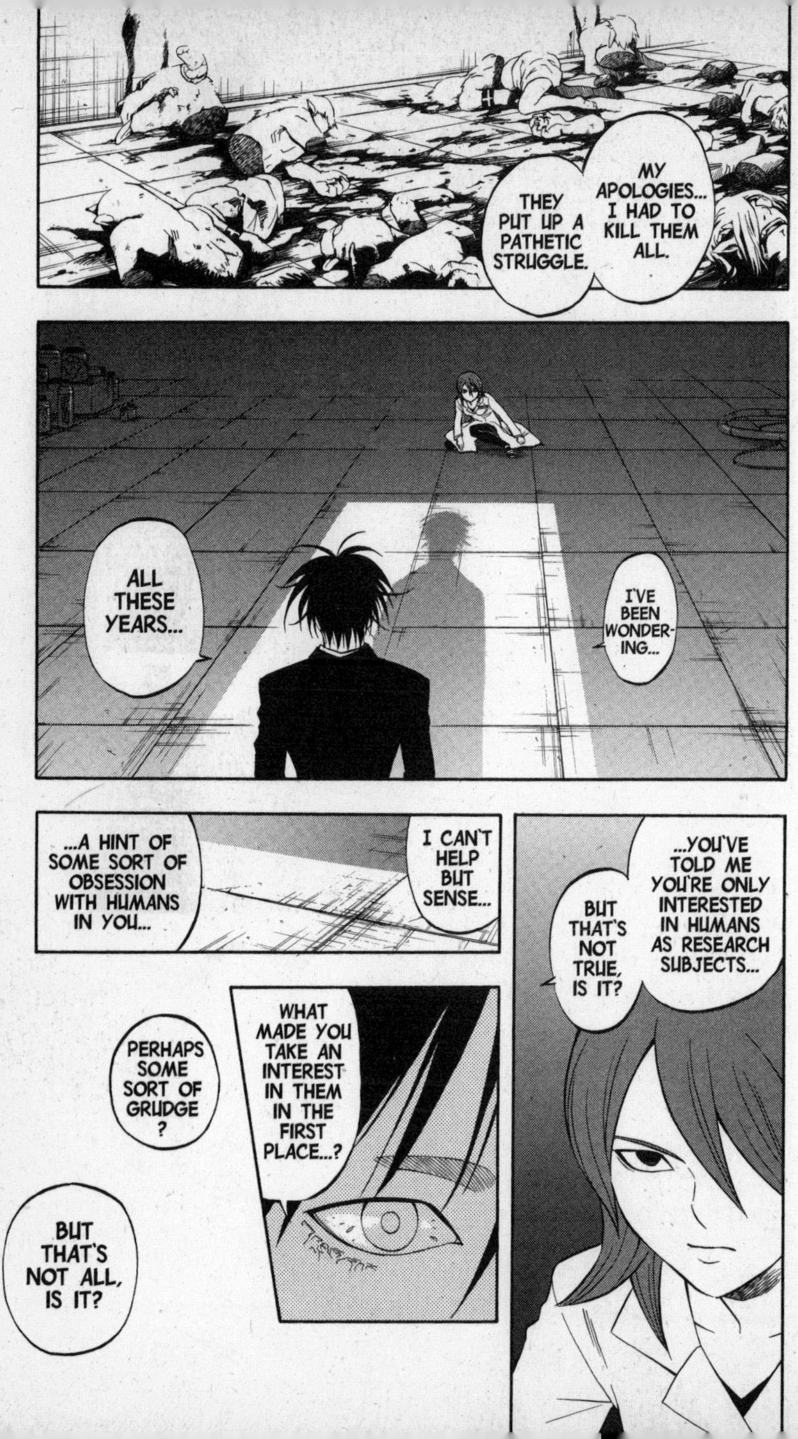
MY APOLOGIES... I HAD TO KILL THEM ALL.
THEY PUT UP A PATHETIC STRUGGLE.
I'VE BEEN WONDERING...
ALL THESE YEARS...
...YOU'VE TOLD ME YOU'RE ONLY INTERESTED IN HUMANS AS RESEARCH SUBJECTS...
BUT THAT'S NOT TRUE, IS IT?
I CAN'T HELP BUT SENSE...
...A HINT OF SOME SORT OF OBSESSION WITH HUMANS IN YOU...
WHAT MADE YOU TAKE AN INTEREST IN THEM IN THE FIRST PLACE...?
PERHAPS SOME SORT OF GRUDGE ?
BUT THAT'S NOT ALL, IS IT?

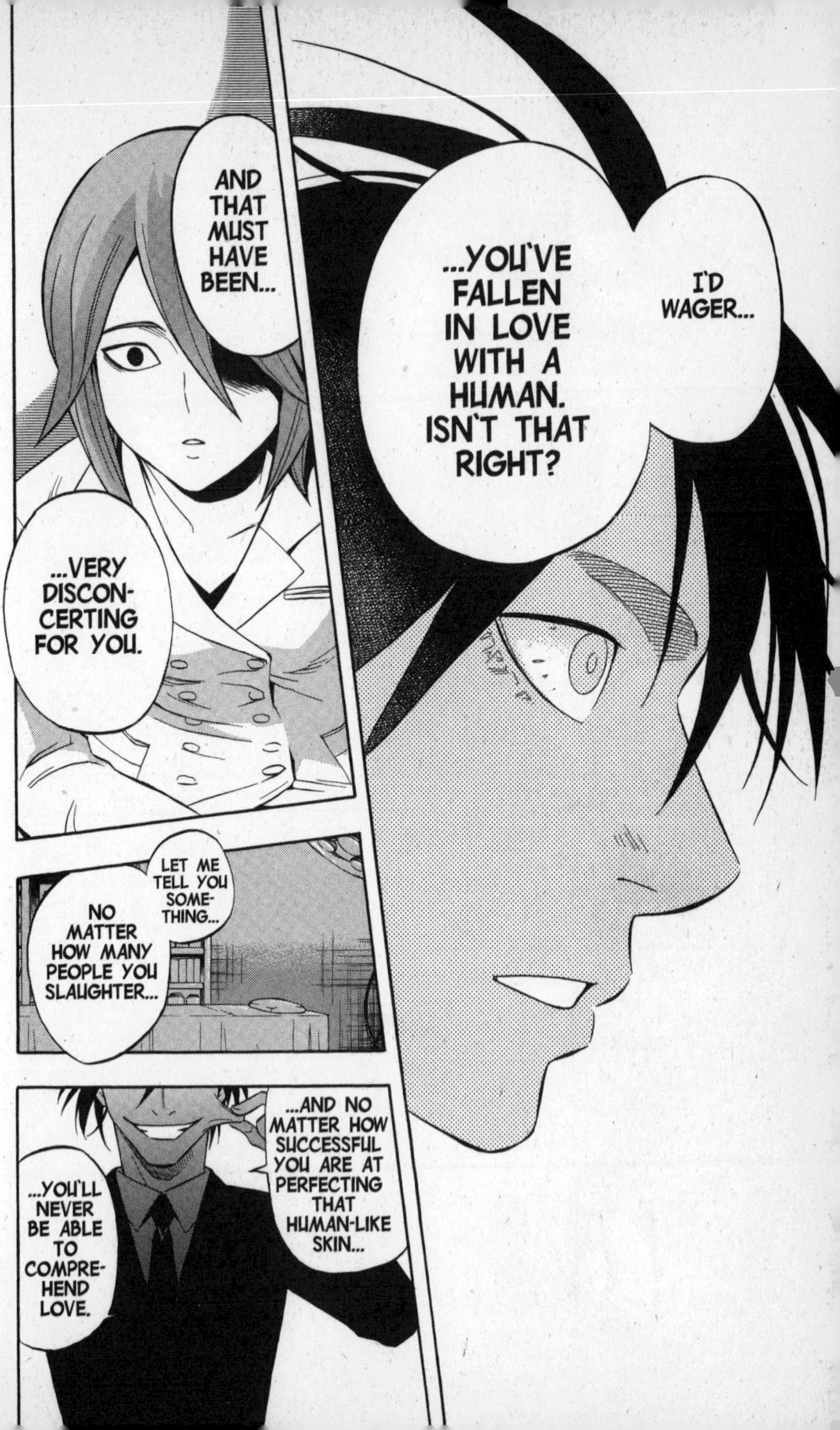
I'D WAGER...
...YOU'VE FALLEN IN LOVE WITH A HUMAN. ISN'T THAT RIGHT?
AND THAT MUST HAVE BEEN...
...VERY DISCONCERTING FOR YOU.
LET ME TELL YOU SOMETHING...
NO MATTER HOW MANY PEOPLE YOU SLAUGHTER...
...AND NO MATTER HOW SUCCESSFUL YOU ARE AT PERFECTING THAT HUMAN-LIKE SKIN...
...YOU'LL NEVER BE ABLE TO COMPREHEND LOVE.

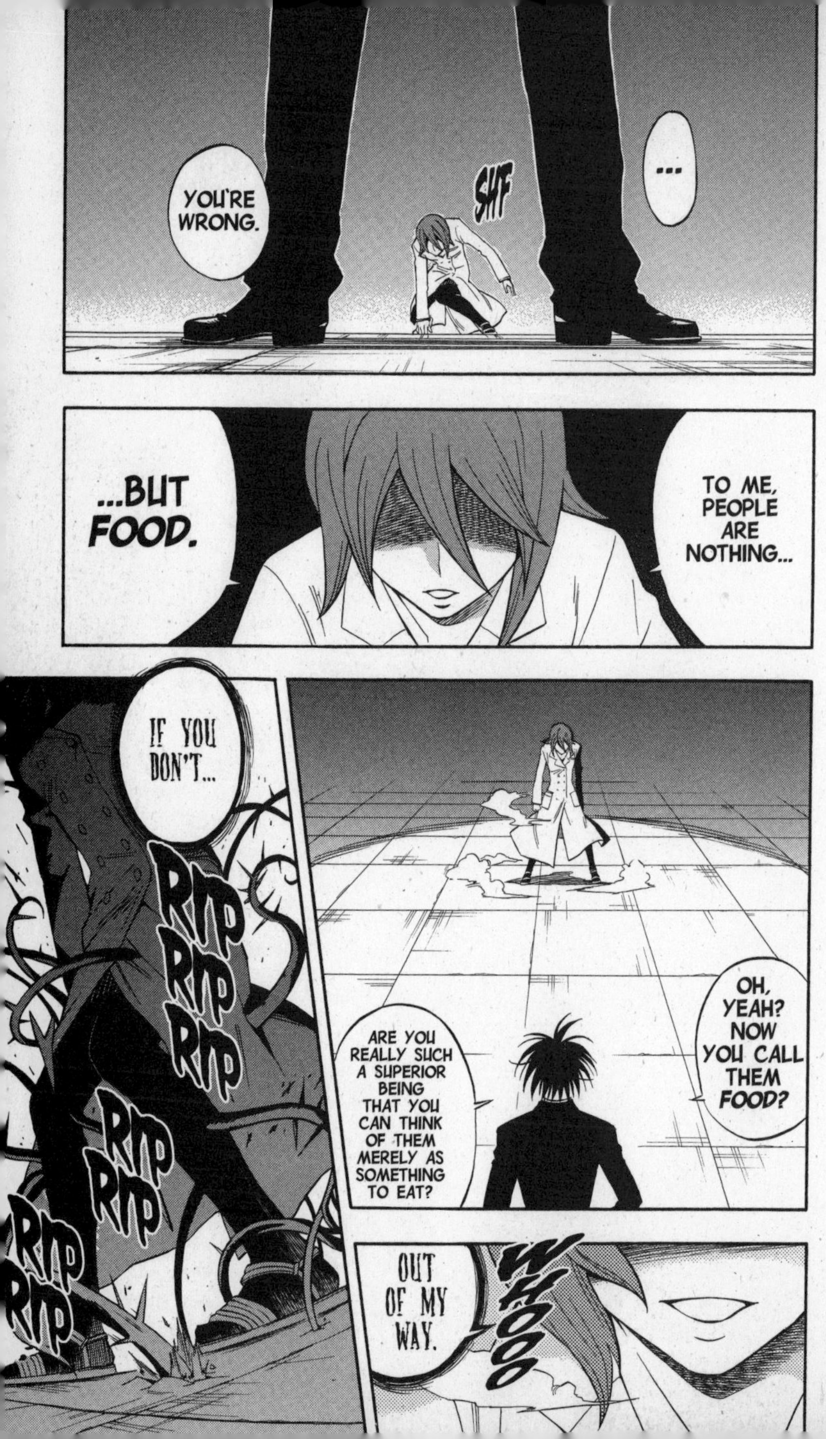
...
SHF
YOU'RE WRONG.
TO ME, PEOPLE ARE NOTHING...
...BUT FOOD.
OH, YEAH? NOW YOU CALL THEM FOOD?
ARE YOU REALLY SUCH A SUPERIOR BEING THAT YOU CAN THINK OF THEM MERELY AS SOMETHING TO EAT?
OUT OF MY WAY.
WHOOO
IF YOU DON'T...
RIP RIP RIP
RIP RIP
RIP RIP

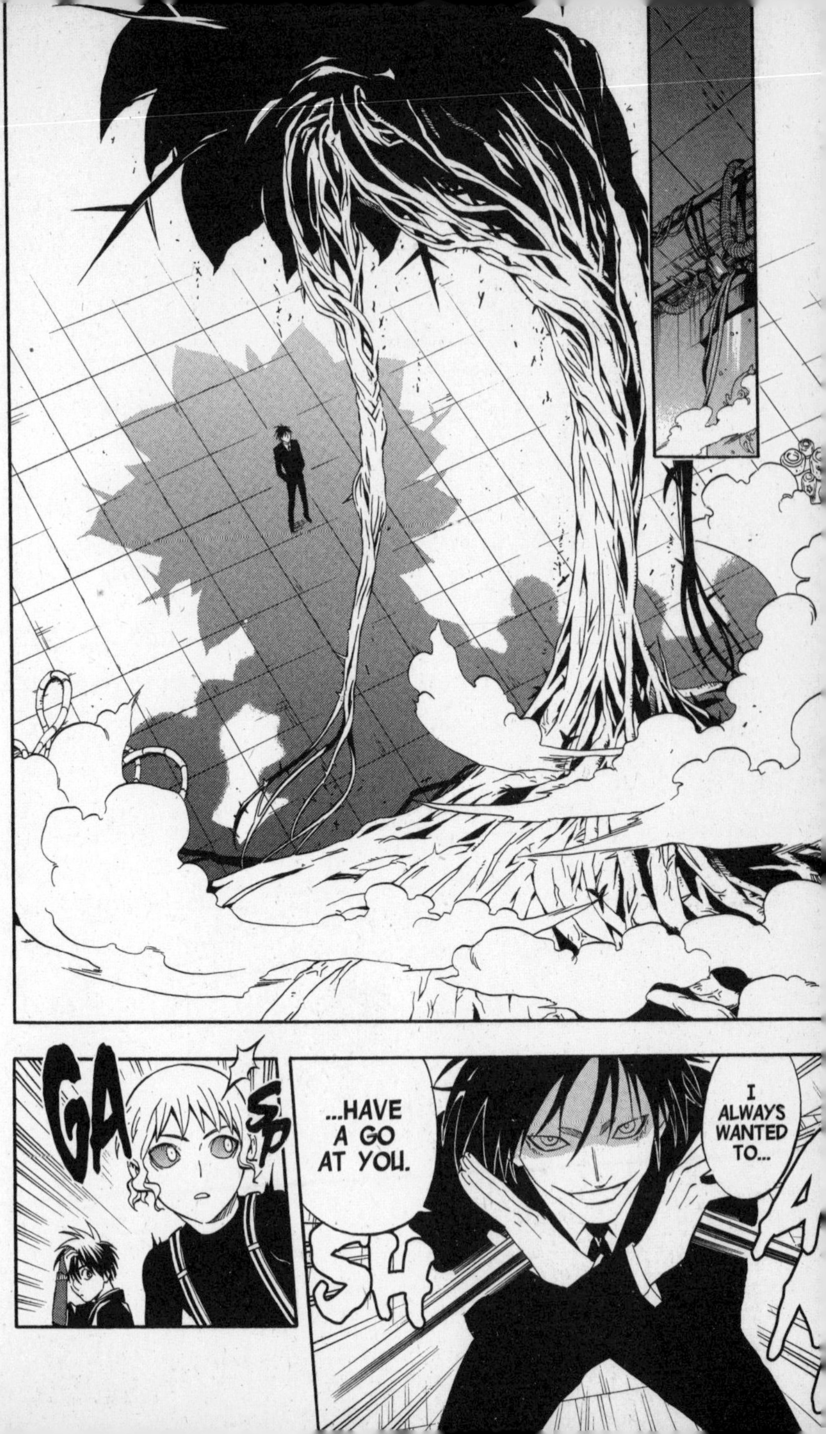
I ALWAYS WANTED TO...
...HAVE A GO AT YOU.
SH
A
GA
SP

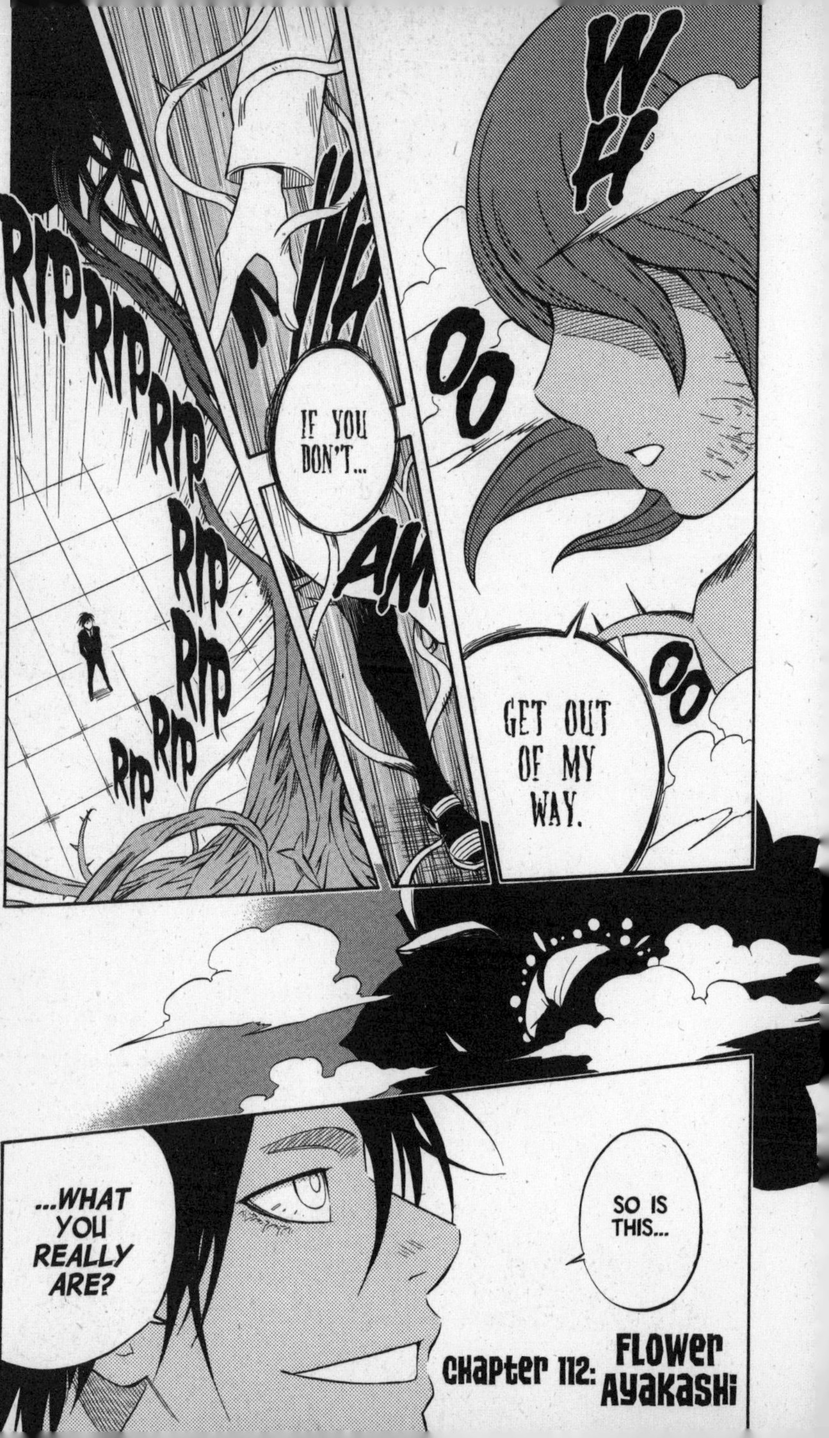
WH
OO
OO
GET OUT OF MY WAY.
IF YOU DON'T...
WH
AM
RIP RIP RIP RIP RIP RIP RIP
SO IS THIS...
...WHAT YOU REALLY ARE?
Chapter 112: Flower Ayakashi

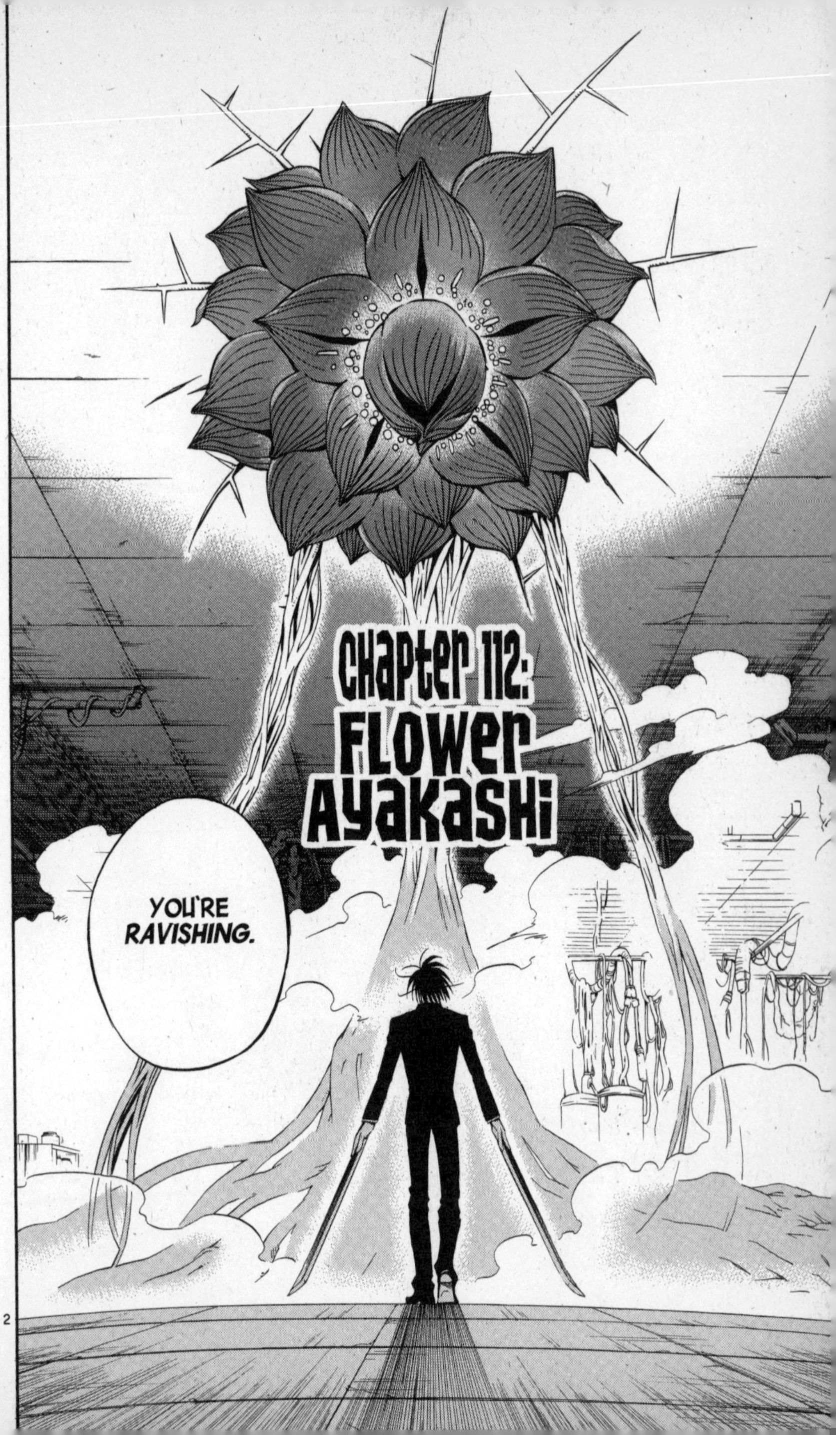
CHAPTER 112:
FLOWER AYAKASHI
YOU'RE RAVISHING.

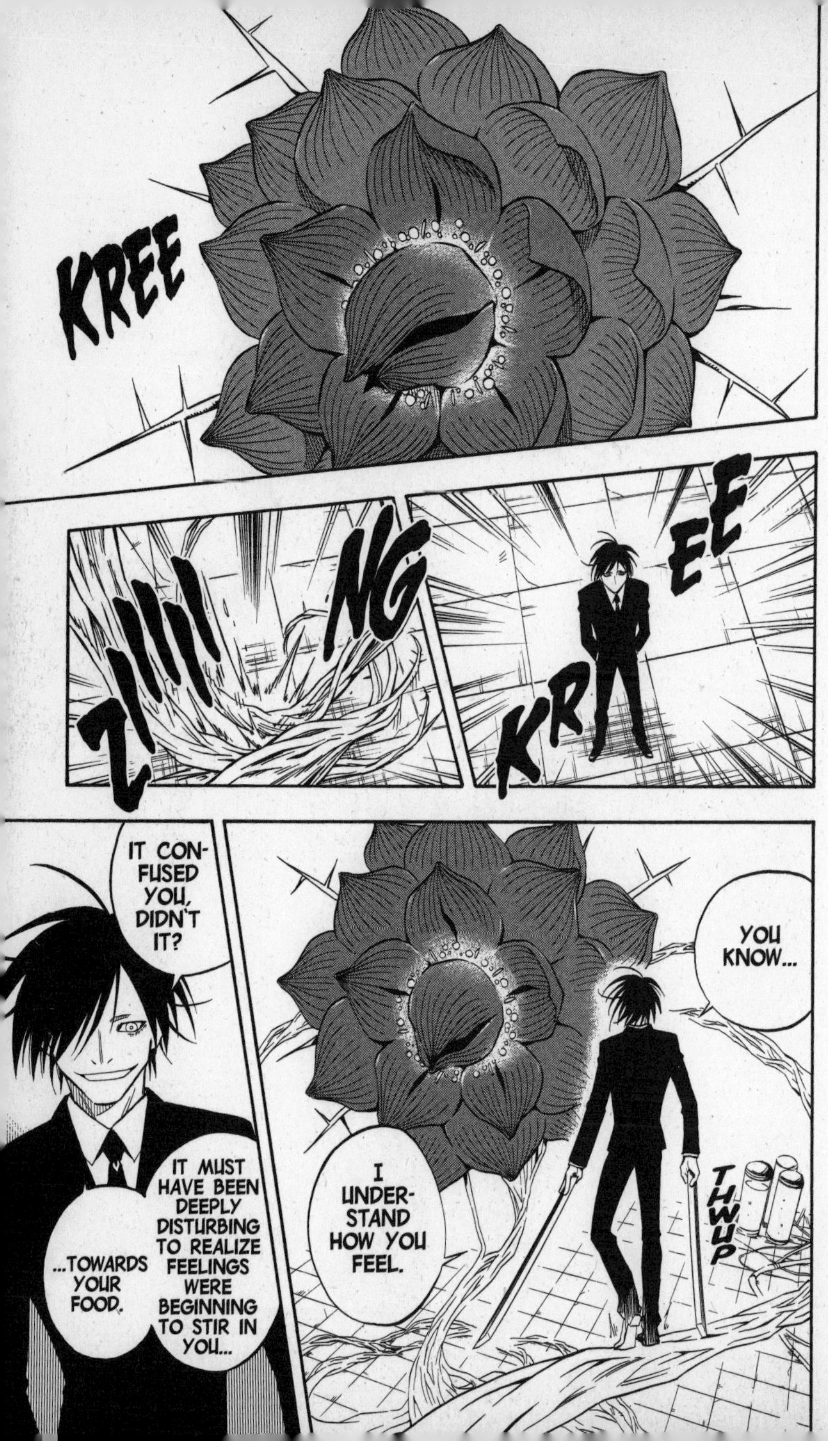
KREE
KREE
ZIIIING
YOU KNOW...
THWUP
I UNDERSTAND HOW YOU FEEL.
IT CONFUSED YOU, DIDN'T IT?
IT MUST HAVE BEEN DEEPLY DISTURBING TO REALIZE FEELINGS WERE BEGINNING TO STIR IN YOU...
...TOWARDS YOUR FOOD.

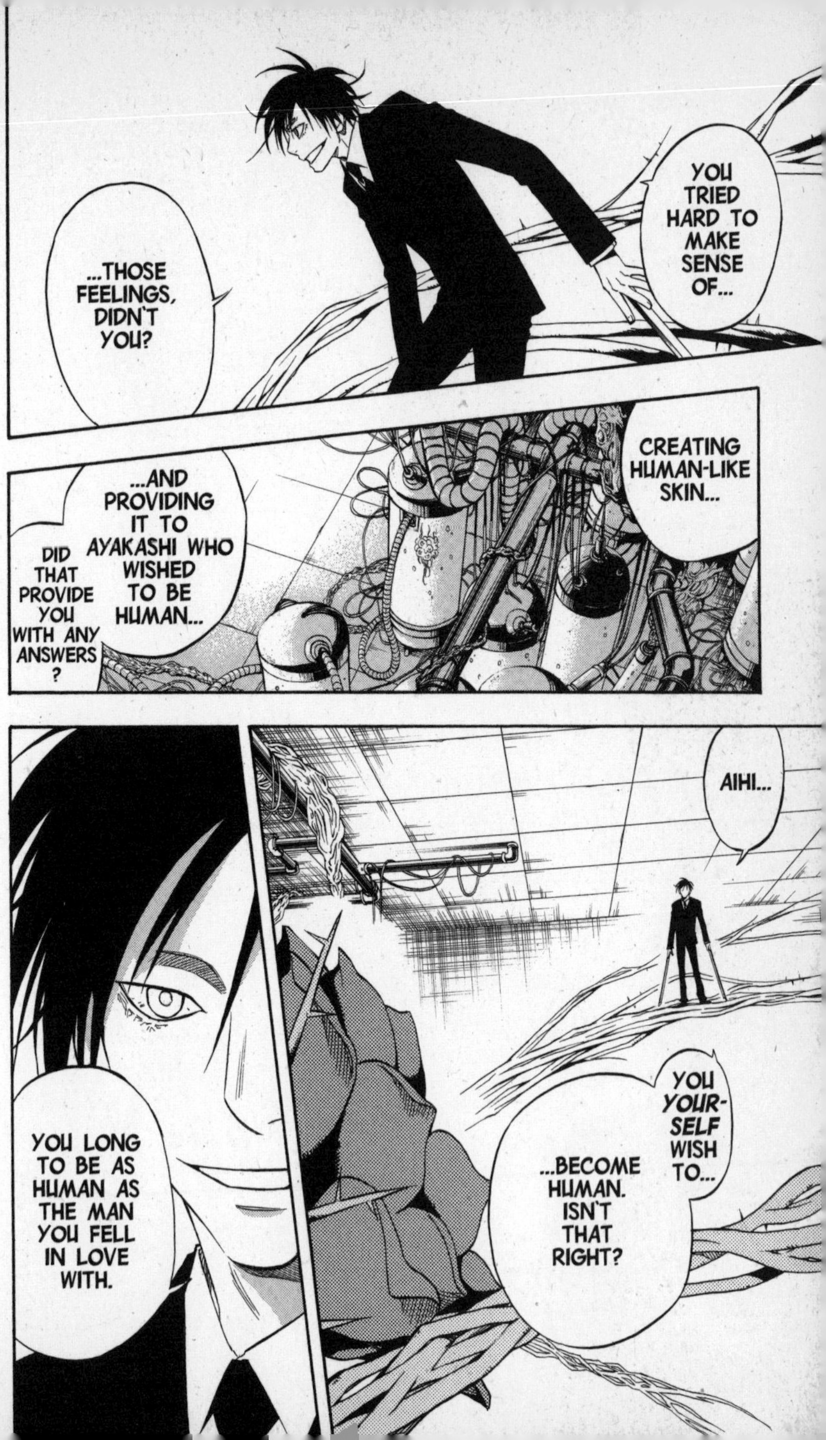
YOU TRIED HARD TO MAKE SENSE OF...
...THOSE FEELINGS, DIDN'T YOU?
CREATING HUMAN-LIKE SKIN...
...AND PROVIDING IT TO AYAKASHI WHO WISHED TO BE HUMAN...
DID THAT PROVIDE YOU WITH ANY ANSWERS?
AIHI...
YOU *YOURSELF* WISH TO...
...BECOME HUMAN. ISN'T THAT RIGHT?
YOU LONG TO BE AS HUMAN AS THE MAN YOU FELL IN LOVE WITH.

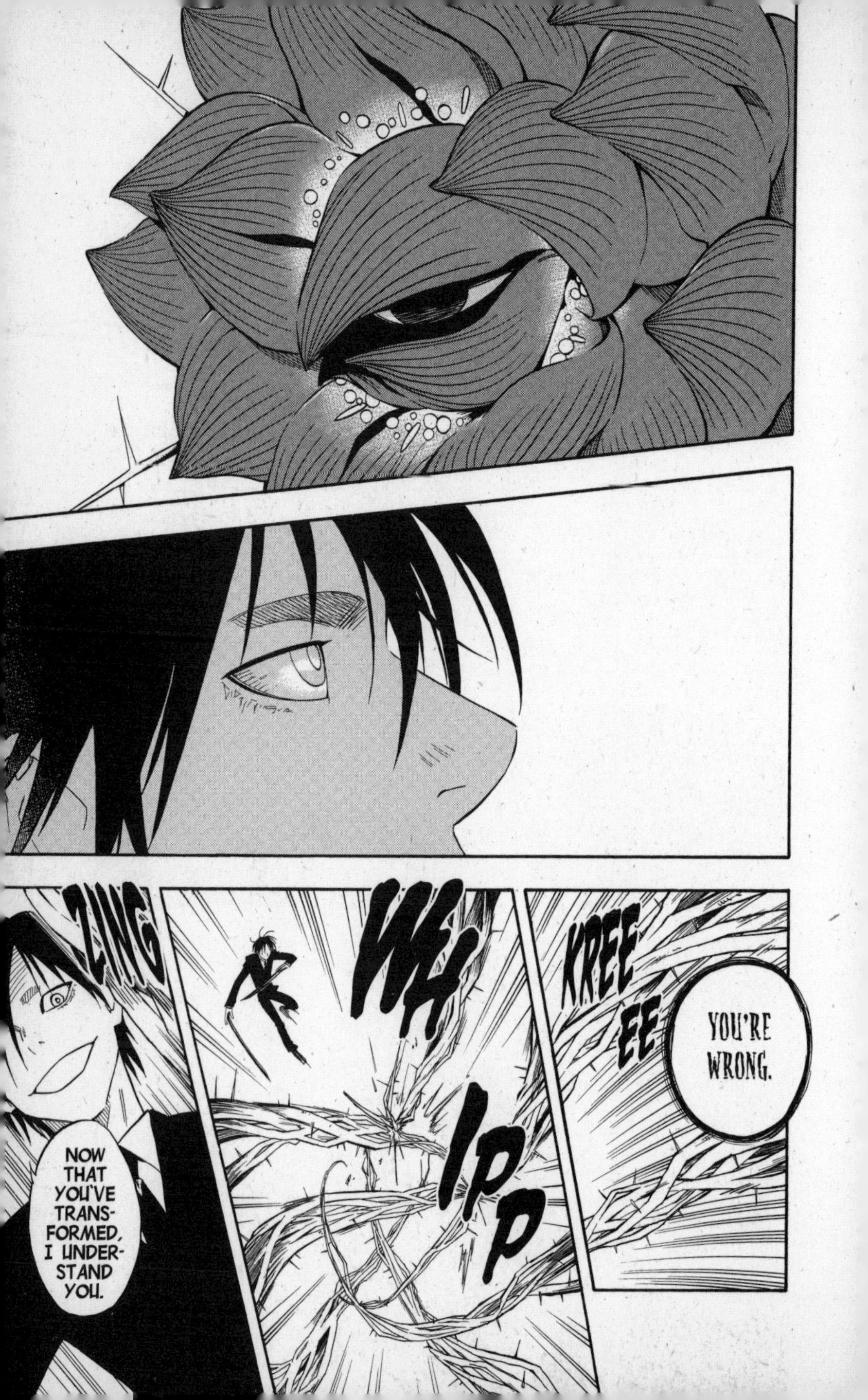
KREEEE
YOU'RE WRONG.
WHIPP
ZING
NOW THAT YOU'VE TRANSFORMED, I UNDERSTAND YOU.

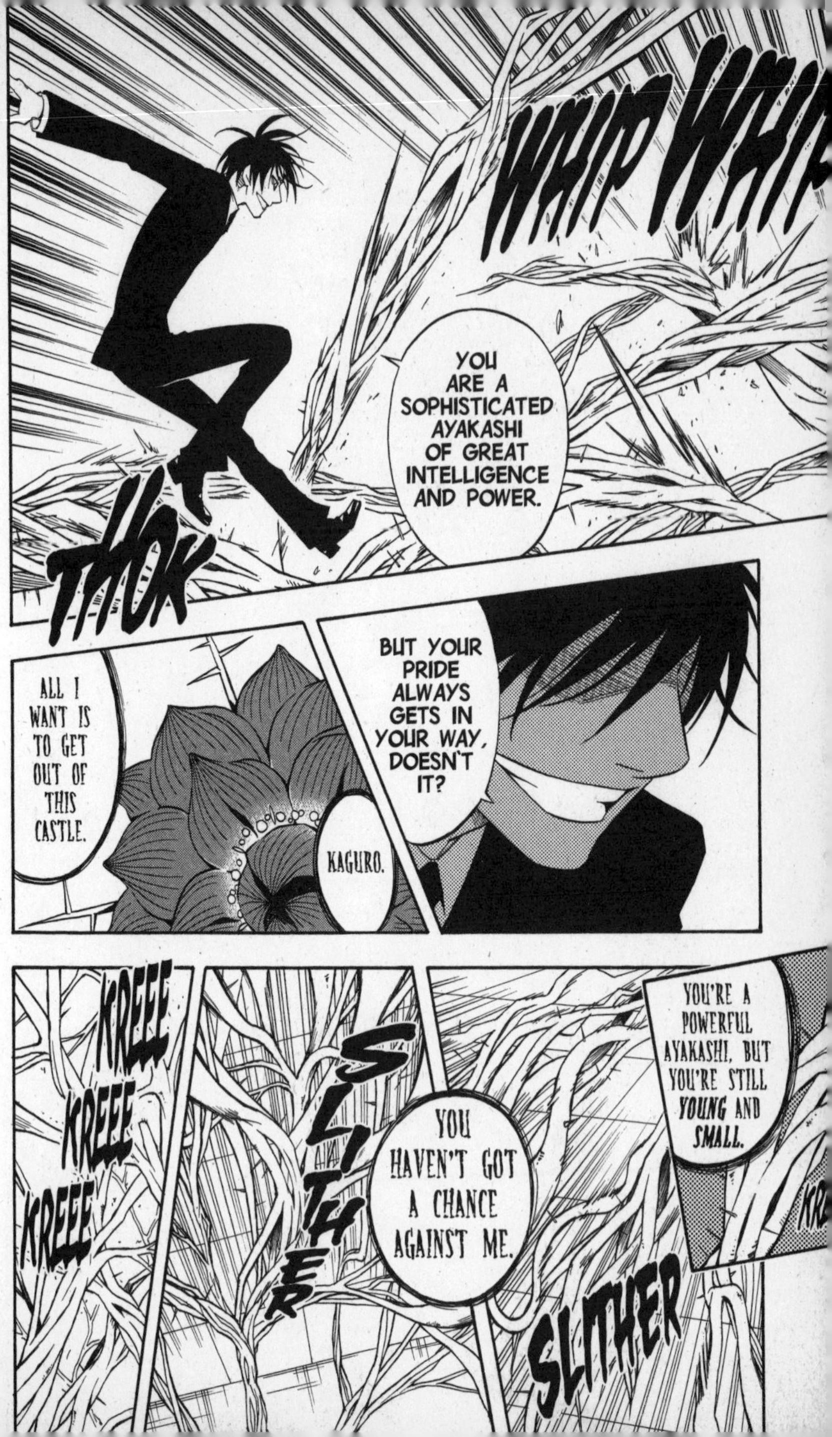
WHIP WHIP
YOU ARE A SOPHISTICATED AYAKASHI OF GREAT INTELLIGENCE AND POWER.
THOK
BUT YOUR PRIDE ALWAYS GETS IN YOUR WAY, DOESN'T IT?
KAGURO.
ALL I WANT IS TO GET OUT OF THIS CASTLE.
YOU'RE A POWERFUL AYAKASHI, BUT YOU'RE STILL YOUNG AND SMALL.
SLITHER
YOU HAVEN'T GOT A CHANCE AGAINST ME.
SLITHER
KREEE
KREEE
KREEE

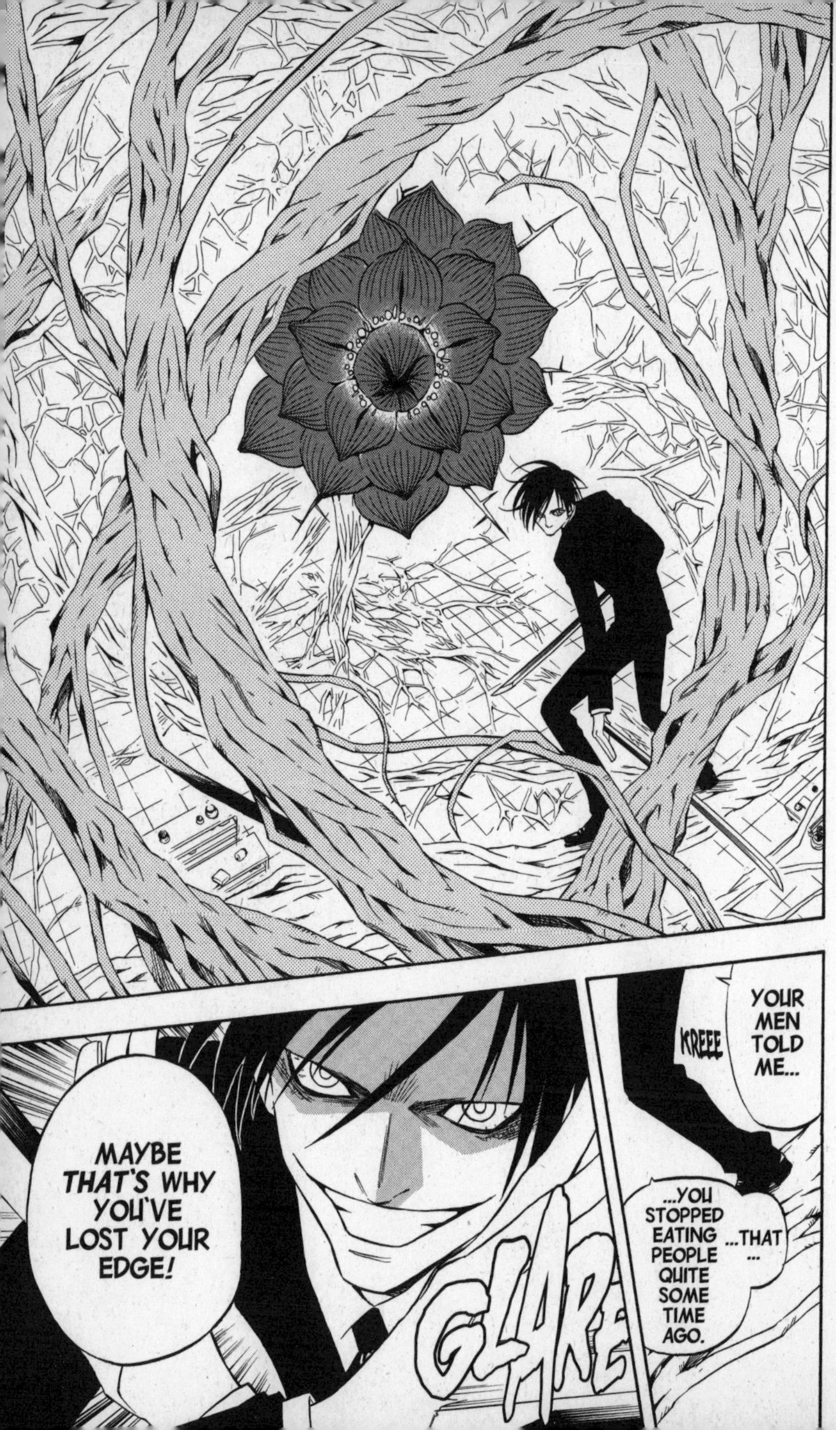
YOUR MEN TOLD ME...
KREEE
...THAT ...
...YOU STOPPED EATING PEOPLE QUITE SOME TIME AGO.
GLARE
MAYBE THAT'S WHY YOU'VE LOST YOUR EDGE!

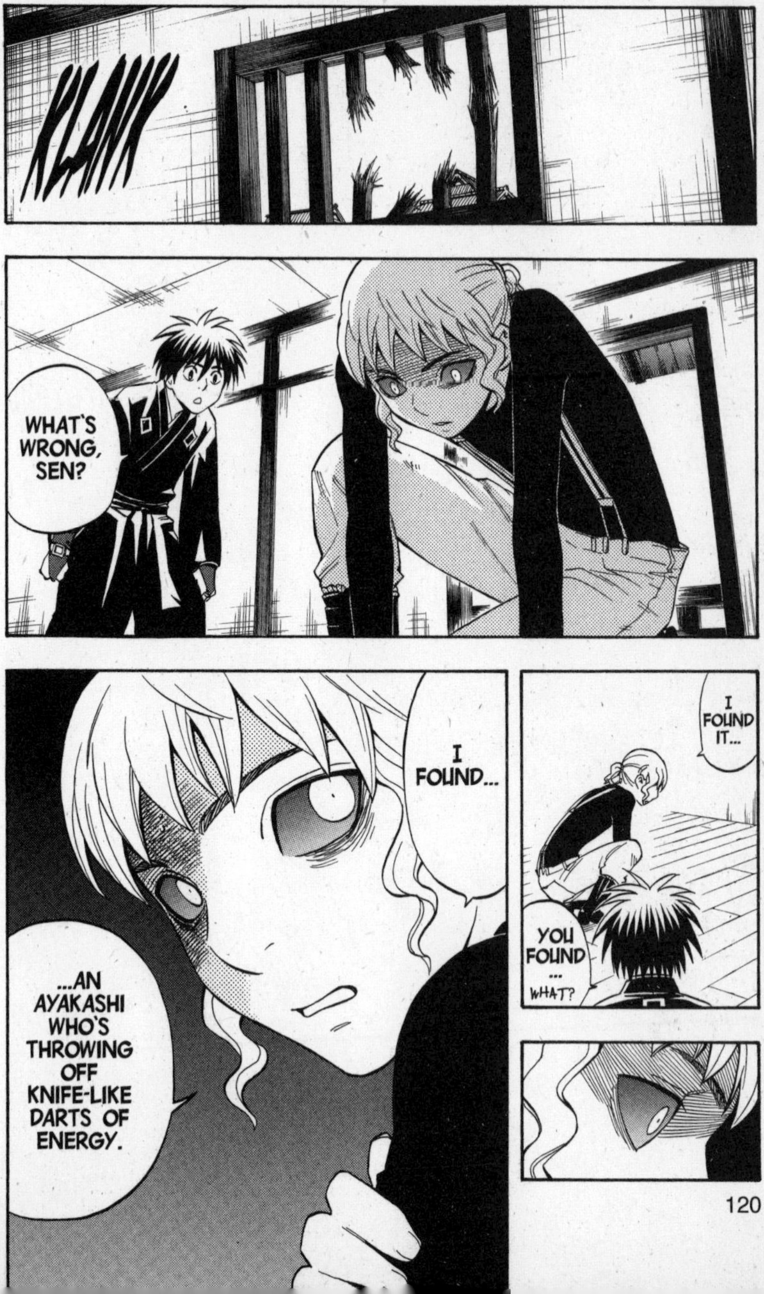
KLANK
WHAT'S WRONG, SEN?
I FOUND IT...
YOU FOUND ... WHAT?
I FOUND...
...AN AYAKASHI WHO'S THROWING OFF KNIFE-LIKE DARTS OF ENERGY.

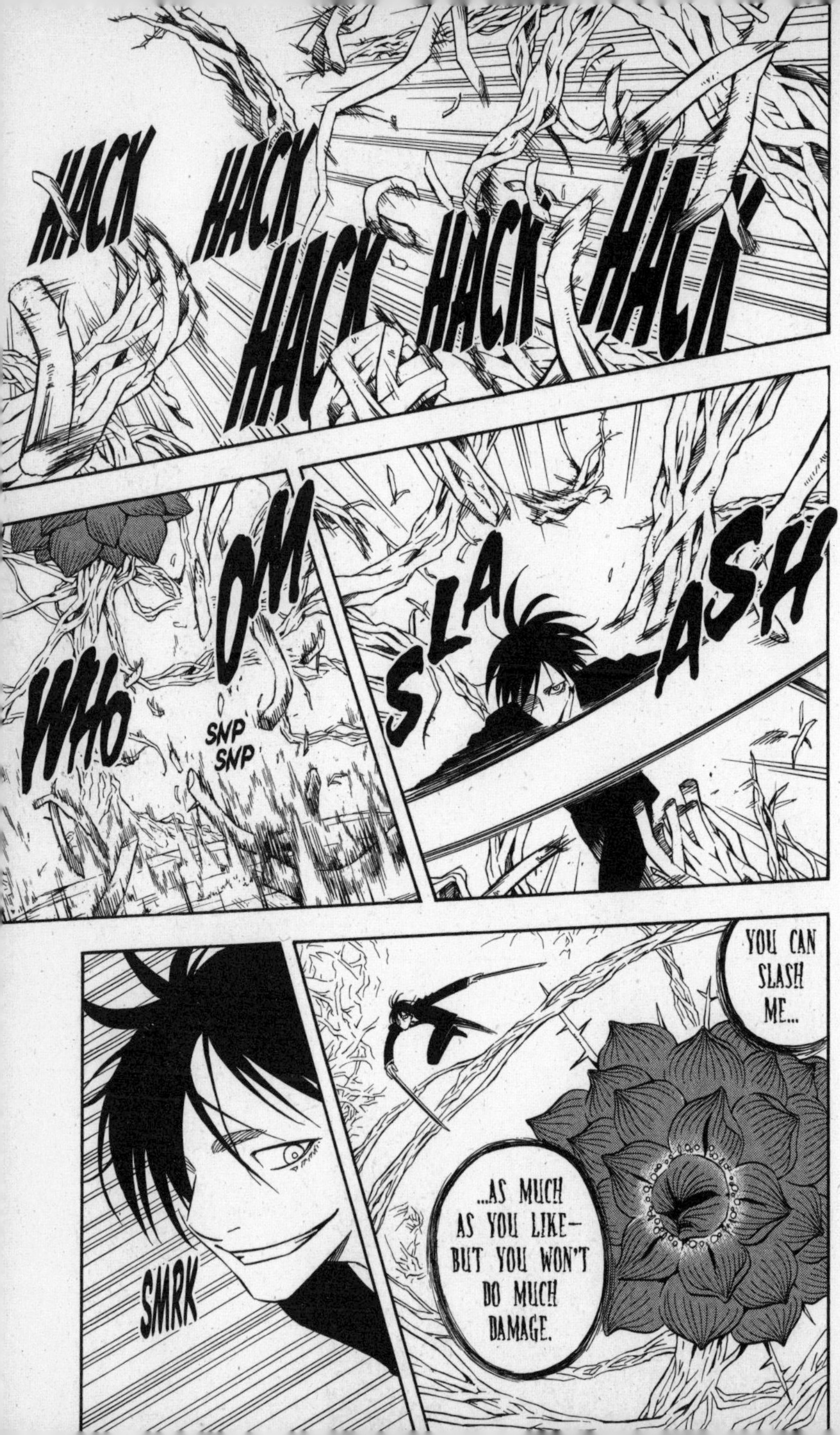
HACK HACK HACK HACK HACK
SLASH
WHOOM
SNP SNP
YOU CAN SLASH ME...
...AS MUCH AS YOU LIKE— BUT YOU WON'T DO MUCH DAMAGE.
SMRK

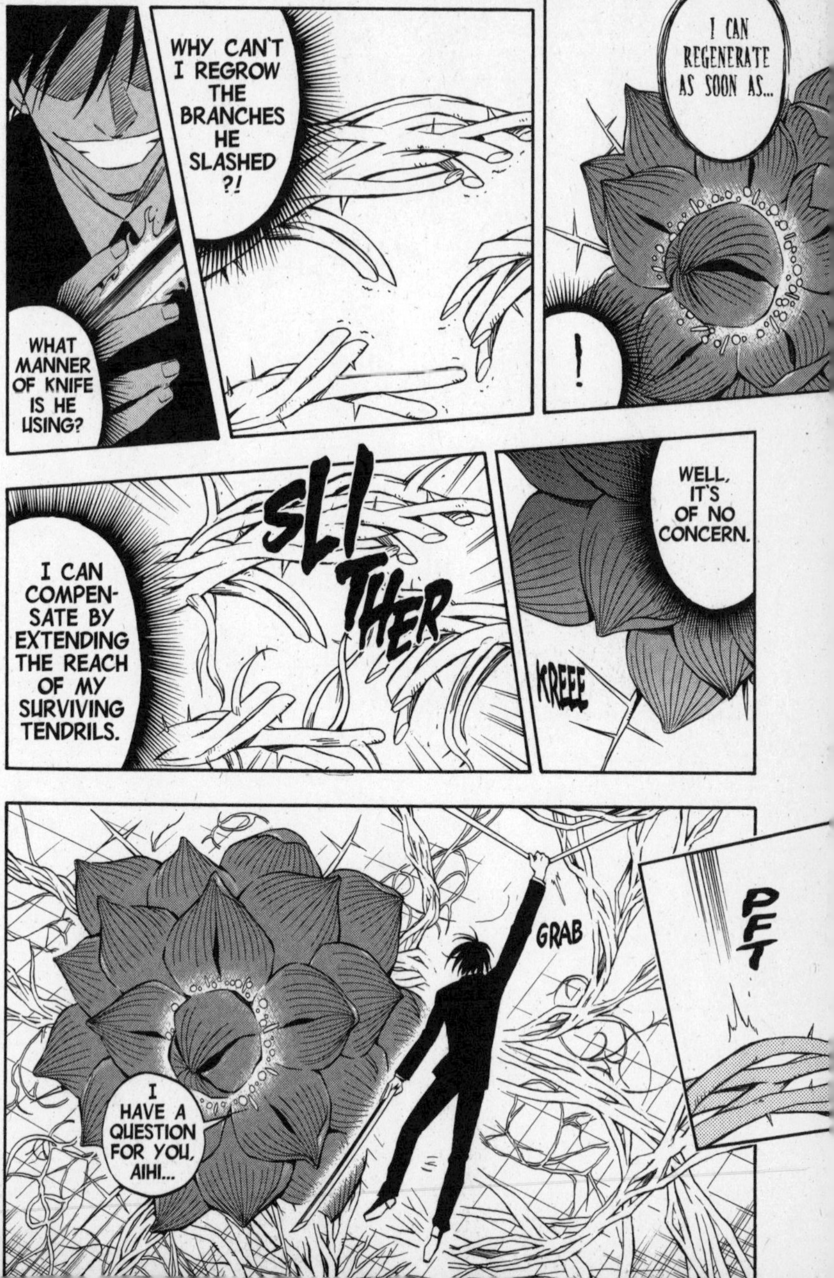
I CAN REGENERATE AS SOON AS...
!
WHY CAN'T I REGROW THE BRANCHES HE SLASHED?!
WHAT MANNER OF KNIFE IS HE USING?
WELL, IT'S OF NO CONCERN.
KREEE
SLITHER
I CAN COMPENSATE BY EXTENDING THE REACH OF MY SURVIVING TENDRILS.
PFT
GRAB
I HAVE A QUESTION FOR YOU, AIHI...

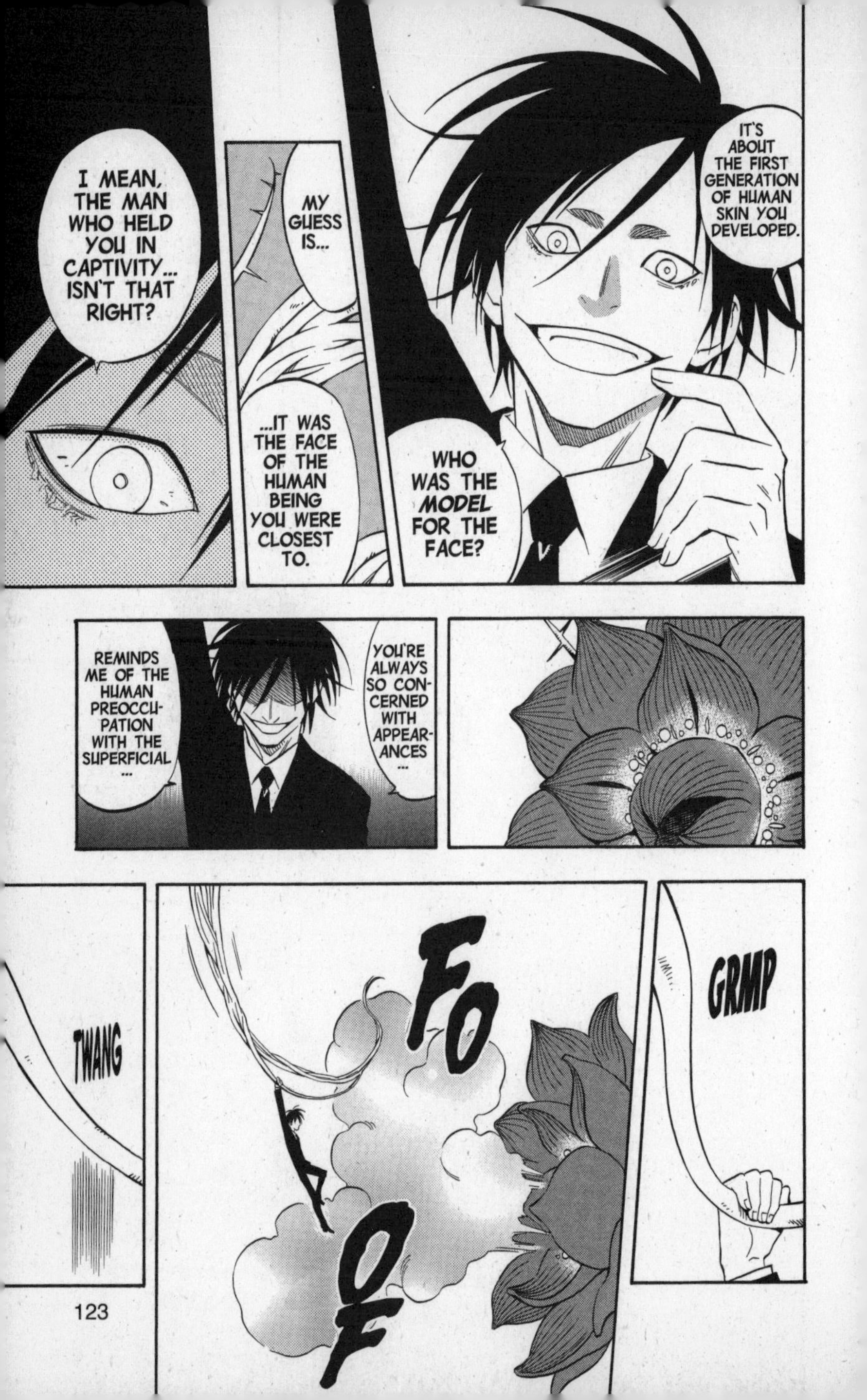
IT'S ABOUT THE FIRST GENERATION OF HUMAN SKIN YOU DEVELOPED.
WHO WAS THE *MODEL* FOR THE FACE?
MY GUESS IS...
...IT WAS THE FACE OF THE HUMAN BEING YOU WERE CLOSEST TO.
I MEAN, THE MAN WHO HELD YOU IN CAPTIVITY... ISN'T THAT RIGHT?
YOU'RE ALWAYS SO CONCERNED WITH APPEARANCES...
REMINDS ME OF THE HUMAN PREOCCUPATION WITH THE SUPERFICIAL...
GRMP
FOOF
TWANG

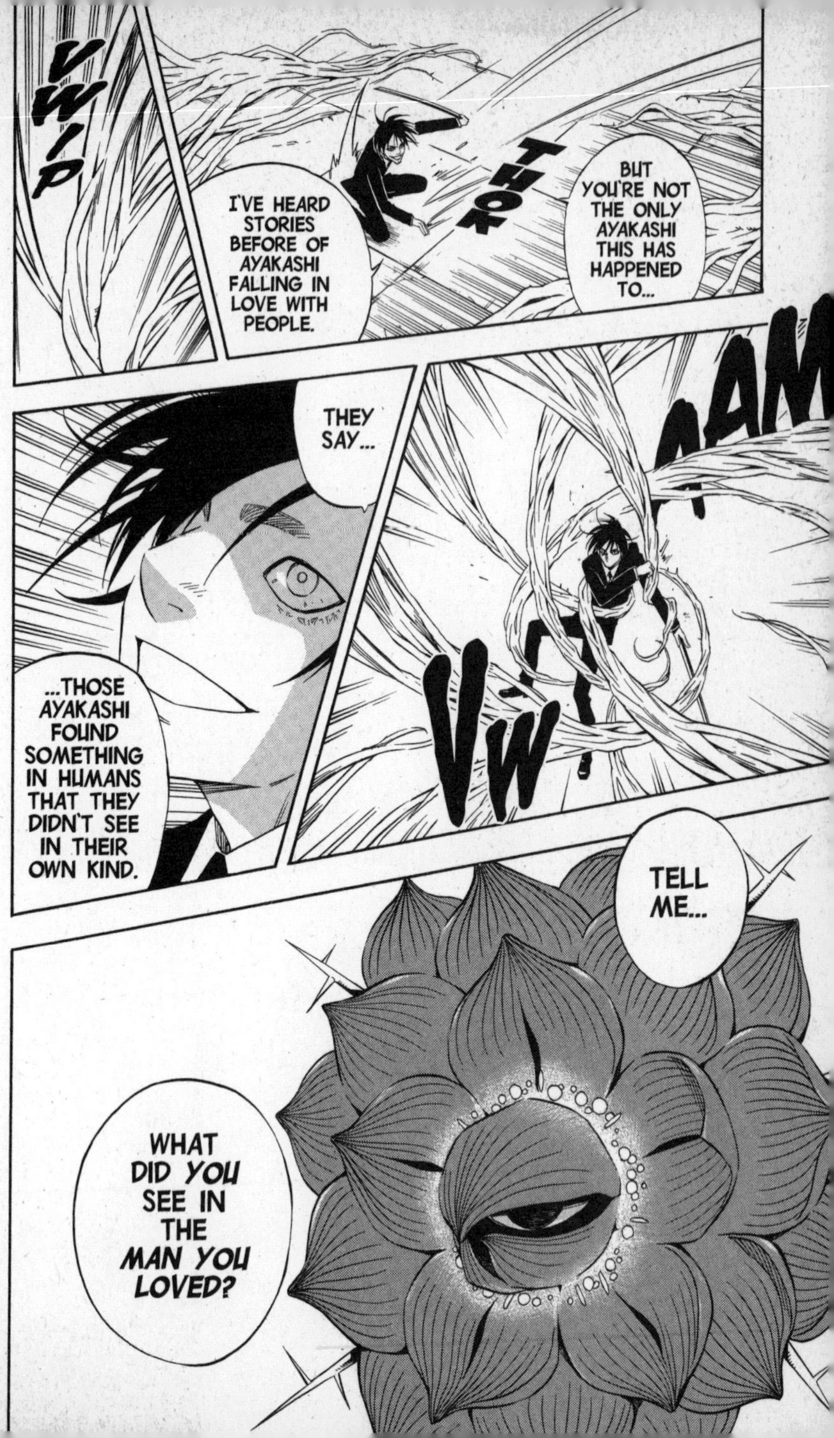
VWIP
THOK
BUT YOU'RE NOT THE ONLY AYAKASHI THIS HAS HAPPENED TO...
I'VE HEARD STORIES BEFORE OF AYAKASHI FALLING IN LOVE WITH PEOPLE.
AAAM
VW
THEY SAY...
...THOSE AYAKASHI FOUND SOMETHING IN HUMANS THAT THEY DIDN'T SEE IN THEIR OWN KIND.
TELL ME...
WHAT DID YOU SEE IN THE MAN YOU LOVED?

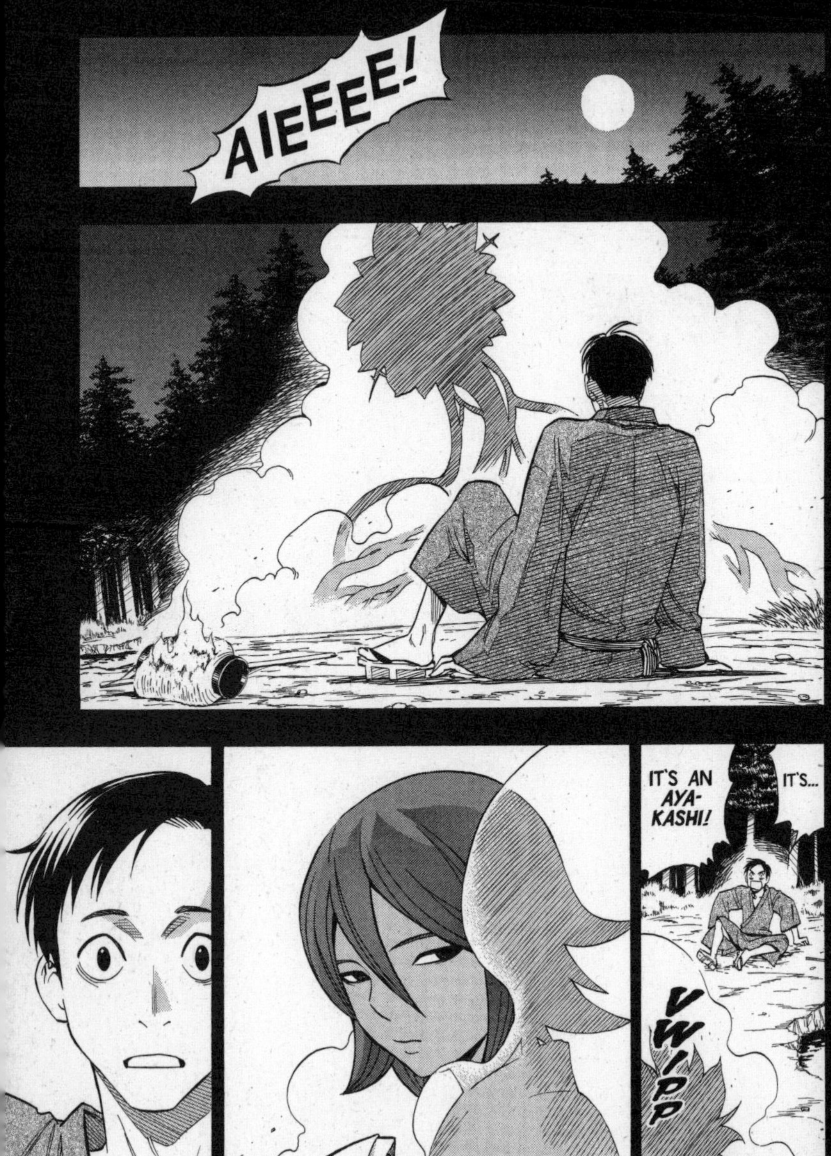
AIEEEE!
IT'S...
IT'S AN AYA-KASHI!
VWIPP

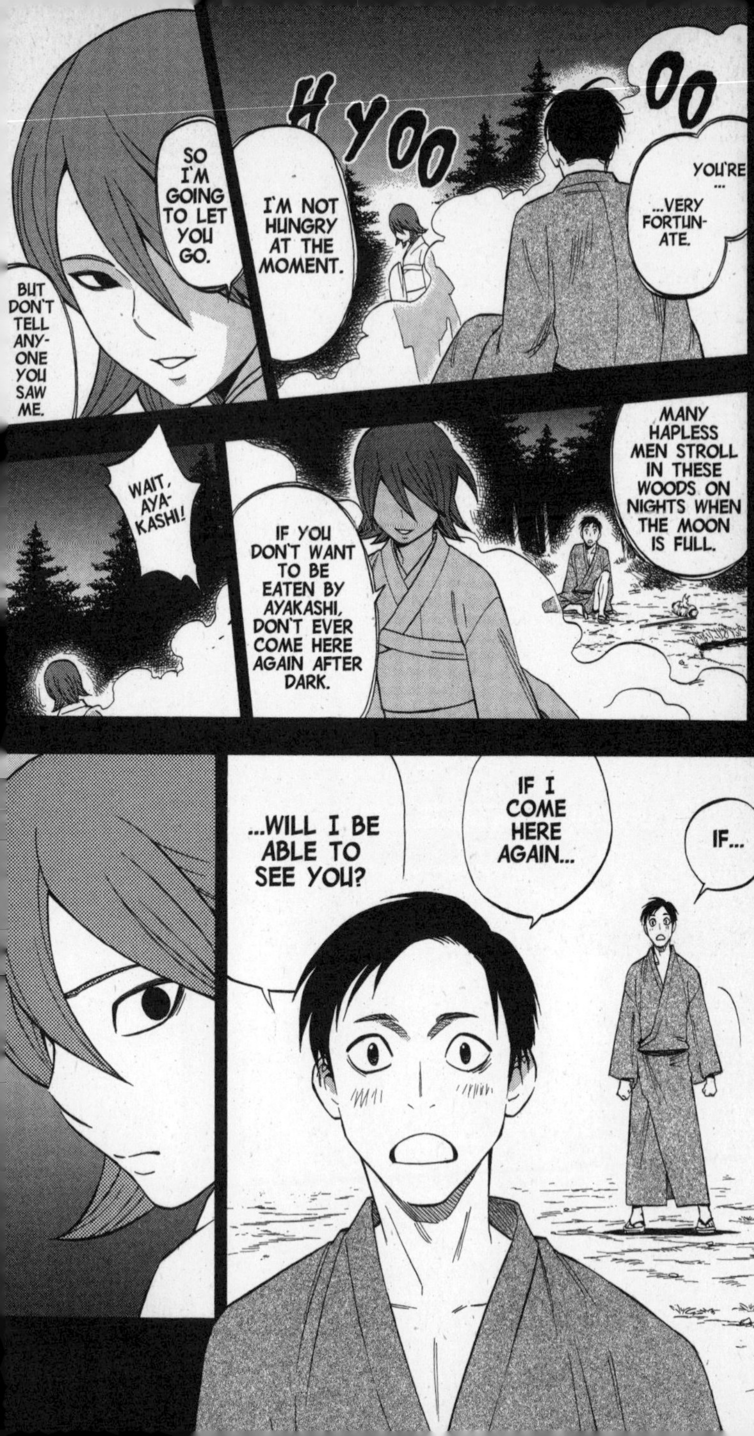
HYOO
OO
YOU'RE...
...VERY FORTUNATE.
I'M NOT HUNGRY AT THE MOMENT.
SO I'M GOING TO LET YOU GO.
BUT DON'T TELL ANYONE YOU SAW ME.
MANY HAPLESS MEN STROLL IN THESE WOODS ON NIGHTS WHEN THE MOON IS FULL.
IF YOU DON'T WANT TO BE EATEN BY AYAKASHI, DON'T EVER COME HERE AGAIN AFTER DARK.
WAIT, AYAKASHI!
IF...
IF I COME HERE AGAIN...
...WILL I BE ABLE TO SEE YOU?

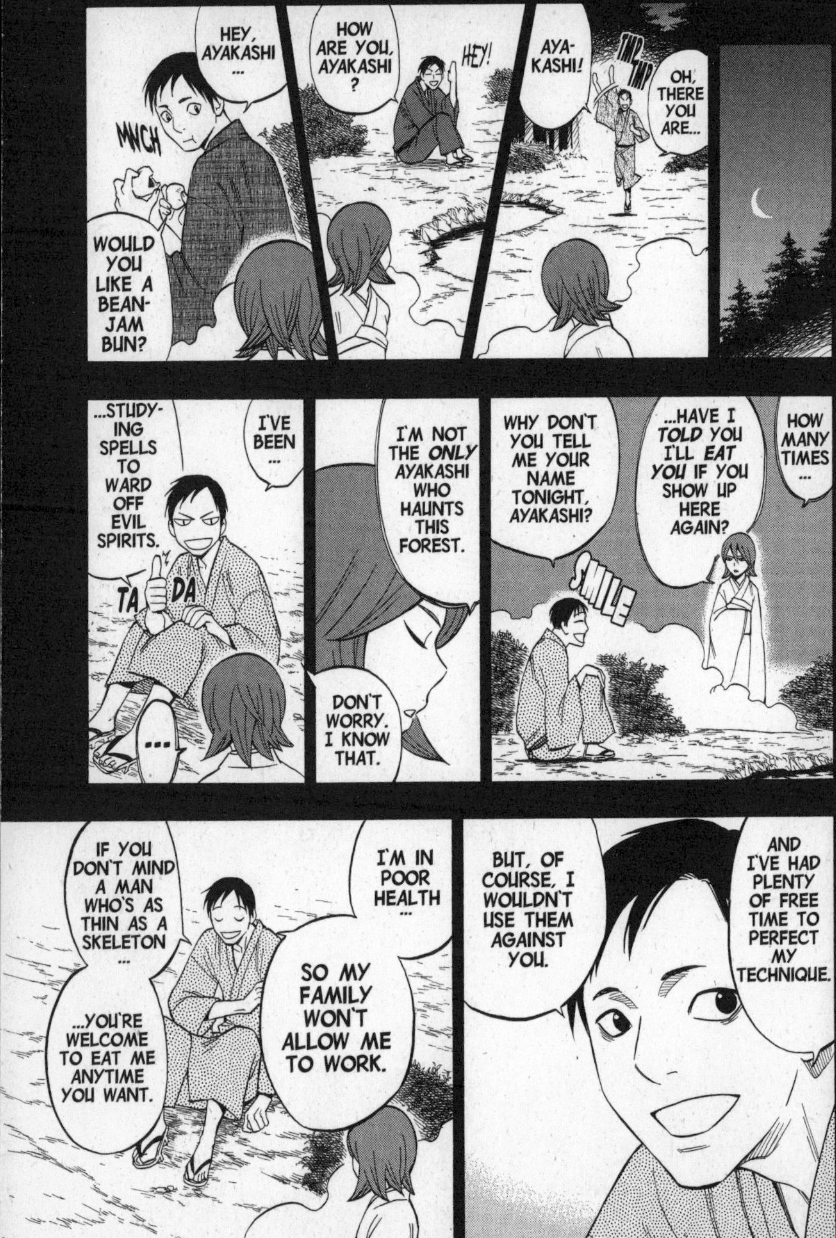
OH, THERE YOU ARE...
TMP TMP
AYA-KASHI!
HEY!
HOW ARE YOU, AYAKASHI?
HEY, AYAKASHI...
MNCH
WOULD YOU LIKE A BEAN-JAM BUN?
HOW MANY TIMES...
...HAVE I *TOLD* YOU I'LL *EAT YOU* IF YOU SHOW UP HERE AGAIN?
WHY DON'T YOU TELL ME YOUR NAME TONIGHT, AYAKASHI?
SMILE
I'M NOT THE *ONLY* AYAKASHI WHO HAUNTS THIS FOREST.
DON'T WORRY. I KNOW THAT.
I'VE BEEN...
...STUDYING SPELLS TO WARD OFF EVIL SPIRITS.
TA DA
...
AND I'VE HAD PLENTY OF FREE TIME TO PERFECT MY TECHNIQUE.
BUT, OF COURSE, I WOULDN'T USE THEM AGAINST YOU.
I'M IN POOR HEALTH...
SO MY FAMILY WON'T ALLOW ME TO WORK.
IF YOU DON'T MIND A MAN WHO'S AS THIN AS A SKELETON...
...YOU'RE WELCOME TO EAT ME ANYTIME YOU WANT.

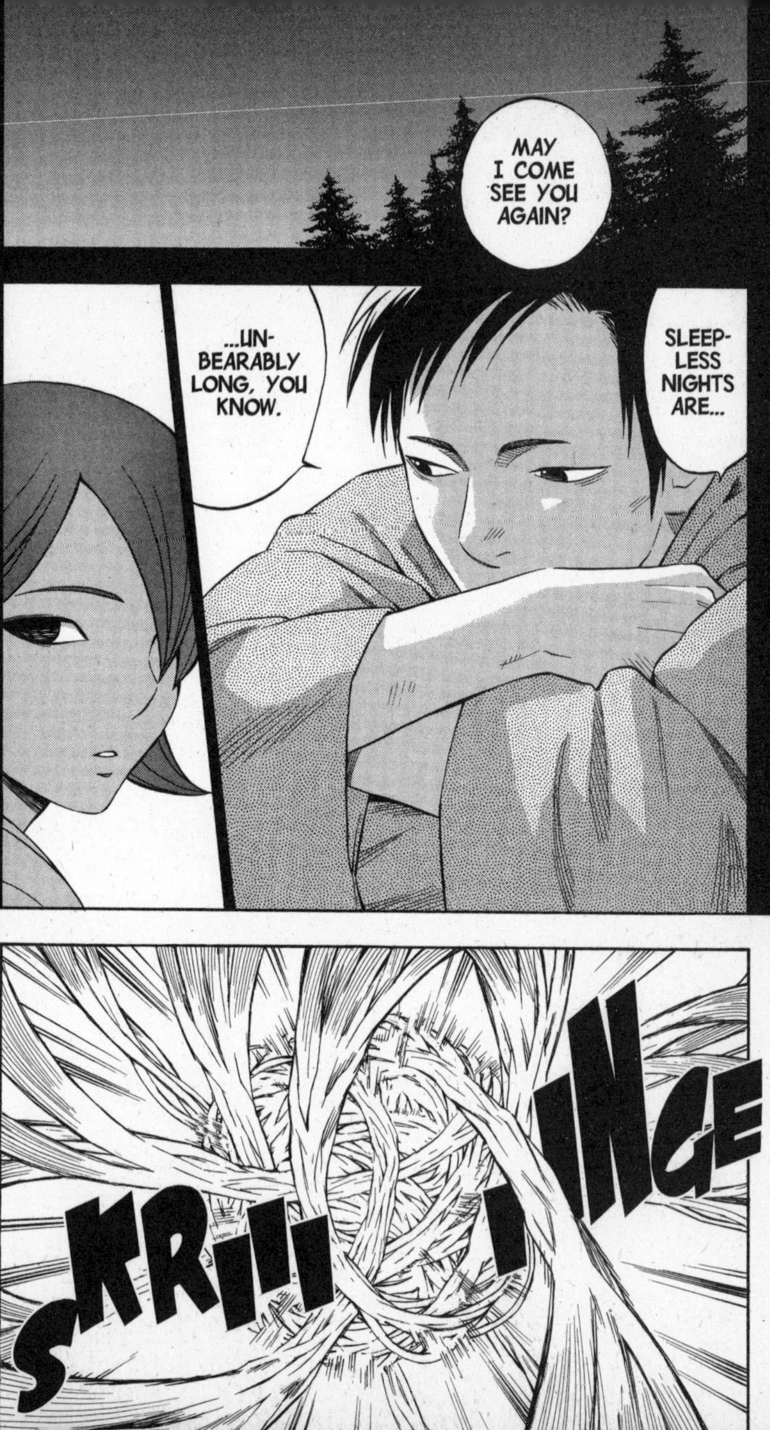
MAY I COME SEE YOU AGAIN?
SLEEP-LESS NIGHTS ARE...
...UN-BEARABLY LONG, YOU KNOW.
SKRIII IINGE

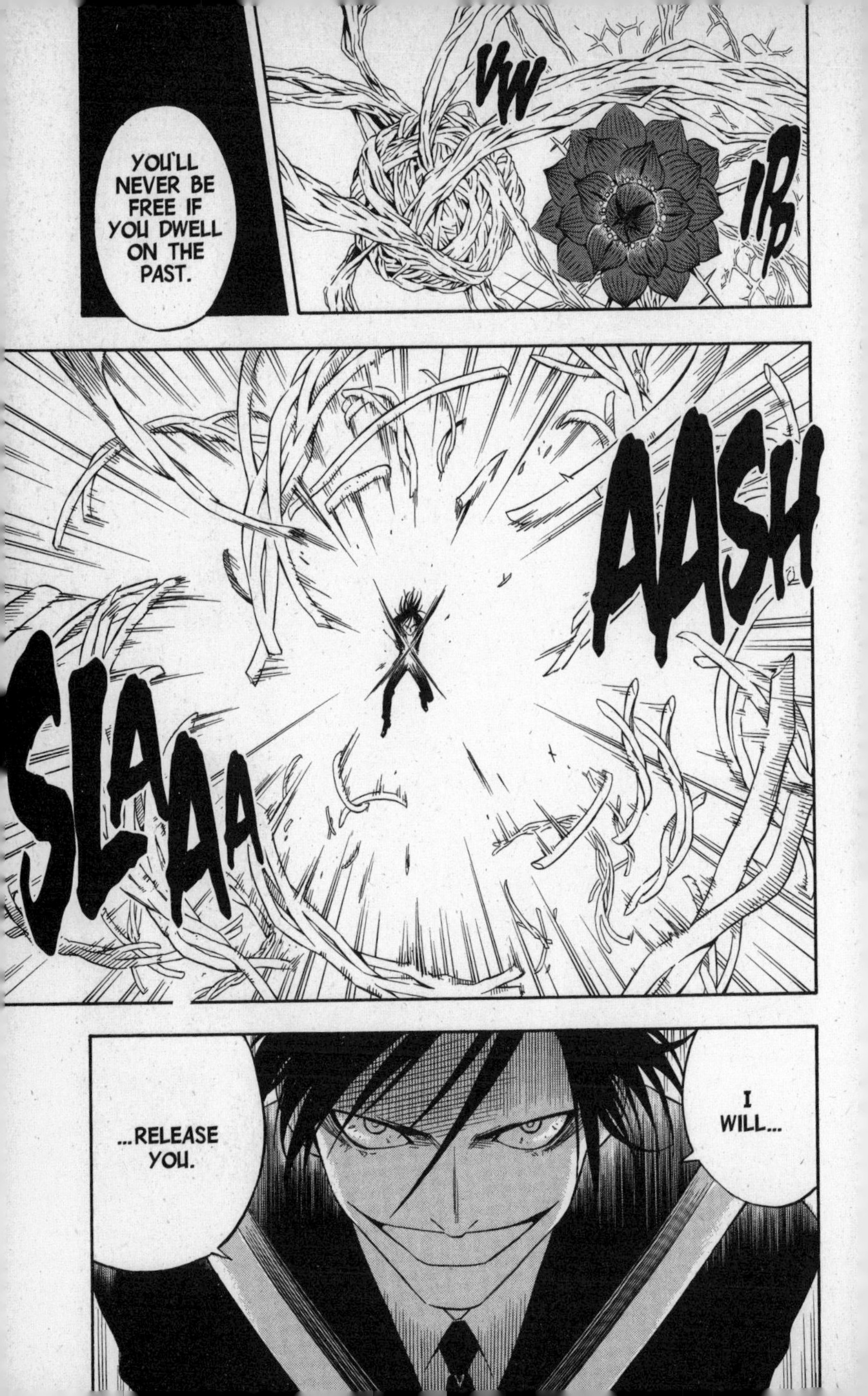

VW
IRP
YOU'LL NEVER BE FREE IF YOU DWELL ON THE PAST.
SLAAA
AASH
I WILL...
...RELEASE YOU.

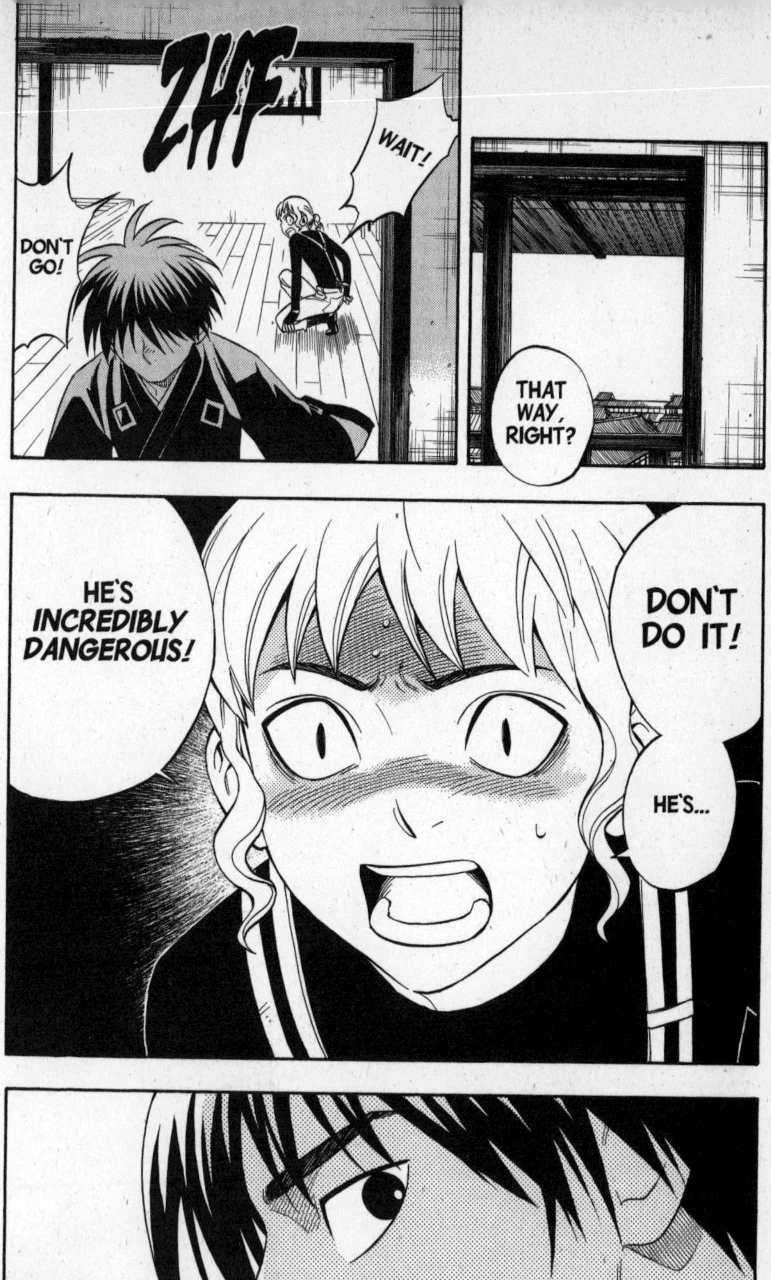
THAT WAY, RIGHT?
WAIT!
ZHF
DON'T GO!
DON'T DO IT!
HE'S...
HE'S INCREDIBLY DANGEROUS!

Chapter 113: The Man Who Would Not Die

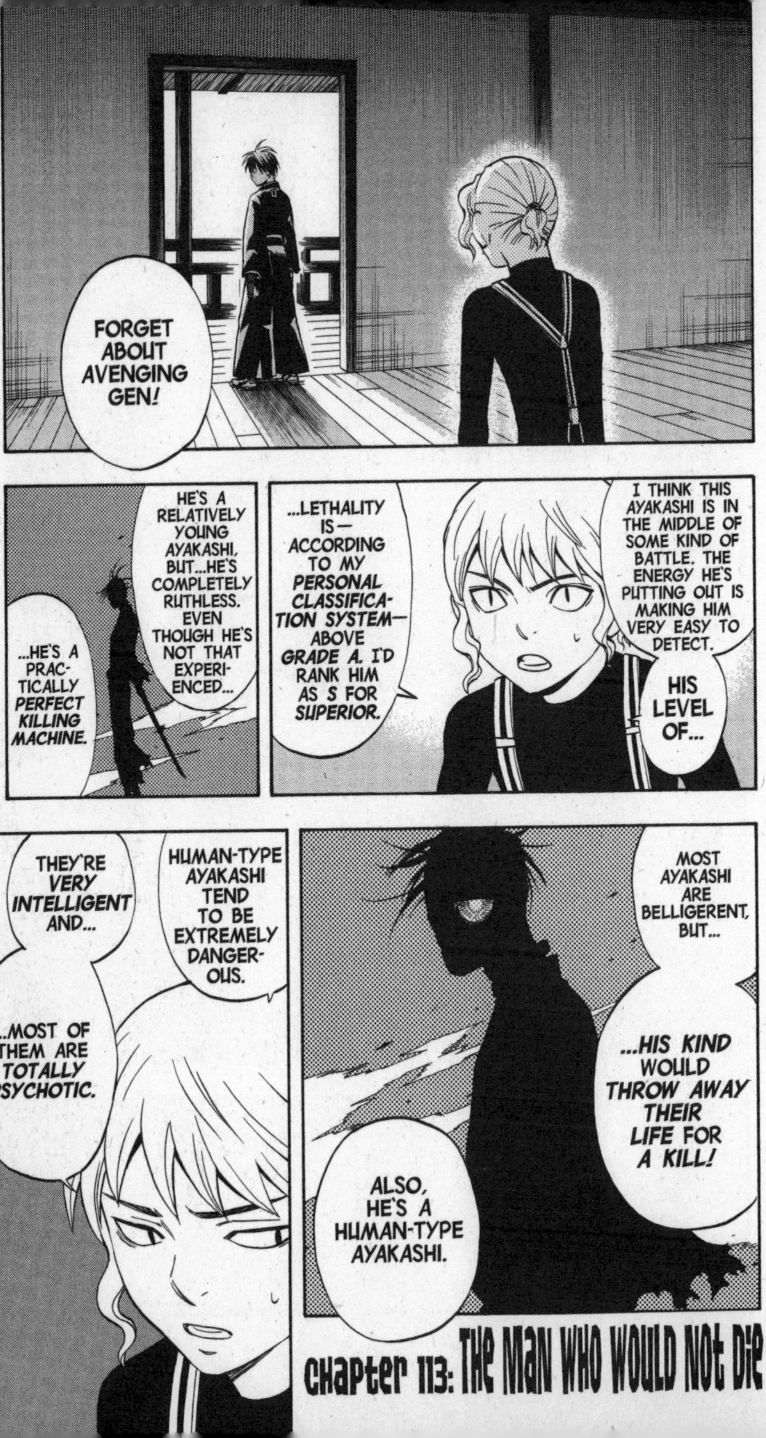
FORGET ABOUT AVENGING GEN!
I THINK THIS AYAKASHI IS IN THE MIDDLE OF SOME KIND OF BATTLE. THE ENERGY HE'S PUTTING OUT IS MAKING HIM VERY EASY TO DETECT.
HIS LEVEL OF...
...LETHALITY IS—ACCORDING TO MY *PERSONAL CLASSIFICATION SYSTEM*—ABOVE *GRADE A*. I'D RANK HIM AS S FOR *SUPERIOR*.
HE'S A RELATIVELY YOUNG AYAKASHI, BUT...HE'S COMPLETELY RUTHLESS. EVEN THOUGH HE'S NOT THAT EXPERIENCED...
...HE'S A PRACTICALLY *PERFECT KILLING MACHINE*.
MOST AYAKASHI ARE BELLIGERENT, BUT...
...HIS KIND WOULD THROW AWAY THEIR LIFE FOR A KILL!
ALSO, HE'S A HUMAN-TYPE AYAKASHI.
HUMAN-TYPE AYAKASHI TEND TO BE EXTREMELY DANGEROUS.
THEY'RE *VERY INTELLIGENT* AND...
...MOST OF THEM ARE *TOTALLY PSYCHOTIC*.

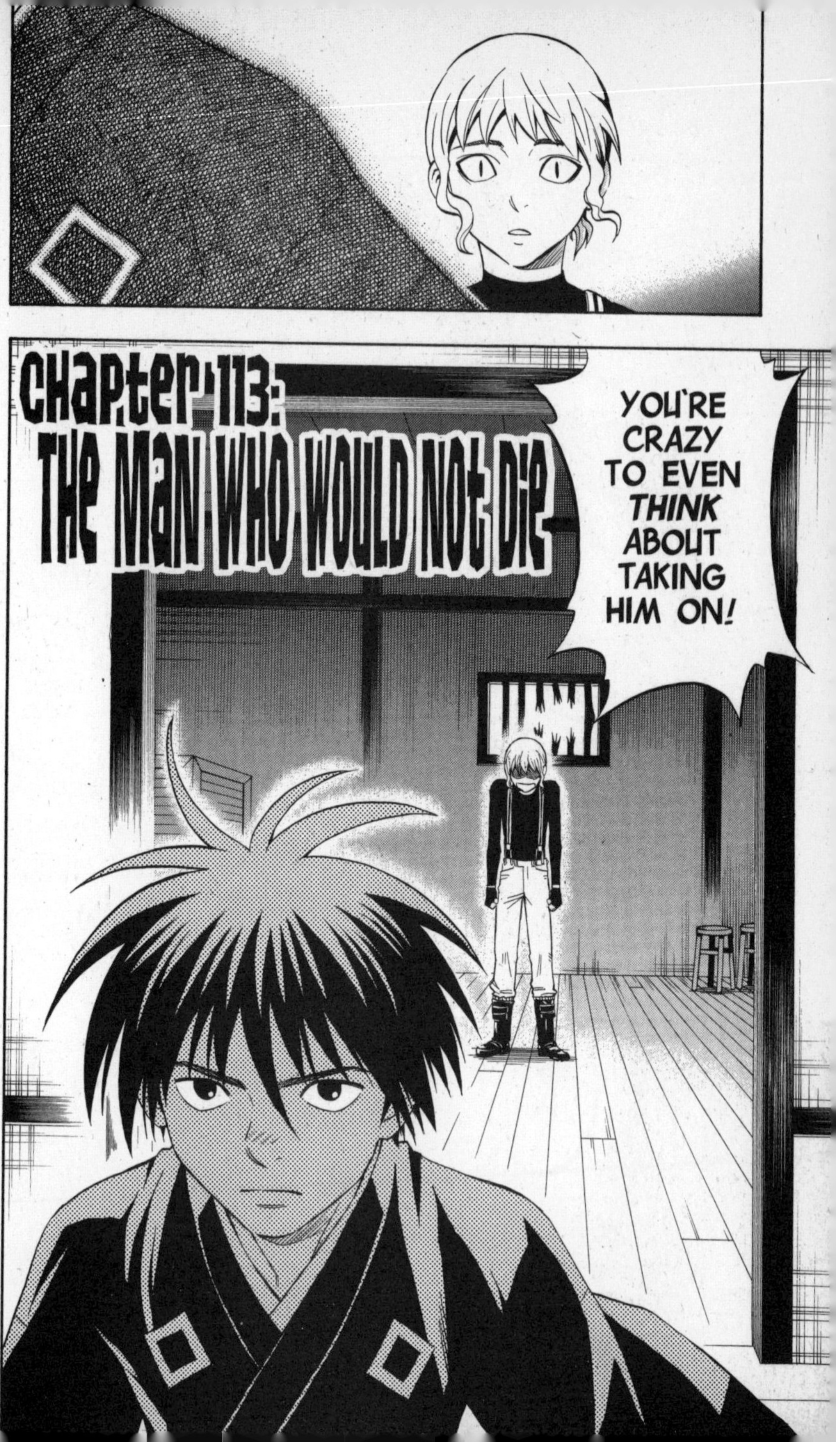
Chapter 113:
The Man Who Would Not Die
YOU'RE CRAZY TO EVEN *THINK* ABOUT TAKING HIM ON!

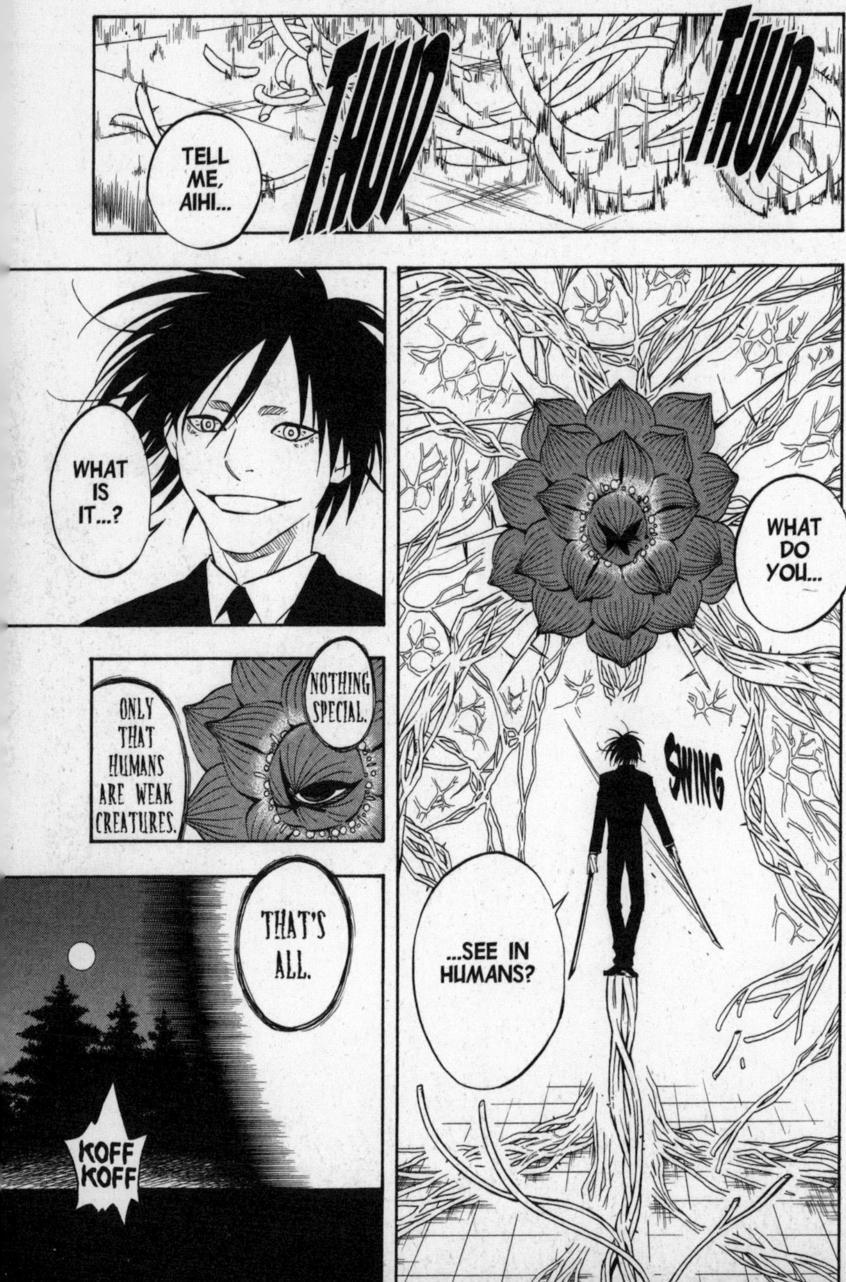
THUD
THUD
TELL ME, AIHI...
WHAT IS IT...?
WHAT DO YOU...
...SEE IN HUMANS?
SWING
NOTHING SPECIAL.
ONLY THAT HUMANS ARE WEAK CREATURES.
THAT'S ALL.
KOFF KOFF

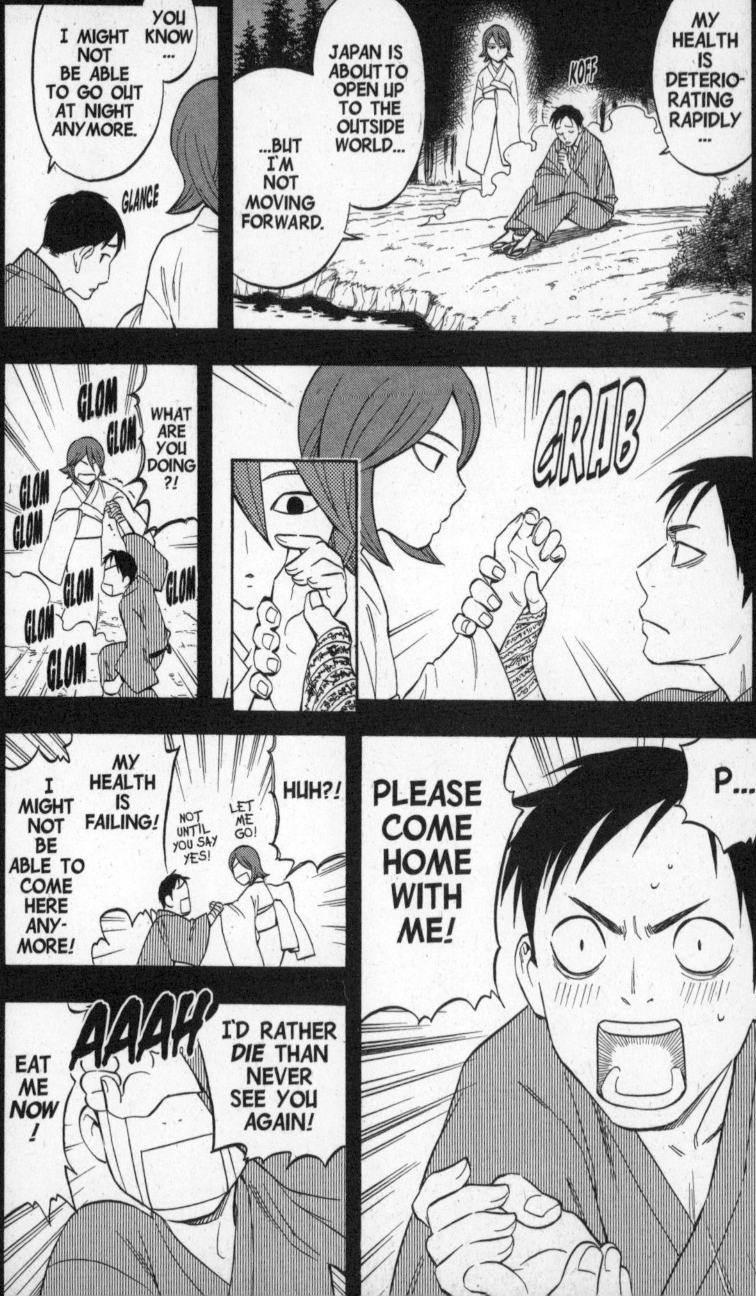
MY HEALTH IS DETERIO-RATING RAPIDLY...
KOFF
JAPAN IS ABOUT TO OPEN UP TO THE OUTSIDE WORLD...
...BUT I'M NOT MOVING FORWARD.
YOU KNOW...
I MIGHT NOT BE ABLE TO GO OUT AT NIGHT ANYMORE.
GLANCE
GRAB
WHAT ARE YOU DOING?!
GLOM GLOM GLOM GLOM GLOM GLOM GLOM GLOM
P...
PLEASE COME HOME WITH ME!
HUH?!
MY HEALTH IS FAILING!
I MIGHT NOT BE ABLE TO COME HERE ANY-MORE!
LET ME GO!
NOT UNTIL YOU SAY YES!
I'D RATHER *DIE* THAN NEVER SEE YOU AGAIN!
AAAH
EAT ME *NOW*!

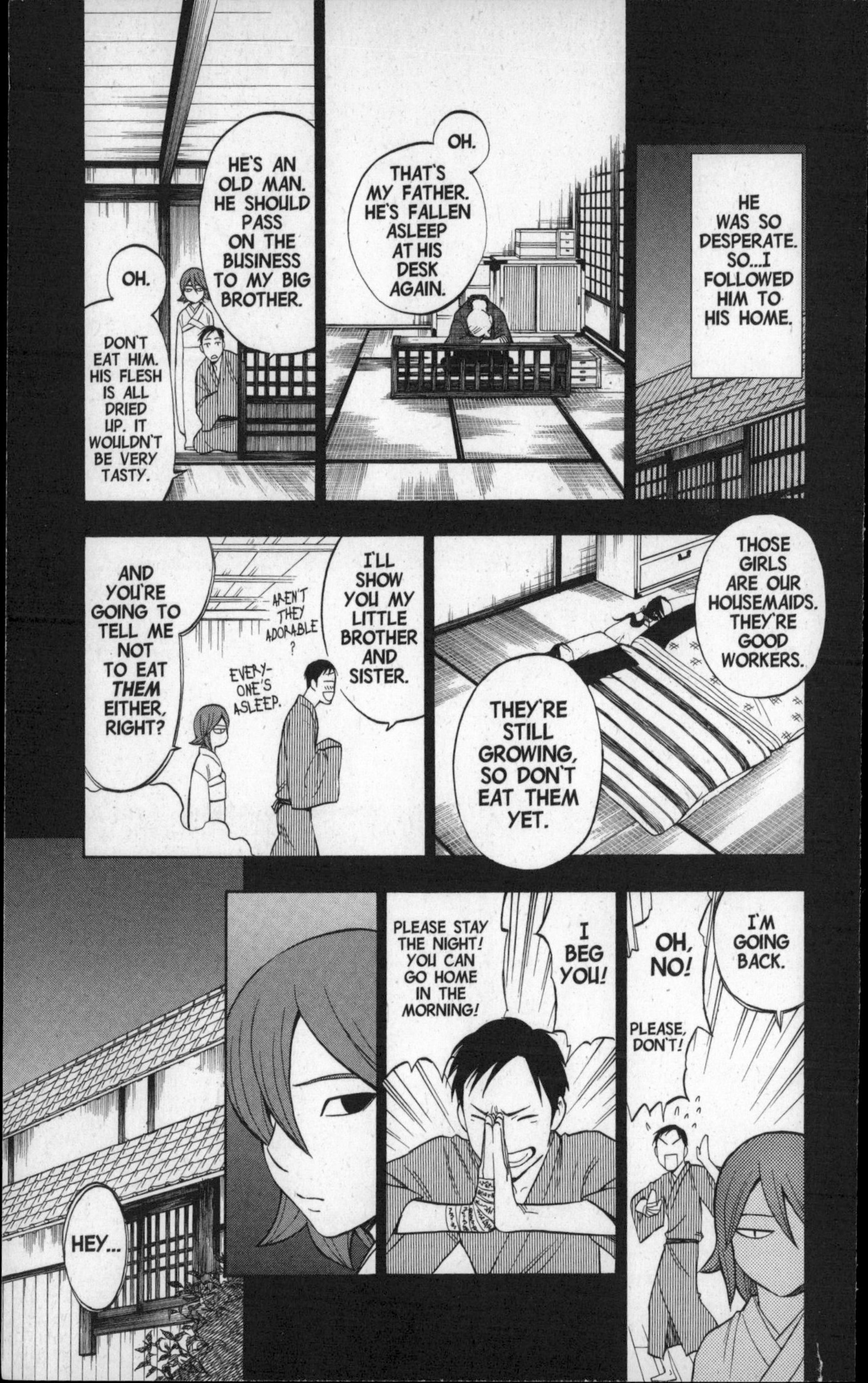
HE WAS SO DESPERATE. SO...I FOLLOWED HIM TO HIS HOME.
OH.
THAT'S MY FATHER. HE'S FALLEN ASLEEP AT HIS DESK AGAIN.
HE'S AN OLD MAN. HE SHOULD PASS ON THE BUSINESS TO MY BIG BROTHER.
OH.
DON'T EAT HIM. HIS FLESH IS ALL DRIED UP. IT WOULDN'T BE VERY TASTY.
THOSE GIRLS ARE OUR HOUSEMAIDS. THEY'RE GOOD WORKERS.
THEY'RE STILL GROWING, SO DON'T EAT THEM YET.
I'LL SHOW YOU MY LITTLE BROTHER AND SISTER.
AREN'T THEY ADORABLE?
EVERY-ONE'S ASLEEP.
AND YOU'RE GOING TO TELL ME NOT TO EAT *THEM* EITHER, RIGHT?
I'M GOING BACK.
OH, NO!
PLEASE, DON'T!
I BEG YOU!
PLEASE STAY THE NIGHT! YOU CAN GO HOME IN THE MORNING!
HEY...

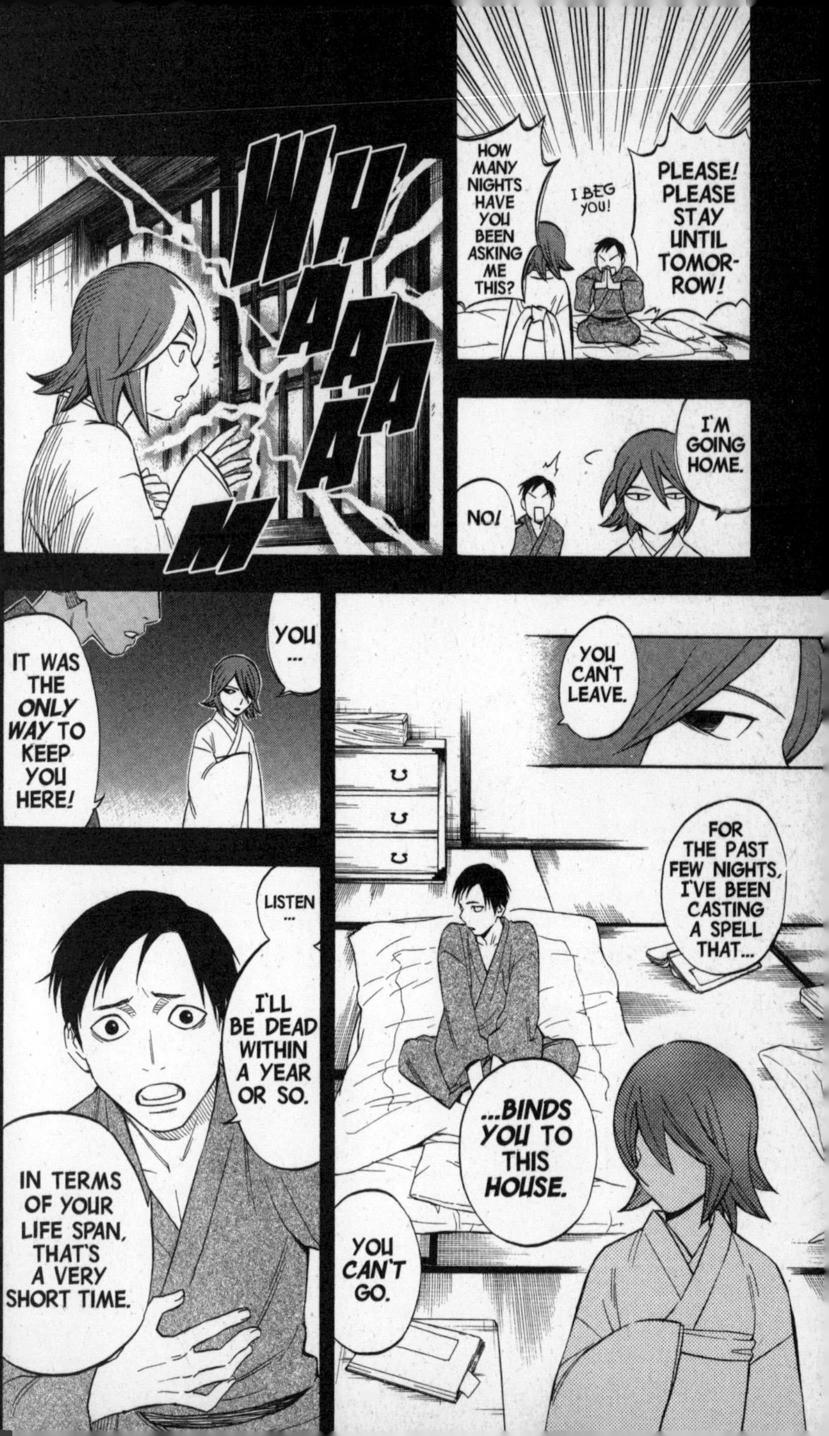
PLEASE! PLEASE STAY UNTIL TOMOR-ROW!
I BEG YOU!
HOW MANY NIGHTS HAVE YOU BEEN ASKING ME THIS?
I'M GOING HOME.
NO!
WHAAAAM
YOU CAN'T LEAVE.
FOR THE PAST FEW NIGHTS, I'VE BEEN CASTING A SPELL THAT...
...BINDS YOU TO THIS HOUSE.
YOU CAN'T GO.
YOU ...
IT WAS THE ONLY WAY TO KEEP YOU HERE!
LISTEN ...
I'LL BE DEAD WITHIN A YEAR OR SO.
IN TERMS OF YOUR LIFE SPAN, THAT'S A VERY SHORT TIME.

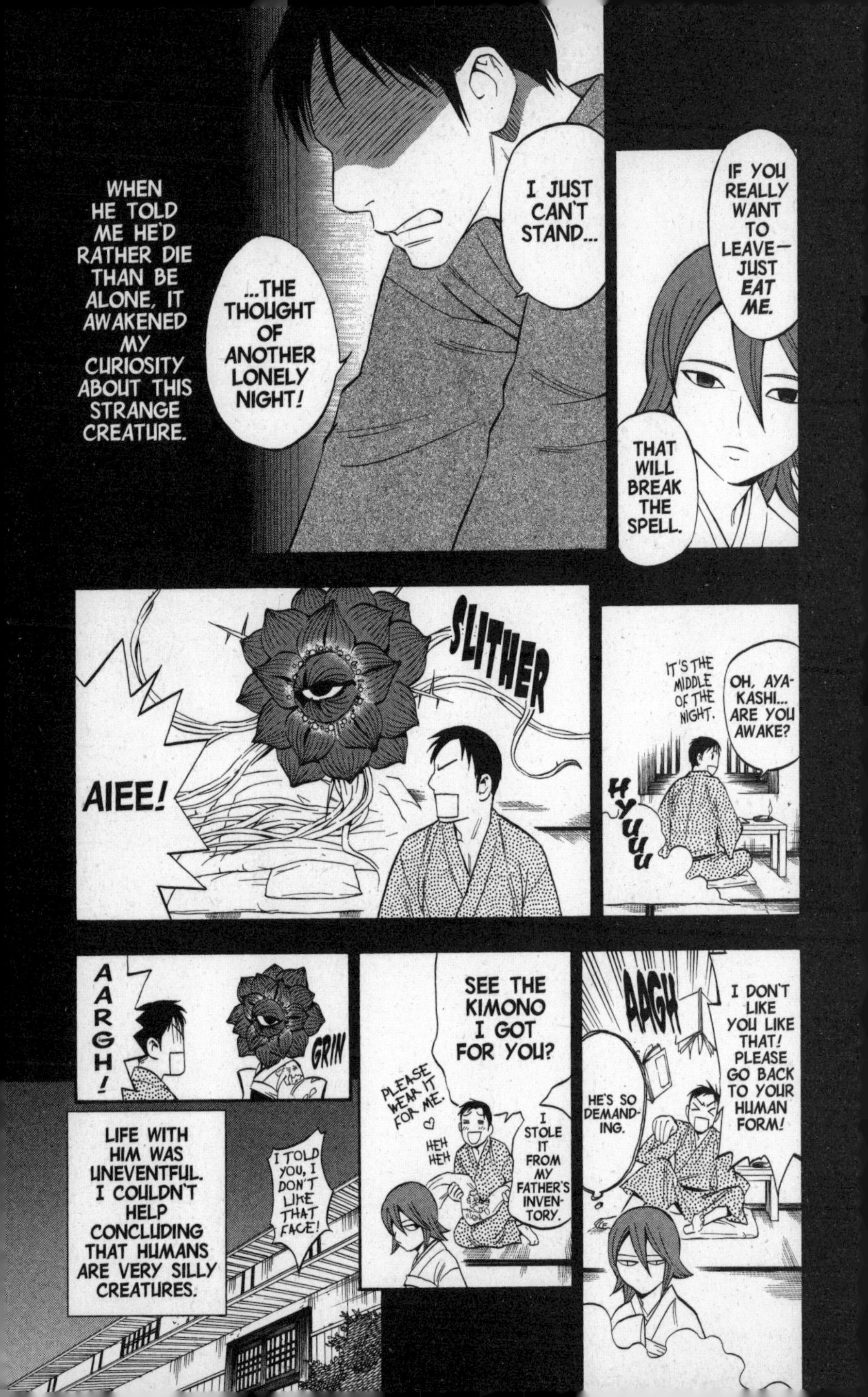
IF YOU REALLY WANT TO LEAVE—JUST EAT ME.
THAT WILL BREAK THE SPELL.
I JUST CAN'T STAND...
...THE THOUGHT OF ANOTHER LONELY NIGHT!
WHEN HE TOLD ME HE'D RATHER DIE THAN BE ALONE, IT AWAKENED MY CURIOSITY ABOUT THIS STRANGE CREATURE.
OH, AYA-KASHI... ARE YOU AWAKE?
IT'S THE MIDDLE OF THE NIGHT.
HYUUU
SLITHER
AIEE!
AAGH
I DON'T LIKE YOU LIKE THAT! PLEASE GO BACK TO YOUR HUMAN FORM!
HE'S SO DEMAND-ING.
SEE THE KIMONO I GOT FOR YOU?
PLEASE WEAR IT FOR ME.
I STOLE IT FROM MY FATHER'S INVEN-TORY.
HEH HEH
AARGH!
GRIN
LIFE WITH HIM WAS UNEVENTFUL. I COULDN'T HELP CONCLUDING THAT HUMANS ARE VERY SILLY CREATURES.
I TOLD YOU, I DON'T LIKE THAT FACE!

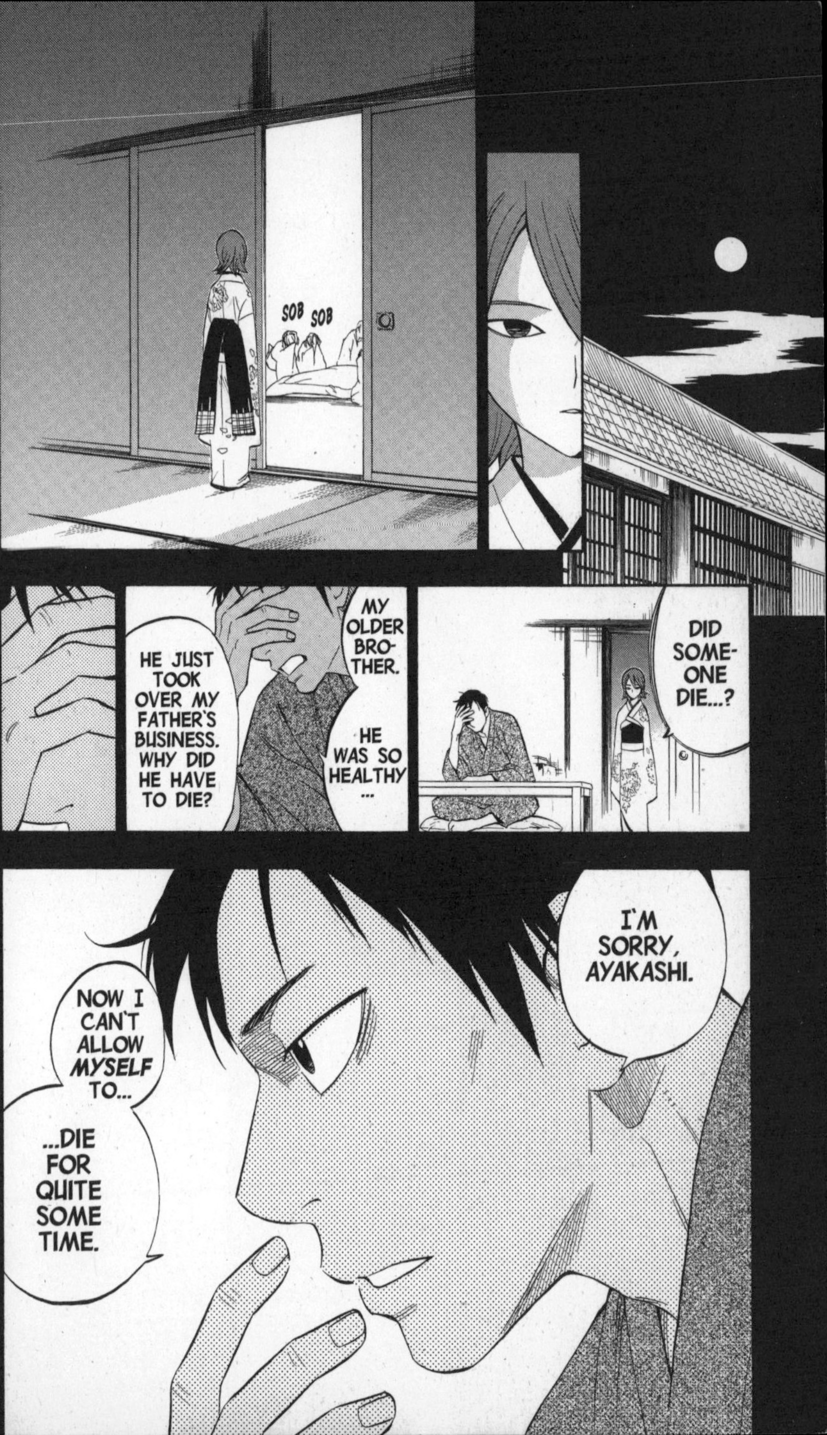
SOB SOB
DID SOMEONE DIE...?
MY OLDER BROTHER.
HE WAS SO HEALTHY...
HE JUST TOOK OVER MY FATHER'S BUSINESS. WHY DID HE HAVE TO DIE?
I'M SORRY, AYAKASHI.
NOW I CAN'T ALLOW *MYSELF* TO...
...DIE FOR QUITE SOME TIME.

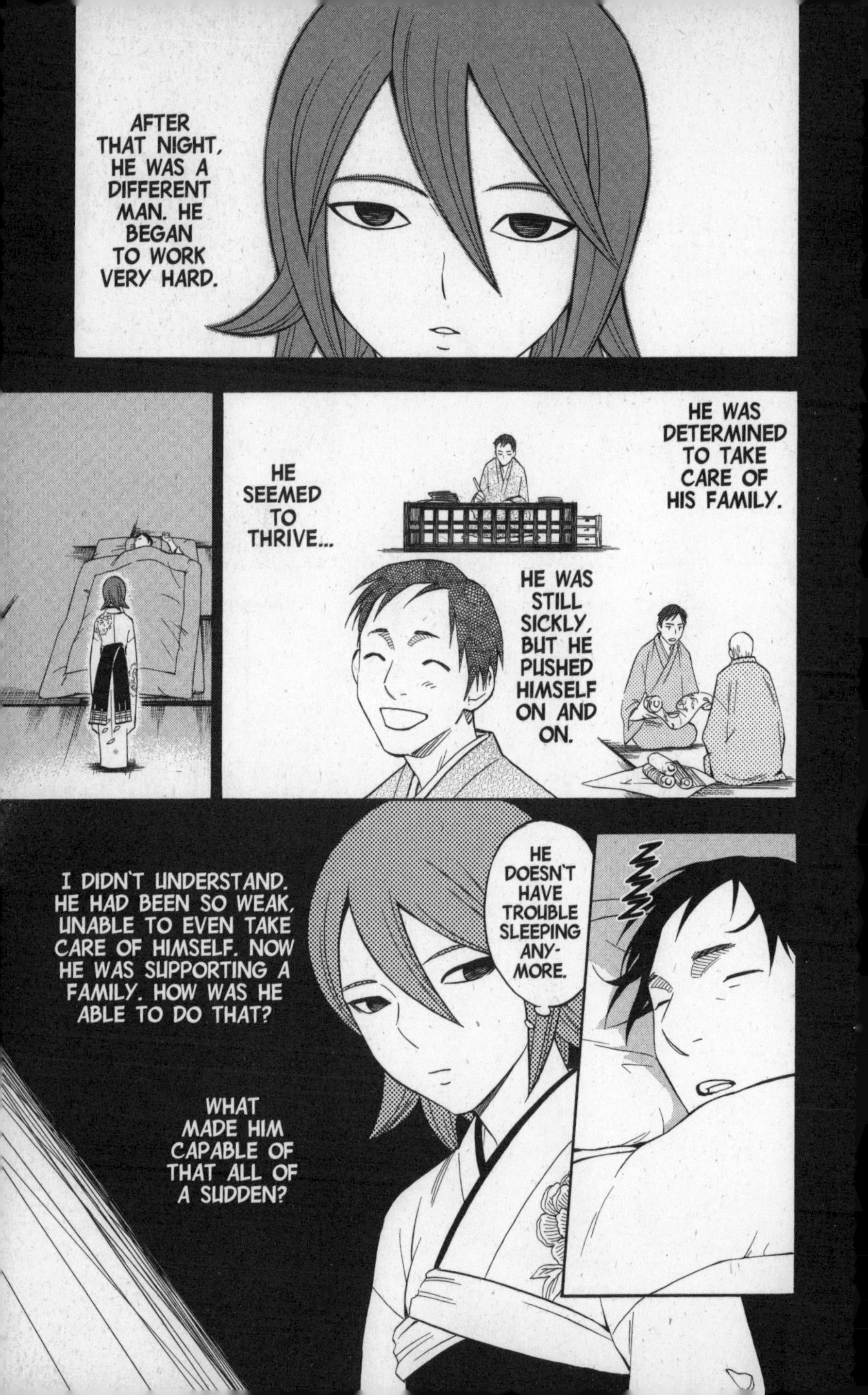
AFTER THAT NIGHT, HE WAS A DIFFERENT MAN. HE BEGAN TO WORK VERY HARD.
HE WAS DETERMINED TO TAKE CARE OF HIS FAMILY.
HE SEEMED TO THRIVE...
HE WAS STILL SICKLY, BUT HE PUSHED HIMSELF ON AND ON.
HE DOESN'T HAVE TROUBLE SLEEPING ANY-MORE.
I DIDN'T UNDERSTAND. HE HAD BEEN SO WEAK, UNABLE TO EVEN TAKE CARE OF HIMSELF. NOW HE WAS SUPPORTING A FAMILY. HOW WAS HE ABLE TO DO THAT?
WHAT MADE HIM CAPABLE OF THAT ALL OF A SUDDEN?

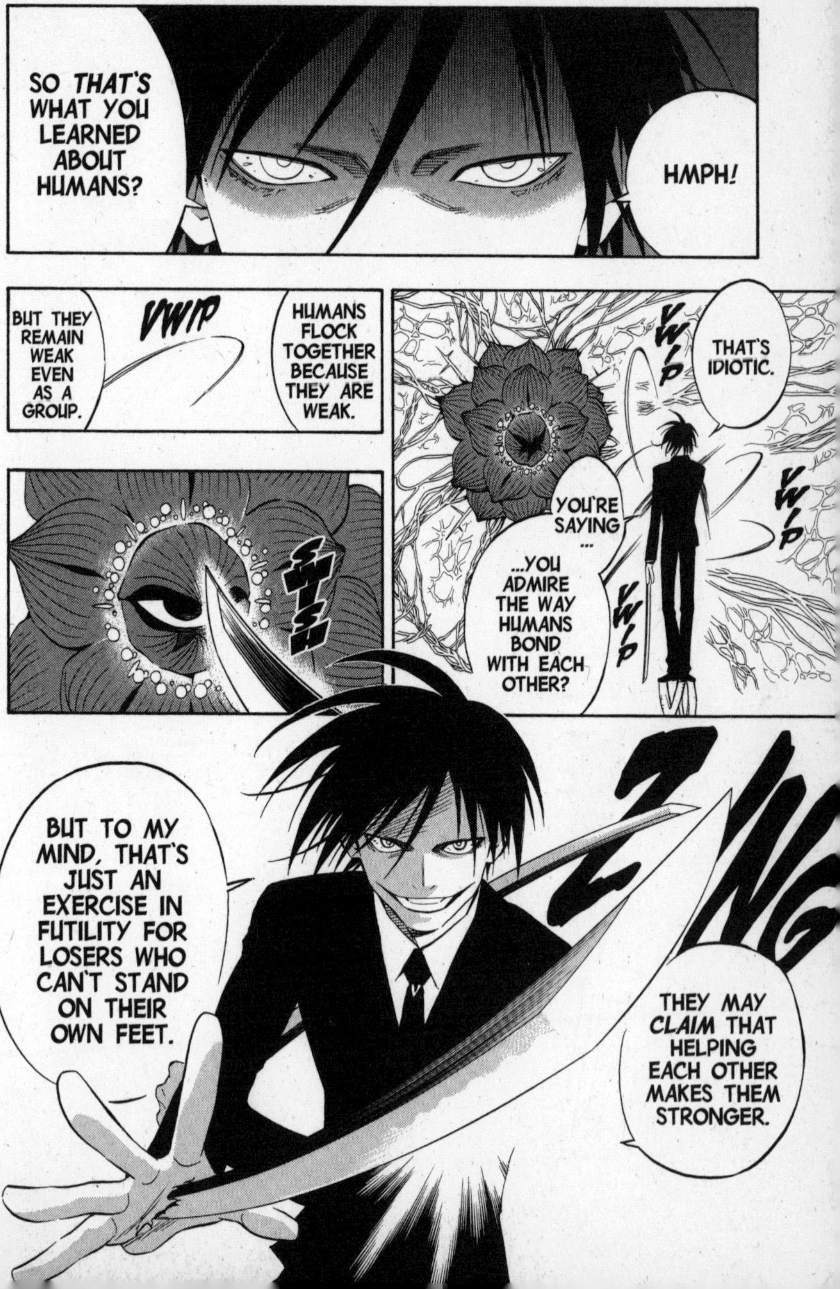
HMPH!
SO *THAT'S* WHAT YOU LEARNED ABOUT HUMANS?
THAT'S IDIOTIC.
VWIP
YOU'RE SAYING ...
...YOU ADMIRE THE WAY HUMANS BOND WITH EACH OTHER?
VWIP
VWIP
HUMANS FLOCK TOGETHER BECAUSE THEY ARE WEAK.
VWIP
BUT THEY REMAIN WEAK EVEN AS A GROUP.
SWISH
ZING
THEY MAY *CLAIM* THAT HELPING EACH OTHER MAKES THEM STRONGER.
BUT TO MY MIND, THAT'S JUST AN EXERCISE IN FUTILITY FOR LOSERS WHO CAN'T STAND ON THEIR OWN FEET.

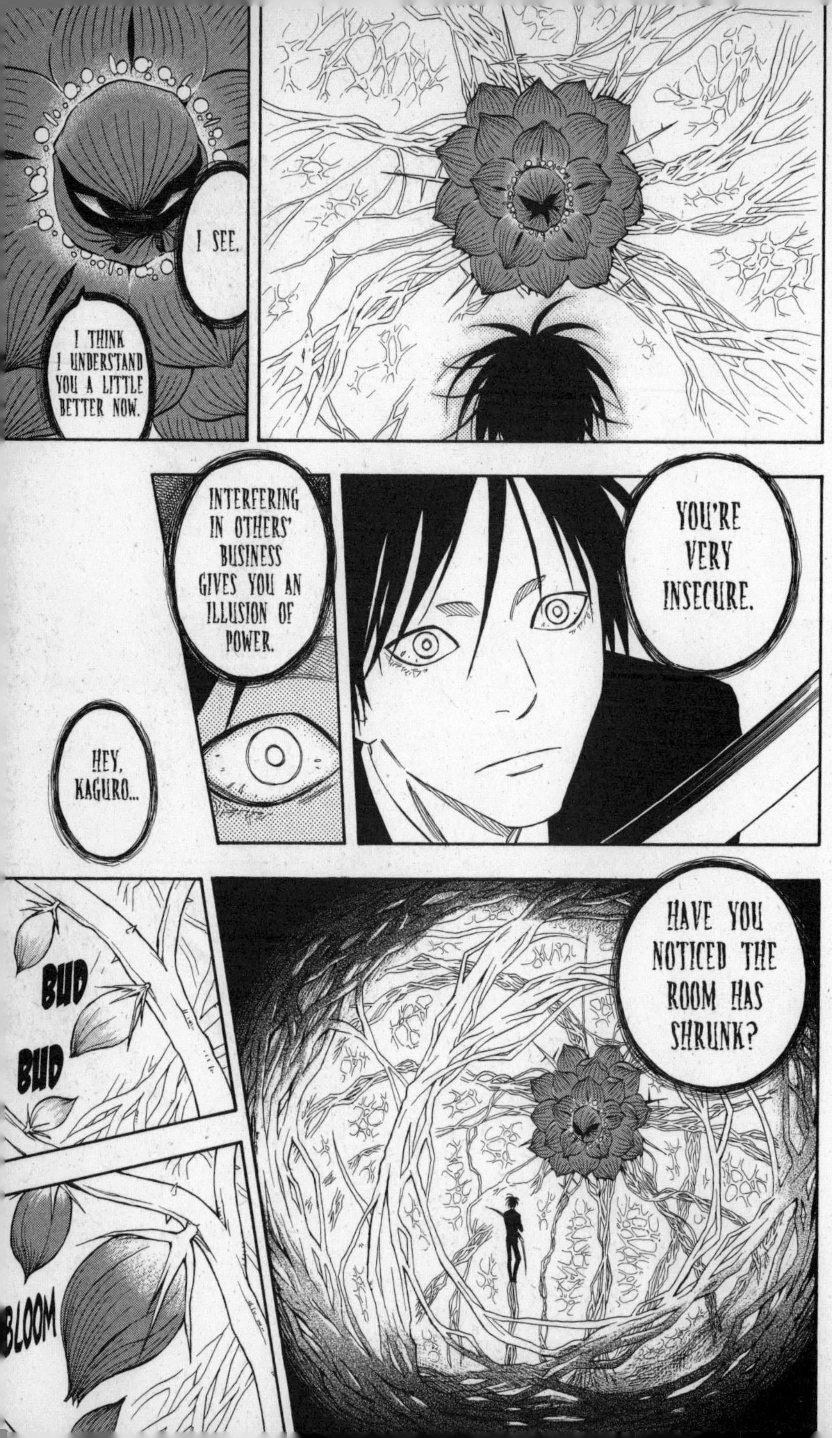
I SEE.
I THINK I UNDERSTAND YOU A LITTLE BETTER NOW.
YOU'RE VERY INSECURE.
INTERFERING IN OTHERS' BUSINESS GIVES YOU AN ILLUSION OF POWER.
HEY, KAGURO...
HAVE YOU NOTICED THE ROOM HAS SHRUNK?
BUD
BUD
BLOOM

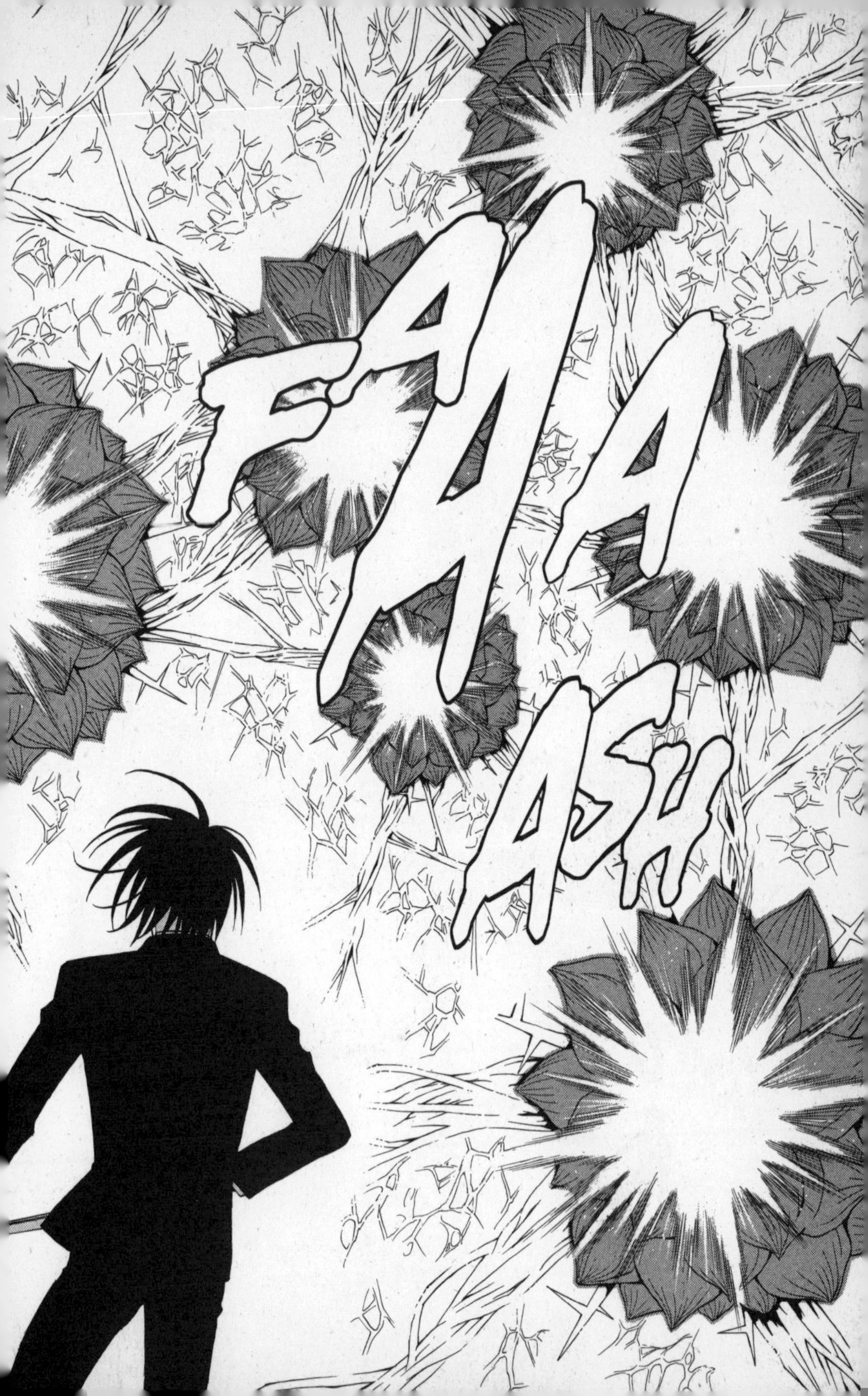
FWAAASH

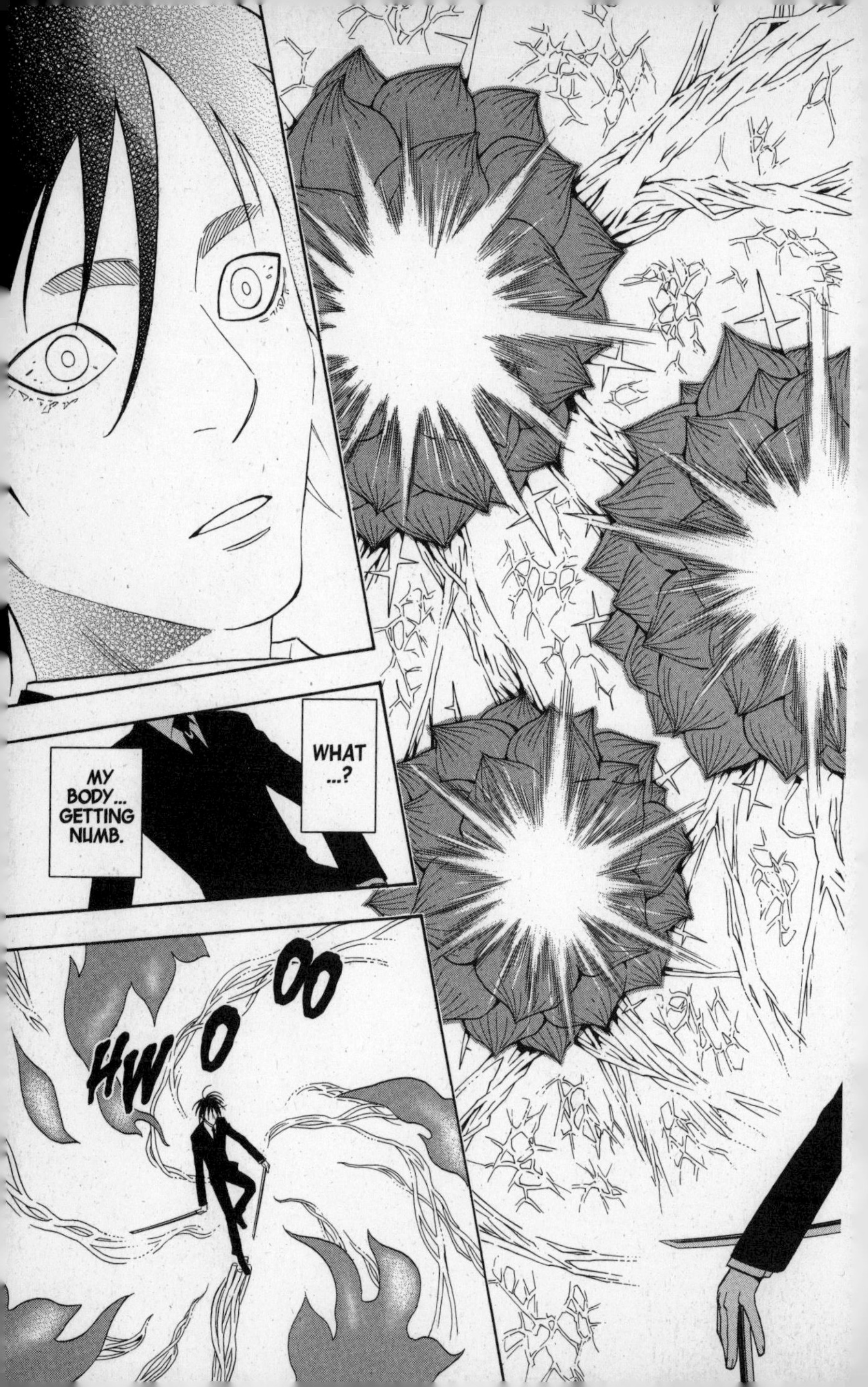
WHAT ...?
MY BODY... GETTING NUMB.
HWOOOO

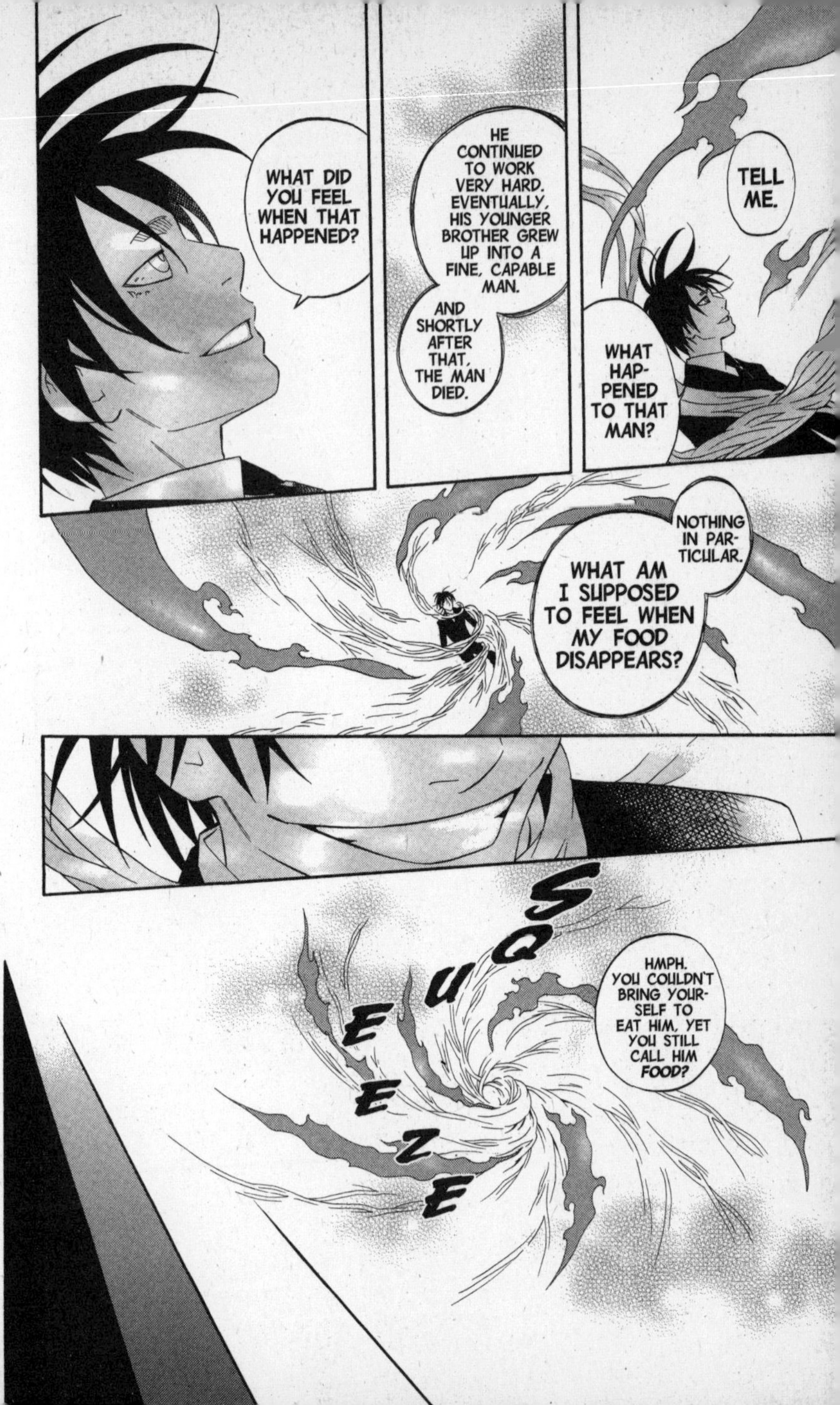
TELL ME.
WHAT HAPPENED TO THAT MAN?
HE CONTINUED TO WORK VERY HARD. EVENTUALLY, HIS YOUNGER BROTHER GREW UP INTO A FINE, CAPABLE MAN.
AND SHORTLY AFTER THAT, THE MAN DIED.
WHAT DID YOU FEEL WHEN THAT HAPPENED?
NOTHING IN PARTICULAR.
WHAT AM I SUPPOSED TO FEEL WHEN MY FOOD DISAPPEARS?
SQUEEZE
HMPH. YOU COULDN'T BRING YOURSELF TO EAT HIM, YET YOU STILL CALL HIM *FOOD*?

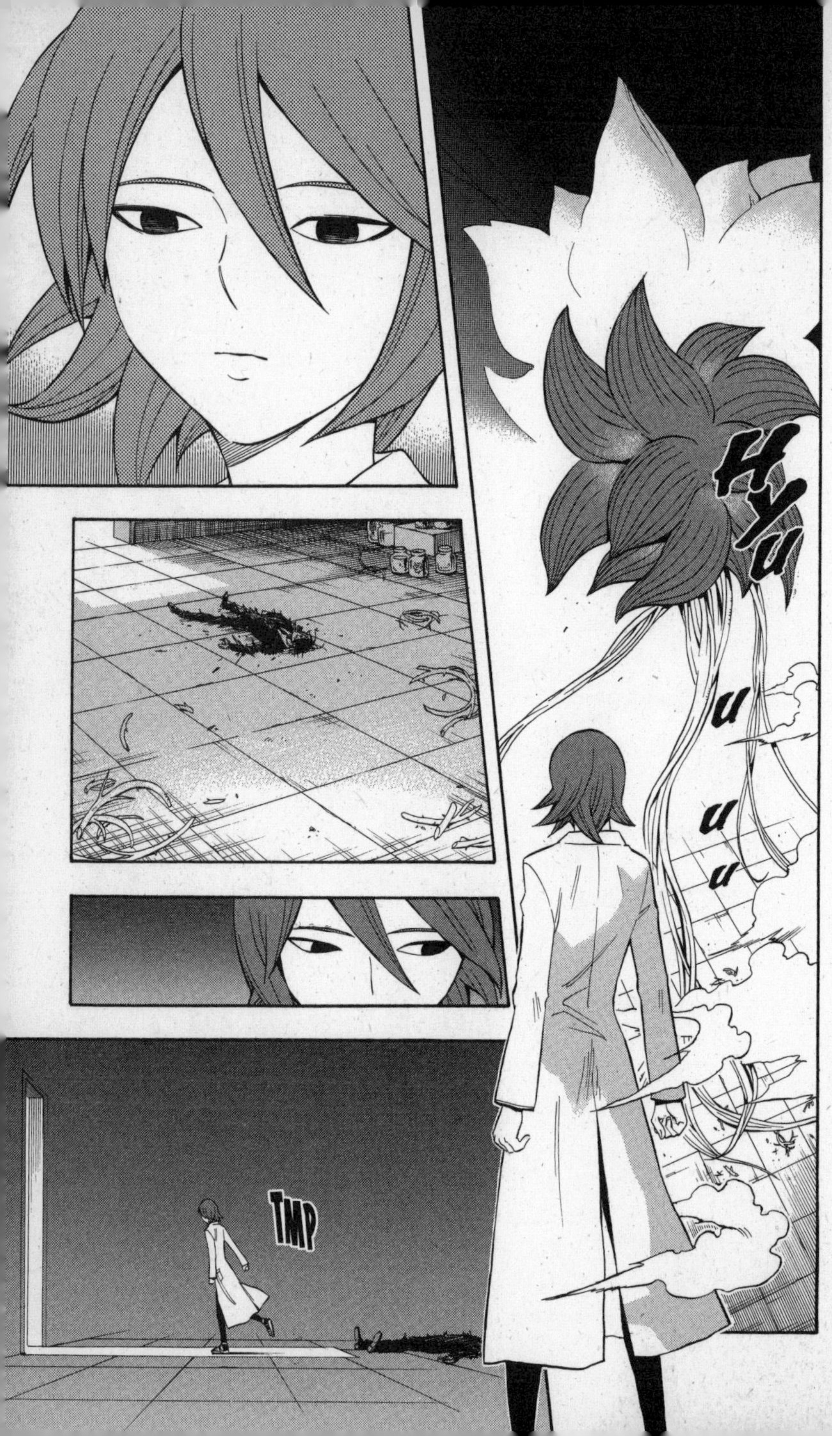
HYUUUUU
TMP

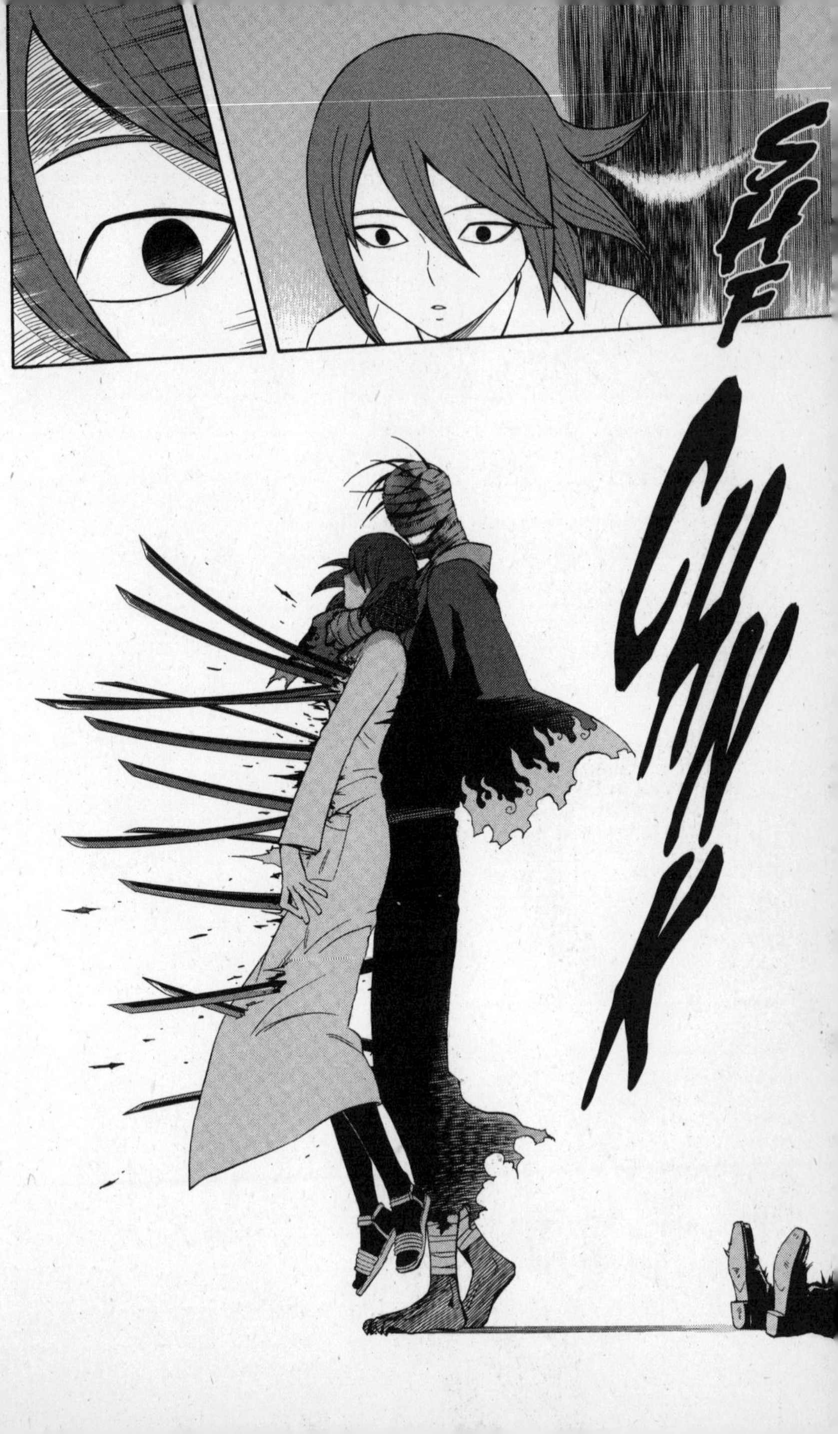
SHF
CHNK

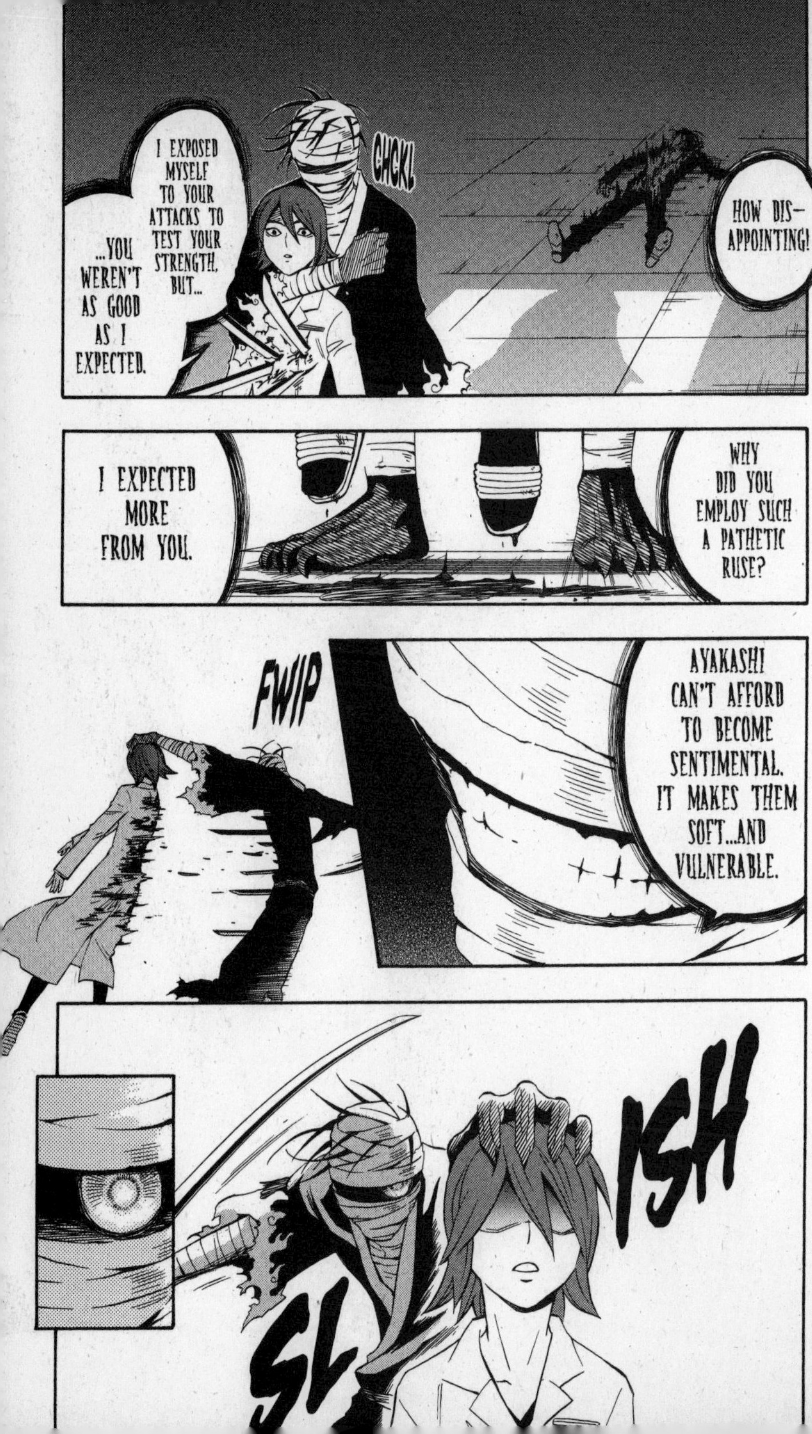
HOW DIS-APPOINTING!
CHCKL
I EXPOSED MYSELF TO YOUR ATTACKS TO TEST YOUR STRENGTH, BUT...
...YOU WEREN'T AS GOOD AS I EXPECTED.
WHY DID YOU EMPLOY SUCH A PATHETIC RUSE?
I EXPECTED MORE FROM YOU.
AYAKASHI CAN'T AFFORD TO BECOME SENTIMENTAL. IT MAKES THEM SOFT...AND VULNERABLE.
FWIP
SLISH

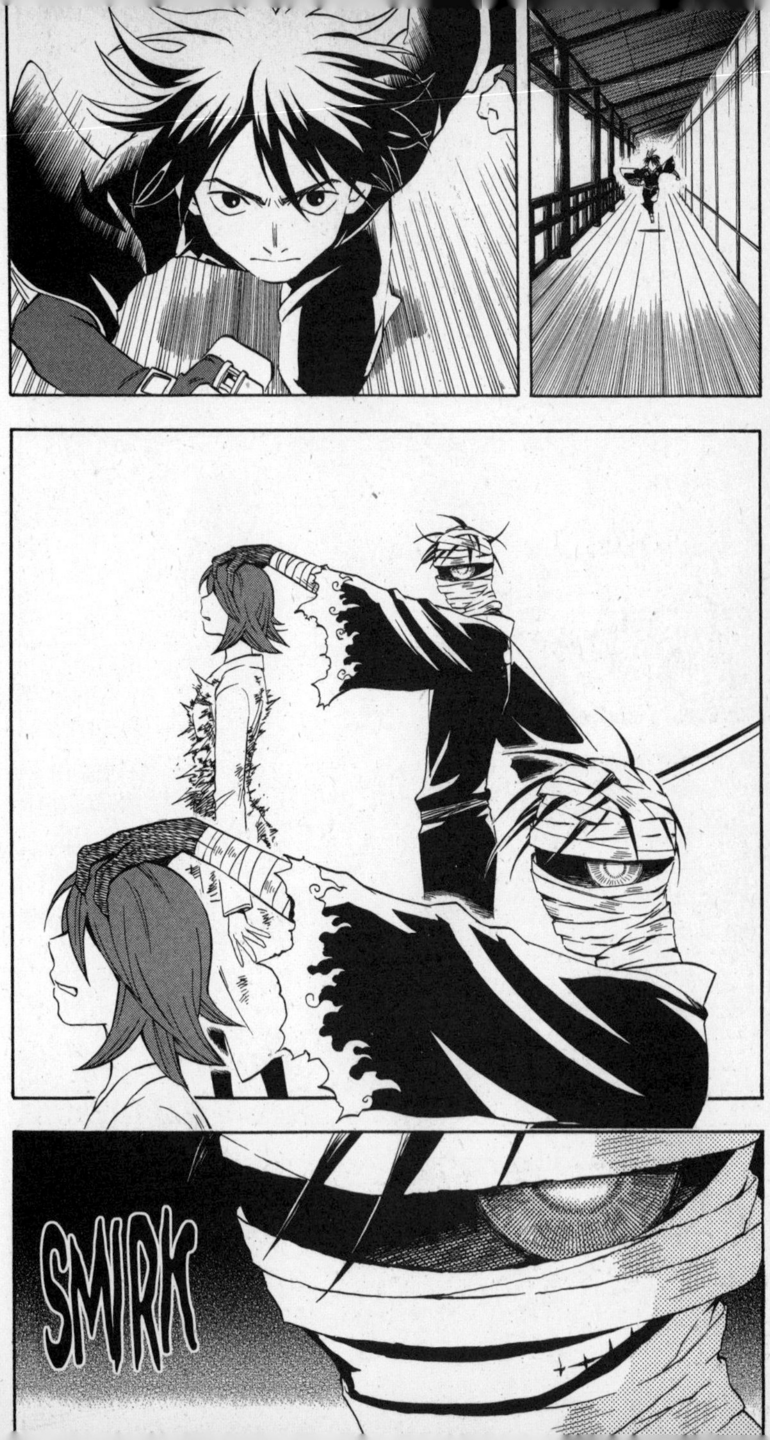
SMIRK

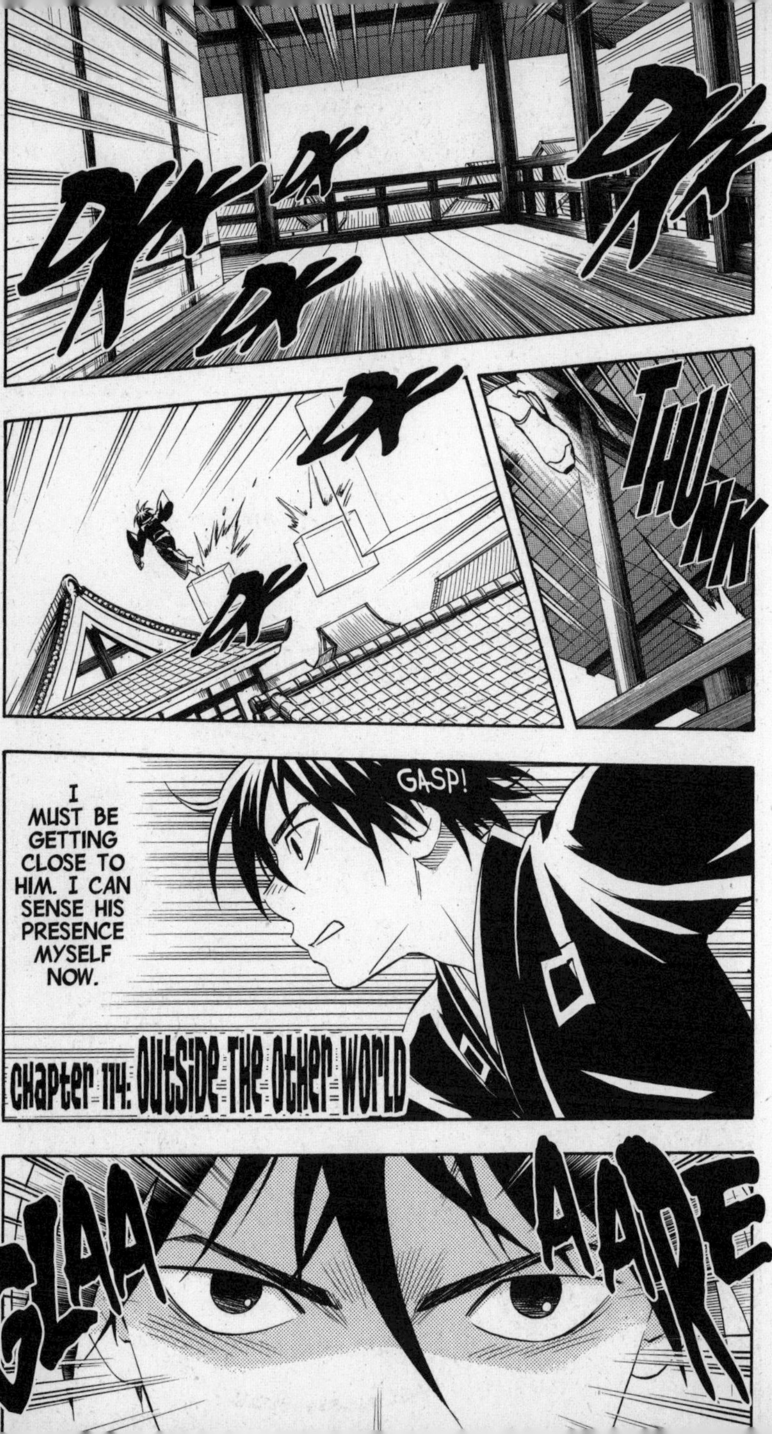
DOK
DOK
DOK
DOK
THUNK
DOK
DOK
GASP!
I MUST BE GETTING CLOSE TO HIM. I CAN SENSE HIS PRESENCE MYSELF NOW.
Chapter 114: Outside the Other World
GLAAAARE

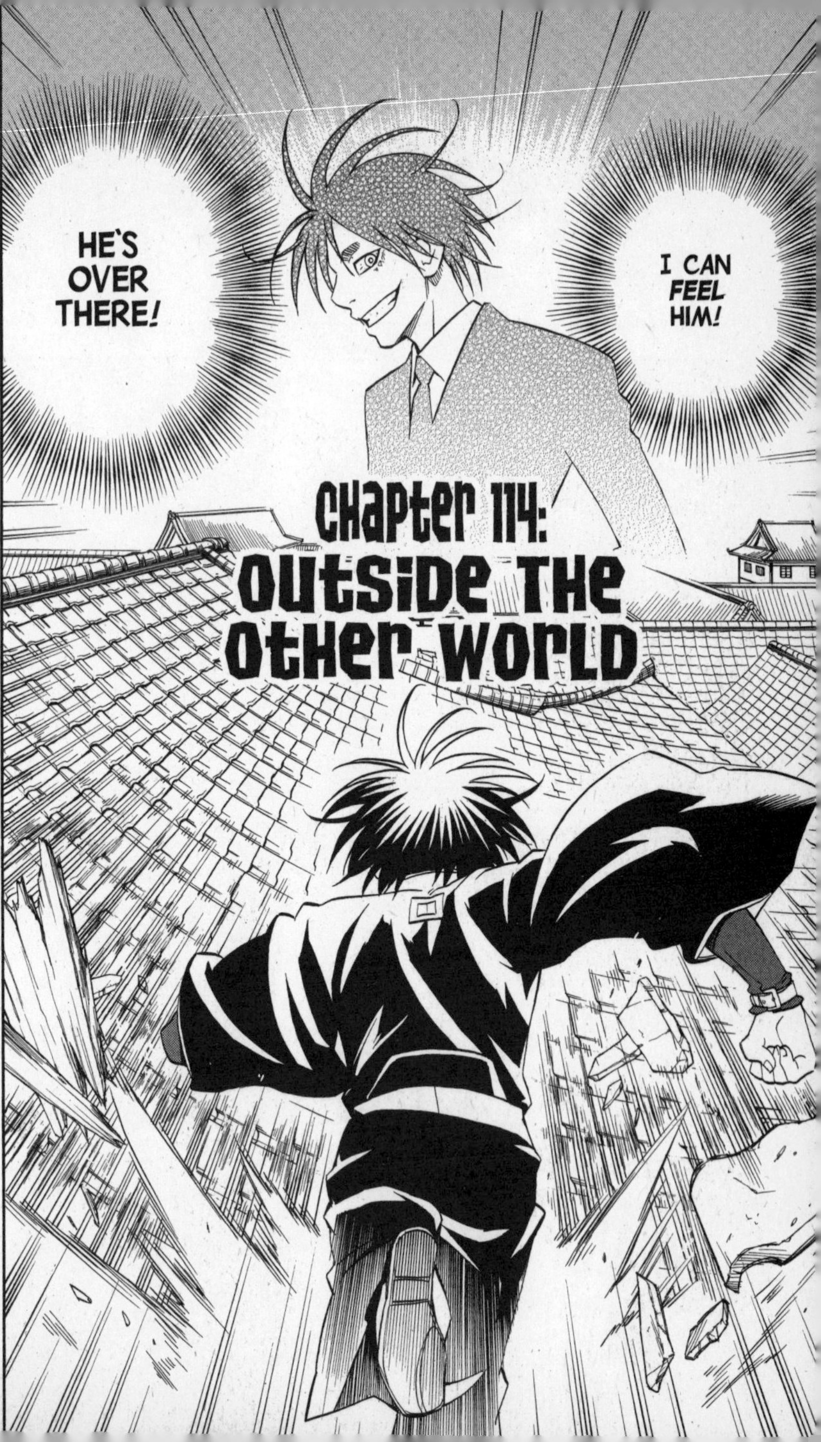
I CAN FEEL HIM!
HE'S OVER THERE!
CHAPTER 114: OUTSIDE THE OTHER WORLD

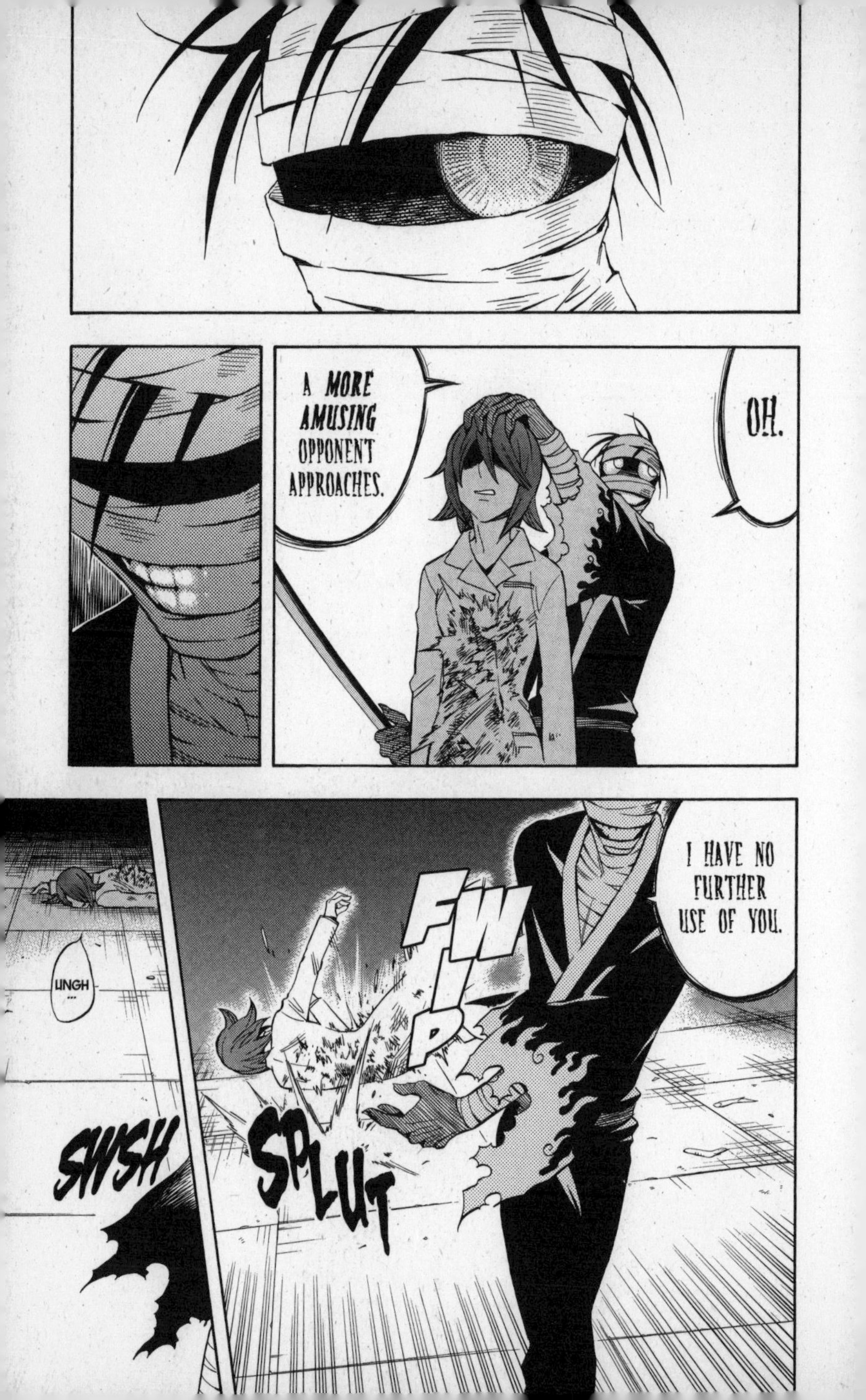
OH.
A MORE AMUSING OPPONENT APPROACHES.
I HAVE NO FURTHER USE OF YOU.
FWIP
SPLUT
UNGH...
SWSH

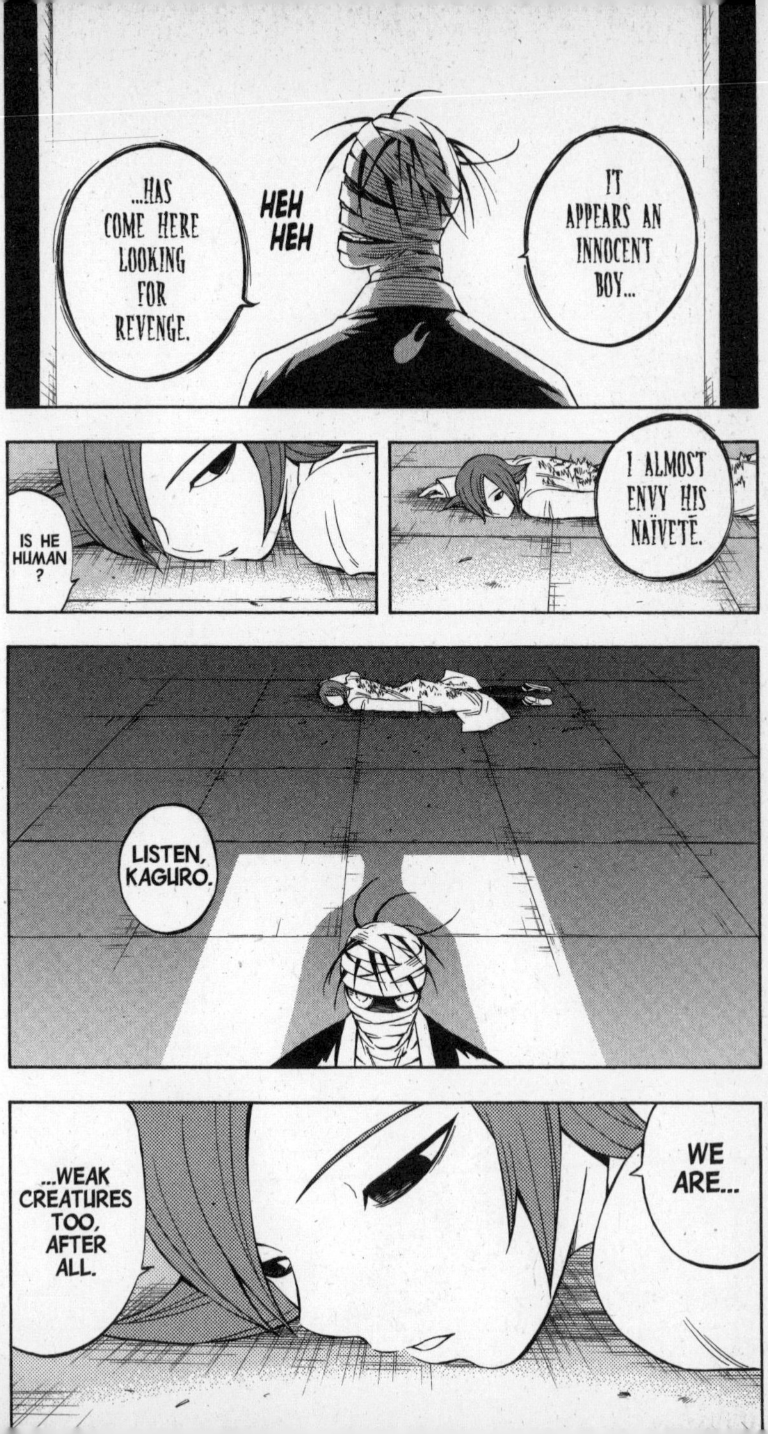
IT APPEARS AN INNOCENT BOY...
HEH HEH
...HAS COME HERE LOOKING FOR REVENGE.
I ALMOST ENVY HIS NAÏVETÉ.
IS HE HUMAN?
LISTEN, KAGURO.
WE ARE...
...WEAK CREATURES TOO, AFTER ALL.

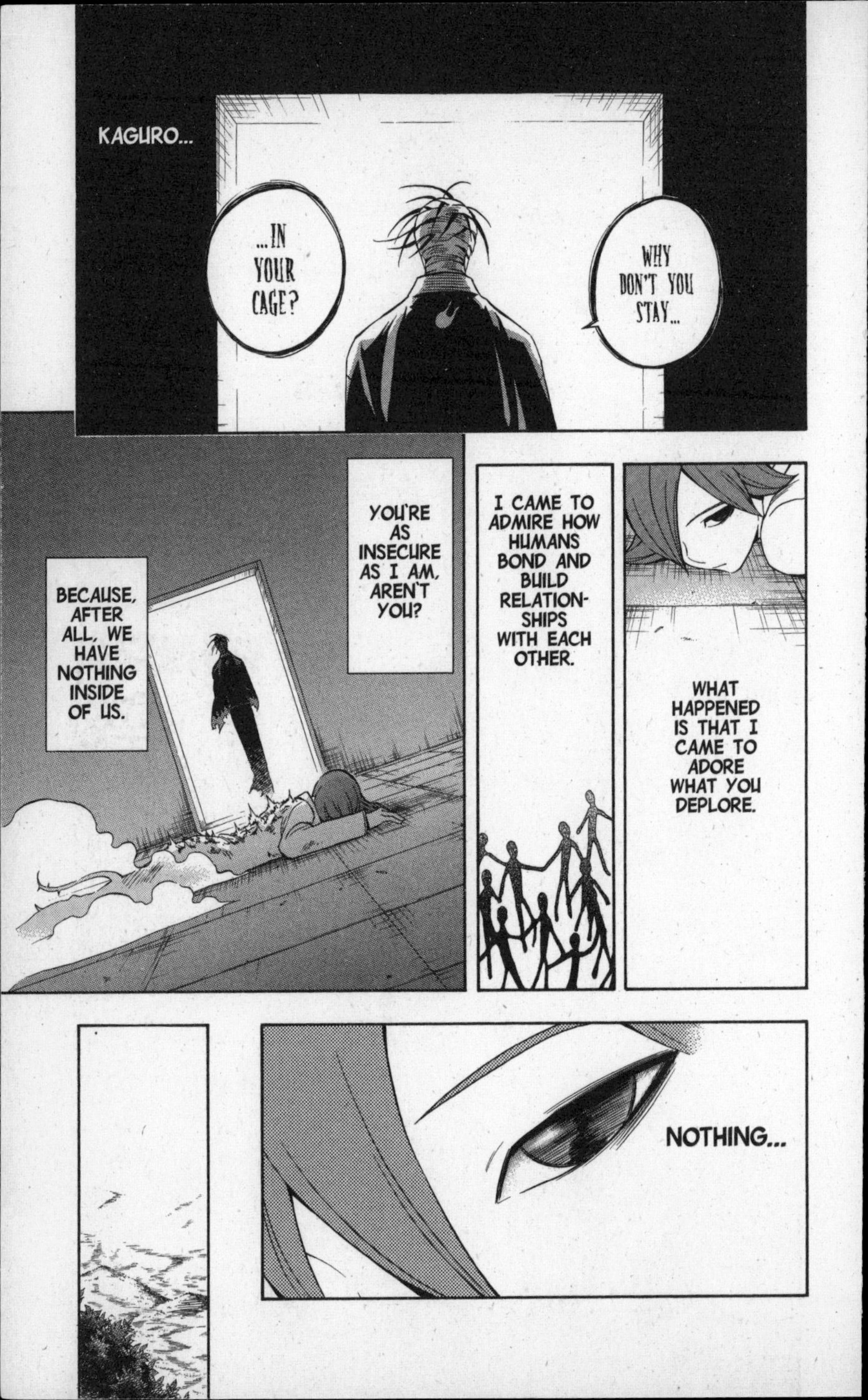
KAGURO...
WHY DON'T YOU STAY...
...IN YOUR CAGE?
WHAT HAPPENED IS THAT I CAME TO ADORE WHAT YOU DEPLORE.
I CAME TO ADMIRE HOW HUMANS BOND AND BUILD RELATION-SHIPS WITH EACH OTHER.
YOU'RE AS INSECURE AS I AM, AREN'T YOU?
BECAUSE, AFTER ALL, WE HAVE NOTHING INSIDE OF US.
NOTHING...

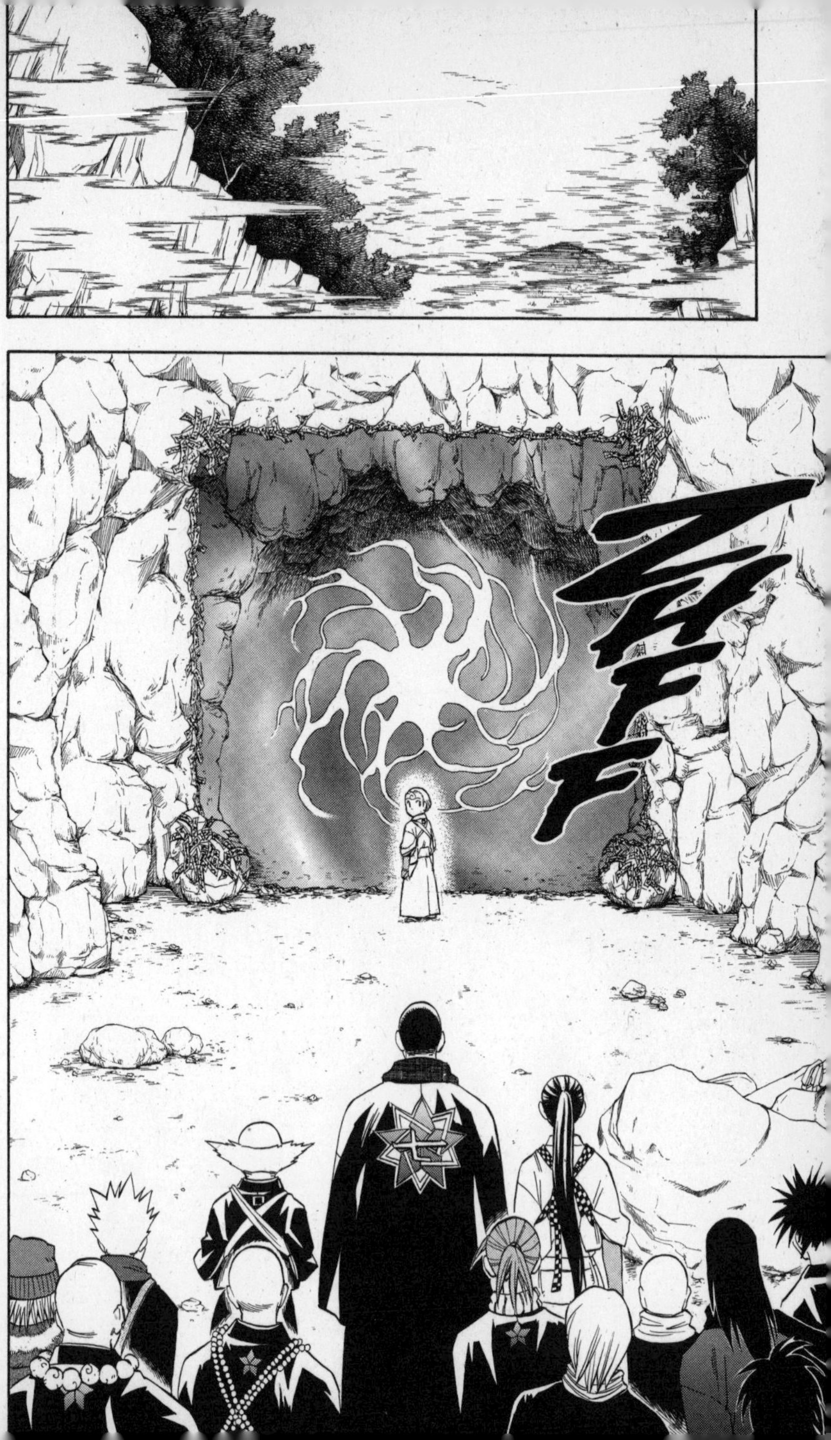

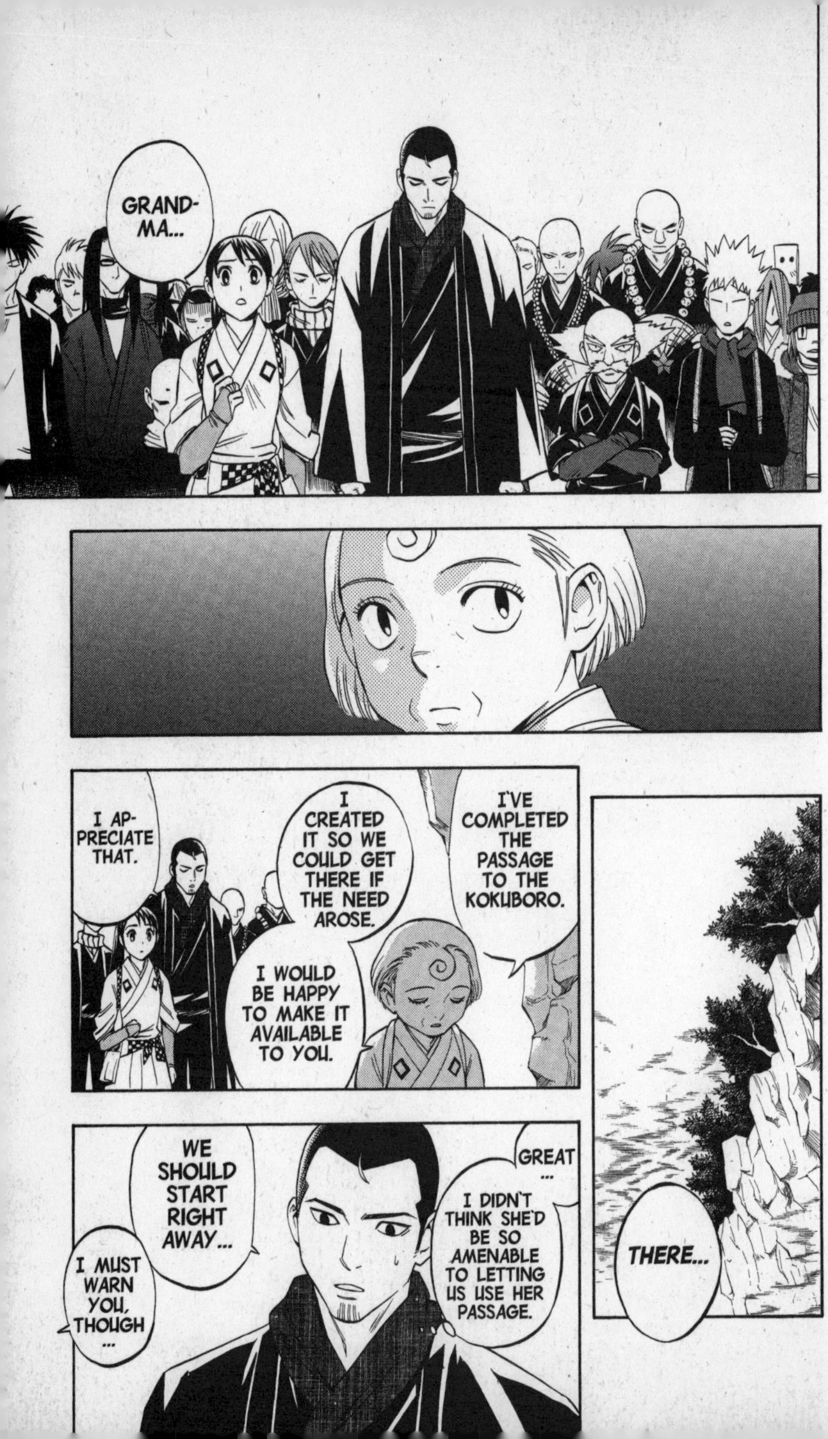
GRAND-MA...
THERE...
I'VE COMPLETED THE PASSAGE TO THE KOKUBORO.
I CREATED IT SO WE COULD GET THERE IF THE NEED AROSE.
I WOULD BE HAPPY TO MAKE IT AVAILABLE TO YOU.
I APPRECIATE THAT.
GREAT...
I DIDN'T THINK SHE'D BE SO AMENABLE TO LETTING US USE HER PASSAGE.
WE SHOULD START RIGHT AWAY...
I MUST WARN YOU, THOUGH...

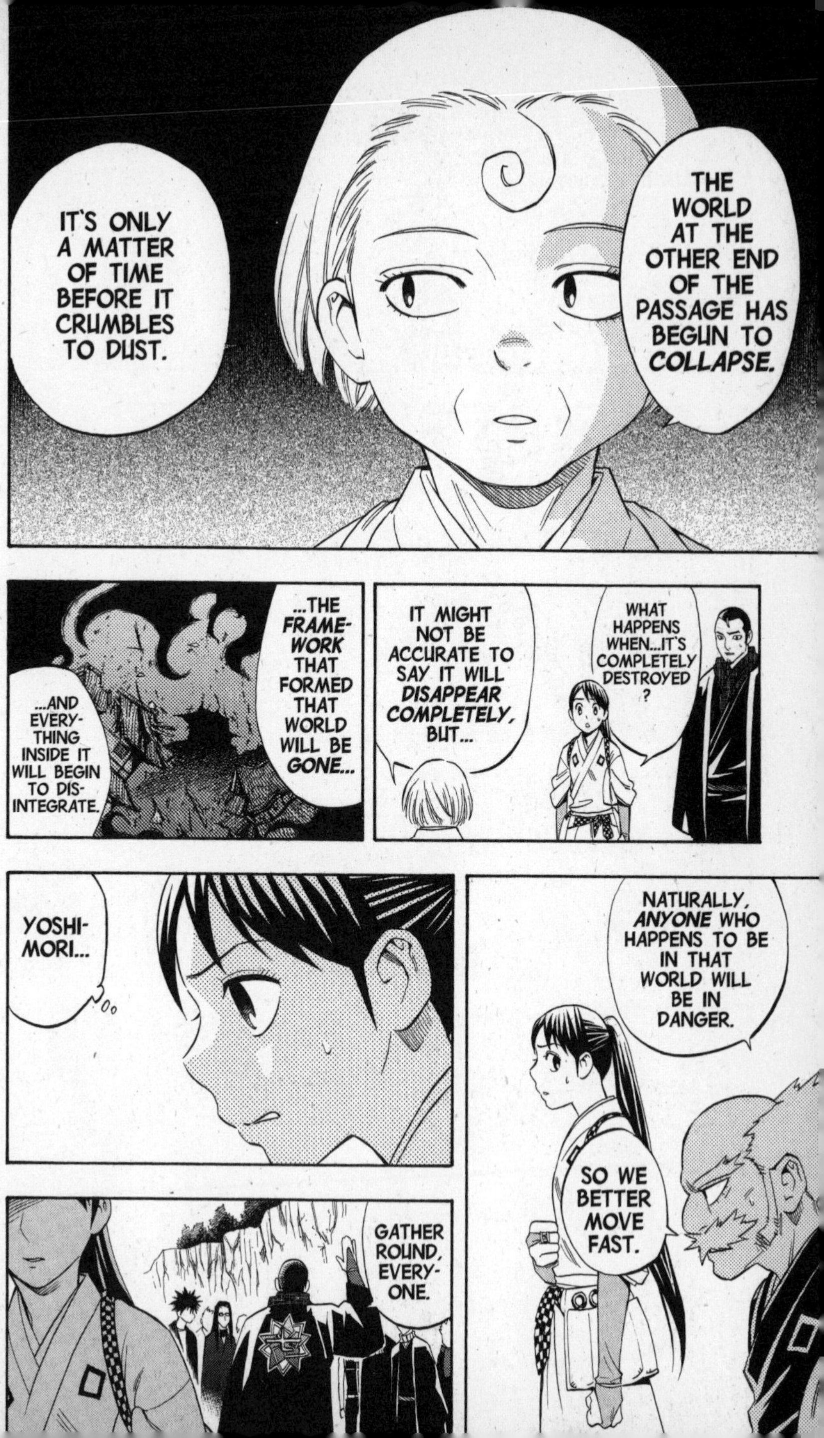
THE WORLD AT THE OTHER END OF THE PASSAGE HAS BEGUN TO *COLLAPSE.*
IT'S ONLY A MATTER OF TIME BEFORE IT CRUMBLES TO DUST.
WHAT HAPPENS WHEN...IT'S COMPLETELY DESTROYED?
IT MIGHT NOT BE ACCURATE TO SAY IT WILL *DISAPPEAR COMPLETELY,* BUT...
...THE *FRAMEWORK* THAT FORMED THAT WORLD WILL BE *GONE...*
...AND EVERYTHING INSIDE IT WILL BEGIN TO DISINTEGRATE.
NATURALLY, *ANYONE* WHO HAPPENS TO BE IN THAT WORLD WILL BE IN DANGER.
SO WE BETTER MOVE FAST.
YOSHIMORI...
GATHER ROUND, EVERYONE.

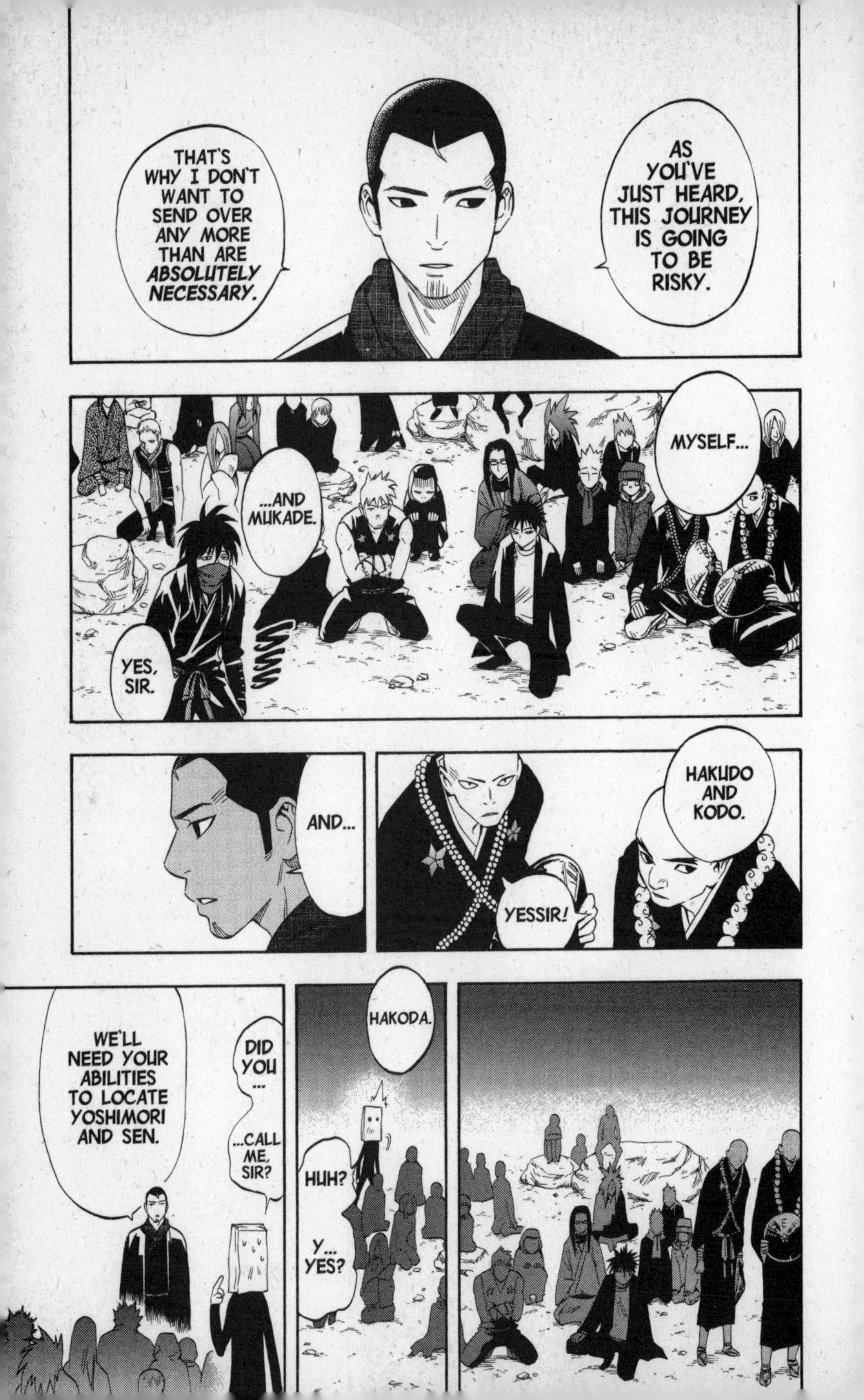
AS YOU'VE JUST HEARD, THIS JOURNEY IS GOING TO BE RISKY.
THAT'S WHY I DON'T WANT TO SEND OVER ANY MORE THAN ARE ABSOLUTELY NECESSARY.
MYSELF...
...AND MUKADE.
YES, SIR.
HAKUDO AND KODO.
YESSIR!
AND...
HAKODA.
HUH?
Y... YES?
DID YOU ...
...CALL ME, SIR?
WE'LL NEED YOUR ABILITIES TO LOCATE YOSHIMORI AND SEN.

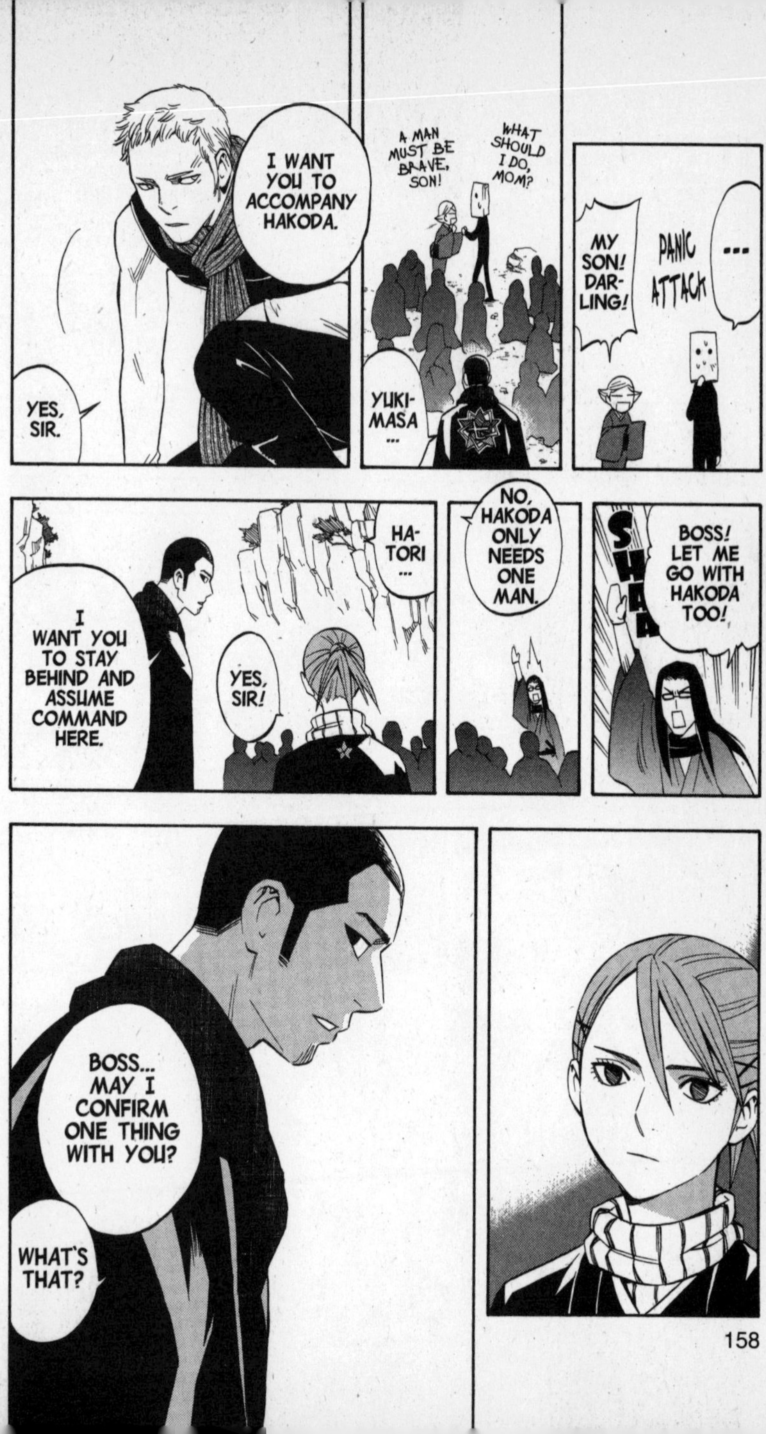
...
PANIC ATTACK
MY SON! DARLING!
WHAT SHOULD I DO, MOM?
A MAN MUST BE BRAVE, SON!
YUKI-MASA ...
I WANT YOU TO ACCOMPANY HAKODA.
YES, SIR.
SHAA
BOSS! LET ME GO WITH HAKODA TOO!
NO, HAKODA ONLY NEEDS ONE MAN.
HA-TORI ...
I WANT YOU TO STAY BEHIND AND ASSUME COMMAND HERE.
YES, SIR!
BOSS... MAY I CONFIRM ONE THING WITH YOU?
WHAT'S THAT?

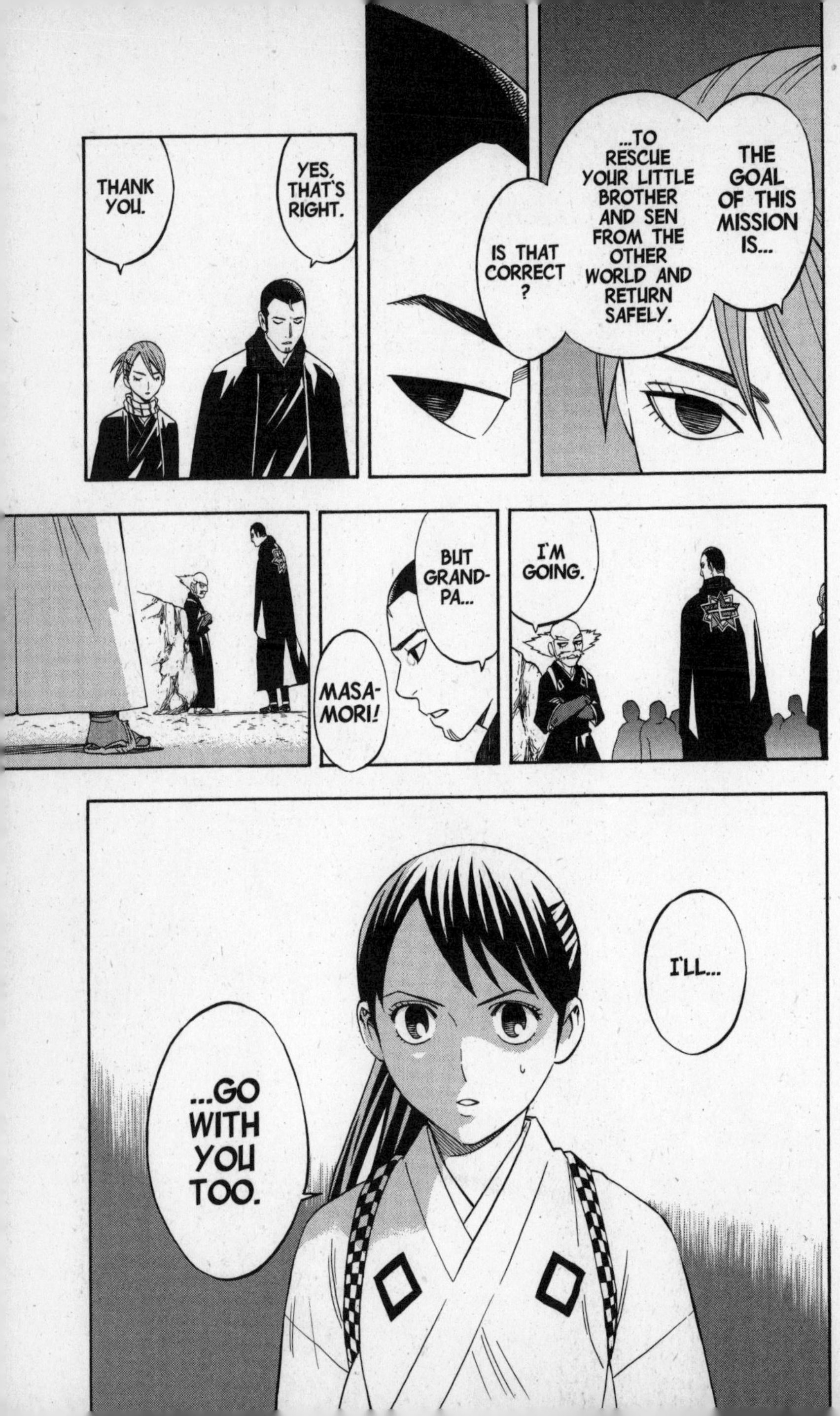
THE GOAL OF THIS MISSION IS...
...TO RESCUE YOUR LITTLE BROTHER AND SEN FROM THE OTHER WORLD AND RETURN SAFELY.
IS THAT CORRECT?
YES, THAT'S RIGHT.
THANK YOU.
I'M GOING.
BUT GRAND-PA...
MASA-MORI!
I'LL...
...GO WITH YOU TOO.

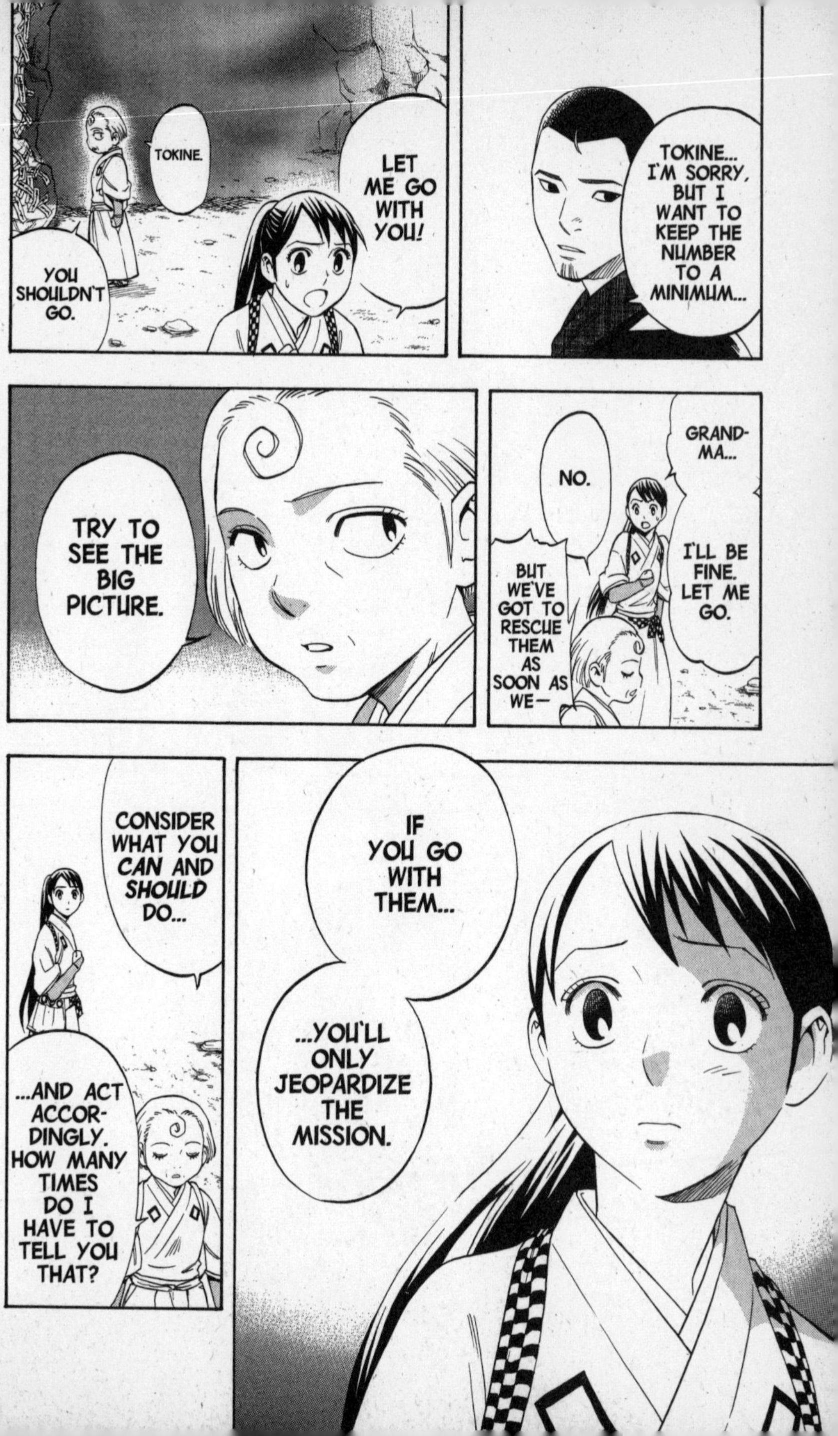
TOKINE... I'M SORRY, BUT I WANT TO KEEP THE NUMBER TO A MINIMUM...
LET ME GO WITH YOU!
TOKINE.
YOU SHOULDN'T GO.
GRAND-MA...
I'LL BE FINE. LET ME GO.
NO.
BUT WE'VE GOT TO RESCUE THEM AS SOON AS WE—
TRY TO SEE THE BIG PICTURE.
IF YOU GO WITH THEM...
...YOU'LL ONLY JEOPARDIZE THE MISSION.
CONSIDER WHAT YOU *CAN* AND *SHOULD* DO...
...AND ACT ACCORDINGLY. HOW MANY TIMES DO I HAVE TO TELL YOU THAT?

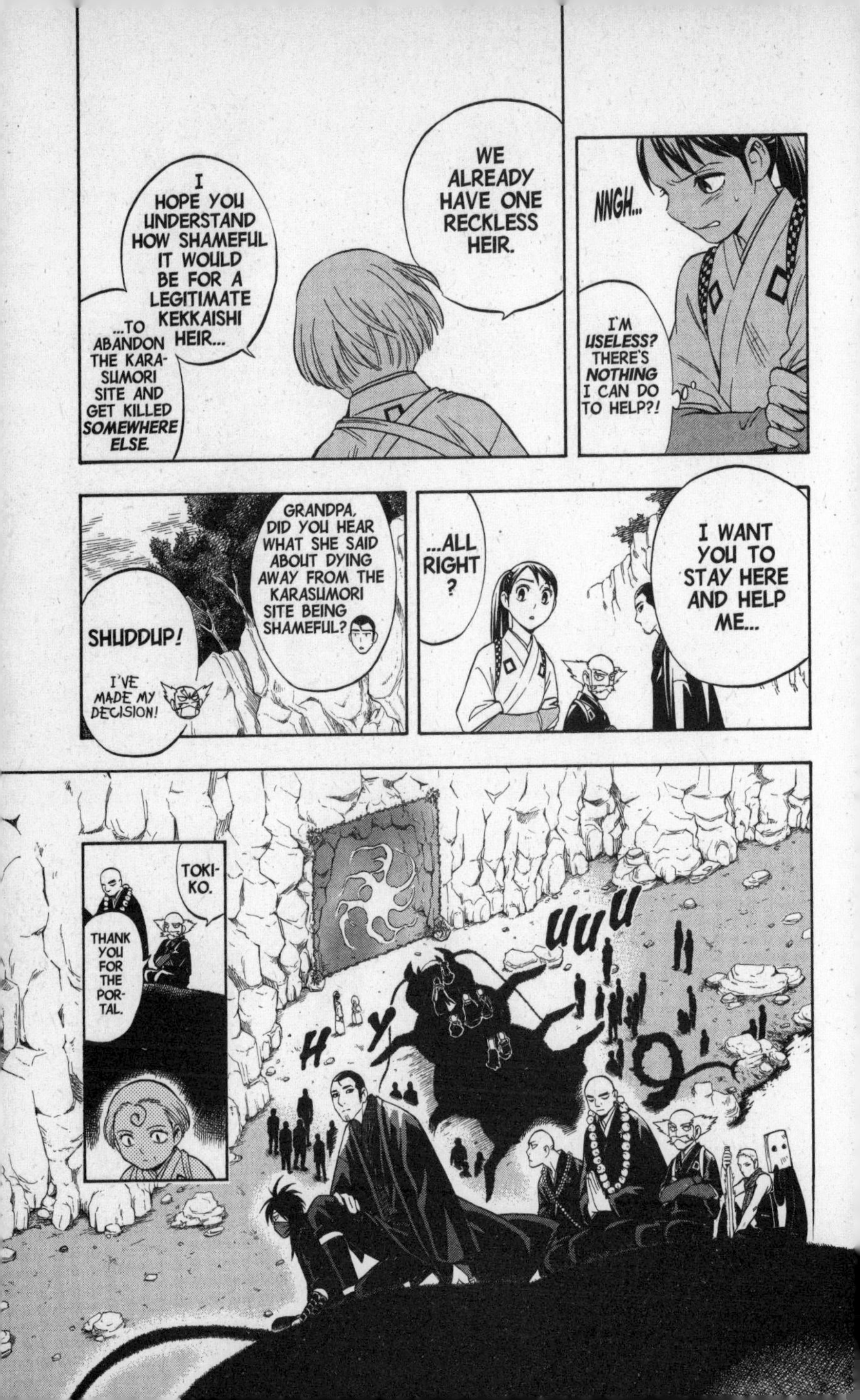
NNGH...
I'M USELESS? THERE'S NOTHING I CAN DO TO HELP?!
WE ALREADY HAVE ONE RECKLESS HEIR.
I HOPE YOU UNDERSTAND HOW SHAMEFUL IT WOULD BE FOR A LEGITIMATE KEKKAISHI HEIR...
...TO ABANDON THE KARA-SUMORI SITE AND GET KILLED SOMEWHERE ELSE.
I WANT YOU TO STAY HERE AND HELP ME...
...ALL RIGHT?
GRANDPA, DID YOU HEAR WHAT SHE SAID ABOUT DYING AWAY FROM THE KARASUMORI SITE BEING SHAMEFUL?
SHUDDUP!
I'VE MADE MY DECISION!
HYUUUU
TOKI-KO.
THANK YOU FOR THE POR-TAL.

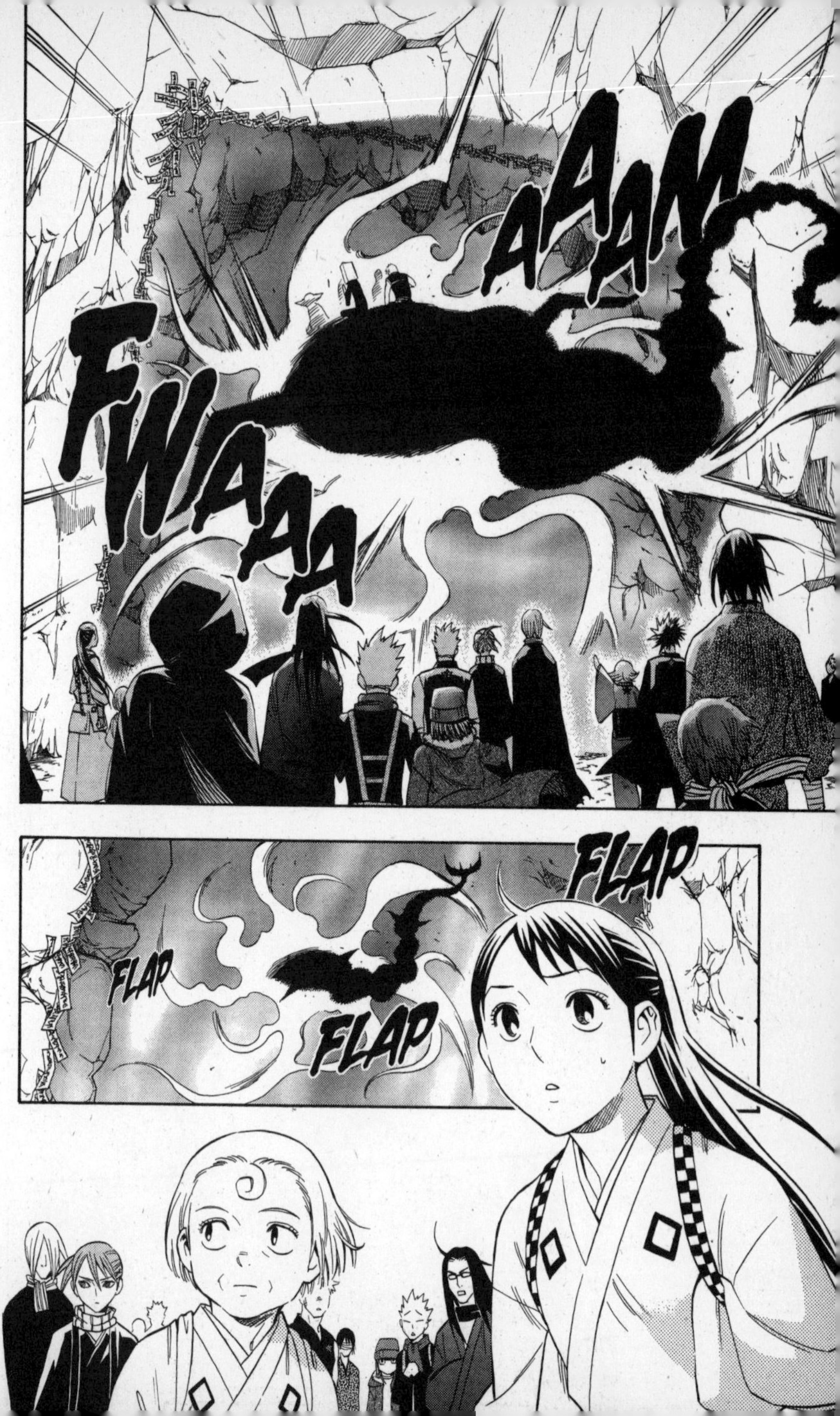
FWAAAA
AAAM
FLAP
FLAP
FLAP

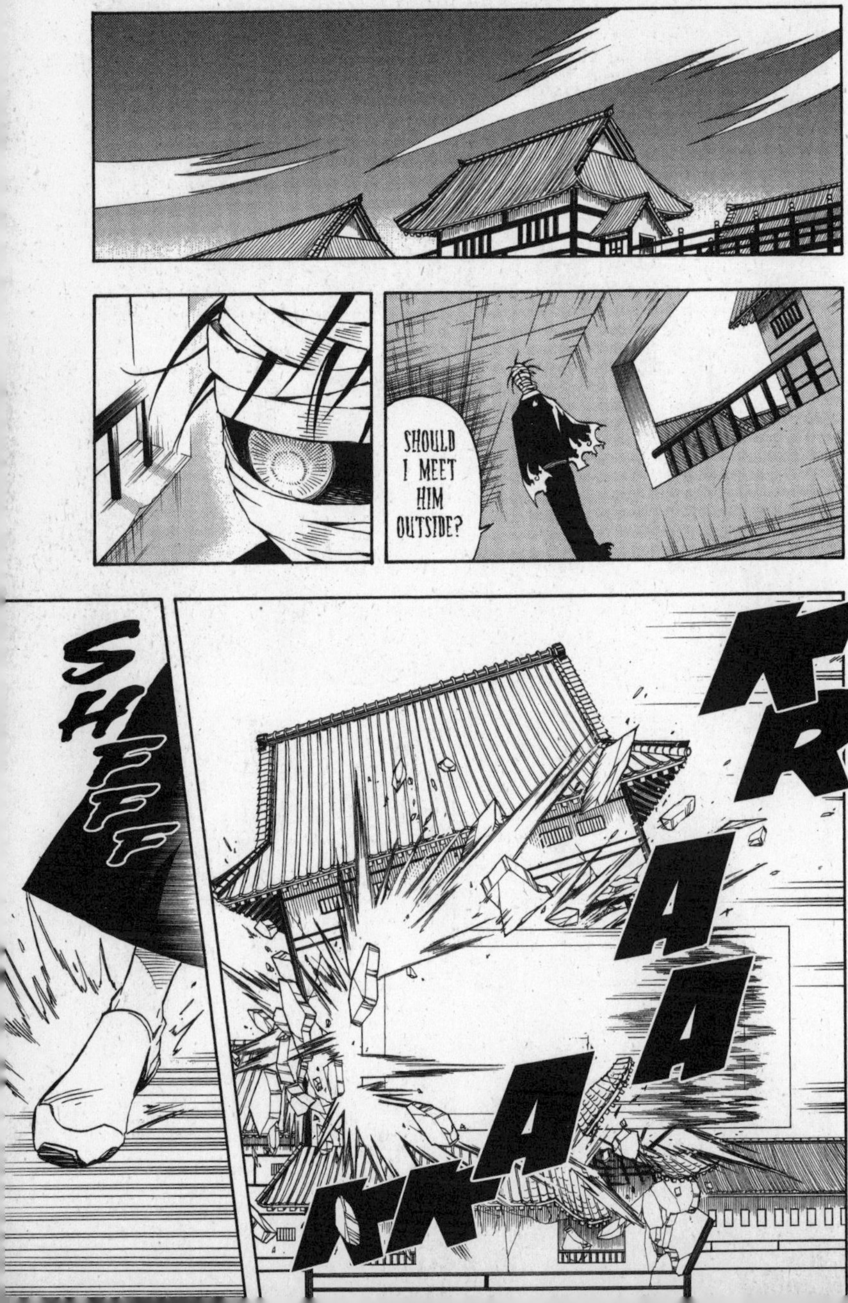
SHOULD I MEET HIM OUTSIDE?
KRAAAAKA
SHFFF

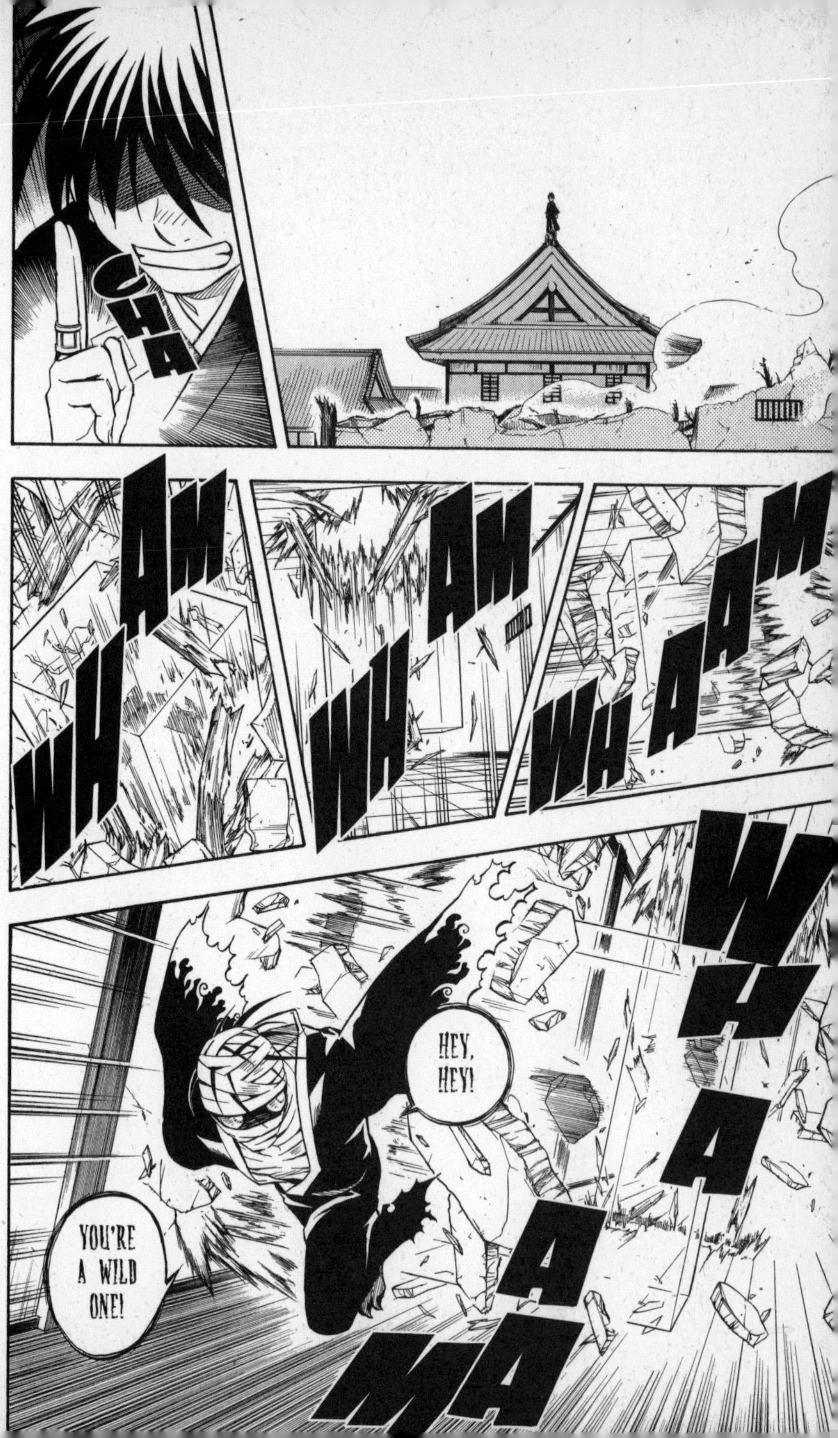
CHA
WHAAAM
WHAM
WHAM
WHAAA
HEY, HEY!
YOU'RE A WILD ONE!

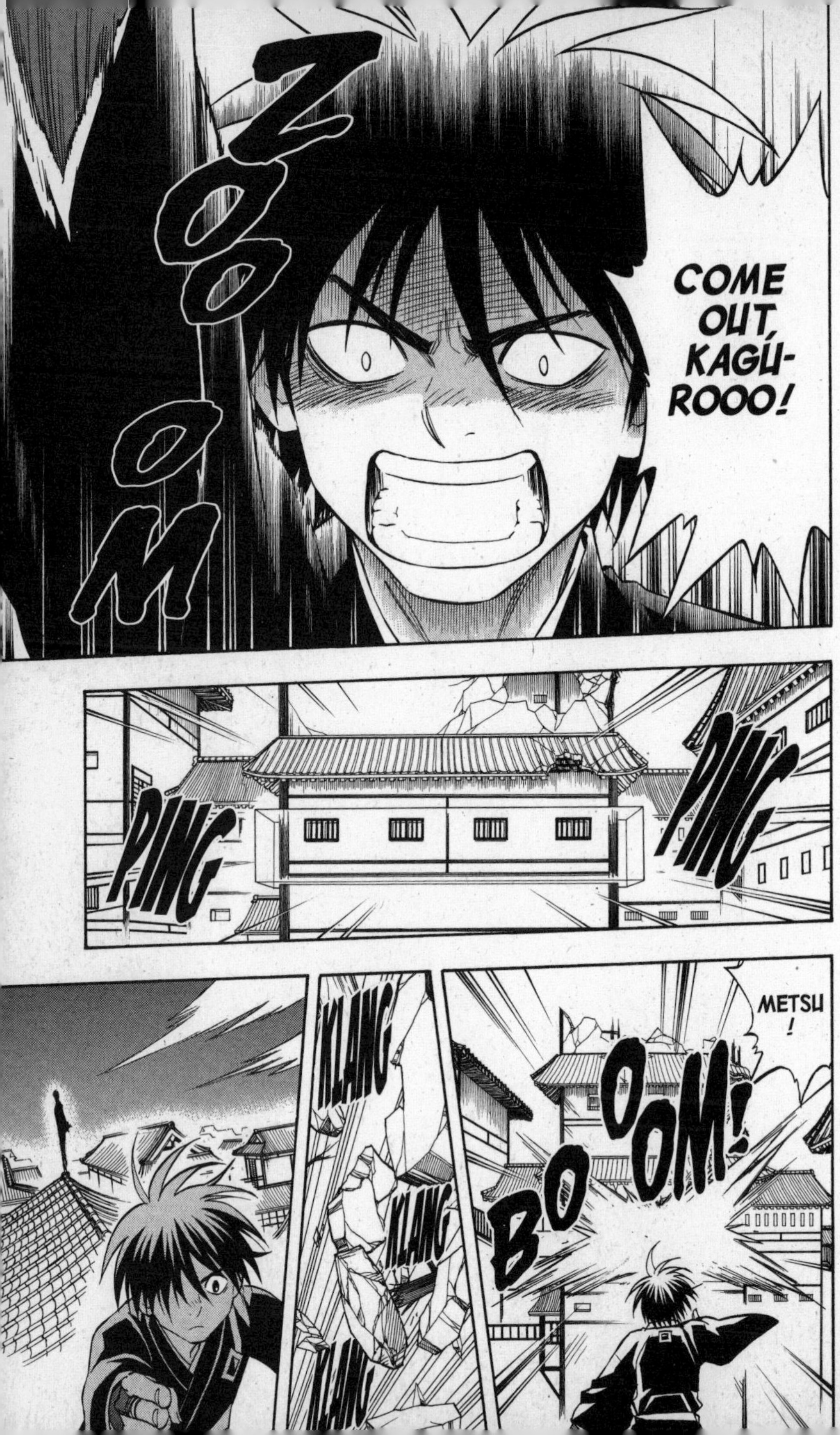
COME OUT, KAGÚ-ROOO!
ZOOOM
PING
PING
METSU!
BOOOM!
KLANG
KLANG
KLANG

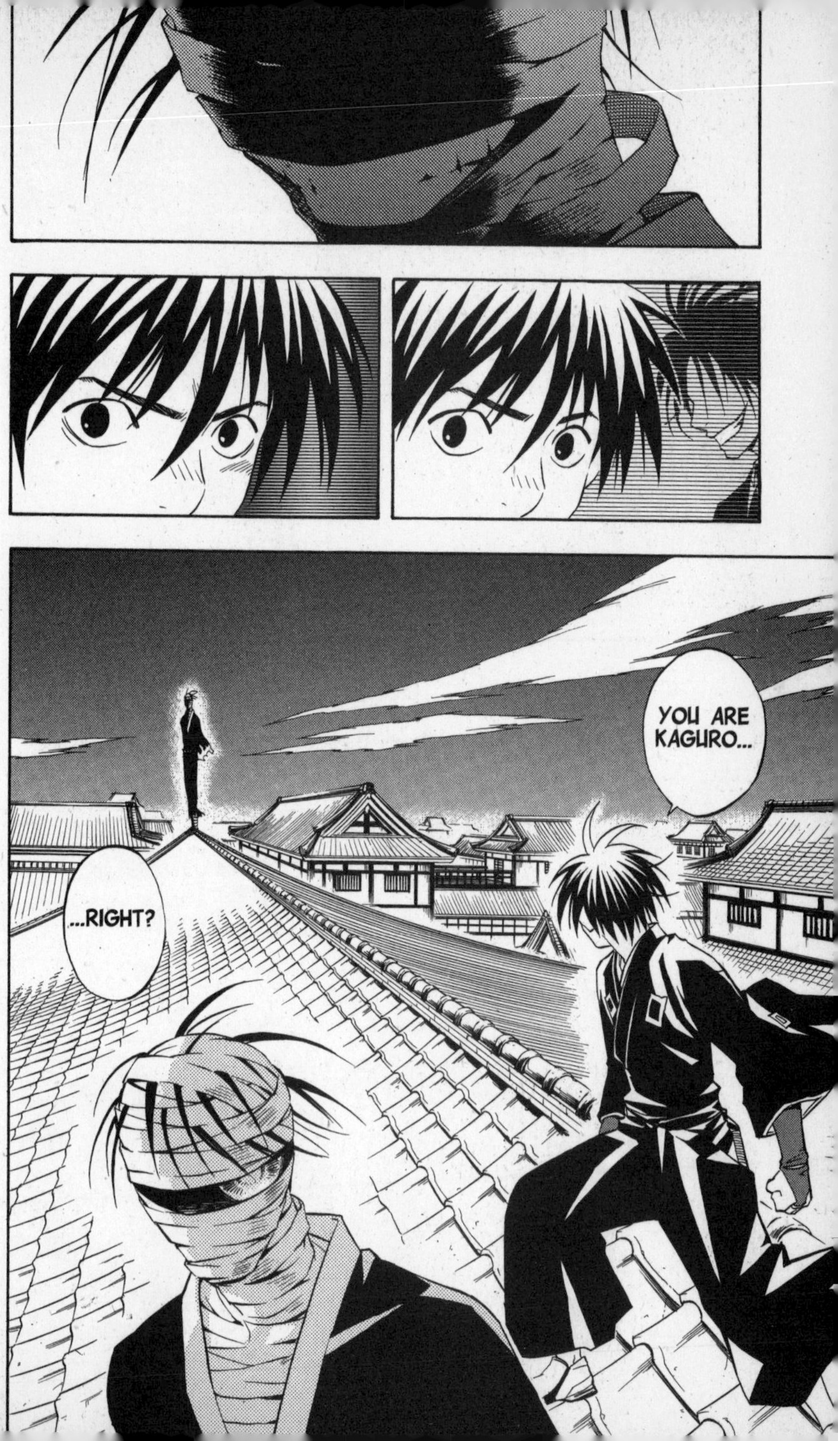
YOU ARE KAGURO...
...RIGHT?

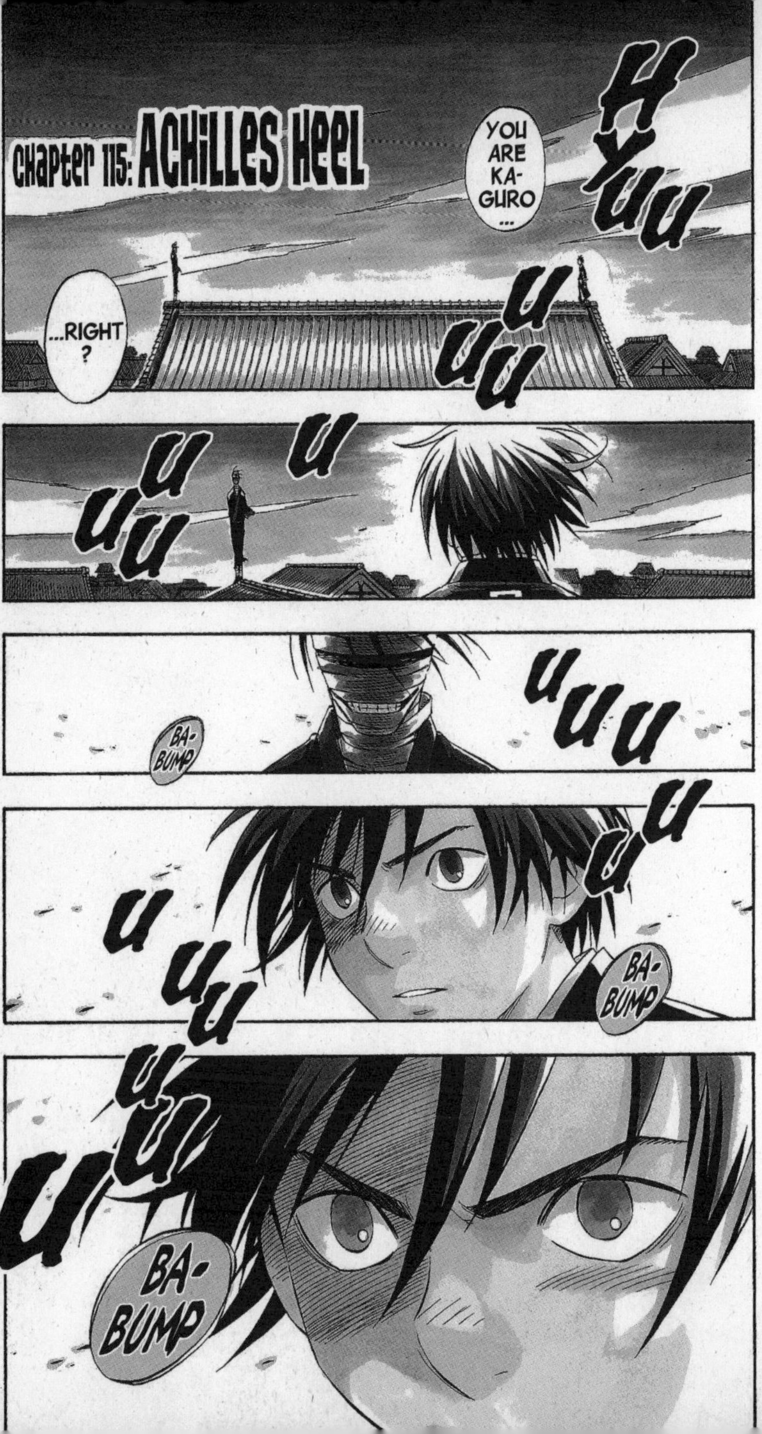
Chapter 115: Achilles Heel
YOU ARE KAGURO...
HYUUUUUUU
...RIGHT?
UUUUU
UUUUUU
BA-BUMP
UUUUUUUU
BA-BUMP
UUUUUU
BA-BUMP

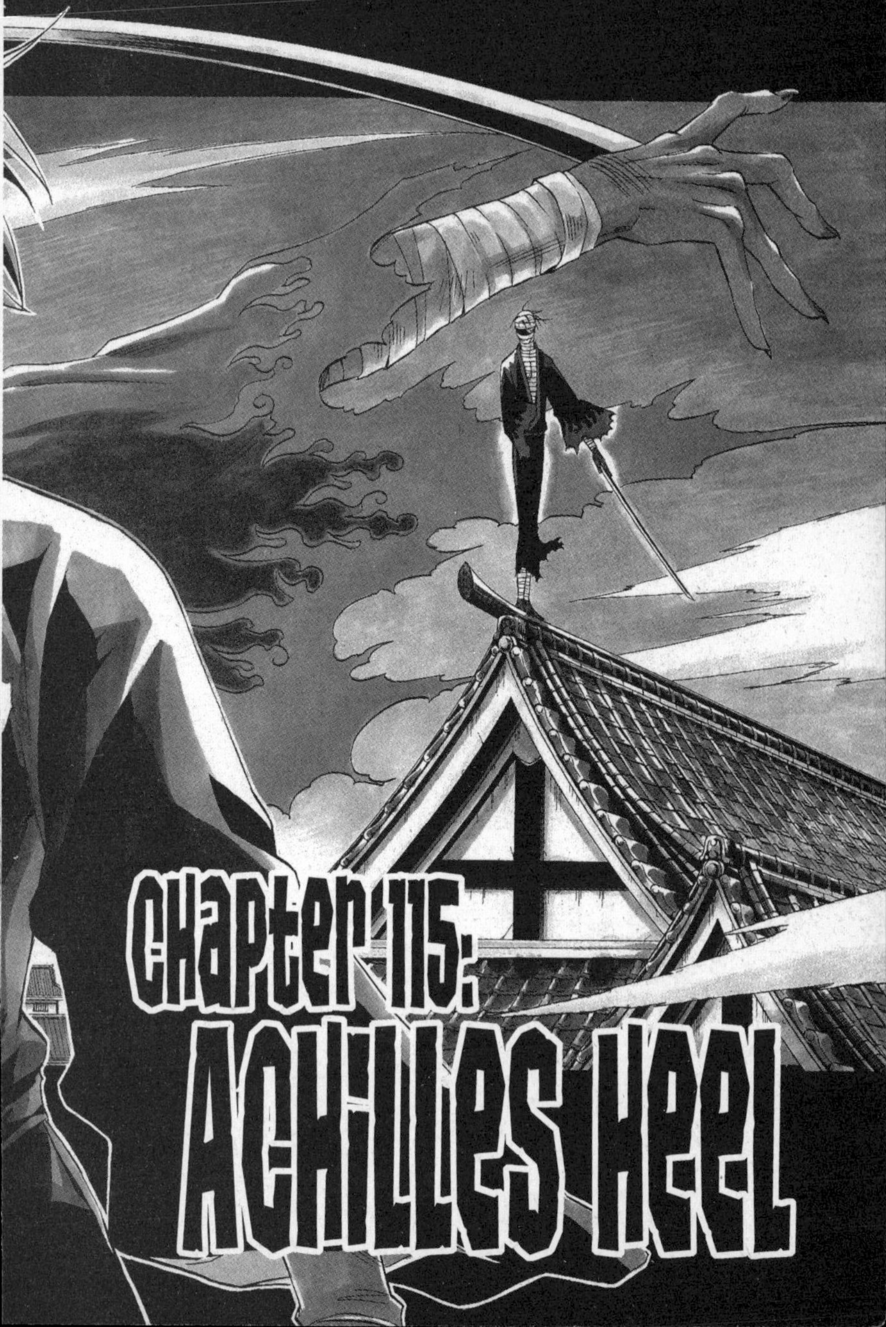
CHAPTER 115:
ACHILLES HEEL

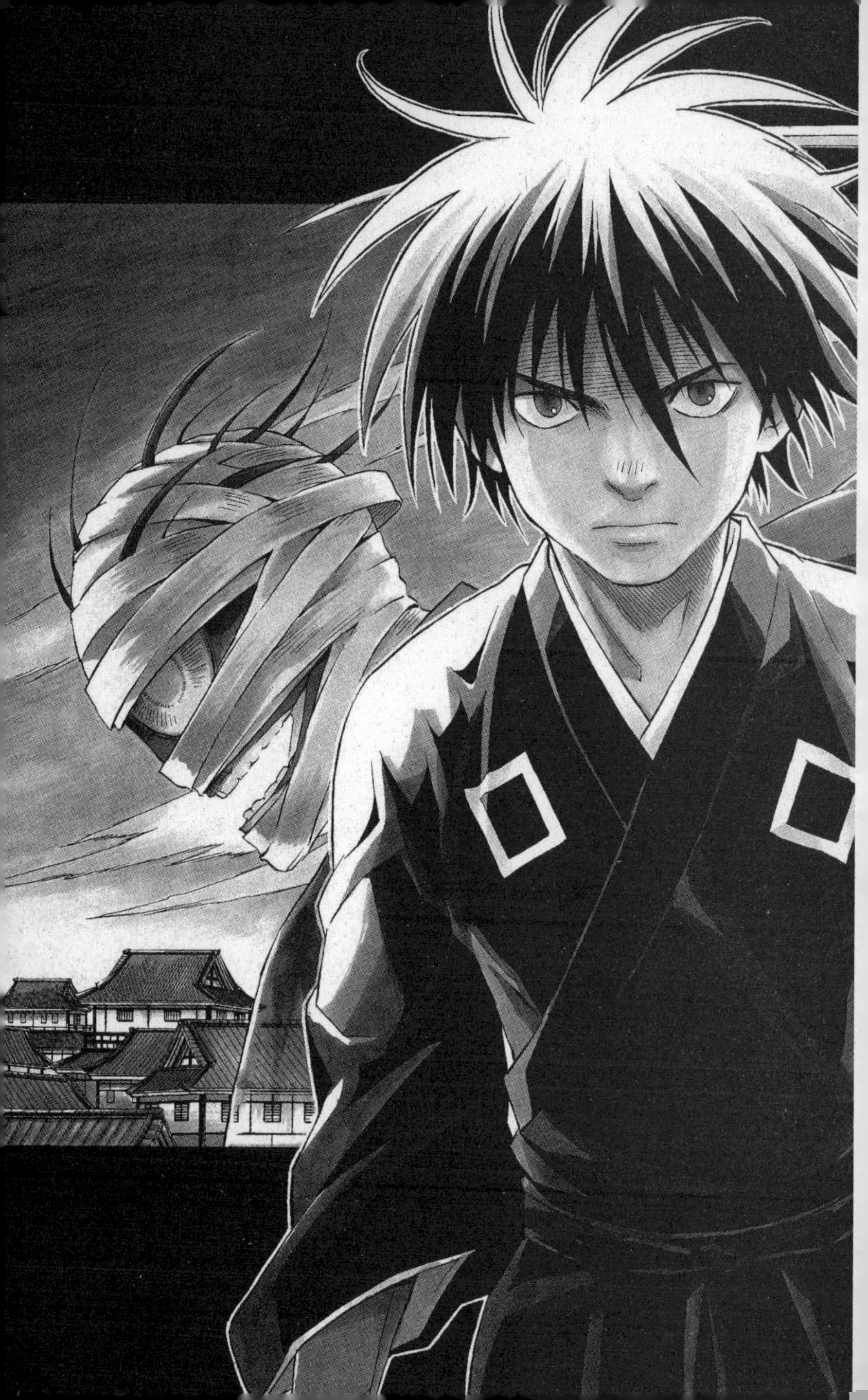

結界師
KEKKAISHI

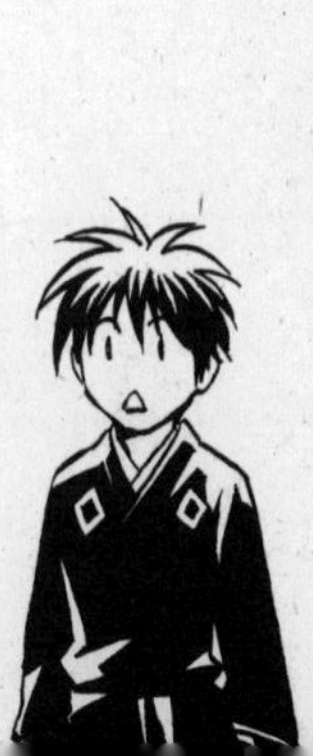

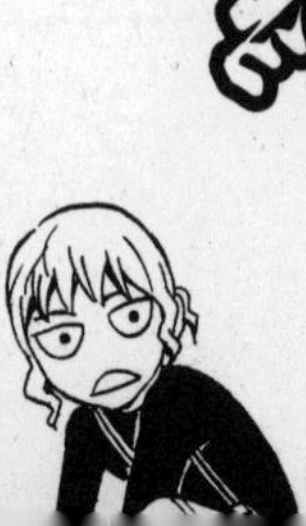

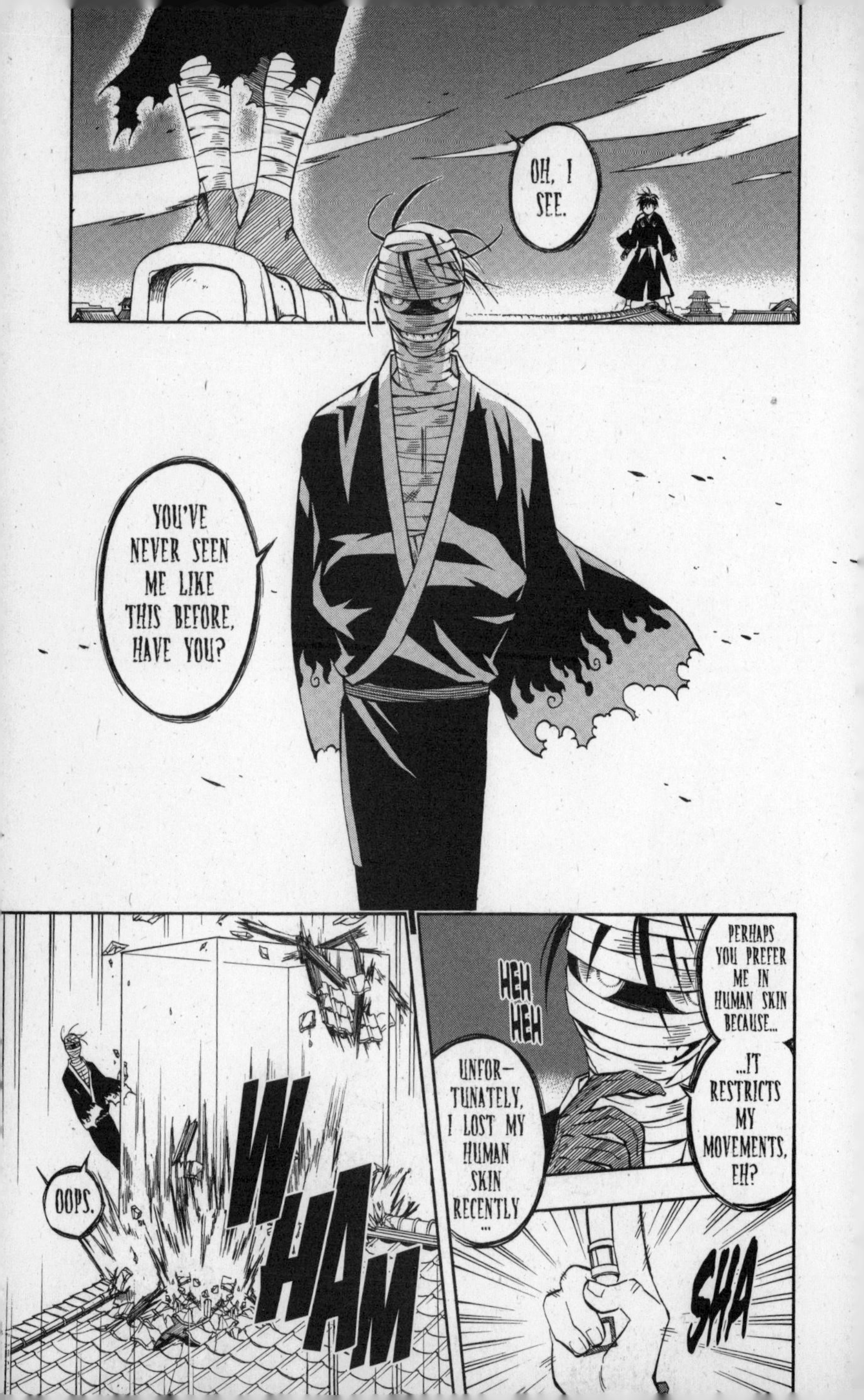
OH, I SEE.
YOU'VE NEVER SEEN ME LIKE THIS BEFORE, HAVE YOU?
PERHAPS YOU PREFER ME IN HUMAN SKIN BECAUSE...
...IT RESTRICTS MY MOVEMENTS, EH?
HEH HEH
UNFOR-TUNATELY, I LOST MY HUMAN SKIN RECENTLY...
SHA
WHAM
OOPS.

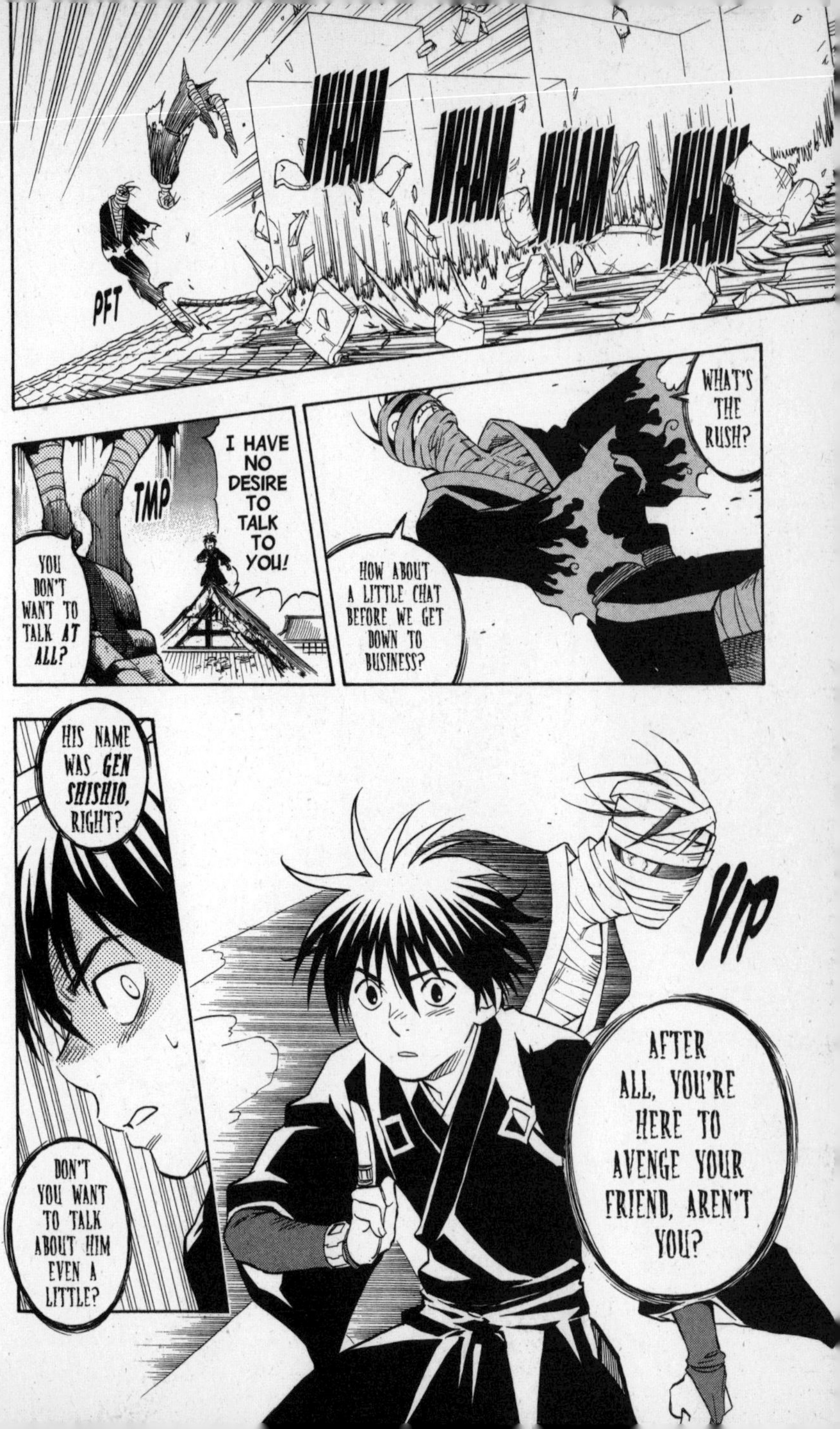
WHAM
WHAM
WHAM
WHAM
PFT
WHAT'S THE RUSH?
HOW ABOUT A LITTLE CHAT BEFORE WE GET DOWN TO BUSINESS?
I HAVE NO DESIRE TO TALK TO YOU!
TMP
YOU DON'T WANT TO TALK AT ALL?
VIP
AFTER ALL, YOU'RE HERE TO AVENGE YOUR FRIEND, AREN'T YOU?
HIS NAME WAS GEN SHISHIO, RIGHT?
DON'T YOU WANT TO TALK ABOUT HIM EVEN A LITTLE?

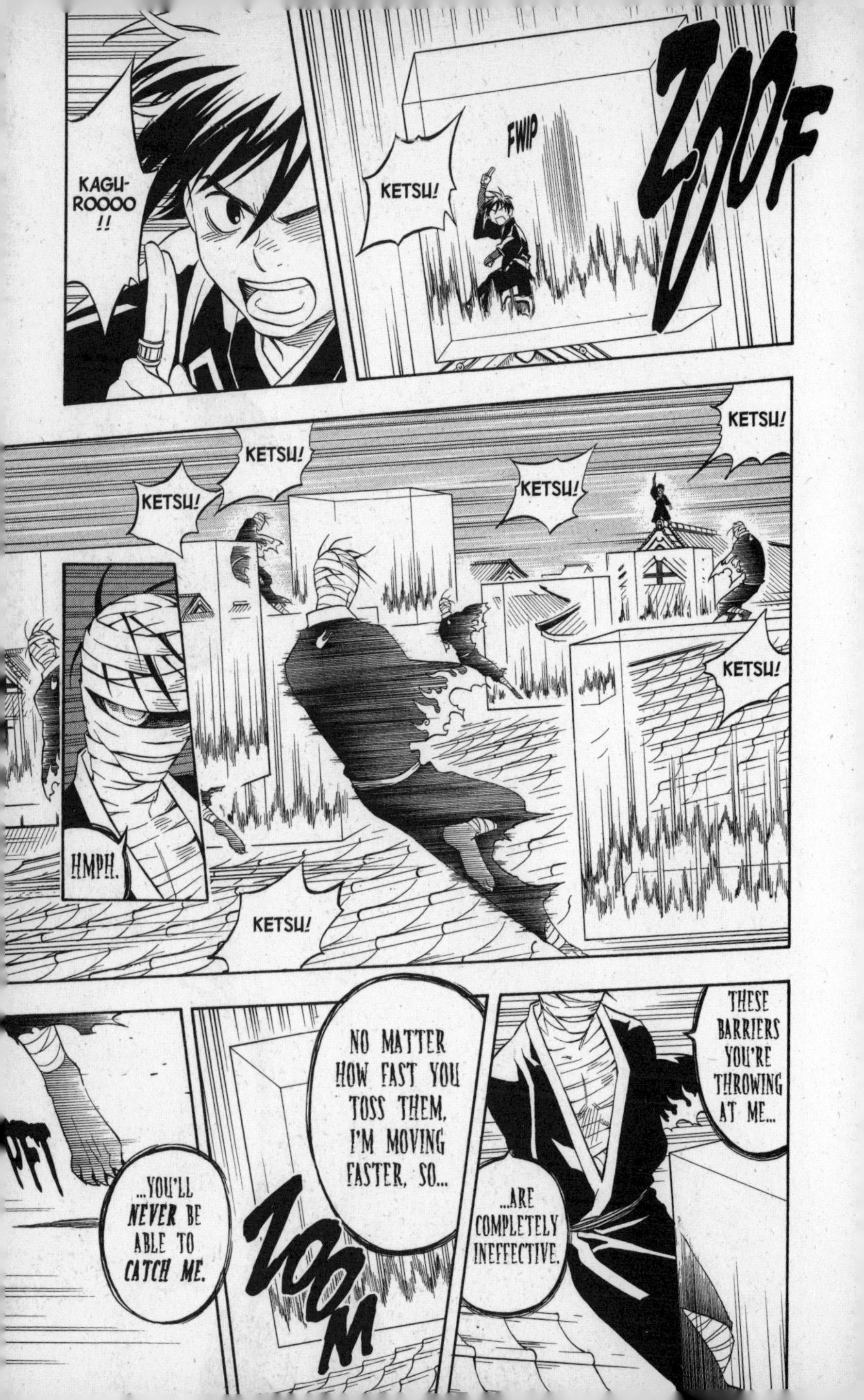
KETSU!
FWIP
ZZOF
KAGU-ROOOO!!
KETSU!
KETSU!
KETSU!
KETSU!
KETSU!
HMPH.
KETSU!
THESE BARRIERS YOU'RE THROWING AT ME...
...ARE COMPLETELY INEFFECTIVE.
NO MATTER HOW FAST YOU TOSS THEM, I'M MOVING FASTER, SO...
ZOOM
...YOU'LL *NEVER* BE ABLE TO *CATCH ME.*

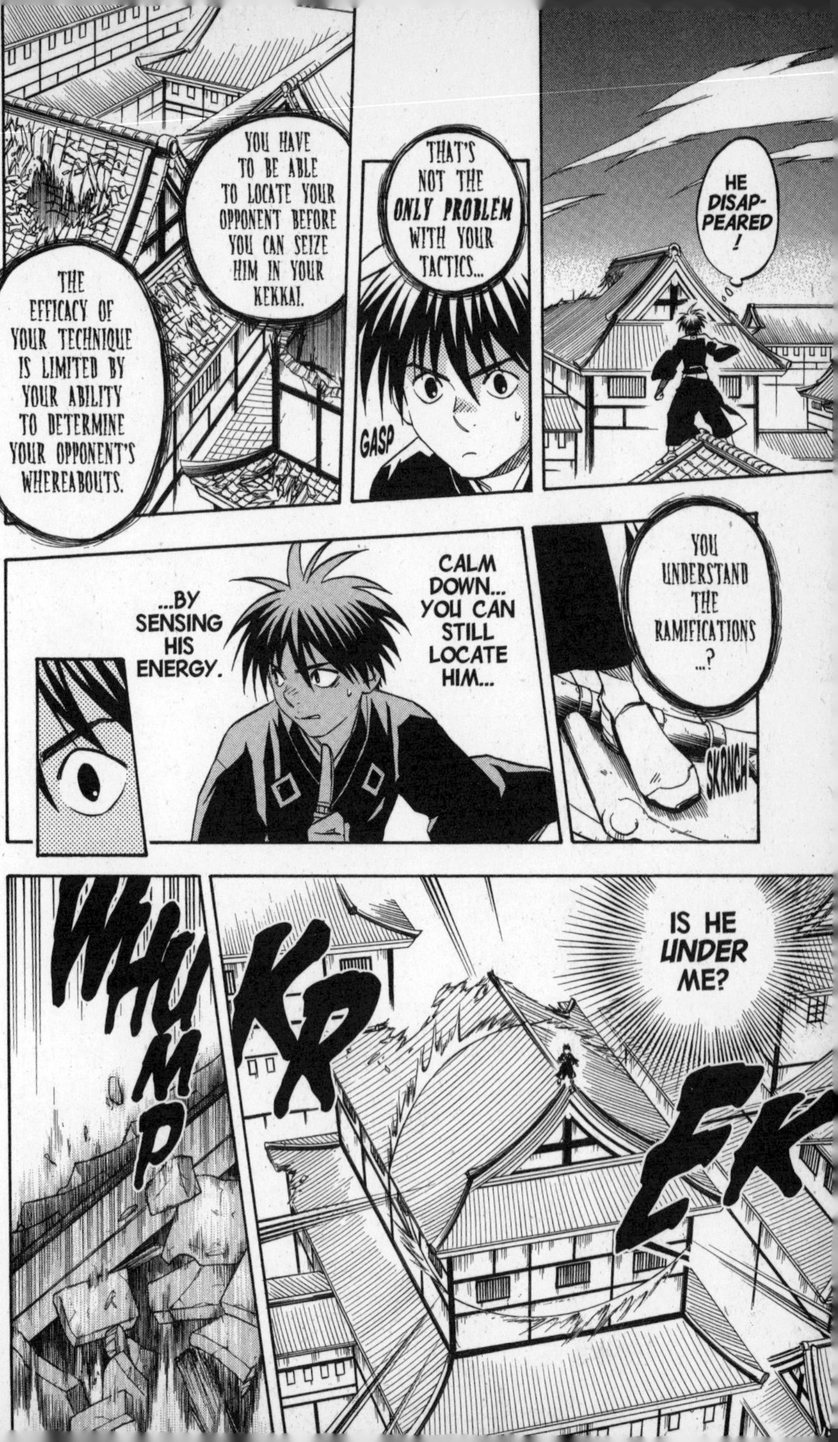
HE DISAP-PEARED!
THAT'S NOT THE ONLY PROBLEM WITH YOUR TACTICS...
GASP
YOU HAVE TO BE ABLE TO LOCATE YOUR OPPONENT BEFORE YOU CAN SEIZE HIM IN YOUR KEKKAI.
THE EFFICACY OF YOUR TECHNIQUE IS LIMITED BY YOUR ABILITY TO DETERMINE YOUR OPPONENT'S WHEREABOUTS.
YOU UNDERSTAND THE RAMIFICATIONS ...?
SKRNCH
CALM DOWN... YOU CAN STILL LOCATE HIM...
...BY SENSING HIS ENERGY.
IS HE UNDER ME?
KR
EK
WHUMP

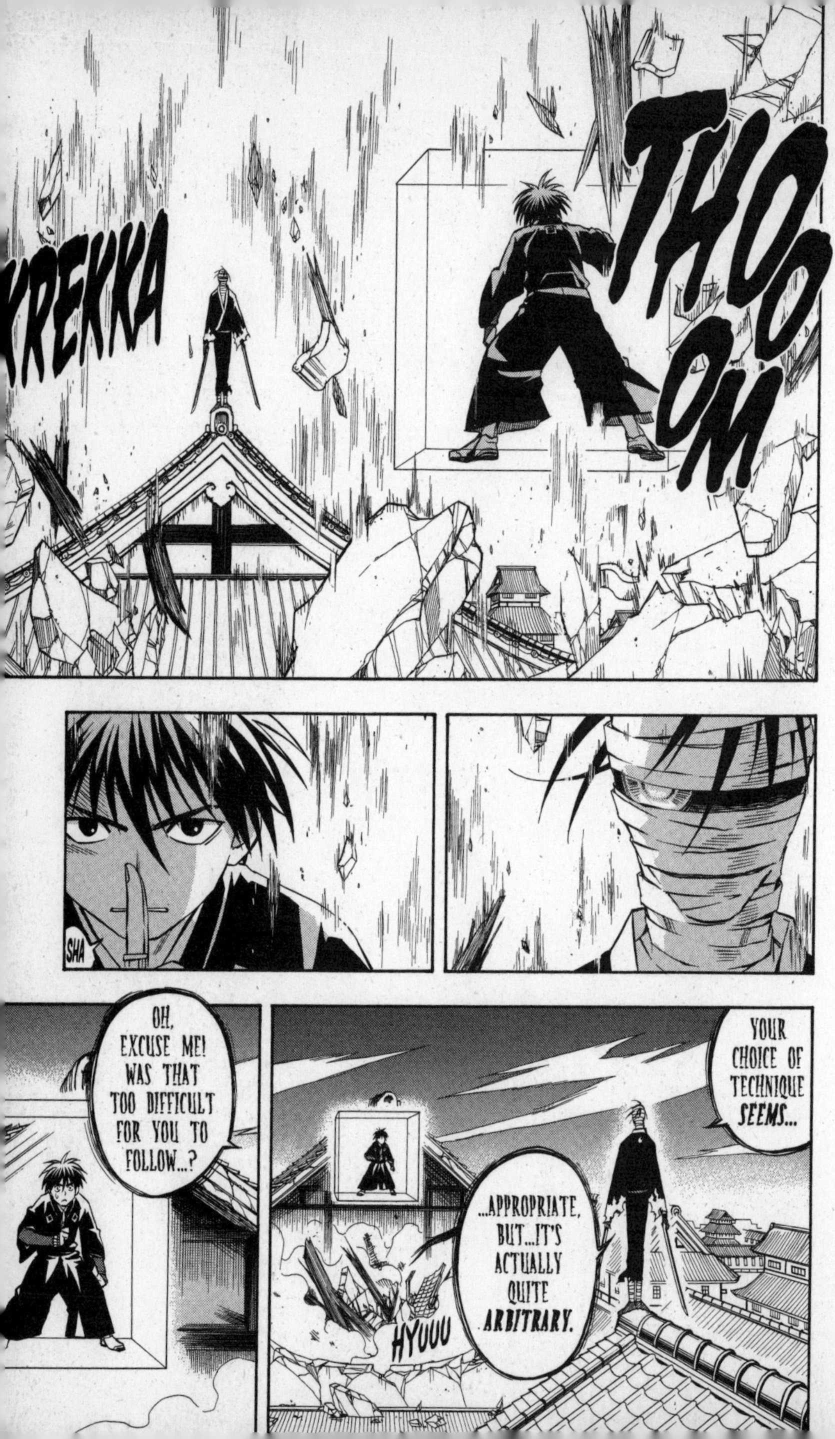
THOOOM
KREKKA
SHA
YOUR CHOICE OF TECHNIQUE SEEMS...
...APPROPRIATE, BUT...IT'S ACTUALLY QUITE ARBITRARY.
HYUUU
OH, EXCUSE ME! WAS THAT TOO DIFFICULT FOR YOU TO FOLLOW...?

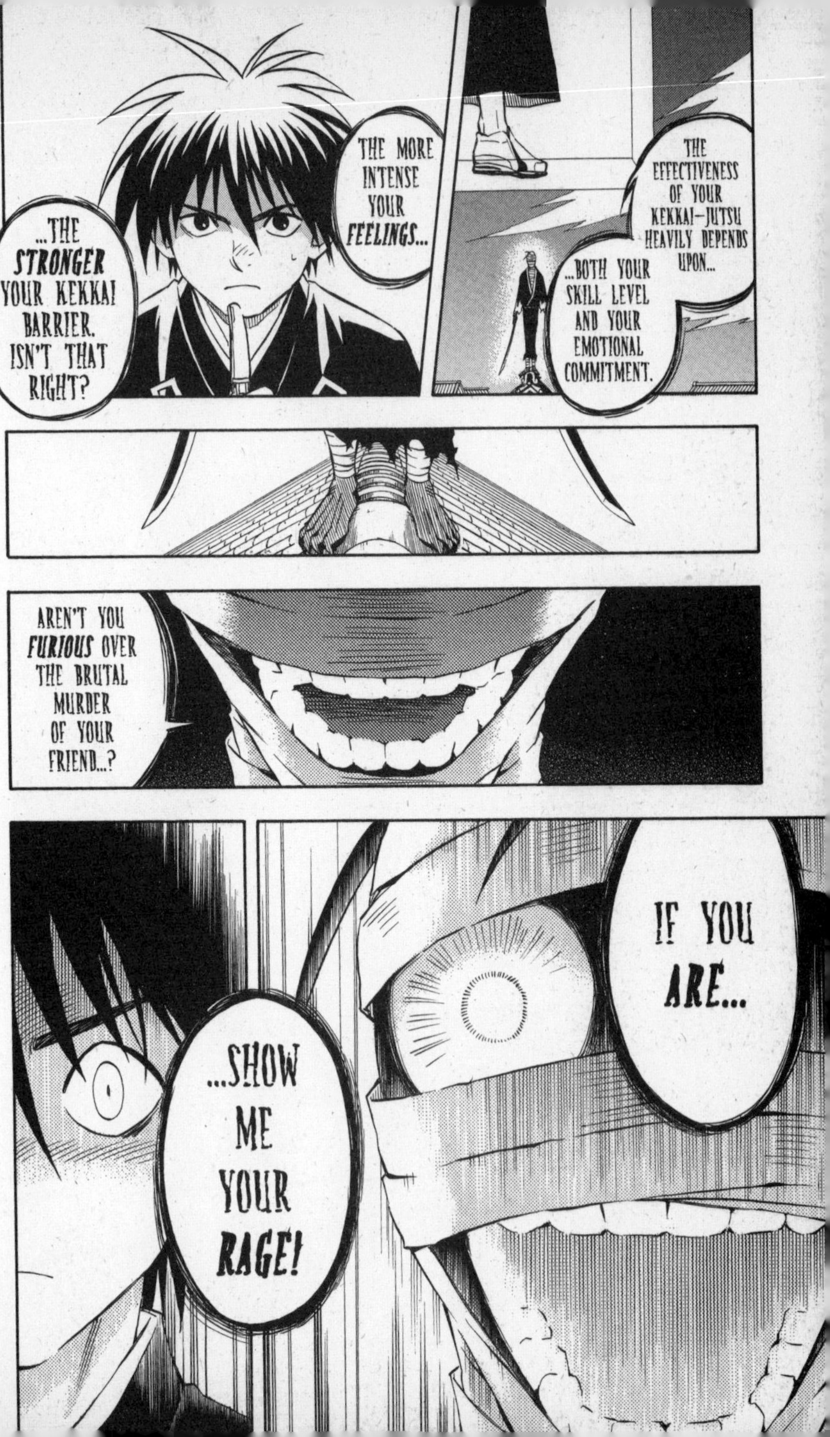
THE EFFECTIVENESS OF YOUR KEKKAI-JUTSU HEAVILY DEPENDS UPON...
...BOTH YOUR SKILL LEVEL AND YOUR EMOTIONAL COMMITMENT.
THE MORE INTENSE YOUR FEELINGS...
...THE STRONGER YOUR KEKKAI BARRIER. ISN'T THAT RIGHT?
AREN'T YOU FURIOUS OVER THE BRUTAL MURDER OF YOUR FRIEND...?
IF YOU ARE...
...SHOW ME YOUR RAGE!

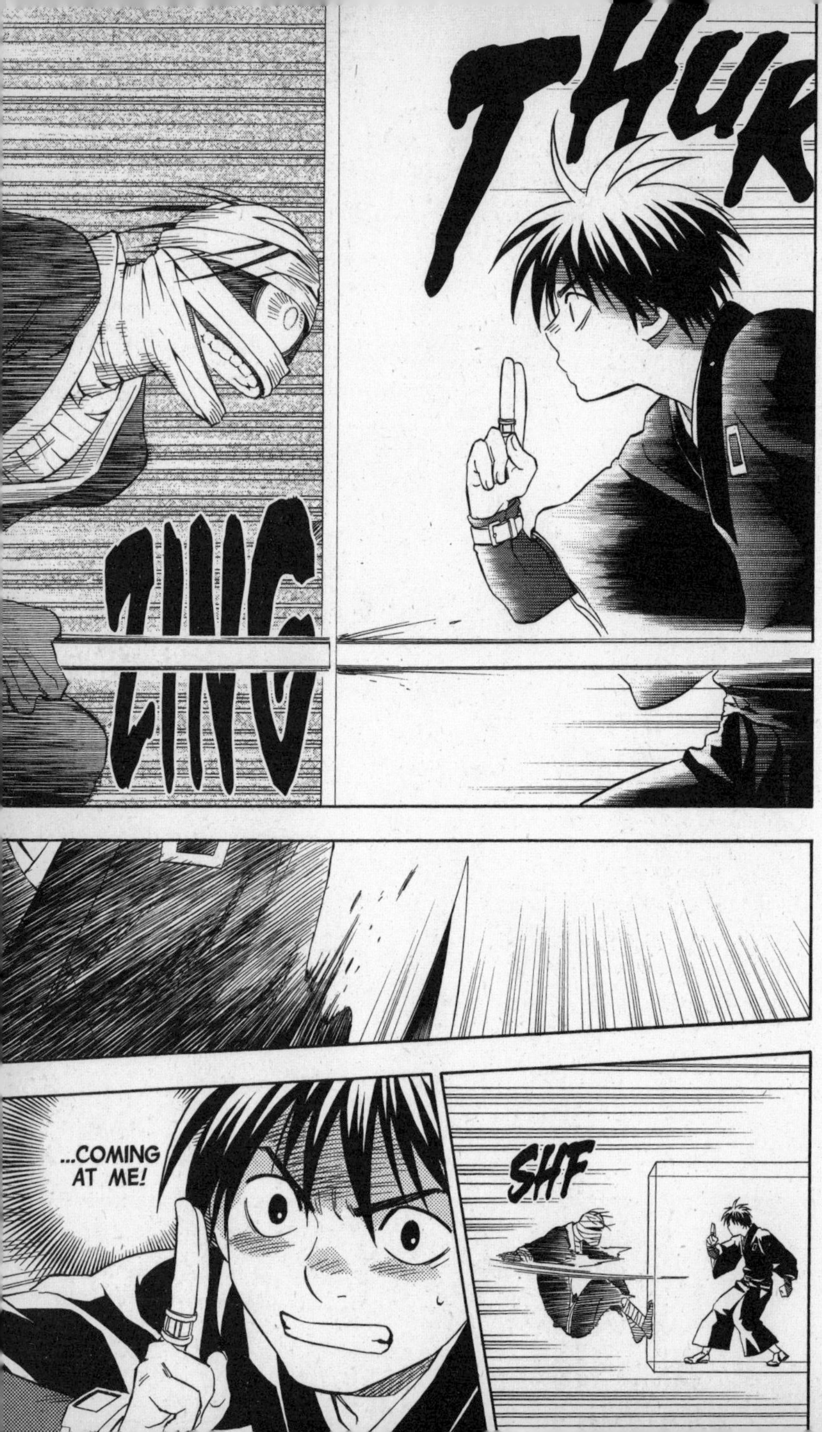
THUR
ZING
SHF
...COMING AT ME!

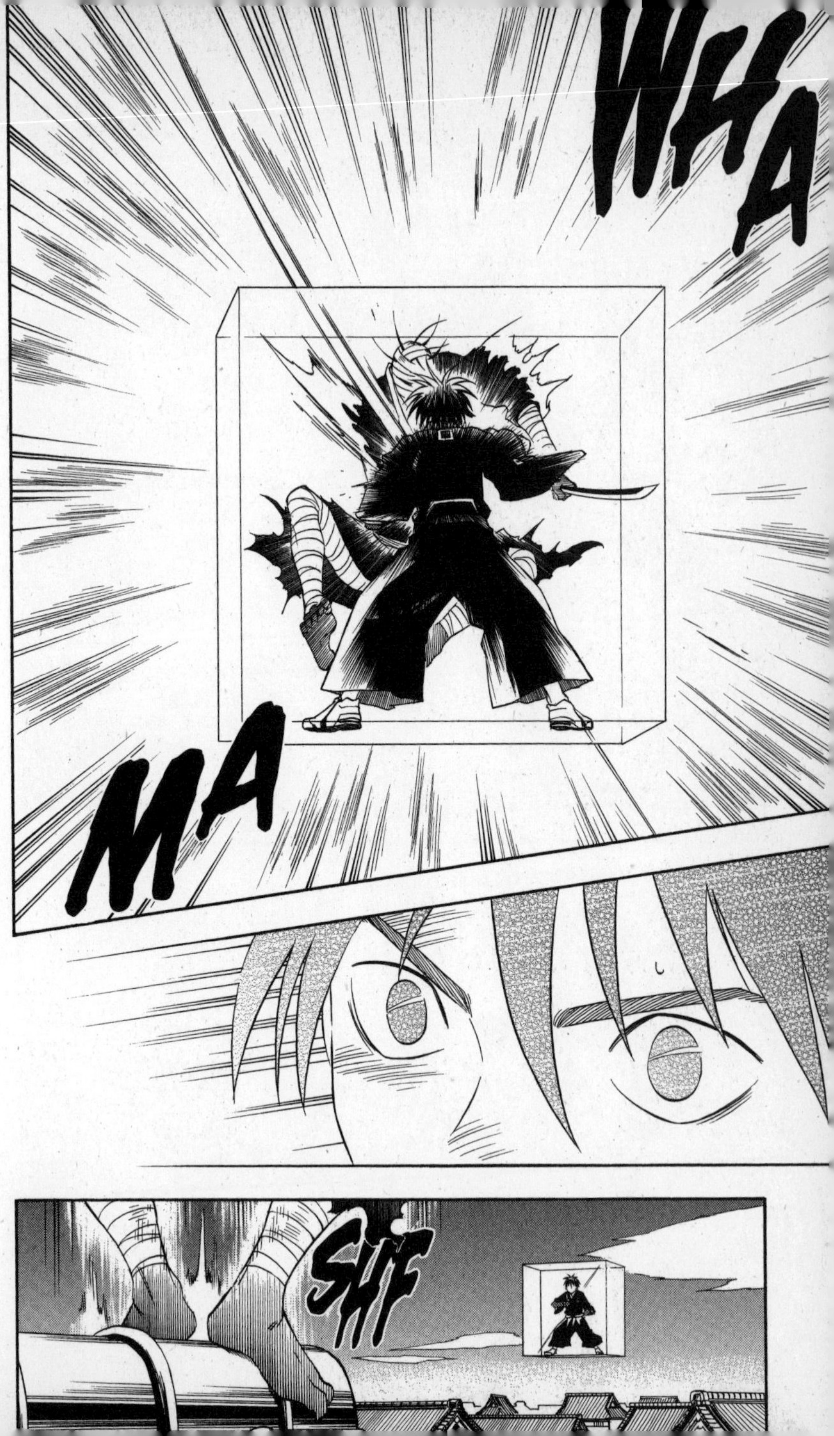
WHA
MA
SHF

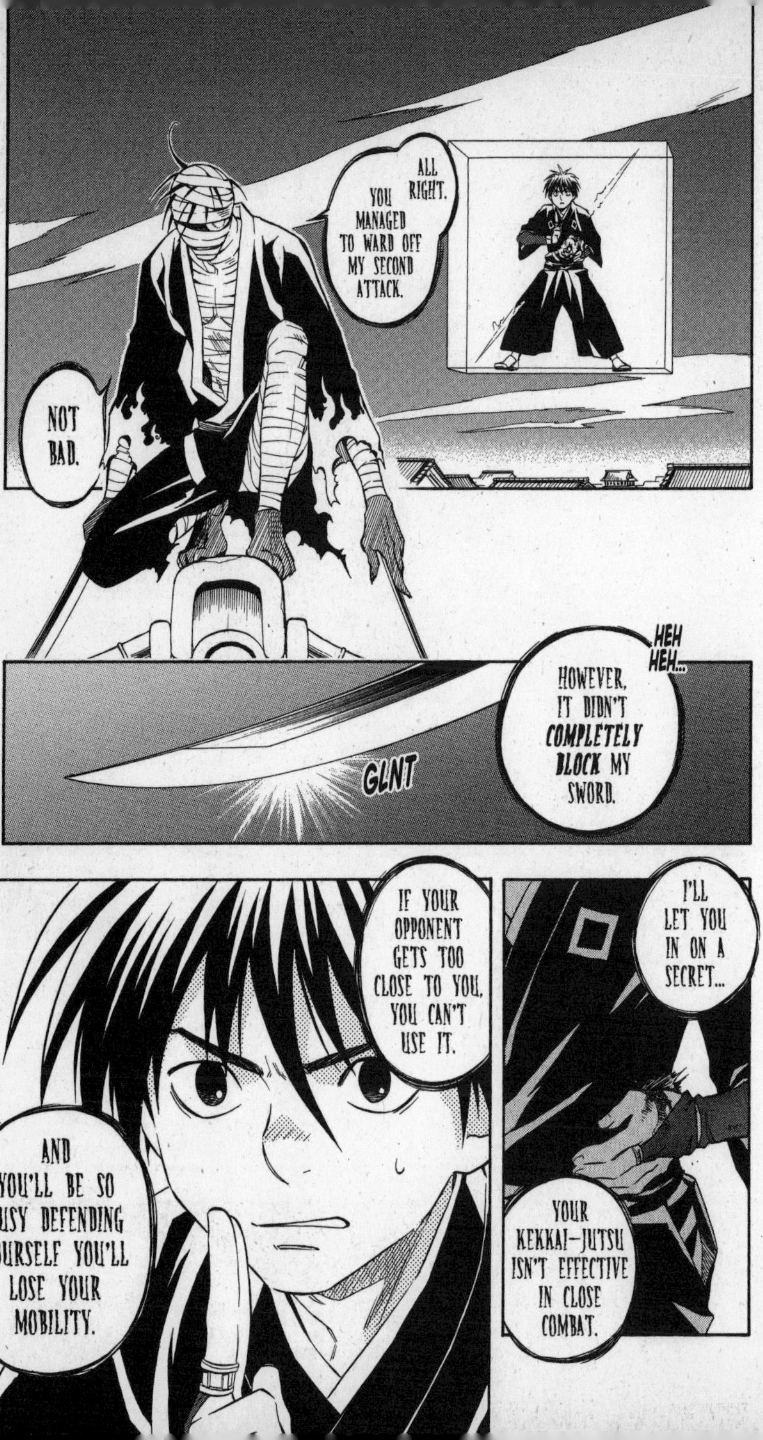
ALL RIGHT. YOU MANAGED TO WARD OFF MY SECOND ATTACK.
NOT BAD.
HEH HEH...
HOWEVER, IT DIDN'T COMPLETELY BLOCK MY SWORD.
GLNT
I'LL LET YOU IN ON A SECRET...
YOUR KEKKAI-JUTSU ISN'T EFFECTIVE IN CLOSE COMBAT.
IF YOUR OPPONENT GETS TOO CLOSE TO YOU, YOU CAN'T USE IT.
AND YOU'LL BE SO BUSY DEFENDING YOURSELF YOU'LL LOSE YOUR MOBILITY.

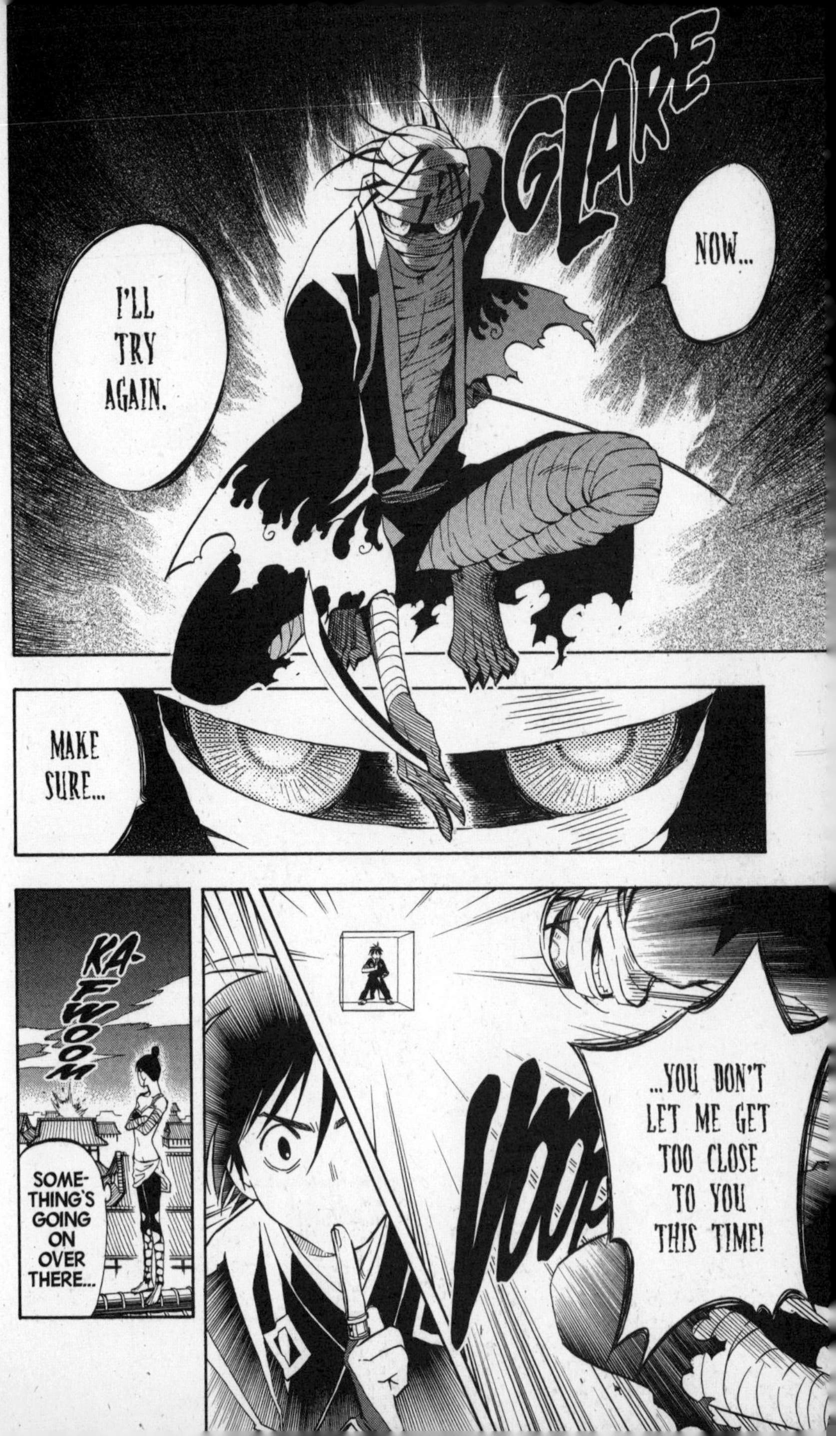
NOW...
GLARE
I'LL TRY AGAIN.
MAKE SURE...
...YOU DON'T LET ME GET TOO CLOSE TO YOU THIS TIME!
KA-FWOOM
SOME-THING'S GOING ON OVER THERE...

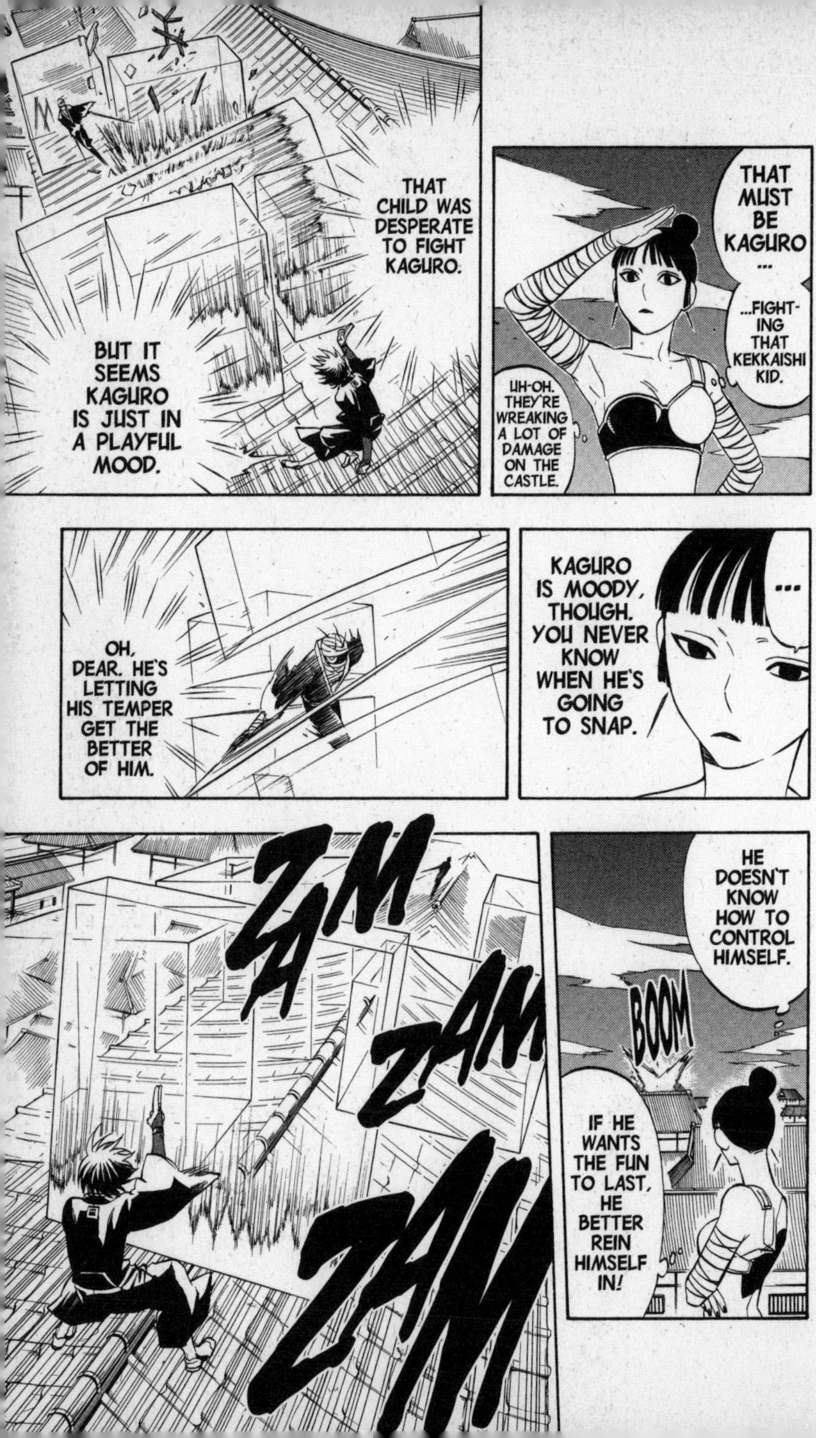
THAT MUST BE KAGURO...
...FIGHTING THAT KEKKAISHI KID.
UH-OH. THEY'RE WREAKING A LOT OF DAMAGE ON THE CASTLE.
THAT CHILD WAS DESPERATE TO FIGHT KAGURO.
BUT IT SEEMS KAGURO IS JUST IN A PLAYFUL MOOD.
...
KAGURO IS MOODY, THOUGH. YOU NEVER KNOW WHEN HE'S GOING TO SNAP.
OH, DEAR. HE'S LETTING HIS TEMPER GET THE BETTER OF HIM.
HE DOESN'T KNOW HOW TO CONTROL HIMSELF.
BOOM
IF HE WANTS THE FUN TO LAST, HE BETTER REIN HIMSELF IN!
ZAM
ZAM
ZAM

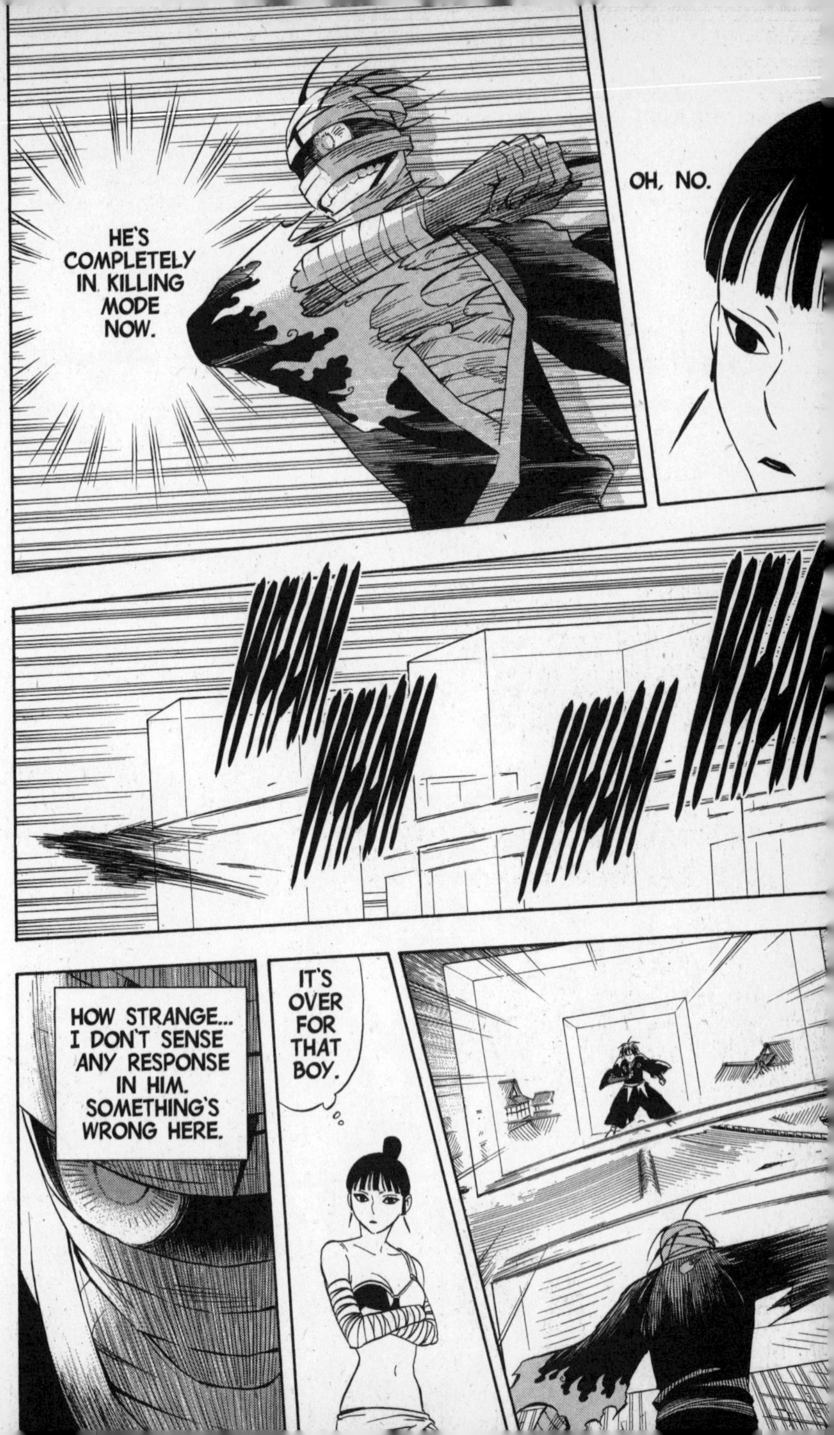
OH, NO.
HE'S COMPLETELY IN KILLING MODE NOW.
IT'S OVER FOR THAT BOY.
HOW STRANGE... I DON'T SENSE ANY RESPONSE IN HIM. SOMETHING'S WRONG HERE.

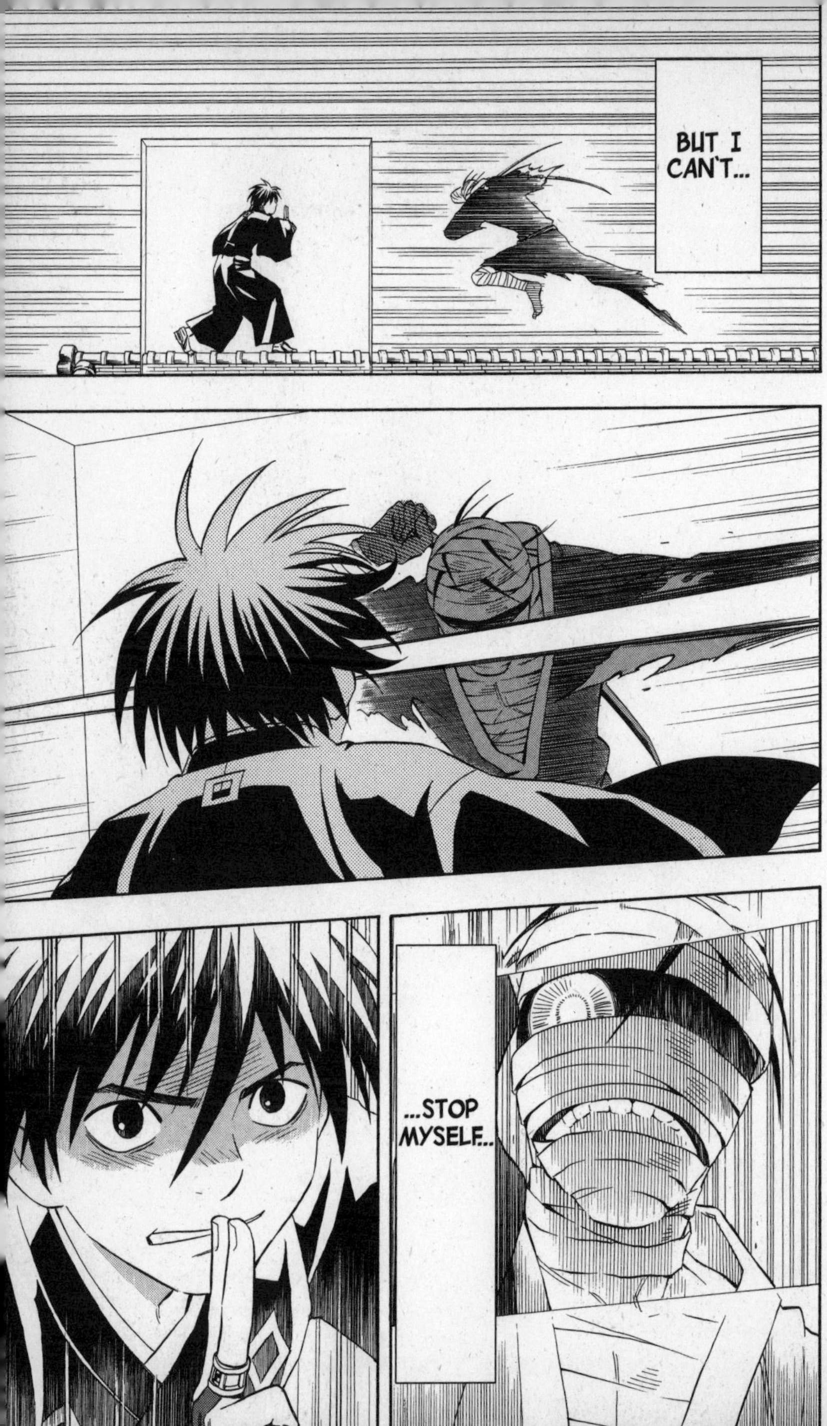
BUT I CAN'T...
...STOP MYSELF...

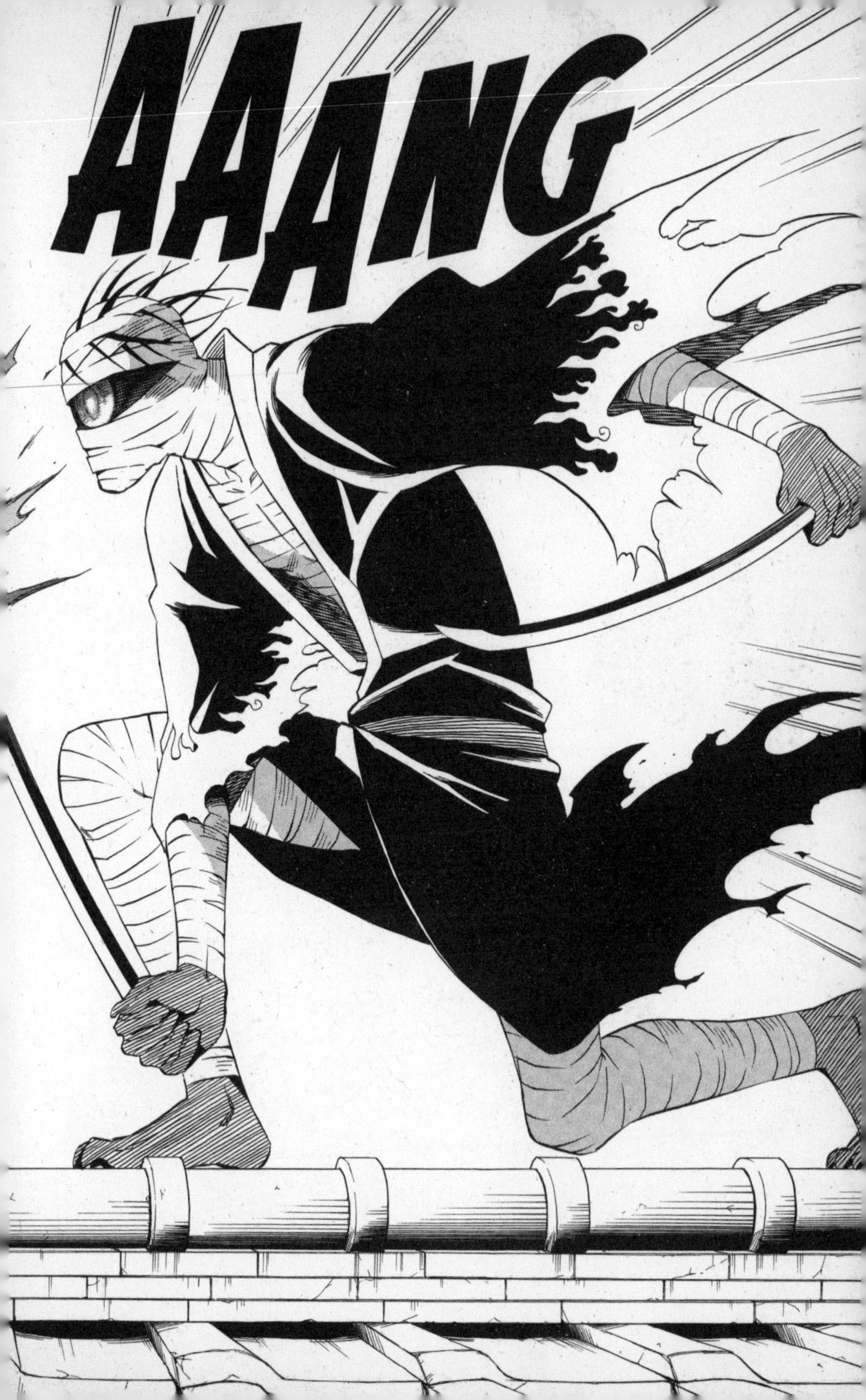
AAANG

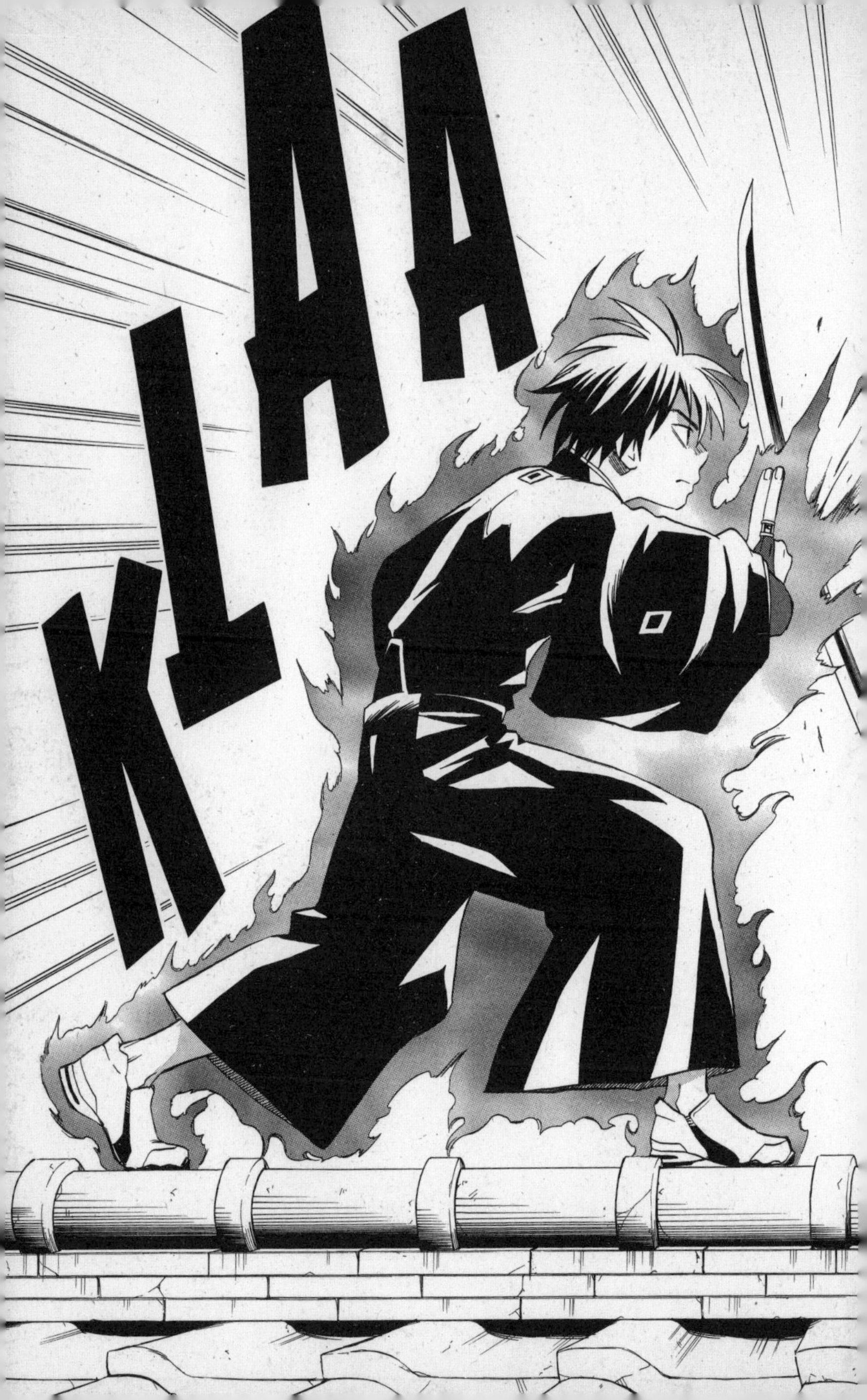
KLAAA

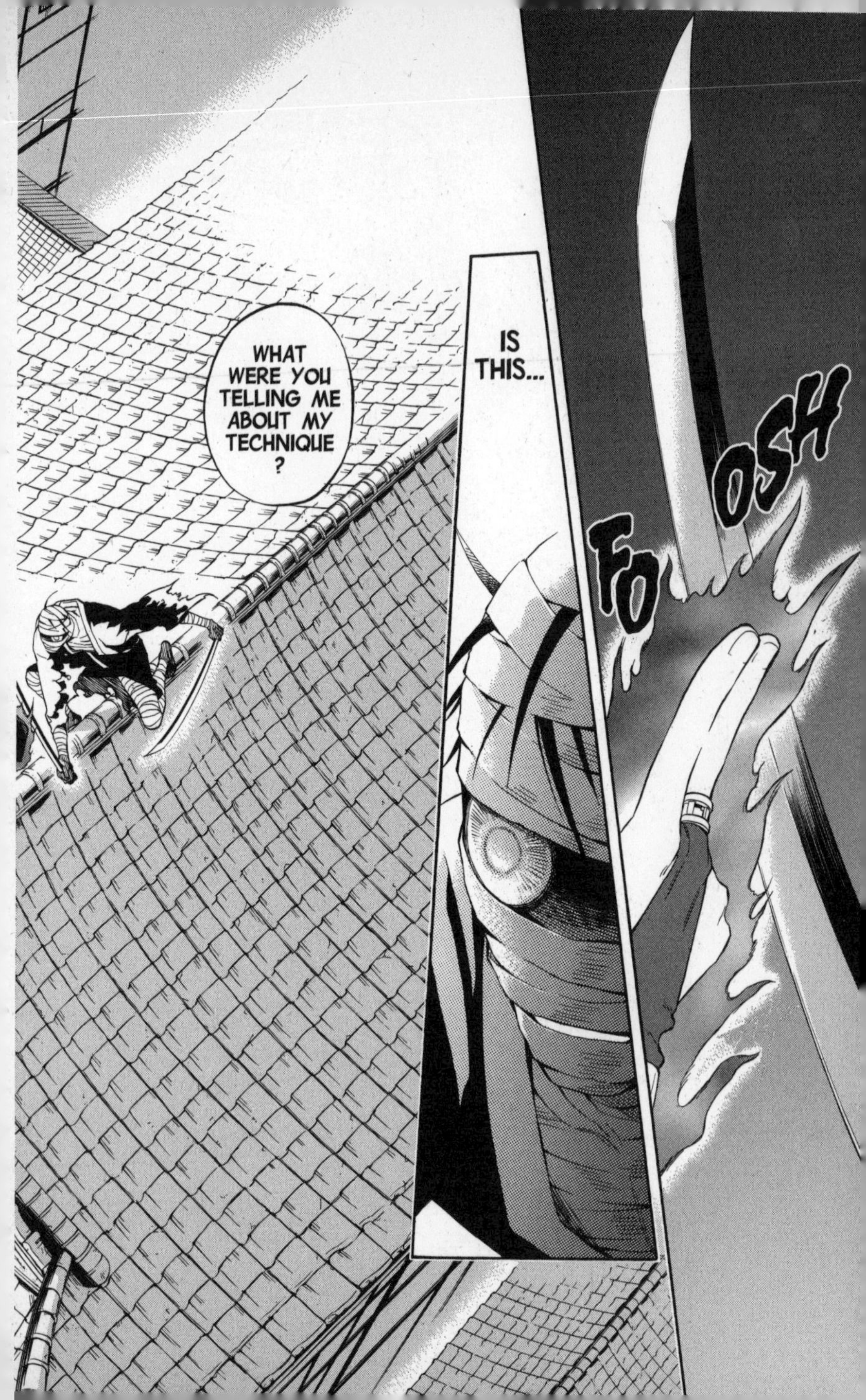
FOOSH
IS THIS...
WHAT WERE YOU TELLING ME ABOUT MY TECHNIQUE?

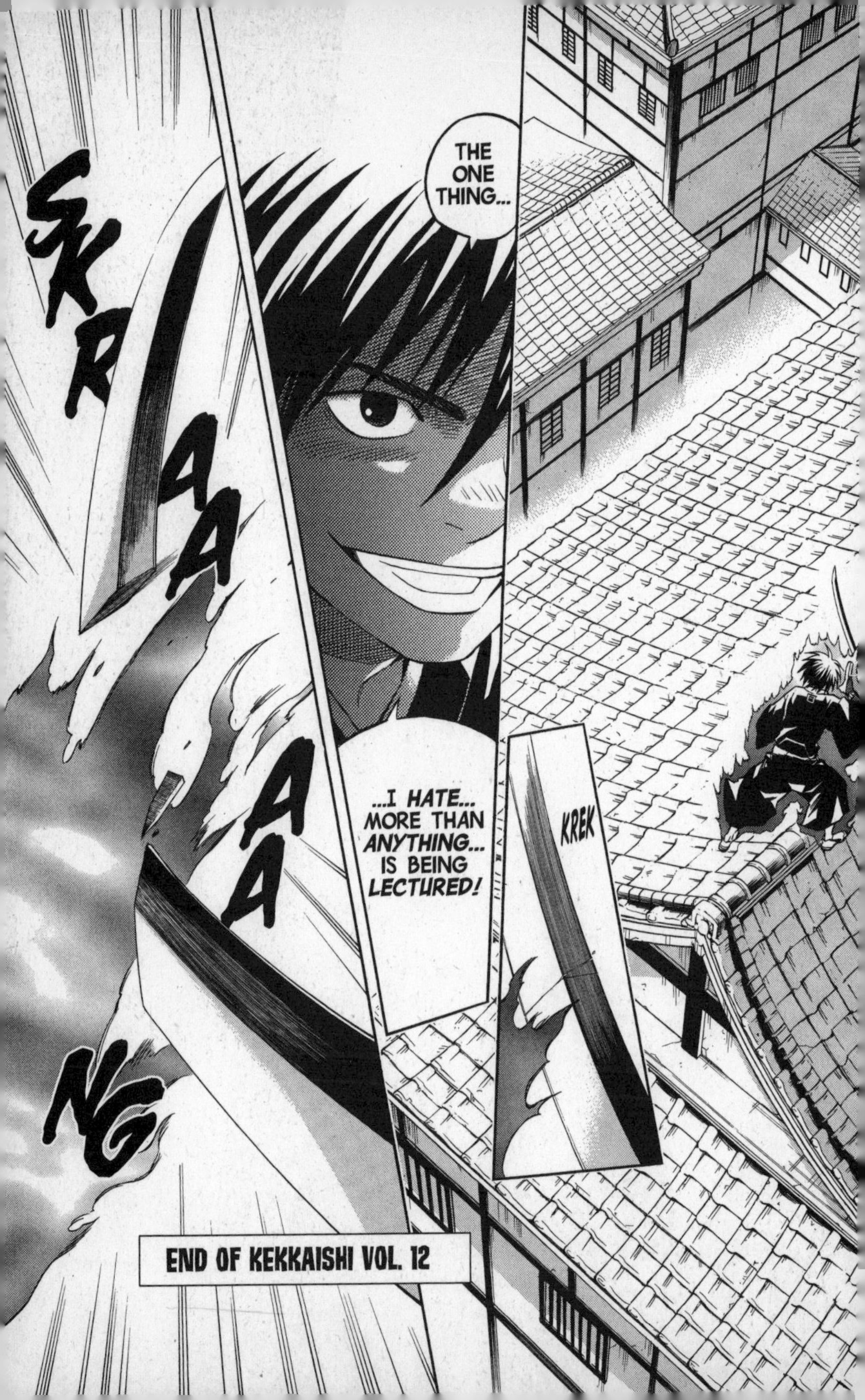
THE ONE THING...
...I HATE... MORE THAN ANYTHING... IS BEING LECTURED!
KREK
SKRAAAAANG
END OF KEKKAISHI VOL. 12

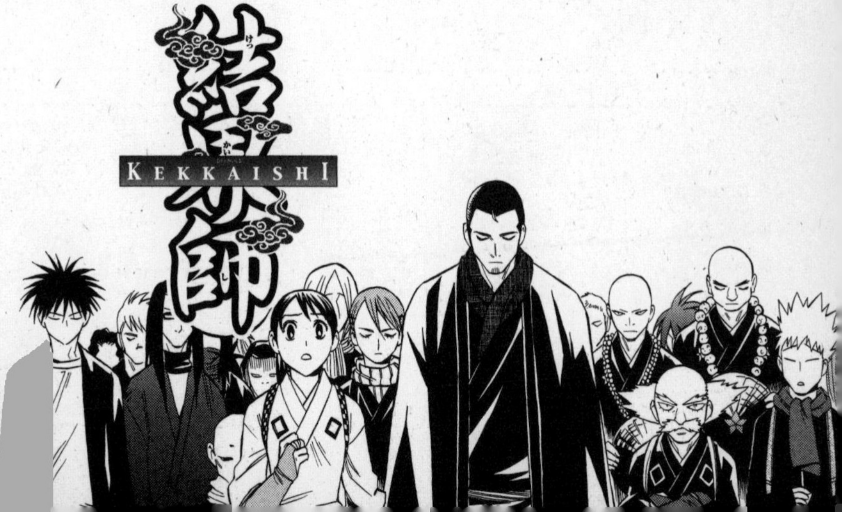
結界師
KEKKAISHI

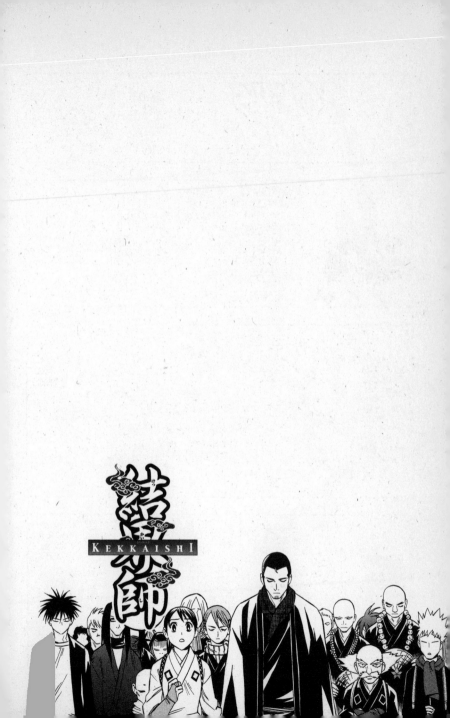

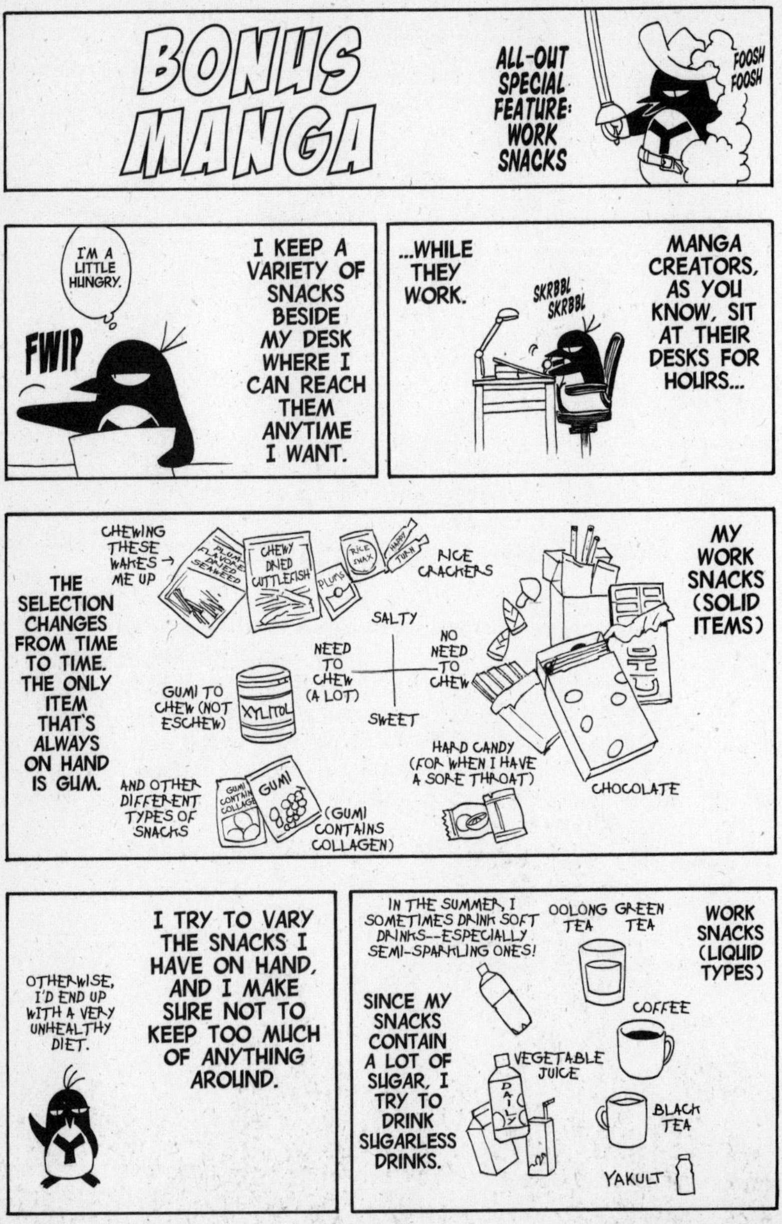
BONUS MANGA
ALL-OUT SPECIAL FEATURE: WORK SNACKS
FOOSH FOOSH
MANGA CREATORS, AS YOU KNOW, SIT AT THEIR DESKS FOR HOURS...
...WHILE THEY WORK.
SKRBBL SKRBBL
I KEEP A VARIETY OF SNACKS BESIDE MY DESK WHERE I CAN REACH THEM ANYTIME I WANT.
I'M A LITTLE HUNGRY.
FWIP
MY WORK SNACKS (SOLID ITEMS)
RICE CRACKERS
RICE SNAX
HAPPY TURN
PLUMS
CHEWY DRIED CUTTLEFISH
PLUM FLAVORED DRIED SEAWEED
CHEWING THESE WAKES ME UP
SALTY
NO NEED TO CHEW
NEED TO CHEW (A LOT)
SWEET
CHOCOLATE
HARD CANDY (FOR WHEN I HAVE A SORE THROAT)
GUMI TO CHEW (NOT ESCHEW)
XYLITOL
GUMI
GUMI CONTAINS COLLAGEN
(GUMI CONTAINS COLLAGEN)
AND OTHER DIFFERENT TYPES OF SNACKS
THE SELECTION CHANGES FROM TIME TO TIME. THE ONLY ITEM THAT'S ALWAYS ON HAND IS GUM.
WORK SNACKS (LIQUID TYPES)
OOLONG TEA
GREEN TEA
IN THE SUMMER, I SOMETIMES DRINK SOFT DRINKS--ESPECIALLY SEMI-SPARKLING ONES!
COFFEE
VEGETABLE JUICE
DAILY
BLACK TEA
YAKULT
SINCE MY SNACKS CONTAIN A LOT OF SUGAR, I TRY TO DRINK SUGARLESS DRINKS.
I TRY TO VARY THE SNACKS I HAVE ON HAND, AND I MAKE SURE NOT TO KEEP TOO MUCH OF ANYTHING AROUND.
OTHERWISE, I'D END UP WITH A VERY UNHEALTHY DIET.

Cross-cultural Connection (not really)

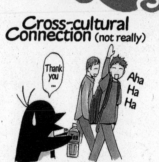

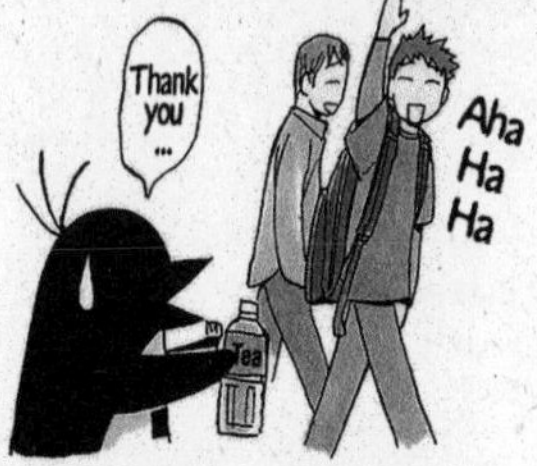
Thank you ...
Aha Ha Ha
Tea

MESSAGE FROM YELLOW TANABE

I once got a foreigner on the street to help me open my bottle of mineral water. Every once in a while, I have trouble opening a bottle. Maybe I should work out to build up my muscles. But I don't think I'd be able to develop much muscle mass, no matter how hard I try, so I should probably be satisfied as long as I can lift a pen and a coffee mug.